photography/politics:one

Dedicated to Terry Dennett and Jo Spence

PUBLISHER'S NOTE

This new edition of *Photography/Politics: One* aims to bring this iconic publication – long out-of-print – to the attention of a new audience.

The original text is reproduced in full as are the images (enhanced from the original 44-year-old publication where possible, though varying in size). The original adverts are included in an Appendix and newly-sourced Notes from some of the authors have been added to provide context.

Grateful thanks is due to the authors and photographers for agreeing to the reproduction of their work, and to Shirley Read who first proposed this new edition.

ORIGINAL COVER

Garment worker, whose wages don't allow her to buy what she makes.
From: *Women – Work in Hackney*, Hackney Flashers Collective, 1976.
Picture: © Michael Ann Mullen.

photography/politics:one

5 x 7 EDITIONS

HOW DOES PHOTOGRAPHY contribute to the defence of the old order? How may it be used to help hasten the arrival of the new?

The attempt to answer these questions is our main excuse for adding to a list of existing photo annuals which is already too long (nine published in London alone at the last count).

In 1839 Sir John Hershel suggested the term *photography* to William Henry Fox Talbot to describe any method of producing a visible image by the action of light. His definition is good enough for us – we are interested in any use of this method. We therefore part company with those who want to privilege certain photographs with the adjective *creative* and want to make them the sole object of analysis. We part company – but are not uninterested in the "creative camera". On the contrary, one concern is the process (usually far from innocent) which results in certain photographic texts being allowed through a "creative" turnstile. John Tagg correctly reminds us that Matthew Brady's Civil War negatives were kept by the US Signal Corps; Henry Jackson's plates of the Far West were in the Bureau of Reclamation; many of the Depression photographs of Evans, Lange and others are to be found filed and indexed in the Library of Congress as part of the work of the Farm Security Administration. Their "re-presentation" as "art", in "art" books and "art" shows is a recent phenomenon.

Our expansive definition of photography is paralleled by an equally expansive definition of politics. Our starting point is the class struggle. We assume that it exists (now hidden, now in the open) and that it has economic, cultural and political sites (all overlapping, all continuously shifting). We assume further that it is a struggle which is ultimately played out in politics, but that the form this takes is always crucially related to the outcome of conflicts in all the other sites. Clearly we reject those concepts of class which stress a hierarchy of separate groups graded according to income or "life style" (popular with market researchers, government statisticians and academic sociologists). We also reject the conventional wisdom which views the economy, society and politics as isolated spheres, to be understood with discrete, respective "disciplines" (a view made concrete in the division of labour between university departments).

Photography, like language, is inscribed in all of these class conflicts. Several examples from the annual suggest some of the ways how. One example is taken from Judith Williamson's discussion of history and advertising in our first section: the family album and the family in advertisements. Outside professional photography, it is within the family that photography is mainly practised, usually to produce images of itself; within advertising photography, it is the image of the consuming (bourgeois) family which is a recurrent theme, a recurrent ideal. Not formally part of the state, the family, and its representations, nevertheless have very pertinent political effects, for their very existence is presented as a denial of class, and therefore as a denial of the primacy of class politics.

But class politics was the core of Worker Photography, the subject of section two. The Worker Photographer movement was related to the various national communist parties, under the leadership of the Third International, between the wars. It sought to turn amateur photographers within the communist and broad labour movement into militant photojournalists, able to supply the left press with pictures revealing working class life and struggles from a Marxist viewpoint.

However, we do not assume that a left photography must be linked to a party or that it must mainly document the working class. Allan Sekula, in an article concluding our third section on left photography today, describes recent American work by photographers on a variety of themes – the self, the family, and labour. What links them is a critical stance to dominant forms of representation and the search for ways of adequately documenting "monopoly capitalism's inability to deliver the conditions of a fully human life." They are all engaged in cultural work which, to use Sylvia Harvey's phrase, seeks to "anticipate future class needs".

Judith Williamson's family example suggests some of the ways in which photography contributes to the maintenance of bourgeois hegemony. The Worker Photographers of the inter-war period and the new American work presented by Sekula suggest some of the oppositional and revolutionary possibilities. Both aspects will be explored in this and future annuals.

THE EDITORS

PHOTOGRAPHY WORKSHOP

A STATEMENT FROM PHOTOGRAPHY WORKSHOP

THIS ANNUAL, the first of a number of publications planned by Photography Workshop, is essentially a continuation of the work we originally attempted to initiate through Half Moon Photography Workshop (HMPW). As co-founders of the Workshop and its magazine *Camerawork* we felt it crucial for us, as socialists, to call into question various institutional photographic practices, and to do everything possible to engage in the widest possible debate of the politics of visual imagery. Important also we felt was the urgent task of attempting to raise from obscurity, and re-examine, the earlier traditions of left-wing photography, before they became elevated and rarefied as part of the bourgeois "documentary tradition" within various art establishments.

In the event, these attempts proved to be premature, for members of HMPW's other co-founding group, Half Moon Gallery Limited, looked upon such activities as "time-wasting", "obscure", or "too theoretical". This rejection of our theoretical and political practice eventually led to Photography Workshop's total exclusion from HMPW and from *Camerawork*, and to the artificial closure of the debates which were just beginning to emerge in embryonic form in that journal. Traumatic though these events have been for us personally they have, nonetheless, had a positive outcome in that our present programme is now more broadly based and is entirely self-supporting. Our thanks to those people who helped us in various ways during this difficult period.

The production of this annual has presented us with many difficulties, not least of which has been the fact that all editorial and production work has been carried out entirely in people's spare time, in addition to their normal work. Finance has come from a variety of sources; from our wages, from donations, and from the proceeds of an out-of-court settlement of £2,000 made to Photography Workshop following Industrial Tribunal proceedings for "unfair dismissal" against Half Moon Gallery Limited.

We would like to extend our thanks to all those who have worked in various stages of production, especially to our fellow editors David Evans and Sylvia Gohl, and to John Myers, our production person.

TERRY DENNETT | JO SPENCE
SEPTEMBER 1979

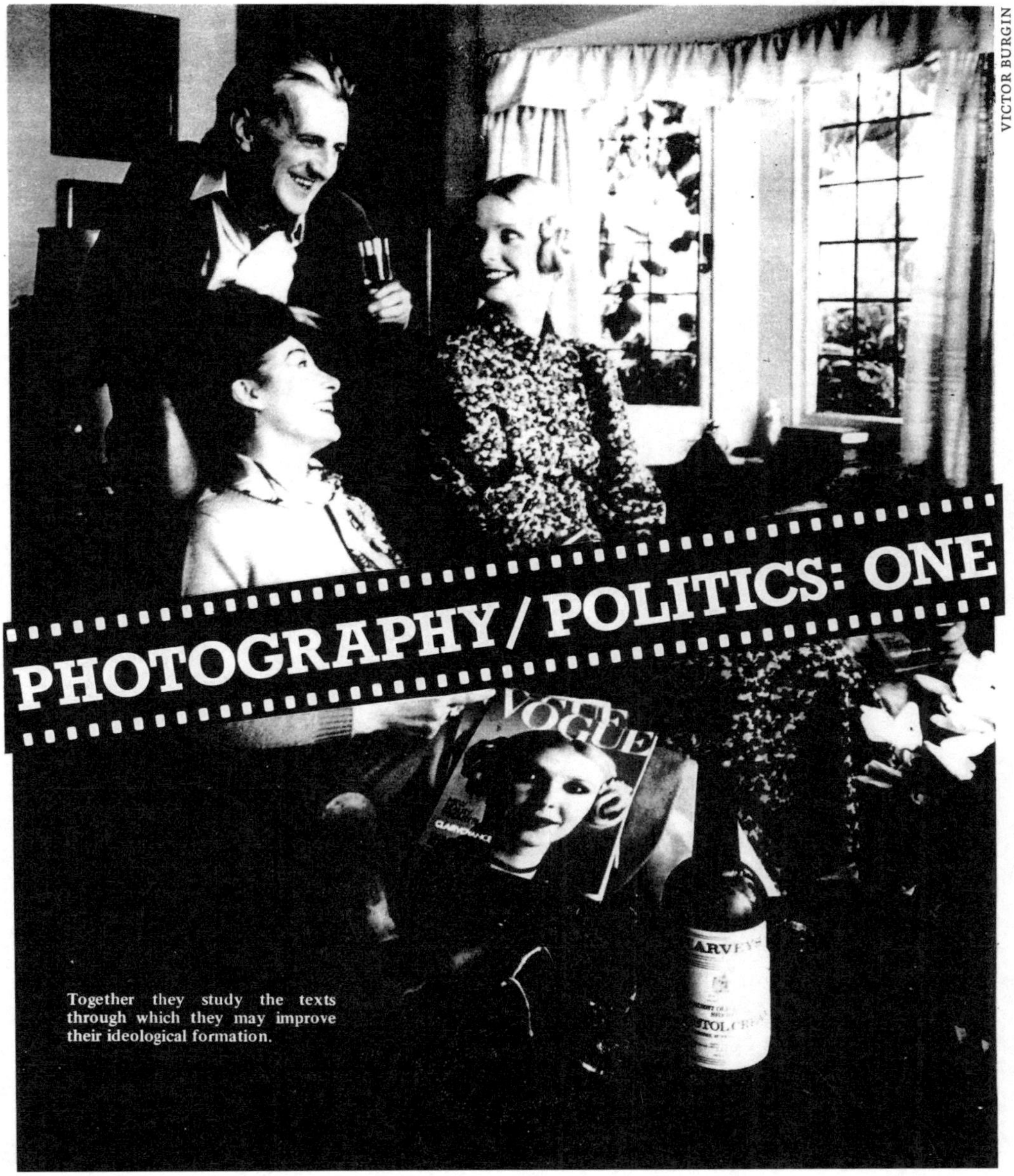

Together they study the texts through which they may improve their ideological formation

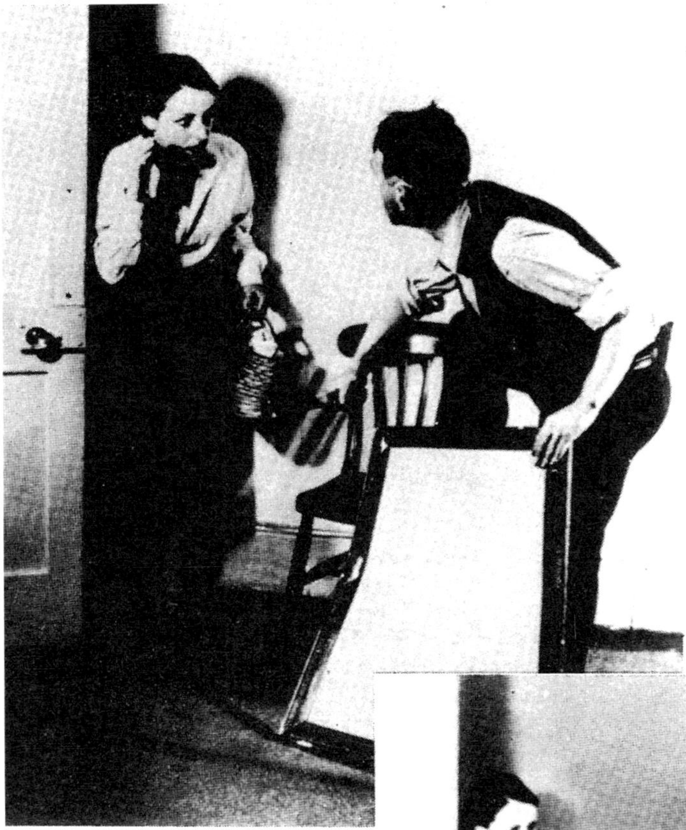

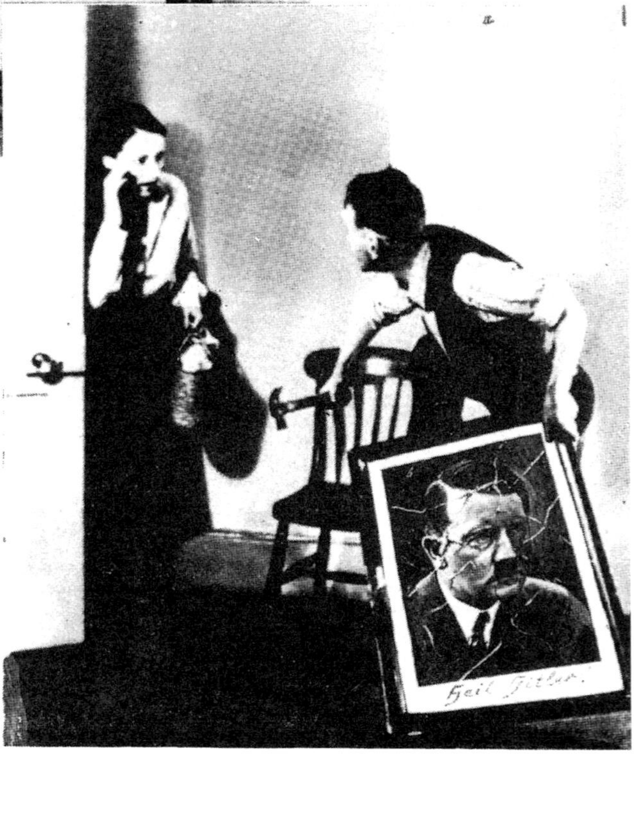

8

ACKNOWLEDGEMENTS

We are grateful for the help of the following people in the production of this book

Editorial Advisory Group
Victor Burgin
Douglas Lowndes
Stuart Hood
Maggie Murray

Production Assistance
Tony Benn, Annie Grove-White, Viv Hollis, Mick Keats,
Lucy Williams, Yanira Codato, Gen Doy, Jenny Kane.

Distribution
PDC, 27 Clerkenwell Close
London EC1

Finally, our thanks to all contributors/translators,especially those listed under whose work did not get into print because we had to restrict the final section of the book to fit in with our budget:
Heather Lloyd, Patricia Holland, Susan Bennett, Larry Herman, Roy Peters/Frank Mort, Les Ruda, Michael Ann Mullen, The Ford Group, Martin Lister/Andrew Dewdney, Grahame White, the Cologne Arbeiter-Fotografie Group.

Paste-up John Myers
Typesetting Ms Shulay
Printing Anvil Printers Ltd (TU)

ISSN: 0142-7865

Photography Workshop
152 Upper Street, London N1

CONTENTS

AGAINST THE DOMINANT IDEOLOGY

LEFT PHOTOGRAPHY BETWEEN THE WARS

LEFT PHOTOGRAPHY TODAY

POSTCRIPT

APPENDIXES

AGAINST THE DOMINANT IDEOLOGY

Ideology: The Base and Superstructure Debate

Sylvia Harvey

THE CENTRAL PROBLEM for those theorists of art or culture operating either within – or in a way that is sympathetic to – the traditions of Marxist thought, has been the question: what is the relationship between cultural production and a society's mode of material production (often referred to as the "economic", the "base" of any social formation)? And, further, what is the relationship between cultural production and that system of class relations which derives from a particular mode of material production? Who produces for whom, and which class interests are served by this production?

Appreciating the debates around these questions must involve a general understanding of certain developments in the Marxist theory of ideology, in particular those developments associated with the name of the French Marxist philosopher Louis Althusser. What characterises these developments is a calling into question of what came to be seen as the increasingly problematic metaphor of "base" and "superstructure" which for so long had been used by Marxists to explain the relationship between cultural production (art) and the mode of material production (economics).

The model of base and superstructure (of a base which determines, and a superstructure which is determined by the base) implied a simple relationship of reflection or correspondence between the base, or what Marx had called the "material foundations" of a society, its mode of producing and distributing wealth, and the superstructure which Marx had referred to as "the social, political and intellectual life process in general", "forms of social consciousness", "the legal political, religious, aesthetic or philosophic in short ideological forms", "modes of thought and views of life".

The rethinking of the categories of base and superstructure over the last 50 years or so (roughly spanning the period that begins in the twenties, or earlier, with the work of the Italian Marxist Antonio Gramsci, and ends in the seventies with the work of Louis Althusser) has resulted in the development of a theory of ideology within Marxism which, its exponents would argue, is rather more comprehensive and complex than the concept of ideology as outlined in the writings of Marx himself. However, since Marx's ideas provide the necessary point of departure for any examination of subsequent developments in this area, a brief account of his formulations around the question of base and superstructure will be offered here. References will be made here to three sources: *The German Ideology* (Marx and Engels, 1846), *The Eighteenth Brumaire of Louis Bonaparte* (Marx, 1852) and *Preface to A Contribution to the Critique of Political Economy* (Marx, 1859).

In *The German Ideology*, and beginning with the statement that:

> "The first premise of all human history is of course the existence of living human individuals"[1]

Marx sets out to relate the modes of social organisation, forms of consciousness etc. to "the way in which men produce their means of subsistence", and to the manner in which they reproduce the conditions for their own existence. In other words he is looking for a method – to be proposed as the materialist method – for linking the analysis of any mode of social organisation to the mode of production and reproduction of the material conditions of existence adopted by these "human individuals".

The crucial point here is that, from a very early stage in human history, men and women enter into social relationships, modes of social organisation, in order to reproduce the conditions for their own existence. The mode of production adopted entails more, Marx argues, than simply "the production of the physical existence of the individuals", it results also in a particular mode of social organisation, a particular way of life:

> This mode of production... is a definite form of activity of these individuals, a definite form of expressing their life, a definite *mode of life* on their part. As individuals express their life, so they are. What they are therefore, coincides with their production, both with *what* they produce and with *how* they produce. The nature of individuals thus depends on the material conditions determining their production.[2]

In searching for an adequate means of describing what he calls "the life-process" of individuals, Marx searches also for a way of making a crucial distinction between individuals "as they may appear in their own or other people's imagination", and individuals "as they *really* are". He defines individuals "as they really are" in this way:

> ...as they operate, produce materially, and hence as they work under definite

> material limits, presuppositions and conditions independent of their will.[3]

In pursuit of this distinction between what men and women think of themselves as being, and what they "really are", he proposes a method of analysis according to which:

> ...we do not set out from what men say, imagine, conceive, nor from men as narrated, thought of, imagined, conceived, in order to arrive at men in the flesh. We set out from real, active men, and on the basis of their real life process we demonstrate the development of the ideological reflexes and echoes of this life process.[4]

It is with the vocabulary of "reflexes" and "echoes" that the problems begin, and subsequent Marxist commentators (writers like Althusser in France, Stuart Hall and Raymond Williams in Britain) have found these terms to be something of an embarrassment, in the belief that they imply far too simple and direct a correspondence between base and superstructure. Frequently Marx's later writings have been cited as a corrective to the too-simple notion of superstructure reflecting, echoing or expressing the base. Antonio Gramsci, for example, in the *Prison Notebooks* written in the early thirties, refers readers to *The Eighteenth Brumaire* in the context of an attack which he launches upon:

> The claim presented as an essential postulate of historical materialism, that every fluctuation of politics and ideology can be presented and expounded as an immediate expression of the structure...[5]

Gramsci here uses the term *structure* in place of the term *base*, but he is clearly thinking in terms of the classic base/superstructure opposition, and he goes on to argue that this "claim":

> ...must be contested in theory as primitive infantilism, and combated in practice with the authentic testimony of Marx, the author of concrete political and historical works.[6]

A little later, in the same passage, he attacks "mechanical historical materialism" on the grounds that it "assumes that every political act is determined, immediately, by the structure". If Gramsci's argument that political acts cannot be accounted for in terms of some immediately determining function of the economic base is accepted, how much more carefully does the concept of cultural production have to be thought through in its complex relationship to a society's mode of material production.

There are other formulations in *The German Ideology* which have come under attack for similar sorts of reasons (that is, that they suggest too simple a correspondence between base and superstructure): Marx's use of the camera obscura model is perhaps the best known of these, though it should be said that this formulation has remained acceptable to some Marxists. In pursuit of the argument that there is a relationship between, on the one hand, "the production of ideas, of conceptions, of consciousness" and, on the other, "material activity" (a proposition to which no Marxist could object), he continues:

> Consciousness can never be anything else than conscious existence, and the existence of men is their actual life-process. If in all ideology men and their circumstances appear upside-down as in a *camera obscura*, this phenomenon arises just as much from their historical life-process as the inversion of objects on the retina does from their physical life-process.[7]

According to this model what men and women "see" in ideology is related to their material conditions, to their "actual life-process", but they simply "see" their real conditions reflected upside-down, inverted. It is then, clearly, not such a difficult task for someone (the materialist philosopher) to come along and turn these reflections the right way up again. The model also suggests that once the "historical life-process" has been adequately understood, presumably through the methods proposed by historical materialism, then there will be no more ideology, no more upside-down seeing, people will see social relations, simply, as they are.

Althusser and others have taken issue with some of the implications of this model on two counts. Firstly that it proposes too simple and direct a relationship (a relationship of reflection) between "ideology" and "mode of production"; they would argue, rather, that ideology has its own specific mode of operation and stands in a highly complex relationship to the mode of production, and that since both ideology and mode of production are to be thought of as *processes*, constantly subject to change, never static moments, that consequently their relationship cannot be conceptualised in terms of "reflection". Secondly, the objection to the *camera obscura* model has been on the grounds that it suggests the possibility of an end to ideology.

The arguments here have been, perhaps, rather more controversial, and Althusser, in speaking of ideology as a "matter of the *lived* relation between men and their world" [8] and therefore as something indispensable to any mode of social organisation, has claimed that ideology as such cannot be thought of as disappearing with the disappearance of class society (the position will be outlined in more detail later in this article). Crucially the objections have been to the notion of ideology as straightforward *distortion*; and in relationship to the statement in *The German Ideology* that:

> The phantoms formed in the human brain are also, necessarily, sublimates of their material life-process, which is empirically verifiable and bound to material premises.[9]

It is the terminology of "phantoms" and "sublimates" that has been fastened on as inadequate. For if ideology is thought of as "something that doesn't really exist" (a phantom) – as, therefore, a species of lie – then the way is left open to the thought that the simple solution to the problem of ideology lies in the advent of the materialist philosopher who, bearing the true image, will be able to uncover the falsity of the upside-down image, to correct the sight of those who previously saw the world askew. Ideology is thus abolished.

But for Althusser and others this abolition is not possible, ideology is seen as performing its own particular kind of work within the complex whole of the social formation, within the complex interaction between those aspects of the social formation traditionally referred to as base and superstructure; ideology cannot be seen as the direct expression or "echo" of any other aspect of the social formation (for example the base). In Althusser's model ideology does not "go away", shrieking like a vampire at the coming of the dawn, when the spotlight of a materialist understanding of the operations of the economic is turned upon it, rather it continues to perform its own "work" only in a different way in a classless society from the manner in which it operates in a class society.

If the vocabulary of phantoms and "upside-down" reflections has proved controversial, *The German Ideology*, in introducing, in addition, the notion of ruling ideas, also stands at the beginning of a long line of discussions and arguments around the question of what is most commonly referred to now as the dominant ideology. Having outlined a method which links the production of ideas, modes of consciousness etc., to a society's mode of material production and reproduction, Marx and Engels then go on to explain what they refer to as the phenomenon of ruling ideas, how it is that in any society certain ideas dominate and succeed in proposing themselves as "the only rationally, universally valid" ideas.[10] The notion of "ruling ideas" is developed in relation to the concept of relative access to the "means of mental production":

> The ideas of the ruling class are in every epoch the ruling ideas, i.e., the class which is the ruling *material* force of society, is at the same time its ruling *intellectual* force. The class which has the means of material production at its disposal has control at the same time over the means of mental production... The individuals composing the ruling class... regulate the production and distribution of the ideas of their age: thus their ideas are the ruling ideas of the epoch.[11]

None of this seems very far removed from the common-sense saying that "He who pays the piper calls the tune". But the statement does raise some important questions as to the absolute, or relative, nature of the control over the means of mental production. What Marx and Engels probably have in mind here is the work of philosophers in constructing certain systems of ideas; but there is clearly a sense in which both philosophers and cultural producers (writers, painters, etc.), who may be "controlled" by the ruling class (in the sense of patronage and censorship of the market) but are certainly not identical with it, have under certain circumstances produced works which do not immediately fulfil the ideological "needs" of the ruling class. Such works call attention to certain contemporary contradictions, and may call into question the legitimacy of the authority of the ruling class. So there is, and has perhaps always been the "space" for certain forms of oppositional cultural practice, which is perhaps not allowed for in the notion of (total?) control over the means of mental production.

The use of the word "control" may in itself imply too simple and direct a fit or correspondence between activities at the level of cultural production (the music of the piper) and the political programmes of a ruling class (the calling of the tune). The word "hegemony" may serve us better, with its sense of the complex orchestration of consent, rather than the more direct, brutal and straightforwardly functionalist notion of control which seems to imply a necessarily conscious activity on the part of the ruling class. Moreover the notion of a tight class control over the production of ideas as proposed by *The German Ideology* needs to be rethought in the context of a society which, unlike the society Marx knew, is characterised by mass literacy, universal secondary education and such peculiar concessions to the notion of feedback from those at the receiving end of the organs of mass communication as the radio phone-in programme, the television access programme, and the letters pages of local and national newspapers. This is not to put forward the argument that our society is in fact characterised by a liberal pluralism founded on the free exchange of ideas among social equals, simply to call into question some of the more obviously functionalist implications associated with the use of the word "control".

Where the operation of hegemony comes in most sharply and most incontrovertibly, is through the mechanisms of regulating production *and distribution* to which Marx and Engels call attention in the passage from *The German Ideology* quoted above. Particularly with the development of cultural production as commodity production under capitalism – that is, the exchange of cultural objects whether books, films, paintings etc., through the market – the most powerful instance of ruling class control lies in the control of the market, the control over *exchange* or distribution. (Though a whole complex theory of mediations obviously needs to be developed to account for the operation of hegemony in a state-owned broadcasting corporation like the BBC which in so far as it produces "for itself" has only an indirect relationship to the market.)

The most obvious question which the statement about ruling ideas in *The German Ideology* seems to leave unanswered is the question: where do ideas which are not the ruling ideas come from, how do they emerge? A little later in the same passage an answer is in fact offered: such ideas do not fall from the sky, are not generated out of the superior wisdom of the philosophers, rather they are developed out of the material conditions of existence of that class (the proletariat) which has the potential for successfully challenging and historically superseding the existing ruling class (the bourgeoisie):

> The existence of revolutionary ideas in a particular period presupposes the existence of a revolutionary class...[12]

The emphasis on class, not on individuals, as the point of origination for the development of systems of beliefs, ideologies, or what Marx calls "illusions, modes of thought and views of life" is continued in a brief but often quoted remark in *The Eighteenth Brumaire of Louis Bonaparte*:

> Upon the different forms of property, upon the social conditions of existence, rises an entire superstructure of distinct and peculiarly formed sentiments, illusions, modes of thought and views of life. The entire class creates and forms them out of its material foundations and out of the corresponding social relations. The single individual who derives them through tradition and upbringing, may imagine that they form the real motives and the starting point of his activity.[13]

This emphasis on the class basis for the production of ideologies, and on the relationship between ruling and subordinate classes and between dominant and subordinate systems of ideas, raises all kinds of further problems and questions, particularly for those who, having accepted the theory which proposes the revolutionary potential of the proletariat, have lived to see not the demise and supersession of the capitalist class in Western Europe and the United States, but rather its continued, apparently successful existence, and the skill with which its corresponding modes of social organisation regulate and contain instances of class conflict.

To put the problem very crudely: why has the revolutionary class not produced revolutionary ideas? Attempts at theorising the operation of what has been called the "dominant ideology" by Marxists over the last 50 years, including Gramsci's development of the notion of hegemony (the means by which one class organises the consent of another class to its rule) can all be related to this central problem. The increasing interest in the development of theories of ideology in France in the period after May 68 (and before, in the case of much of Althusser's work) can be related to this obvious fact or problem – the continued existence or dominance of the capitalist class in Western Europe, 50 years after the overthrow of that class in the Soviet Union. This interest can also be related to the concern expressed by those both inside and outside the French Communist Party to "explain" the deviations and deficiencies of the Stalinist era, the period of the "cult of the personality" (a concept which is criticised by Althusser as a reversion to non-materialist modes of thinking) in Russia.

This explanation was in some cases undertaken on the basis of a theoretical acknowledgement of the possibility of a radical *discrepancy* between base and superstructure, between mode of production and a mode of social existence; and it was not only the *gauchistes*, the radical left, who expressed the dissatisfaction that the quality of social life in the Soviet Union was by no means fully commensurate with that state's revolutionising of its mode of material production. It is in pursuit of a solution to this particular problem that we find Althusser arguing (in a formulation rejected as inadequate by many of the non-communist left) that it is the theory of the "relative autonomy" of superstructure from base which "explains very simply... how the socialist *infrastructure* has been able to develop without essential damage during this period of errors affecting the superstructure".[14]

To the problem of the longevity of Western capital, and the difficulties entailed in the analysis of Russian society under Stalin, can be added an interest in the principles behind the Chinese Cultural Revolution. For it is clear that the revival of interests in problems of ideology in France was in certain respects fostered by an encounter with the ideas of the Chinese communists who were emphasising, at the time of the Cultural Revolution, the importance of a struggle consciously conducted by the proletariat within the sphere of culture and cultural production even *after* the taking of power by a proletarian party and the revolutionising of the relations of production.

The notion of a "dominant ideology" ushers in numerous problems for the radical theorists of cultural production. The most serious problems arise in relation to the examination of its "effects" within a subordinate working class culture, what Marx called "a definite form of expressing their life, a definite mode of life on their part". We shall return to this problem later. But even the endeavour to think through the relationship between "ruling ideas" and the "ruling class" is a difficult one. In the formulation of *The German Ideology* the position of the ruling class in relation to the dominant ideology would seem to be a relatively straightforward one: this is the class which has access to the means of mental production, and which therefore controls the dissemination of ideas. But, as has already been indicated, the situation may be more complex than this. For we would run into severe difficulties and be taking the chance of a disastrous oversimplification if we proposed the organs of mass communication in Britain, for example, as simply and directly under the control of the ruling class, and as expressing in a unified and monolithic fashion only those systems of values and beliefs which are supportive of the status quo. The notion of a single ruling class ideology organising and uniting the organs of mass communication ignores both the presence of divisions within the ruling class, and the extent to which the ideology of free speech does open up a space for progressive journalists and media practitioners. One example of divisions within the ruling class, divisions which through a complex series of mediations might eventually find themselves transformed and reproduced within a media discourse, would be the sometimes conflicting interests of finance capital and industrial capital, a conflict between the "free-trade" programmes of international monopoly capital and the tendency towards a policy of national protectionism – the imposition of import controls etc. – of local, national, industrial capital.

A related problem concerns the relationship between proletariat and cultural production in a post-revolutionary situation. After the revolutionising of the ownership of the means of production will the "ruling ideas" necessarily be the ideas of the proletariat in the period of its political ascendancy: will the proletariat necessarily generate its own revolutionary culture?

Despite the evident complexities in that area which has to do with the analysis of the relationship between ruling ideas and ruling class, the problems entailed in the theorising of the relationship between ruling ideas and the working class in capitalist society are in many ways very much more pressing, for such theorisation is a precondition for the development of any programme of radical cultural practice. A first question here would be this: to what extent is a particular national working class (or fraction of that class) held within the sway of ruling ideas? To what extent does a dominant ideology penetrate or suffuse, like the air that is breathed, the mode of living of the working class? This notion of an "omnipresent ideology" is very strong in Althusser's formulation of its role: "Human societies secrete ideology as the very element and atmosphere indispensable to their historical respiration and life." [15] There are two extreme positions which can be taken up in relation to this question of the extent to which a dominant ideology penetrates or suffuses the culture of a subordinate class.

The first position proposes the notion that the working class, considered as an undifferentiated whole, is simply dominated by the dominant ideology, which is conceived of as an undifferentiated unity. The implication of this position is that only after a revolution with respect to the ownership of the means of production would the stranglehold of the dominant ideology be broken. Moreover, it would then necessarily be broken at the level of the superstructures as the superstructures reflect and reproduce the "break" constituted at the level of the base. This position allows no "relative autonomy" to the superstructures. Without a revolutionising of the mode of production and therefore of the relations of production (the relations between classes) the power of the dominant ideology cannot be called into question. This position would regard the notion of cultural struggle within capitalism as theoretically inconceivable, as at best a deviation from the main line of attack, the assault on the economic base. It might be difficult to find any exponents adhering in all respects to this position, laid out in an extreme, almost caricatural version as it is here.

The second position taken up on the question of the relationship between ruling ideas and subordinate classes suggests (in complete contrast to the first position) that the working class, through or because of the specificity of *its own* life experience under capitalism, as it were naturally and spontaneously produces, along with its own culture, its own ideology which is frequently inferred to be oppositional. To put the position most crudely: the eating of fish and chips in a working class community is not only different from but also aggressively in opposition to the forms of culinary pleasure of the middle and upper classes. This position both assumes that there is a one-to-one correspondence between the cultural form and the class which produces or consumes it, and that the act of production or consumption is an act of resistance to dominant cultural forms.

A related position speaks of the need for workers' self-expression. The assumption that the working class will be able to express itself, its own needs, ignores the problem that the working class does not live in its own world, but in a world organised by capital and the needs of capital. When it expresses its needs, therefore, there is a sense in which these needs are not "its own" but its needs understood only as they can be expressed through the structures (whether the forms of mass communication or the structures of wage-bargaining) produced by the existing relations of production and by the corresponding forms of social organisation. Any consideration of the concept of workers' self-expression must encounter, and find, ways of dealing satisfactorily with, the twin dangers of unprincipled populism (if a worker says it, it must be right) and vanguardist elitism (the workers don't know what's good for them, and must on all occasions be spoken for by the vanguard/ Party which does know).

The problem of developing cultural forms which will permit a subordinate class to "express itself" is an enormous one, since it has to confront not only the difficulty of distinguishing the expression of "real needs" from the expression of "false needs", but also the existing limitations on access to a language, to a means of representation: the difficulty of "mastery of a language" referred to in an extraordinarily acute comment made by a group of Italian peasant school children:

> True culture, which no man has yet possessed, would be made up of two elements, belonging to the masses and mastery of the language.[16]

To summarise then, briefly, these two positions on the relationship between a dominant ideology and a subordinate class: the first assumes that the dominant ideology is completely in control of the subordinate class, and that the mechanism of control is guaranteed by the mode of production, by the economic base. The second suggests that the subordinate class "escapes" the control of the dominant ideology by virtue of its own specific life experience, and that furthermore it necessarily generates oppositional ideologies out of this differentiated life experience. Of these two extremes the first tends to a sort of quietism with respect to cultural production for the cultural is placed firmly beneath the economic, and activity is directed primarily at the revolutionising of the economic, the base. The very possibility of cultural struggle, under capitalism and within capitalist institutions, is lobotomised out of the mind of the political activist. The second extreme offers us a very much more productive error; for it is incorrect only in assuming that the cultural forms of the working class are necessarily in a relationship of resistance to those of the ruling class. What is to be salvaged from this position is the proposition that these cultural forms are *potentially* in a relationship of resistance to those of the ruling class; but that this potentiality can be developed only in a particular historical conjuncture, and only in relationship to an understanding of other elements or aspects (to include the apparatuses of cultural exchange) of contemporary class struggle.

The summary offered above of two extreme positions on the question of the relationship between a dominant ideology and a subordinate class may help to clarify certain tendencies. But it has the great disadvantage of presenting ideology as an entity, a quantity, a thing, rather than as a process, an operation, a kind of work. For the positions outlined above rely upon the idea of the presence or absence of the dominant ideology; like a vast oil slick it either contaminates the whole sea, or leaves certain sheltered bays untouched. It should therefore be noted here that the dominant ideology may more usefully be thought of as a process, constantly changing as all aspects of social reality change, and that its operations may be thought of as being negotiated in different ways by those occupying different class positions. The dominant ideology may thus be thought of as working to contain the potentially oppositional cultural forms of subordinate classes. It cannot, as it were, obliterate these forms, make them vanish, any more than it could make the class which generates them vanish. Rather it works to bring these cultural forms within that vast arena of consent which enables a ruling class to assert its authority without the show of naked force. That is to say, the dominant ideology "gathers" these subordinate cultural forms and class forces containing them within the hegemony (to use Gramsci's term) of the ruling class.

If there has been a tendency in more recent discussion of cultural production to call attention to the inadequacy of a theory of superstructure directly determined by base and in turn simply reflecting the operations of the base, Marx and Engels also expressed certain reservations about what they saw as misleadingly mechanical interpretations of the base/superstructure model. In his 1859 Preface to *A Contribution to the Critique of Political Economy*, Marx discusses the changes effected at the level of both base and superstructure during a period of social revolution, and while pointing out the relative ease with which changes in the base, the "economic foundation" can be discerned, clearly sees the analysis of transformations at the level of the superstructures as a rather more complex and difficult business:

> With the change of the economic foundation the entire immense superstructure is more or less rapidly transformed. In considering such transformations a distinction should always be made between the material transformation of the economic conditions of production, which can be determined with the precision of natural science, and the legal, political, religious, aesthetic or philosophic – in short, ideological forms in which men become conscious of this conflict and fight it out.[17]

The forms of struggle at the level of ideology thus have their own specificity, and are more difficult to analyse than transformations of the base. This specificity of the ideological is often discussed in terms of the notion of the "uneven development" of the different levels of a social formation. The expression is to be found in Marx's 1857 Introduction to the *Critique of Political Economy* (also referred to as the *Grundrisse*), where in a very schematic form he notes the problem of the uneven development of forms of art and modes of social organisation:

> the uneven development of material production relative to, e.g., artistic development. In general the concept of progress not to be conceived in the usual abstractness...[18]
>
> In the case of the arts, it is well known that certain periods of their flowering are out of all proportion to the general development of society, hence also to the material foundation, the skeletal structure as it were, of its organisation.[19]

Engels, introducing in 1890 the notion, though not the vocabulary, of the specific effectivity of the superstructures, criticises the notion of the economic base as the only determining factor in social change, and emphasises the way in which the operations at the level of the superstructures in turn react upon, have an effect upon the base. Here he proposes a rather more interactive model than that suggested by the image of the camera obscura:

> According to the materialist concept of history, the *ultimately* determining element in history is the production and reproduction of real life. More than this neither Marx nor I have ever

> asserted. Hence if somebody twists this into saying that the economic element is the *only* determining one, he transforms that proposition into a meaningless, abstract, senseless phrase. The economic situation is the basis, but the various elements of the superstructure ... also exercise their influence upon the course of the historical struggles and in many cases preponderate in determining their *form*. There is an interaction of all these elements...[20]

Engels' insistence that the economic is not to be seen as the only determining factor, and his allocation of "influence" to the elements of the superstructure, introduces the notion of a highly complex differentiated social formation, with each of the elements of that formation accorded a certain effectivity. Moreover, it is Althusser's contention[21] that, by implication, this notion breaks with the idea of a tightly-knit, entirely unified social formation in which each of the upper levels of the grand edifice (the superstructures) exactly corresponds to, reflects, expresses or echoes the foundation of that edifice (the base). In other words what is implied is a notion of the social formation, comprised of the economic, political and ideological levels, which, operating in a complex and contradictory fashion, cannot be thought of as a single "expressive totality"[22] It is Althusser's view, however, that Engels – caught within an earlier and inadequate theoretical paradigm – lacked both the concepts and the vocabulary to think through these implications to a new and adequate formulation. It is to this task (among others), of providing a more adequate theorisation of the base/superstructure relationship, that Althusser addresses himself.

The tendency of Althusser's discussion of ideology is to insist that far from being a phantom-like illusion, a straightforward lie or distortion, a thin and easily-to-be-pierced veil that covers the truth, ideology has, rather a reality, a materiality even, of its own. So he argues, in a 1965 article, against the notion that:

> ... the whole social function of ideology could be summed up cynically as a myth (such as Plato's "beautiful lies" or the techniques of modern advertising) fabricated and manipulated from the outside by the ruling class to fool those it is exploiting...[23]

It cannot be explained away as a device employed by one class to "fool" another; rather, as has already been indicated, it is more like the air that is breathed ("Human societies secrete ideology as the very element and atmosphere indispensable to their historical respiration and life")[24]; and as such it is not consciously "noticed". Warning against the notion "that ideology belongs to the region of 'consciousness' "[25] he argues that it is, rather, "profoundly unconscious", and calls it paradoxically that "form of specific unconsciousness called 'consciousness' "[25] It is concerned with the way in which men and women experience or negotiate their world, "a matter of the *lived* relation between men and their world", and as such it is seen as "a structure essential to the historical life of societies". Because it works to adapt men and women to the conditions of their existence, Althusser argues that it is a necessary part of all societies, including communist society. It is that which, as it were, connects men and women to the real conditions of their existence, and which expresses this connection in one way or another depending upon the nature of the society. Thus:

> In a class society ideology is the relay whereby, and the element in which, the relation between men and their conditions of existence is settled to the profit of the ruling class. In a classless society

> ideology is the relay whereby, and the element in which, the relation between men and their conditions of existence is lived to the profit of all men.[26]

The notion that ideology connects men and women to their world, expresses their relationship to that world, with the implication that it *might* therefore say something about the real conditions of their existence, receives a further gloss as Althusser proposes the dual nature of this connection. Because ideology is the "expression of the relation between men and their 'world'" it brings together and unites both a "real relation" and what Althusser calls an "imaginary" or "lived" relation. Or, to use the better known formulation of his 1970 essay *Ideology and Ideological State Apparatuses*:

> What is represented in ideology is therefore not the system of the real relations which govern the existence of individuals, but the imaginary relation of those individuals to the real relations in which they live.[27]

Furthermore, ideologies are not mere "lies", not the upside-down reflections of "real relations", but systems of representations with their own complex and internally consistent (their own "logic and rigour") mode of operating; the precise nature of their relationship to "real relations" has to be carefully, and with difficulty, traced out. For this "tracing out" to occur ideology has to be understood as a system in its own right, not as merely homologous with or reflexive of the base. To summarise the point in Althusser's words:

> An ideology is a system (with its own logic and rigour) of representations (images, myths, ideas or concepts, depending on the case) endowed with a historical existence and role within a given society.[28]

> Ideology is indeed a system of representations but in the majority of cases these representations have nothing to do with 'consciousness': they are usually images and occasionally concepts, but it is above all as *structures* that they impose on the vast majority of men, not via their 'consciousness'. They are perceived – accepted – suffered cultural objects and they act functionally on men via a process that escapes them.[29]

The fact of its omnipresence, and its operation at an unconscious level, however, does not seem to mean for Althusser that it cannot be known, analysed; though he suggests that it is only when the necessity of the existence of ideology is recognised that it can then be used (presumably in a newly "conscious" way?) for certain defined ends. Certainly the notion of a possible (conscious) ideological struggle is introduced in the statement that:

> ...ideology is not an aberration or a contingent excrescence of History: it is a structure essential to the historical life of societies. Further only the existence and the recognition of its necessity enable us to act on ideology and transform ideology into an instrument of deliberate action on history.[30]

Despite the importance of the arguments about the specific effectivity of the superstructures, and the valuable way in which these serve to counteract any overly mechanical or crudely determinist notion of the action of the base, these arguments can lead to certain difficulties on the very question of determination. While not wishing to accord a simple primacy to the economic, Althusser is content with the formulation of a determination "in the last instance" by the economic.[31] Elsewhere in an endeavour to explain the concept of complex contradiction in relationship to the social formation, he speaks of it as being: "complexly-structurally-unevenly-determined", and proposes to substitute for this inelegant expression the term "over-determined".[32] The difficulties of this whole endeavour have been very usefully summarised by Stuart Hall:

> ... how does Marxism enable us to "think" the complexities of a modern capitalist social formation? How can we conceptualise the relationships between the different levels which compose it? Further, can we "think" this problem in such a way as to retain a key premise of historical materialism: the premise of "determination in the last instance" by what is sometimes misleadingly referred to as "the economic"? Can this be done without losing one's way in the idea of the *absolute* autonomy of each of its levels...?[33]

This danger of "losing one's way in the idea of the *absolute* autonomy of each of its levels" needs to be taken up in relation to the notion of cultural production. And there is a problem here. For once we begin to think of the superstructures as more than the reflection, as more than the echoes of a vigorous base, once they are allowed a certain independence to, as it were, speak for themselves, then what is to prevent us from thinking of these superstructures as completely autonomous from the base? Some recent Marxist commentators moving down the primrose pathway of non-correspondence between the different levels or instances of the social formation, in pursuit of the unique specificity of each instance, have gone as far as to suggest a necessary "non-correspondence" between the levels.[34] Where there is a notion of necessary non-correspondence, there can hardly be a concept of determination of any kind. And while much energy has been devoted to conducting an absolutely necessary attack on crude economic determinism, it is difficult to see how any proposition which finally refuses the notion of a determination in the last instance by the mode of production (considered in its most general sense), can properly be regarded as Marxist. Althusser himself, while persisting in the criticism of what he sees as the basically Hegelian notion of the social formation as "expressive totality", in which all the elements are homologous with each other, correspond directly with each other, fit exactly as a unified totality, nevertheless pulls back from the brink of asserting a complete autonomy for these elements:

> ...I talked about a *whole*, to make it clear that in the Marxist conception of a social formation everything holds together, that the independence of an element is only ever the form of its dependence, and that the interplay of the differences is regulated by the unity of a determination in the last instance; but that is why I did not talk about a *totality*, because the Marxist whole is complex and uneven, and stamped with this unevenness by the determination in the last instance.[35]

This argument about the autonomy/relative autonomy of the elements of the social formation has certain fairly practical consequences for any attempts at progressive cultural production. An emphasis on the autonomy of the elements would tend to result in a cultural practice which in concentrating upon the specificity of art, sees radical practice in terms of certain advances at the level of the formal operations of the text, advances which have to do with the specific history of the art form; the radical is defined in terms of that which is radical in relation to the particular history of the system (element of the social formation) "art". Thus it is that the French critic and semiotician Roland Barthes emphasises in his earlier work the importance of studying "the system's own particular time, the history of forms."[36]

The real difficulty, however, may be posed by the need to understand the *relationship* between different "histories", different elements of the social formation (each with their own specific history and mode of operation) at a particular historical moment. It could be argued that the position which speaks of the *relative autonomy* of the elements would be more likely – at the level of cultural production – to be concerned with these relationships between elements at a particular historical moment; that, to be more specific, the exponents of the semi-autonomous status of art/film would be more interested in developing an understanding of the relationship between cultural production and class struggle at other levels of the social formation. Such exponents might, therefore, be less likely to pose aesthetic strategies divorced from an accompanying analysis of the configurations of contemporary political life and an assessment of the most pressing problems currently confronting a particular national working class.

For the exponents of complete autonomy, by contrast, who see neither the feasibility nor apparently the desirability of assessing the relationship between the elements of the social formation (in this context the relationship between art/politics/economics), the specificity of the cultural is permitted to float elegantly free from the exigencies of the political. No attempt is made to theorise the relationship between cultural production and class struggle.

While (as has already been indicated) the operation of a dominant ideology makes it extremely difficult to speak of a subordinate class "expressing itself", it must be emphasised that the various elements of the social formation (including, of course, class relations) are not static in their relationship to each other, but constantly subject to change. It is the acceptance of this principle of change which allows and encourages Gramsci to affirm the "possibility and necessity of creating a new culture". Indeed, there is a sense in which this "new culture" with its alternative sets of beliefs and values is constantly in the process of being produced. The arguments must be about its extent (for whom?), efficacy and relationship to the balance of class forces. Gramsci outlines the relations between the interests of dominant and subordinate groups in society as being in a state of constant tension:

> ...the dominant group is co-ordinated concretely with the general interests of the subordinate groups, and the life of the state is conceived of as a continuous process of formation and superseding of unstable equilibria... between the interests of the fundamental group and those of the subordinate groups.[37]

If this notion of there being a fundamental instability about the balance of forces within the social formation is accepted, with the dominant group, as it were, working overtime to assert its hegemony and produce the social equilibrium which stems from that successful assertion, it can be argued that a theoretical justification is available for believing in the possibility of productive work, or struggle, within the ideological field. What we find in Gramsci's formulations is a theory that underwrites and encourages a programme of political and cultural action in a pre-revolutionary period. Thus, for example, he argues:

> ...even before attaining power a class can (and must) "lead"... there can and must be a "political hegemony" even before the attainment of governmental power...[38]

And the importance of a programme at the level of ideological and cultural struggle is made rather more explicit in the remark:

> Every revolution has been preceded by hard critical thinking, the diffusion of culture, and the spread of ideas among men who are at first unwilling to listen.[39]

To return briefly to the concept of the "uneven development" of the social formation, we may note that just as there is a possibility that a particular form of cultural production may be a "survival", an anachronistic hangover from the class needs of an earlier epoch, so also it is theoretically possible for cultural production to anticipate future class needs, and to play a part in the transference of political hegemony from one class to another in advance of a radical change in the relations of production. This possibility produces that optimism which looks for the emergence of oppositional cultures and of dominated but "protesting" ideologies. It is only this hope which justifies the continued discussion of and search for radical aesthetic practices within a social order that operates according to the exigencies of monopoly capital. The importance of this work of struggle at the level of cultural production to represent new needs and values, in advance of a radical change in the relations of production, has been usefully outlined by the English historian E. P. Thompson, in the context of a defence of the writings of the poet and political essayist William Morris:

> Morris sought in every way to implant, encourage and enlarge new "wants" in the present, and imbue the socialist movement with an alternative notation of value, *before* the "rupture"; and he judged that socialist success or failure in this enterprise would affect not only when the revolution came but what form it would take. In any event, Morris saw (although unclearly) that "ruptures" in values are taking place *all the time*, and not only during moments of strike and rebellion.[40]

NOTES

1. Marx/Engels, *The German Ideology*. London: Lawrence & Wishart, 1974, p. 42.
2. Ibid.
3. Ibid., pp.46-47.
4. Ibid., p.47.
5. Antonio Gramsci, *Selections from the Prison Notebooks*. Edited and translated by Quintin Hoare and Geoffrey Nowell Smith. London: Lawrence & Wishart, 1971, p. 407.
6. Ibid.
7. *The German Ideology*, op. cit., p.47.
8. Louis Althusser, *For Marx*. Translated by Ben Brewster. London: New Left Books, 1969, p.233.
9. *The German Ideology*, op. cit., p.47.
10. Ibid., p.66.
11. Ibid., p.64.
12. Ibid., p.65.
13. Marx, The Eighteenth Brumaire of Louis Bonaparte. In Marx/Engels, *Selected Works in One Volume*. London: Lawrence & Wishart, 1970, p.117.
14. Louis Althusser, *For Marx*, op. cit., p.240.
15. Ibid., p.232.
16. *Letter to a Teacher, by the School of Barbiana*. London: Penguin, 1970.
17. Marx, Preface to A Contribution to the Critique of Political Economy. In: Marx/Engels, *Selected Works*, op. cit., p.182.
18. Marx, *Grundrisse*. Translated by Martin Nicolaus. London: Penguin, 1973, p. 109.
19. Ibid., p.110.
20. Engels to Bloch, 1890. In: Marx/Engels, *Selected Works*, op. cit.
21. cf. Louis Althusser, Contradiction and Overdetermination. In: *For Marx*, op. cit.
22. For Althusser's discussion of the

Hegelian notion of totality, cf. On the Materialist Dialectic. In: *For Marx*, op. cit,. pp.202-204.
23. Louis Althusser, Marxism and Humanism. In: *For Marx*, op.cit., p.235.
24. Ibid., p.232 and p.240.
25. Ibid., p.232-233.
26. Ibid., p.236.
27. Louis Althusser, Ideology and Ideological State Apparatuses. In: *Lenin and Philosophy and Other Essays*. London: New Left Books, 1971, p.155.
28. Louis Althusser, Marxism and Humanism, op. cit., p.231.
29. Ibid., p.233.
30. Ibid., p.232.
31. Louis Althusser, Contradiction and Overdetermination, op. cit., p.113.
32. Louis Althusser, On the Materialist Dialectic. In: *For Marx*, op. cit., p.209.
33. Stuart Hall, Re-thinking the Base-and-Superstructure Metaphor. In: John Bloomfield (ed.), *Class, Hegemony and Party*. London: Lawrence & Wishart, 1977, p.44.
34. See, in Britain, the debate between Ros Coward and the Birmingham Centre for Contemporary Cultural Studies. Ros Coward, Class, 'Culture' and the Social Formation. In: *Screen*, vol.18 No.1, Spring 1977, pp. 75-105. And the response from the Centre, Marxism and Culture, in *Screen*, vol.18 No.4, Winter 1977-78 pp.109-119.
35. Louis Althusser, Is it Simple to be a Marxist in Philosophy? First published in France in 1975; published in English in: *Essays in Self Criticism*. Translated by Grahame Lock. London: New Left Books, 1976, p.183.
36. Roland Barthes, *Elements of Semiology*. London: Jonathan Cape, 1967, p.98.
37. Antonio Gramsci, *Prison Notebooks*, op. cit., p.182.
38. Ibid., p.57, footnote.
39. Antonio Gramsci, Socialism and Culture. In: *Avanti*, June 1916. Quoted and translated in: John M. Cammett, *Antonio Gramsci and the Origins of Italian Communism*. Stanford University Press, 1967, p.42.
40. Edward Thompson, Romanticism, Utopianism and Moralism: The Case of William Morris. In: *New Left Review*, No. 99, Sept-Oct 1976, p.111.

· This article first appeared in: Sylvia Harvey, *May '68 and Film Culture*. London: British Film Institute, 1978, pp. 87-105. We thank Sylvia Harvey and the British Film Institute for permission to reprint this adapted version.

The Camera Against the Paris Commune

Gen Doy

TWO MYTHS ABOUT photography have had a long history: that the camera is objective; and that the camera has had a democratizing effect on the production and consumption of visual imagery. It was precisely during the period of the Second Empire in France (1852-1870) and the Commune (1871) that these very concepts of objectivity and democratization were being constructed around the growing social significance of photography. However, they were by no means fixed, and the following study attempts to investigate this intermediate stage in the evolution of the photograph as a record of historical events, and the uses of such visual documentation. First of all, it is necessary to summarize the historical and technical information relating to photography in 1871. The following account of the Paris Commune is intended to give a brief account of the historical data, concentrating on aspects which are relevant to the photographs reproduced here.

After an economically prosperous start, the Second Empire in France was beset by increasing financial difficulties in the later

1860s. Bonapartism, personified by Louis-Napoleon Bonaparte, was forced to make mildly liberal concessions to the working classes and bourgeois-liberal reformers. Its function was to maintain, as Marx correctly saw, a precarious equilibrium between classes under developed capitalism. However, the disastrous imperialist war between France and Prussia in 1870 led to the rejection of the Empire by France, and a chauvinist Government of National Defence was formed by Adolphe Thiers. France continued to fight the Prussians, and the working classes of Paris under siege were thus isolated from the more reactionary rural areas of the country. When Paris heard that the Government had negotiated a peace with the enemy, an alliance formed between the working people of Paris and the nationalistic lower bourgeoisie against the reactionary Adolphe Thiers. Thiers surrendered to the Prussians leaving the Parisian National Guard as the most powerful armed body remaining in France. Following an abortive attempt to disarm the Parisian populace, Thiers and his supporters withdrew to Versailles in order to marshal forces to crush insurgent Paris. Generals Thomas and Lecomte had been dispatched to Montmartre on 18 March 1871 to seize the cannons of the National Guard. Local people had protested, and the troops of the line had refused the generals' command to fire on the crowd of protesters, including many women and children. They had instead turned on their commanders and eventually shot them. This so-called barbarity on the part of the insurgents was frequently referred to by Thiers in his speeches, and was also mentioned on numerous occasions by the anti-Communard press. In fact it was one of the few occasions during the Commune period when the Parisians had not been sufficiently disciplined to spare their hostages. The other occasions when this occurred were during the bitter fighting in late May, when the Versailles troops retook Paris, and slaughtered indiscriminately all those suspected of being Communards. In retaliation, the Communards shot hostages they held in prison. During the short life-span of the Commune, declared on March 18 and brutally suppressed by force during *Bloody Week* in late May, strategies for a working class government were put into practice. Obviously the historical significance of the Commune has been differently interpreted according to the political views of its commentators. For Marxists, the Commune became the touchstone for the analysis of practice and theory in revolutionary government. For the right, the Commune was to be either reviled or else ignored, and any traces of its existence quickly blotted out. For those who claimed to have no political affiliation, the "facts" and "documents" of the Commune and its existence could be presented "objectively" in words or images. Many of these "objective" images are, of course, photographs.

What technology was available for recording contemporary events in 1871 and how accurate was it? Photographers already had experience of recording contemporary history under conditions similar to those which were to be encountered in the Paris Commune. Roger Fenton had been dispatched on an official mission to the Crimea in 1855 to provide visual proof that the British Government was not mismanaging the war. He was told "No dead bodies" in no uncertain terms. What appeared in his photographs may have been accurate enough, but the images themselves cannot tell us what is not included in them. In the days before photojournalism proper, the diffusion and marketability of "news" photographs was uncertain. In addition to his government payments, Fenton had arranged with the dealer Agnew to publish a portfolio of the photographs on completion of the mission. Meantime, public interest was kept alive by Agnew who sold to the *Illustrated London News* on the condition that their wood-engravers preserved the character of the photograph, and a

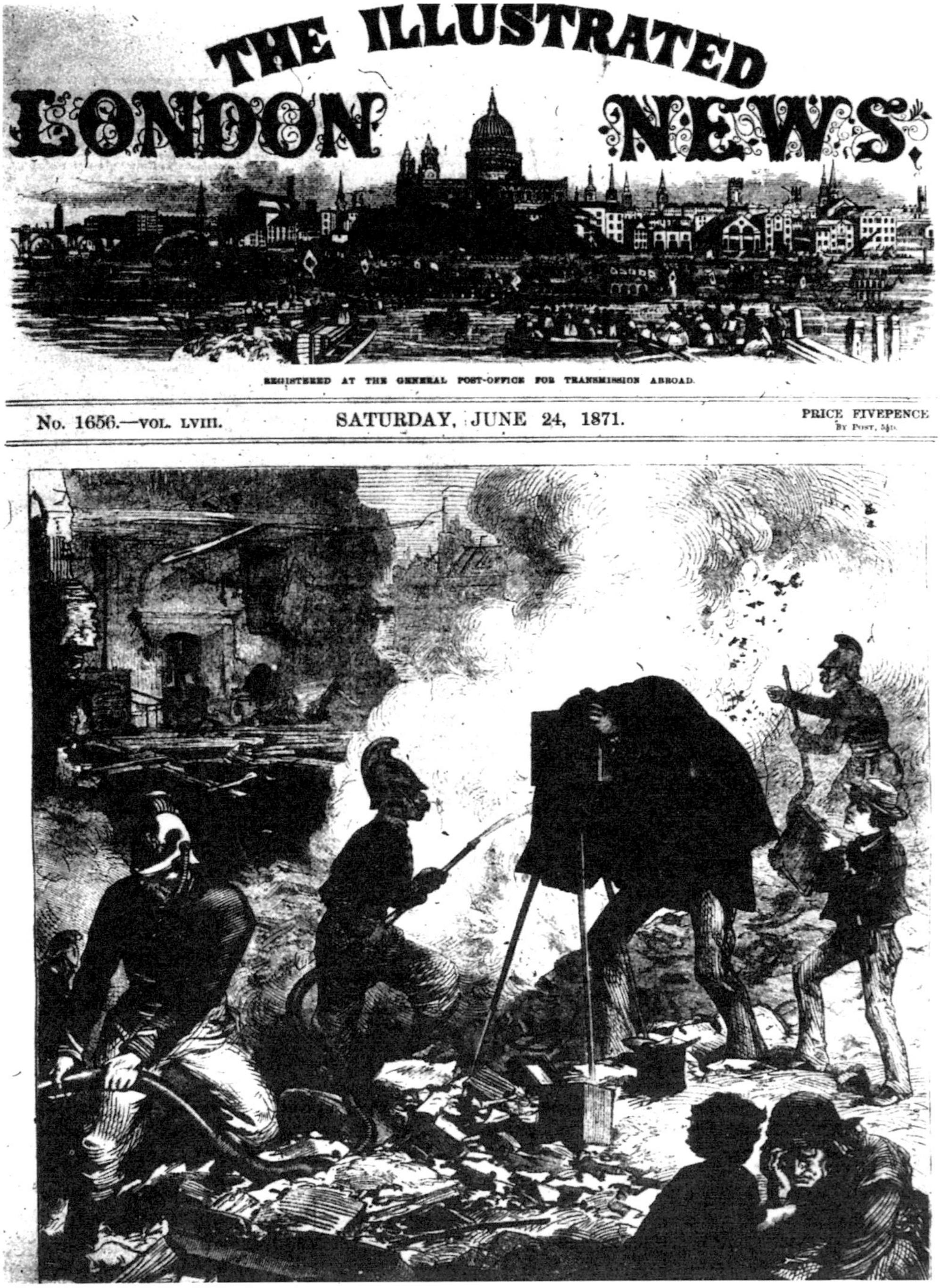
THE ILLUSTRATED LONDON NEWS.

REGISTERED AT THE GENERAL POST-OFFICE FOR TRANSMISSION ABROAD.

No. 1656.—VOL. LVIII. SATURDAY, JUNE 24, 1871. PRICE FIVEPENCE BY POST, 5½D.

1. Cover from *The Illustrated London News*, wood engraving.

credit was given to Fenton.[1] At this time, the function of photographs in the illustrated press was limited to the role of the artist's sketch as a similar basis for the production of a wood-engraving to illustrate the report of a special correspondent who provided an "eye-witness" account. The report and the illustration were intended to enhance one another. In the case of important events both were considered necessary. It was by this time technically possible to print photograph and text together in the paper, but newspaper proprietors were unwilling to make the considerable financial commitments required for the development of the new machinery.

Thus in 1871 the large newspapers illustrated their coverage of the Paris Commune with wood-engravings executed by craftsmen after the drawings of artists present in Paris, who sent out their work from the besieged city either by balloon or through the lines of the troops surrounding the city. Many of the Parisian papers used photographs of ruined buildings as a basis for their illustrations reporting the aftermath of the Commune, but for technical reasons it was not possible in 1871 to photograph anything but static scenes. Fenton's Crimean War pictures tend to be posed and static, not only because he had been told to keep away from images of violence and bloodshed, but also because exposure times and the use of wet-plates requiring careful preservation and development made it impossible to take action pictures. This stage of photographic technique persisted during the Commune period. Consequently photographs taken of the Communards and their activities tend to be static, posed and out-of-doors, apart from true studio portraits of individuals, or "faked" photographs, which sometimes show indoor scenes. (This last point is a good indication as to whether a photograph might be a fake or not.) One tends to find images which show groups of Communards lined up on barricades, corpses ranged in their coffins, mug-shots of Communard prisoners, or desolate ruins of deserted burnt-out buildings.

At a time when the events taking place in Paris cried out for visual reporting, photography did not possess the technical means to do this. Some of the difficulties encountered by the news press in this situation can be seen in a cover from the *Illustrated London News* of June 24, 1871 (plate 1). In fact the editors have cleverly exploited the technical deficiencies of photography in the wood engraving on the cover. A photographer attempts to photograph the scene as firemen try to extinguish the flames which have already destroyed the building. The photographer stands in the midst of the chaos, accompanied by his young assistant who holds the plate ready for him. Neither the firemen nor the homeless mother and child in the foreground pay any attention to him. The "objectivity" of the camera in this case suggests its invisibility, or perhaps even its irrelevance. In this case, the graphic artist gives a "truthful" account of the scene, which also includes, and comments on, the role of the photographer within it. Yet even so, the scene depicted probably occurred at the end of May, when the reactionary troops entered Paris, and the Commune was crushed during bitter fighting. It has taken roughly a month for the "news" to appear on the cover of the paper.

In 1871, therefore, photography did not enjoy the powerful position vis-a-vis other graphic media which it enjoys today. While contemporaries accepted, for example, that the photograph would show a scene which "really" took place, they obviously also accepted that a hand-drawn image could give a truthful account of events. What tended to happen was that photographs were sold as historical souvenirs, to back up the information that the public had already read and seen in the press.

What was the purpose of this visual material and what was its public? The answers to these questions are complex, and not always possible to answer fully. In purely economic terms, for example, it would be fair to say that working class people would not have been able to afford either photographs or illustrated papers except as a luxury. To give some examples – Disdéri brought the price of photographic portraits down dramatically in the early 1850s by exploiting the *carte-de-visite* format, 6 x 9 cms, and by using glass negatives to give multiple prints. This meant that twelve portrait photos now cost twenty francs as opposed to the previous rate of one large portrait for 50-100 francs.[2] As Gisèle Freund points out, quoting Disdéri, this brought photographic portraiture within the grasp of the petty bourgeoisie. However, it certainly did not bring it within the reach of the working classes. The average daily wage of a working man at the end of the Second Empire was three francs, sufficient to buy six kilos of bread.[3] Jules Simon estimated at this time that a family of four living in Paris needed an income of 32-33 francs a week in order to live just above starvation level, and pointed out that only a minority of working-class families made even this amount of money.[4] Wages in craft-type work were, for example, bookbinding: men 3-8 francs a day, women 1-3.50 francs.[5] Photography itself was economically in the class of craft work. For workers in photographic establishments the wages were: men 3-20 francs, women 1.25-6 francs a day.[6] This compares with wages of workers in printing trades. From this we can see that it was most unlikely that the working classes of Paris were used to visiting photographers' studios or buying photographs very frequently. Similarly, the illustrated newspapers were probably beyond their reach, although the most expensive, *L'Illustration*, sold for 75 centimes a copy. Like photography, the illustrated newspaper was the newly created province of the petty bourgeoisie, and all of the French illustrated papers (and indeed the foreign ones) were resolutely anti-Communard. As a comparison, Communard newspapers cost around five centimes, or ten centimes for the illustrated *Caricature*.

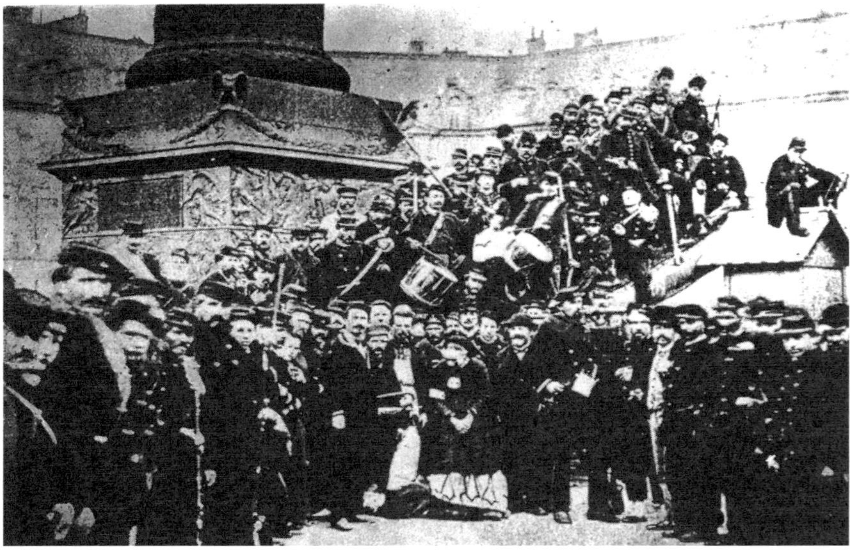

2. Group of Communards at the foot of the Vendôme Column, May 16, 1871, photograph.

It is also difficult to say who worked in photography during the Second Empire and Commune period. Fenton was the son of a wealthy mill-owner, banker and MP, and many of the early pioneers of photography had private means. However in the Second Empire in France, under the impetus of Disdéri's enterprising business sense, photography became a commercial success. Freund quotes Nadar in pointing out that all kinds of people now proceeded to set themselves up in the photography "industry" (bohemians, drop-out students, failed lawyers, and so on) but since it was necessary to buy a camera and rent a studio, it is not likely that there were "working-class" photographers.[7] However, we should beware of a strictly economistic approach to the status and role of the photographer during the Commune. Many of the members of the Commune were obviously not working-class in origin, but this did not prevent their commitment to the emancipation of working-class people.

The function of the photographic material varies and the following attempts to investigate the uses of photographs in the Commune period do not pretend to be exhaustive. It will be helpful to deal with them under several categories, although, as we shall see, these categories overlap.

Firstly, there are photographs which might be loosely termed documentary records (bearing in mind reservations as to the problematic nature of documentation.) These images showed people taking an active part in the construction of their own history and proud to be shown in the act of doing so. As we have seen, for many of the people in these images, it would be a novelty and a privilege hitherto reserved for another class simply to appear in a photograph. They may have felt that the very fact of being photographed conferred a permanency on their achievements. For example the Commune decreed the destruction of the Vendôme column, which commemorated the military conquests of Napoleon I during the First Empire. On May 16 the Commune demanded that the column should be pulled down as "a monument of barbarism, a symbol of brute force and false glory, an affirmation of militarism, a denial of international law,

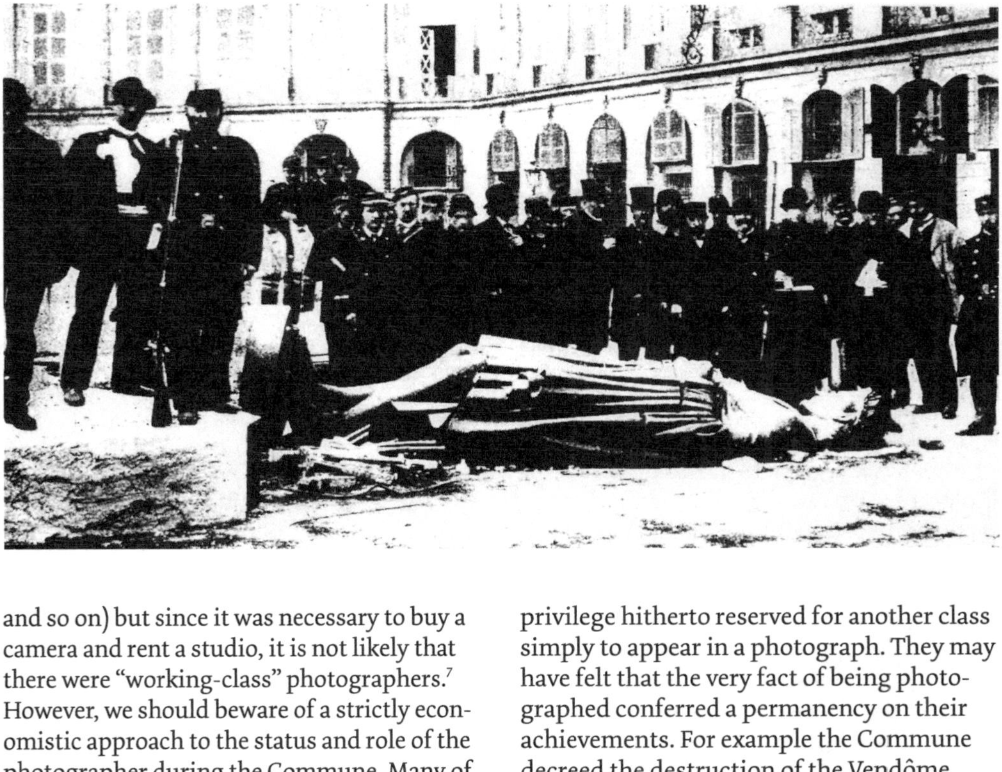

3. Group of Communards surrounding the demolished Vendôme Column, May 16

a permanent insult directed at the conquered by their conquerors, a perpetual attack upon one of the three great principles of the French republic..."[8] The Communards were obviously fully conscious of the important historical and political implications of this decision. A large number of photographs were taken of the actual destruction of the column, and the participants were carefully posed by photographers both before and after the operation to dismantle the monument (plates 2 and 3). What the proud Communards did not realize was that only a few weeks later, the same photographers who had been so eager to immortalize them for revolutionary posterity were more than willing to hand over their prints to the authorities, so that the insurgents could be identified by the Versailles prosecutors from photographs such as those illustrated as plates 2 and 3.[9] Thus what might have been envisaged as the original purpose of the photographs could easily be subverted as soon as they were utilised for different political ends.

Similarly, the Communards were photographed on May 15 when they demolished the private residence of Thiers (plate 4). Thiers' possessions were auctioned in aid of the poor and bed linen and household utensils from the house were given to hospitals. The Communards were aware of the significance of this step and the appropriateness of their decision to destroy Thiers' property. During the Second Empire, Thiers had been receiving 200,000 francs a month from his official government appointments and his income from shares in the mine at Azin, where he had ordered the murder of several strikers. This monthly income represented the salary of a faceworker at the mine over a period of 24 years, supposing that the person's working life extended that long.[10]

Yet here again the intention of documentation can be subverted and reappropriated when the image is used in a different context. The Communards' attack on capitalist

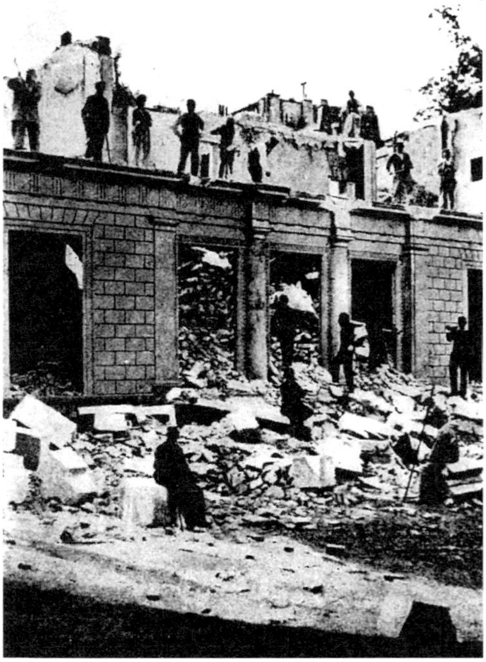

4. Demolitionof the Their's house in Paris, May 15, 1871. Photgraph by C.Soulier.

property was carried out consciously and hit their enemy where it hurt, i.e. in his pocket. A huge body of photographic material related to the Commune in fact went on sale after the repressive measures of Bloody Week, and were photographs of ruined buildings, either entirely deserted, or else with ghostly images of passers-by who had been too quick for the exposure time of the plate (plate 5). These photographs were sold either in albums or else in smaller *carte-de-visite* format, as rather gory souvenirs of the disasters which had taken place during the Commune.

The finance ministry and debtors courts, for example, were obvious candidates for petrol bombs. However the bourgeois press recounted the destruction of the buildings as entirely the work of the vandals of the Commune, devoid of respect for the architectural achievements of civilised society, and bereft of a healthy respect for property. The Hôtel de Ville and the Vendôme column, destroyed by the Communards, were rebuilt afterwards in exactly the same way so as to efface memories of the Commune's existence as much as possible. Because of this

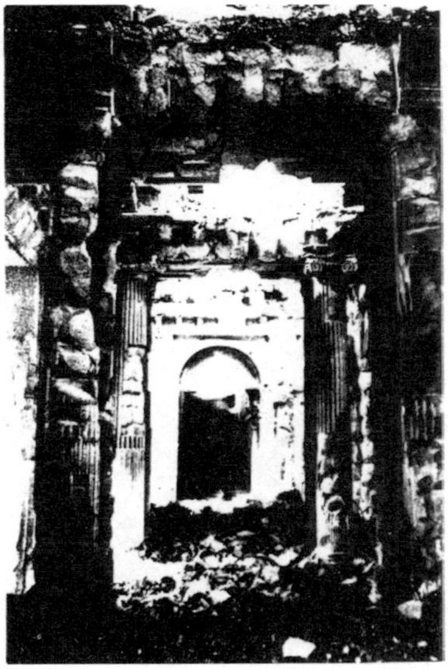

Photographs had been taken of ruined buildings during the Franco-Prussian War, but their function was rather different from the Commune ruins. Although the Versailles troops had shelled Paris for weeks during the Commune, the conservative press conveniently played this down, while emphasising the damage caused by the strategic burning of buildings carried out by Parisians during the last week of the Commune. Most of the buildings were burnt for military reasons, but some were obviously abhorrent to the Communards for ideological reasons.

the photographs of the burnt-out buildings preserve the memory of the Commune at the same time as they attempt to present the ruins as an indictment of their actions. It is important to note the large number of photographs taken of the ruined buildings. On the one hand, it should be borne in mind that technical considerations encouraged such subject matter. On the other, it indicates the concern for the material and for property which occupied the opponents of the Communards. Cluseret, a military leader of the Commune, stressed precisely the

5. Burnt out ruins of Tuileries after the Commune. Photgraph by C. Soulier.

shift in emphasis between the war waged by the imperialist powers in 1870 and the struggle of the Communards in the following year. Their theatre of war was the city, where property, rather than people was at risk: "This is the reverse of bourgeois warfare where men, who cost nothing, are destroyed, and property, which costs a great deal, is respected... To ruin confidence in capital in all its forms should be the constant aim of class warfare."[11]

It seemed to some contemporaries that the photograph was too "objective". It did not state its allegiances clearly enough and was perhaps too accessible. Was it not perhaps safer to use a medium which was traditionally associated with the property owning classes if one wished to illustrate the attack on property during the Commune? Why not revert to oil painting, even when basing your picture on a photograph, and add an obscure caption for good measure? Then perhaps one can be sure of reaching only the "right" public. This was the tactic of the reactionary academic painter Meissonnier, a favourite of the Emperor Napoleon III, who produced a commemorative painting after the Commune which he based on a photograph of the ruins of the Tuileries palace (plate 6). The photograph reproduced here as plate 5 is from the same album as the one actually used by the painter, though not the actual print. The ruined palace is made to look "sublime" and tragic in the manner of the ruins of ancient Greece or Rome. The classical heritage of civilized Europe lies in ruins, wasted by barbarian vandals. The imposing ruins are accentuated by the viewpoint, which exaggerates the scale of the buildings as we look upwards at them. Meissonnier preserves this perspective in his painting, adding a plaque and an inscription at the foot of the painting, which moralizes in Latin about vulgar mobs attempting to destroy the immortal values of culture. In the original photograph used by the painter, the chariot and figures are indeed seen through the framing arch, but the horses and figure have their backs to the viewer as s/he looks through the Tuileries to the Arc du Carrousel. Meissonnier has executed the painting as if it were a photograph, therefore "true" and "real" but has

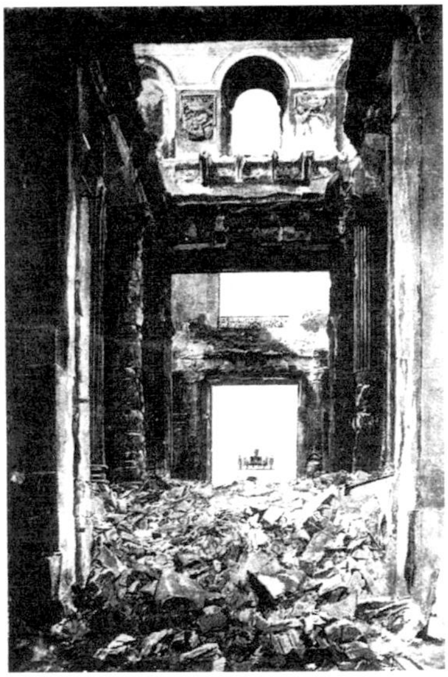

6. E.Meissonnier, *The Ruins of the Tuileries after the Commune*, oil on canvas.

turned the chariot and the victorious figure round to face the spectator in a much more effectively optimistic stance, coupling this with the addition of the plaque proclaiming, in the language of the educated upper classes, the ultimate defeat of the vandals.

Just as tourists flocked to visit the ruins of Paris after the defeat of the Commune, such images were intended as a terrible memento of the Communards' lack of respect for property, and the fate that awaits those who have the misfortune to share their misplaced ideals. Within a few weeks of the suppression of the Commune individual prints of ruins and albums of souvenir photos were listed in the *Bibliographie de la France*, which lists all books, prints and photos published in Paris. The text of one of these albums gives the general tone:

> "Forever accursed be the evil days we have just traversed, and forever let the memory of them be preserved, by the pen, by the pencil, by the burin, by the camera, by the spoken word, by every means, so that generations to come may never forget the lesson of such events!" [12]

However there is another category of photographic material from the Commune period which does attempt to manipulate photographic "objectivity" consciously. This category is made up of photographs composed from a number of negatives, sometimes from drawings or sketches with photographed figures stuck onto them and rephotographed, or even sometimes from photographs of streets with the characters painted onto them and then rephotographed. Many purported to show events and personalities of the Commune as they "truly" existed and selected "events" which could be used as propaganda for the Right. For example the killing of the two Generals Thomas and Lecomte was chosen to demonstrate "evidence" of the brutality of the Communards (plate 7). This composite photograph and the others illustrated here (plates 8, 9, 10) are among many produced during the Commune by one Appert, whose address is given on the back of his prints as 24 Rue

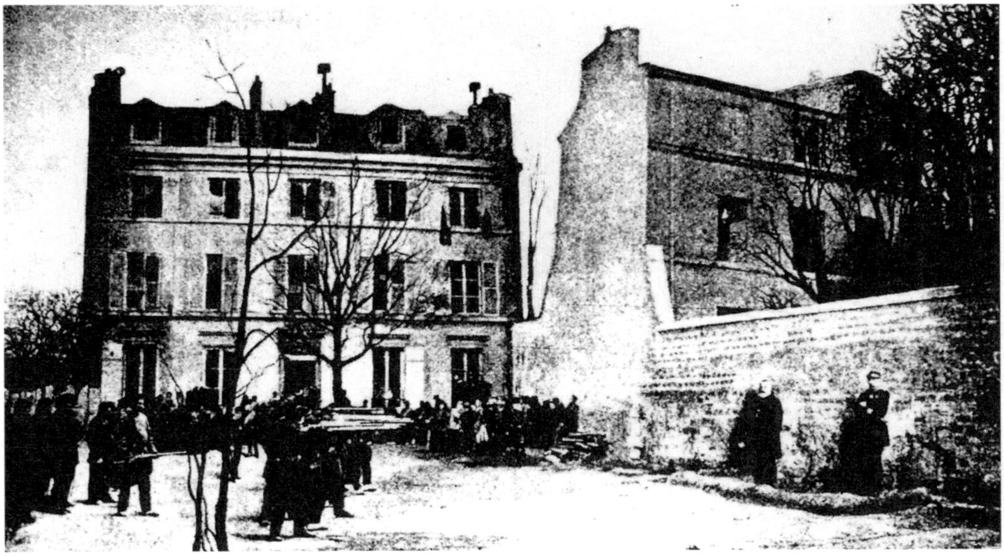

7. Execution of Generals Thomas and Lecomte by supporters of the Commune. Composite photograph by Eugène Appert.

Taitbout. He was active both before and after the Commune, and his work includes studio portraits of dignitaries of the Second Empire as well as prominent members of the Central Committee of the twenty districts of Paris during the Commune, and the Commune executive itself. Some indication of his political allegiances can be gained from an inscription on the reverse of one of his prints in the Victoria and Albert Museum, which proudly proclaims his official appointment to such governmental bodies as the magistrature and the legislative body of the Empire, material from the barricade photos.[13] Within a few weeks of the suppression of the Commune, these photos were on sale. Obviously they were intended for the supporters of the Versailles government, probably as a memento of the terrible fate they might have met at the hands of the Commune, and to justify the scale of the killings during Bloody Week, when the Versailles forces killed between 25,000-40,000 Parisians. This figure puts the event presented to us in Appert's image into a context that is not, of course, suggested by the single photograph.

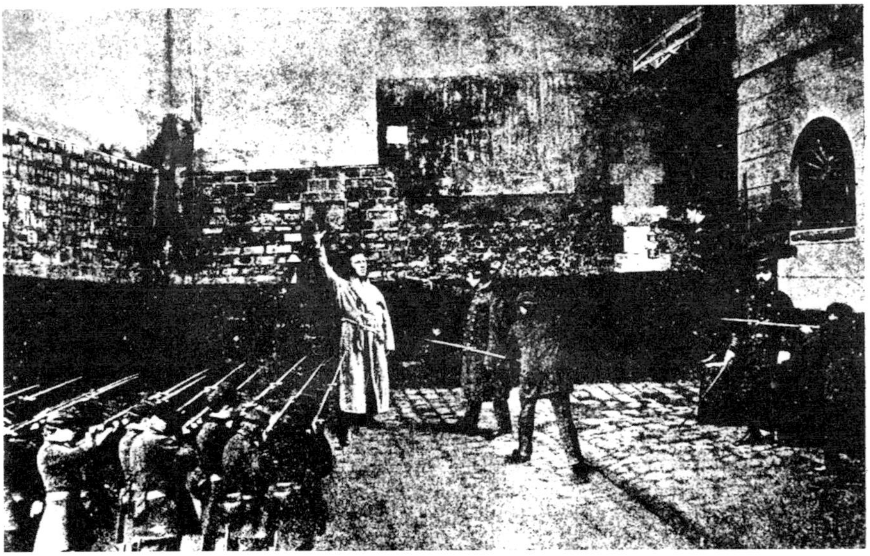

as well as his position as the painter-photographer to the Queen of Spain. Appert was among those photographers who were made welcome by the Communards – eager to pose for posterity on barricades and in ruins – but who later used the pictures for very different ends.

Appert was in fact one of the photographers who took mug-shots of the Communard prisoners at Versailles after the repression of the Commune, and these prints are among those he later used to manufacture his composite photographs, as well as

In the first of the execution scenes (plate 7), Appert has inserted the figures posed in the studio into a photograph of the street where the execution took place. Technically, as well as historically, the image is at fault. The exposure time required would have meant that at least some of the figures would have been blurred, and contemporary accounts state that the execution of the two generals was a much less orderly event than the "posed" scene in this photograph. Yet to a public who, for the most part, believed the myth of the objectivity of the

8. Execution of Gustave Chaudey in the courtyard of St. Pelagie prison, 2 a.m. May 24 1871. Composite photograph by Eugène Appert.

camera, and who, in any case, would be predisposed to accept this image as "factual", Appert's photograph would reinforce anti-Communard prejudice.

Even more damning as an indictment of the actions of the Communards is the second photograph (plate 8). This composite print shows the execution of the lawyer Gustave Chaudey, who had worked with the Commune in spite of some dubious actions on his part before March 18, e.g. ordering riflemen to fire on a crowd of demonstrators outside the Hôtel de Ville on 22 January 1871. As the Versailles troops threatened the city, Chaudey's opponents were prepared to sacrifice him while they had the chance. This image of the evil Communards, prepared to turn on their own supporters, was given the full treatment by Appert. Chaudey strikes a melodramatic pose in the courtyard of the prison where he is about to be executed. Within the rather doubtful box-like space of the enclosure, an impossibly located firing squad level their guns somewhere in the direction of the victim. The scale of the various figures as well as the difficulties which would have been involved in the lighting again indicate a faked photograph. Chaudey's execution did take place, but it was certainly not one of the most important events of the Commune period, and its selection as a moment worthy of documentation is certainly ideological and propagandist. Again it seems that the photograph would sell to a public who wanted visual confirmation of what they already believed.

The final example of Communard execution scenes illustrated here (plate 9) shows Communards shooting 48 hostages in the Rue Haxo on May 26. By this time the Versailles troops were in Paris shooting thousands of victims indiscriminately. In desperation, and against the advice of members of the Central Committee, Parisian militants gave vent to their frustration and despair and shot some of the hostages they held. Appert's composite photo purports to show us this event as an example of the cruelties of the Communards, without any suggestion that in comparison, the atrocities perpetrated by the so-called legal government were far worse.

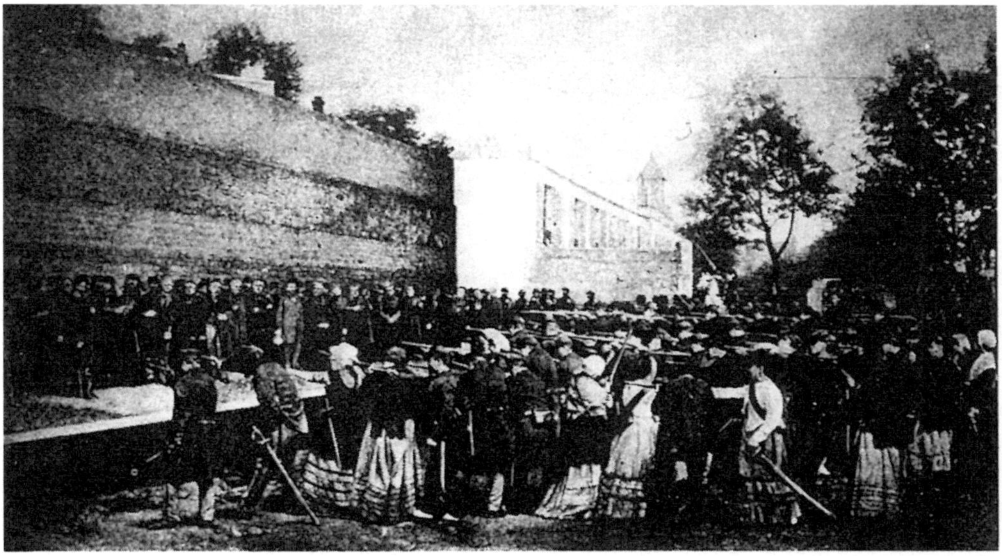

9. Execution of hostages by Communards in the Rue Haxo, May 26, 1871. Composite photograph by Eugène Appert.

Once again, Appert's image presents a carefully constructed, orderly scene. Crowds of neatly dressed women line up with their male comrades to take aim at the hostages. Although more successful than the scene with the execution of Chaudey, the precision and clarity of the picture at once arouses suspicion. As mentioned above, technical considerations prohibited the choice of scenes of action and movement. Appert's fakes were the only photographs on sale after the Commune which purported to show such events.

would give this away, even if the original prints did not exist.[14] The pseudo-documentary quality of the image is underlined by the caption, which gives an exact place and date for the scene, and some of the main characters in the picture are identified by name below. For example, seated third from the left in the foreground is the *cantinière* Anna Rotchild. As she leans back, about to fall over backwards it seems, it is obvious that the chair back from the studio-portrait has been obliterated by Appert. Immediately to her left, two women are shown drinking,

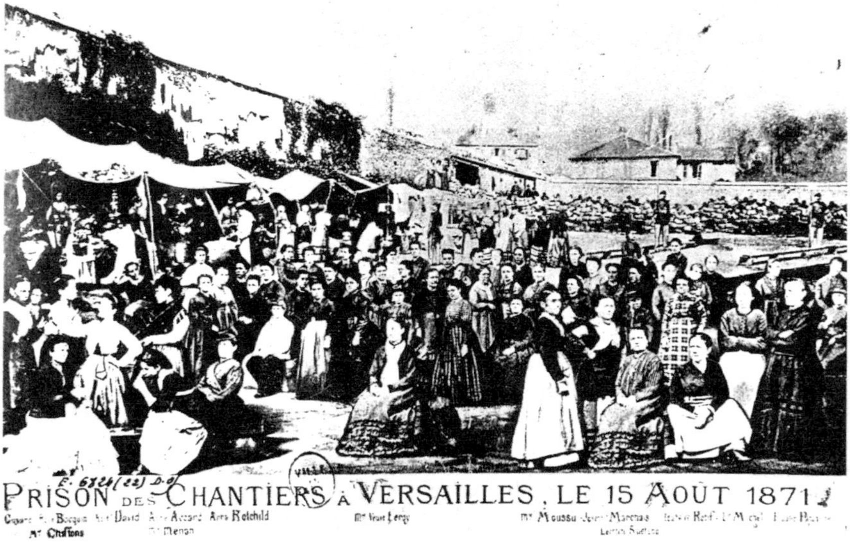

Appert certainly had a shrewd sense of what was topical in the weeks following the repression of late May. The activities of the Communards were sensational, but doubly so if they were carried out by women. The final composite photo by Appert illustrated here (plate 10) supposedly shows the compound of the women's prison at Versailles. In fact it uses the photographs which Appert took in studio conditions for the Versailles authorities and re-assembles the individuals portrayed. The seated poses of many of the figures with folded arms

one straight from a bottle, and are no doubt intended to show the vulgar morals of the women of the Commune, and an antidote to the neatly dressed and attractively presented Mme Leroy, who is seated in the centre of the picture.

Unfortunately many of the Communards photographed after the suppression of their government were in more tragic circumstances still. Those prisoners who had escaped summary execution were marched off to Versailles only to face firing squads there. Those who could not be

10. Communards at the Women's Prison at Versailles, August 15, 1871. Composite photograph by Eugène Appert.

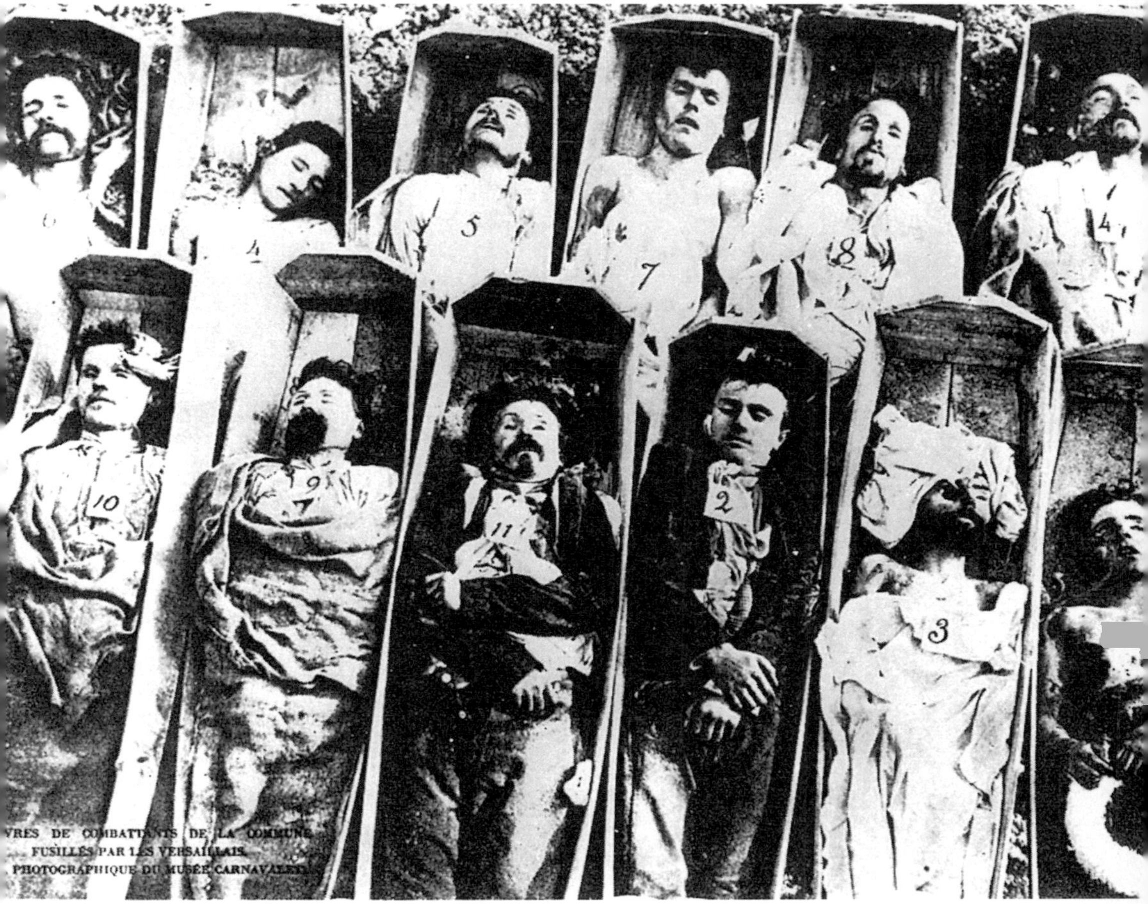

Above: 11. Corpses of unknown Communards shot by Versailles firing Squads, 1871. Photographer unknown.

identified were photographed for police records (plate 11). The original purpose of this image, then, was to furnish "objective" recording of information. Ironically these mutilated corpses are the elite of the thousands shot by the Versailles government, most of whom were thrown half-dead into communal graves, quickly covered with quicklime, not even a statistic in the death toll, let alone recorded by an image and a number. The number of Communards shot during Bloody Week cannot even be established to the nearest 10,000. Possibly there are among these corpses faces who were identified from earlier photographs and shot for that precise reason. Their very immobility tragically guarantees them perfect technical reproduction. They are orderly and carefully posed for the camera. In less perfect conditions, reliance on more traditional methods of visual representation was still necessary. For example the Communard illustrator and caricaturist Pilotell recorded the dead body of Raoul Rigault, a member of the Commune, as it lay in a gutter (plate 12). The body lay exposed to the ridicule of passers-by, spat upon and defiled. In the circumstances, Pilotell had to make a quick recording of the scene without attracting too much attention to himself – photography would have been impossible. Hence the sketch. Yet Pilotell's attitude was very much that of the photojournalist. He inscribes the lower corner of the image: *Seen by the author on the 24 May at 5pm in the Rue Gay-Lussac*. The scene is thus securely documented. As mentioned above, photography had not yet monopolised the aura of credibility at the expense of other media. In circumstances when photography could not be used, the spectator was still prepared to believe the truth of a drawing, or a wood-engraving, provided additional information was given by an accompanying newspaper report or an eye-witness.

Many other photographs of the corpses of Communards still exist (plate 13). In view of their numbers it seems likely that they were on sale to the public, as well as furnishing information for police files. In this respect it is worth speculating as to the function they performed. They obviously made money for the photographer, for one thing. Perhaps also they were intended to

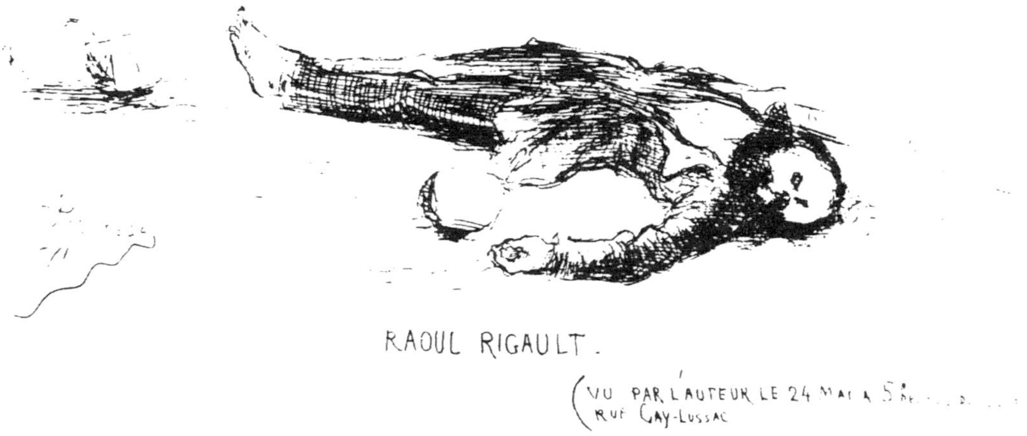

Above: 12. Pilotell, Sketch of the corpse of Raoul Rigault in the Rue Gay-Lussac, 5 p.m. May 24 1871.

serve as a warning, to set an example, much as the trials of Communard prisoners at Versailles were intended to do. However the real repression had been carried out in the form of executions in the working-class areas of Paris during Bloody Week. The aftermath was only a tiny side show in terms of numbers of executions, but was crucial as a public demonstration of the triumph of the forces of reaction. Yet this is a dangerous manoeuvre. The images give the victims a tragic status and importance which goes against the intention of the authorities. In retrospect, these mangled corpses are a condemnation of the victors of 1871, not the victims.[15] Just as these images can have no unambiguous meaning for spectators who saw them in 1871, so their meaning changes for us according to our historical and ideological position today.

Just as "objectivity" must be rejected when we discuss these images, so must the idea that photography democratised the production of visual imagery. As we have seen, probably the only time any of the working class Parisians went anywhere near a camera was during the Commune, perhaps on barricades or at the destruction of the Vendôme column. Far more likely, their only encounter with the new "democratic" medium was as dead bodies in police files. Gisèle Freund writes:

> The camera had definitely democratised the portrait. Before the camera artists, intellectuals, statesmen, white collar workers, employees of very modest means, were all equal. The desire for equality was satisfied at the same time as a desire for representation in all strata of the bourgeoisie... Henceforth on mantelpieces, coffee tables, display cabinets, and walls, the bourgeois smiled benignly from his frame, and surrounding him were his favourite statesmen, men of letters, actresses etc... The photograph owed its popularity not only to the fact that it could furnish its public with a faithful image of individual appearances, but also because it had become the symbol of democracy.[16]

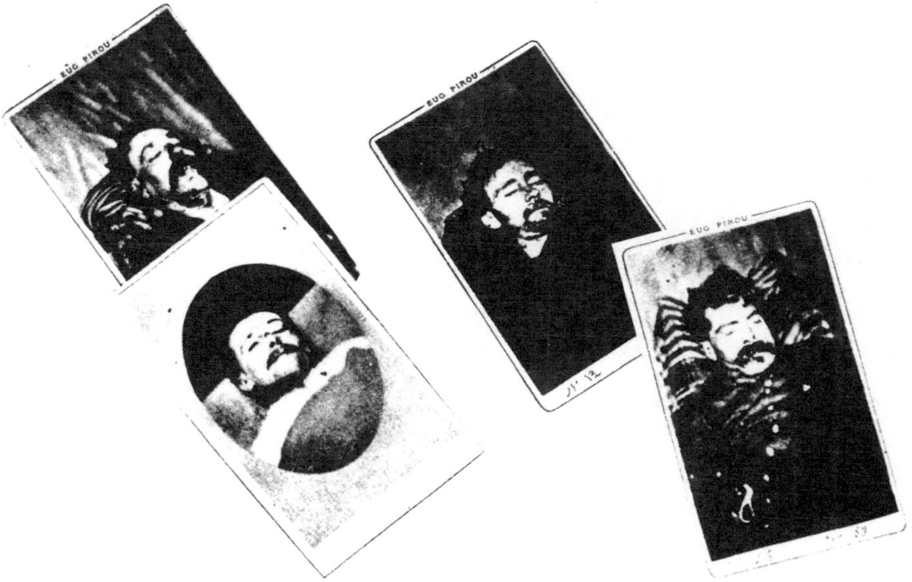

Above and overleaf: 13. Carte de visite photographs of unknown Communards, Eugene Pirou.

In some respects one is tempted to agree with this statement, but confronted with the images of the dead Communards one is forced to conclude that the "democracy" of the photograph in 1871 was of a similar kind to the political "democracy" of the bourgeoisie of the Versailles government. It worked within limits set by the class who owned it, and was intended to further bourgeois economic and ideological aims. The Commune itself had been foolish enough to play the game of bourgeois democracy, holding elections in Paris so that it might

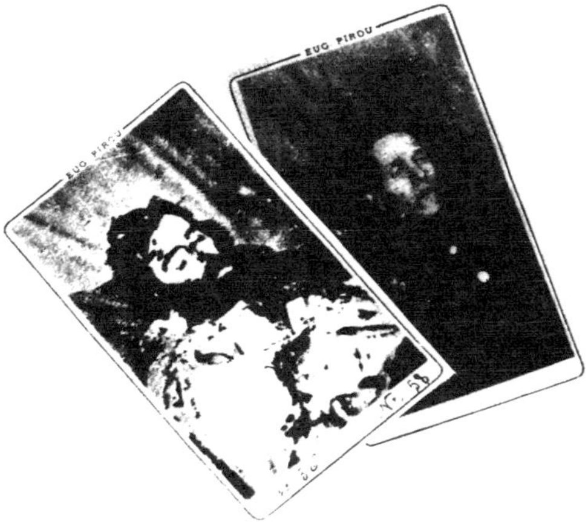

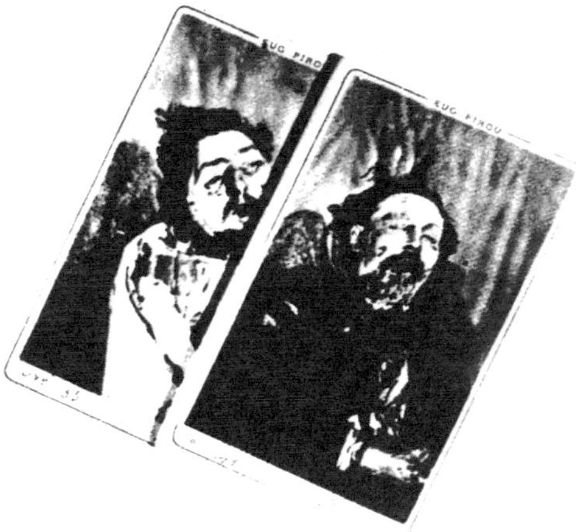

prove its "legality", instead of organising its military campaign and appropriating the capital deposited in the banks.

Appert's "faked" photographs look so obviously propagandist to anyone who knows the background to the events they depict that it is difficult to imagine that they were accepted as faithful recordings of actual incidents. However, it may be that the political stance of the people who bought such prints made them want to believe the reality of what they saw depicted, even if they did realize the images had been manipulated. Also, given the relationship of photography to other visual media available at the time, it may be that contemporaries in a materialistic and positivistic age were not inclined to question apparently transparent mechanisms of understanding visual images which were mechanically recorded. The status of the photograph at this time is an intermediate one. It can, at the same time, exploit and negate the myth of its perceptual innocence, its "democratisation" of what it records.

In situating ourselves in relation to a photographic image, we cannot avoid the recognition of our own ideological and political situation, in spite of the original purpose of the photograph. We have seen that, for example, the same images of Communards on the barricades in 1871 meant very different things, to different groups in 1871. Similarly from a Marxist perspective we see the images produced during the Commune in a different way from the participants. Perhaps the most historically poignant image produced during the Commune is significant in what must surely be an unconscious way (plate 14). This photograph was taken by Langerock of 29 Bld. des Italiens, and shows a Communard barricade on the Rue des Batignolles. In the deserted street are cannons and shells, neatly stacked, ready and waiting in front of some shop-fronts owned by someone by the name of Marx. The shops are inscribed *Au Nouveau Né*, literally *At the sign of the new-born baby*, and presumably selling baby clothes and nursery articles. The scenario aptly suggests the birth pangs of the new-born proletarian govern-

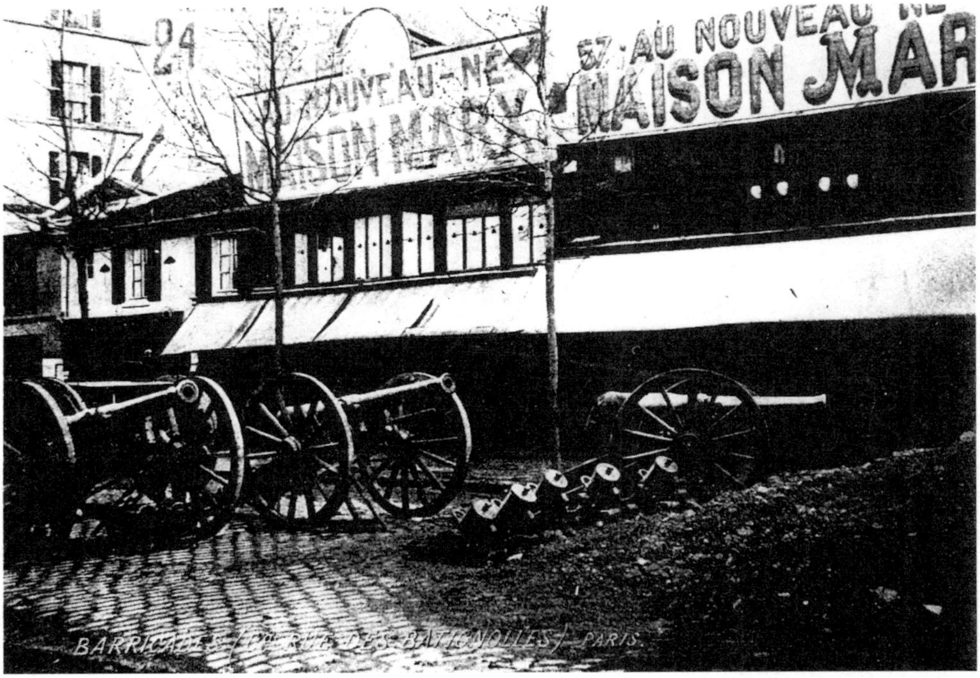

ment during the Commune, with the cannon silently overlooked by the name of Marx in giant letters. Very few of the Communards were Marxists, although Marx was quick to support the Commune in his address to the First International, published soon after the fall of the workers' government. There were far more followers of Proudhon and Blanqui among the Communards than disciples of Marx and Engels. Nevertheless, the photographer has unconsciously captured what proved to be the true historical significance of the Commune in his image of this particular barricade. The Commune's significance has been fully understood only by the Marxist tradition, and its status as the first working class government is due to the lessons it bequeathed to the Russian revolutionaries of 1917.

The reproduction of this print has been taken from a profusely illustrated book on the Franco-Prussian War and the Commune, published in 1901 by Armand Dayot, inspector of the Ministry of Fine Arts. The title page of his comprehensive work is headed by a quotation which proclaims:

> "One day, the visual image will revolutionize the study of history". Indeed this is true, if we can apply a politically conscious view of visual imagery to our contemporary situation, as well as to the past.

14. Barricade in the Rue de Batignolles, 1871. Photograph by E. Langerock.

NOTES

1. For useful information and illustrations relevant to Fenton's trip to the Crimea as a war photographer cf. John Hannavy, *The Camera Goes to War. Photographs From the Crimean War 1854-1856*. Edinburgh: The Scottish Arts Council, no date. Further fascinating material on the whole question of the "documentation" of war can be found in: P. Knightley, *The First Casualty*. London: 1975. Now published in paperback by Quartet books.
2. Gisèle Freund, *Photographie et Société*. Paris: 1974, p.60.
3. J. Bruhat, J. Dautry, E. Tersen *et al.*, *La Commune de 1871*. Second edition. Paris: 1970, p.31. For those who read French, this is the best single book on the Commune.
4. Ibid., p.36.
5. J. Daubié, *La Femme Pauvre au XIXe Siècle*. Paris: 1866, pp. 50-51.
6. Ibid., pp.294-295.
7. Gisèle Freund. Op. cit., pp.61-62.
8. E. Schulkind (ed.), *The Paris Commune of 1871. The View from the Left*. London: 1972, p.159.
9. Gisèle Freund, op. cit., p.104, states that this is the first time photographs were used in this way. By now, of course, this is common practice.
10. J. Bruhat, J. Dautry, E. Tersen *et al.*, op. cit., p.36.
11 S. Edwards (ed.), *The Communards of Paris 1871*. London: 1973, p.166.
12. From: *Paris Incendié. Album Historique*. Paris: 1871, introduction by H. de Bleignerie, commentary by E. Dangin.
13. Many of these photographs taken for the Versailles police authorities are reproduced among the many useful illustrations in: A. Dayot, *L'invasion, le siège, la commune 1870-1871. D'apres des peintures, gravures, photographies, médailles, autographes, objets du temps*. Paris: 1901.
14. An album of the original photographs of women prisoners taken by Appert at Versailles is in the Bibliothèque Marguerite Durand, Place du Pantheon, Paris V. This library has lots of valuable information on women's history in France.
15. L. Chevalier, *Labouring Classes and Dangerous Classes in Paris During the First Half of the Nineteenth Century*. London: 1973, pp. 83 ff., produces some useful information concerning public executions in France. In the early 1830s, public executions were moved from the Town Hall square out into the slum areas of working class Paris. Also, they were held at dawn instead of in the afternoons. Various reasons were given by the authorities for these changes, but the general idea seems to have been to make the death of the criminal a sordid, degrading, surreptitious event, as opposed to a public spectacle which conferred a certain status on the victim. Chevalier quotes Delvau, writing in 1865, towards the end of the Second Empire, who compares most unfavourably the "illustrious criminals" traditionally executed in front of the Town Hall, with the "scum" now put to death ignominiously in the slum districts to the south of Paris. This perhaps gives some indication as to why the Versailles authorities made a public example of so few Communards (relatively speaking). They were unwilling to give them publicity beyond what was absolutely necessary as a warning to would-be socialists. For example the courts at Versailles passed 270 death sentences on Communards, whereas somewhere between 25,000 and 40,000 had been killed on the spot in working class districts during Bloody Week. For statistics cf. P. Lissagaray, *Histoire de la Commune de 1871*. Paris: Maspero, 1976, pp. 25-26.
15. 16. Gisèle Freund, op.cit., pp.60, 69.

The Social Eye of Picture Post

Stuart Hall

PICTURE POST, in photographs and text, registered with remarkable veracity the substance and quality of ordinary life. Its mode of "telling" was direct. It was strongest in capturing the native strengths of English life "under pressure". Its "social eye" was a clear lens. But its "political" eye was far less decisive. It pinpointed exploitation, misery and social abuse, but always in a language which defined these as "problems" to be tackled and remedied with energy and goodwill: it was instinctively reformist – in both a good (humanist) and bad (humanist) sense. It never found a way (this is a matter of technique as well, to which we shall come in a moment) of relating the surface images of these problems to their structural foundations. In this dimension, we can see a clear continuity between *Picture Post* and the "social problem" area of television documentary in a later period. There is a highlighting in a *Picture Post* photograph – of the blitz, of unemployment, of people's everyday pursuits: an accenting of the essential human and the essentially ordinary qualities of experience. There is a rhetoric of change and improvement there, of people capable of resilience and courage; but there isn't anywhere a language of dissent, opposition or revolt. Neither pictures and text, even when they "hit" straight and hard, can enclose the domain of contradiction, of internal conflict, of contrary interests. Potential conflict registers here as active variety. *Picture Post*, as George Orwell saw, could retain its authenticity only because it was constantly and resolutely in touch with a movement for change which had surpassed "party labels" and "the old distinction between Right and Left", and because it spoke straight to "multitudes of unlabelled people who have grasped... that something is wrong." But what was wrong *Picture Post* had no language for.[1]

It might be easier to say what the rhetoric of *Picture Post* could not do, by means of a comparison. On the cover of its issue for 23rd September 1939, *Picture Post* used a sort of "composite photograph" which showed Hitler as if dressed in the plumed helmet and bedecked uniform of the Kaiser. It was entitled *Kaiser Adolf*. This was the work of a refugee German artist, John Heartfield, who arrived in England the previous year, and whose work had been illustrated in an issue of *Lilliput* earlier that year, and twice exhibited (at the London and the Arcade Galleries).

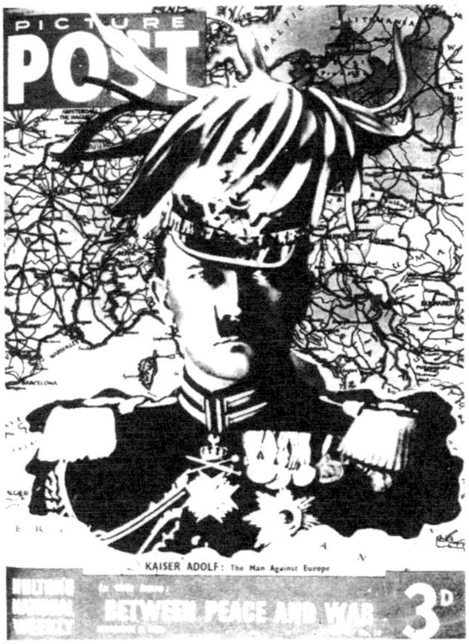

Stefan Lorant, first editor of *Picture Post*, must have known of Heartfield's work: apart from anything else, Lorant edited the Munich edition of a workers' illustrated magazine at the same time as Heartfield who did some of his most important work in a similar medium. In fact, Heartfield was the leading figure in the photomontage movement and his work was widely used and exhibited in Germany in the early 1930s. It was almost certainly Lorant's influence which got Heartfield into *Lilliput*; it was almost certainly his choice of *Kaiser Adolf* for the cover of *Picture Post*. Yet neither *Picture Post*, nor any other British journal, made much use of Heartfield during his long residence in Hampstead.

The neglect of Heartfield was, in retrospect, a disaster; but that is not precisely

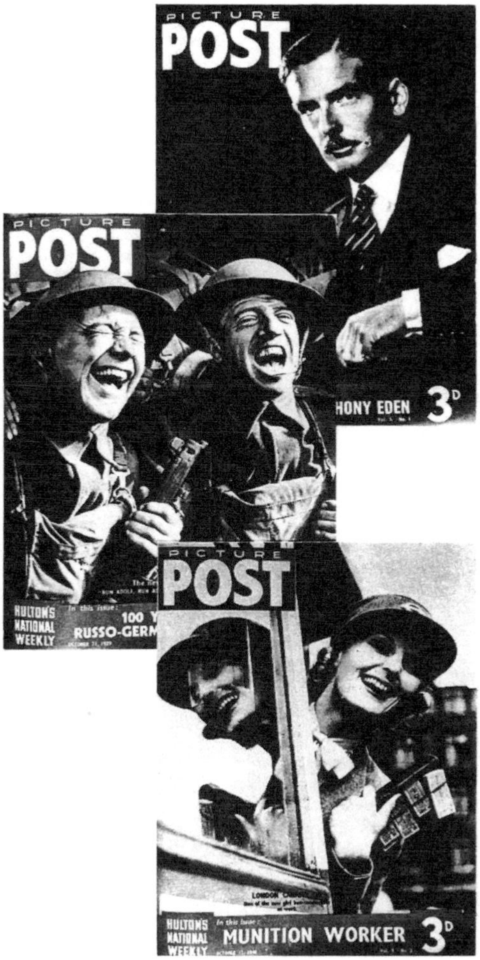

what concerns us here. We have used the existence of Heartfield 's work in order to suggest *what was already possible*, in terms of the development of the exposition of the still photograph: and thus to place and situate the *Picture Post*. We must be careful here. Heartfield was not working in a popular and commercial setting, and his idiom was almost certainly not immediately transferable into such a context. *Picture Post* had something quite unique of its own to do – namely, to adapt the photograph to the dramatic events of war, and to depict the everyday life in graphic images. Moreover, it was obliged to develop its own idiom in a specific historical setting – in Britain in the late thirties and forties: a society relatively untouched and isolated from the whole climate of artistic innovation which overflowed into European art. There was no British Dada, no British Surrealism, no British Eisenstein or Pudovkin: think of the way British documentary naturalised and domesticated the montage impulse. In short, no easy transplant was possible here – it would have gone right against the historical grain. Set against the prevailing orthodoxies, *Picture Post* itself was a remarkable evolution of existing traditions and possibilities, an extension of them into the domain of popular journalism and informal education. And yet, our sense of what *Picture Post* did not – could not – do is inevitably altered by our knowledge of what else was possible in the handling of these new techniques: pointed up by the very presence, in London, of an artist who had already decisively *gone beyond* the limits of the "news photograph". Heartfield's work, then, gives an edge to our considered sense that what the rhetoric of *Picture Post* could not do was to use photographs and text in such a way as to "make the invisible social relations visible". That, in essence, was the outer edge of social democracy as a form of political consciousness. The two are linked, then, not in a mechanically causal or determinist way, but at the level of modes of collective perception, of "structure of feeling" – in terms of their "social eye". The collective consciousness of social democracy and the social eye – the social -democratic eye – of *Picture Post* belong to the same historical "project" and were formed in the same conjuncture. We should make it clear that what concerns us here is not simply the manifest political content of *Picture Post*. As Walter Benjamin[2] correctly observed:

> The political line alone cannot organize. The tendency is the necessary but never sufficient condition of the organizational function of a work... The determinant factor is the exemplary character of a production.
>
> Here I will limit myself to indicating the decisive difference between merely transmitting the apparatus of production and transforming it... I would like to set forth the notion that transmitting an apparatus of production without – as much as possible – transforming it is a highly debatable procedure even when the content of that apparatus which is transmitted seems to be revolutionary in nature.

Picture Post "transmitted" with a striking fidelity and impact. Especially in the war years its sheer transparency to reality was remarkable. What it could not do was to "alienate the apparatus of production (i.e. photography, the magazine) from the ruling class in favour of socialism, by improving it". The fact that most modern examples of the rhetoric of the still photograph are even further away from this aim and purpose gives us some standard by which to measure *Picture Post's* true achievement.

NOTES
1. George Orwell, *Collected Essays*. Harmondsworth: Penguin, 1970.
2. Walter Benjamin, The Author as Producer, in: *Understanding Brecht*. London: New Left Books, 1973.

· We thank Stuart Hall for giving us permission to reprint this extract from Stuart Hall, The Social Eye of Picture Post, in *Working Papers in Cultural Studies* 2, Birmingham: CCCS. Spring 1972.

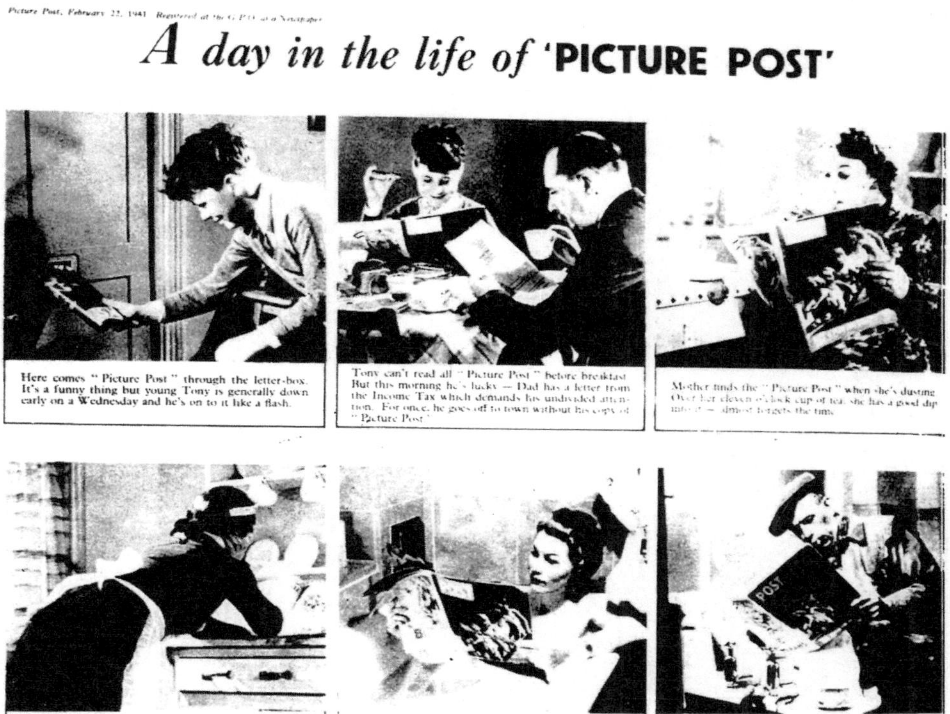

57

How *Picture Post* advertised itself 22.2.41

What Did You Do in the War Mummy? Class and Gender in Images of Women

Jo Spence

MUCH OF THE current work on images of women has been based on two concepts:

1 That there is a binary opposition within systems of signification in which what is present is definable only in relation to what is absent [1]: thus "woman" is signified in relation to "man", or "feminine" in relation to "masculine".

2 That we decode images by looking at what is present in the image itself, trying to locate its various "signs and meanings"; a process of selective remembering and selective forgetting. This decoding process usually obscures from us the fact that we are looking not at real things, but at socially and culturally constructed and learned concepts (or formulations), which may or may not have a basis in reality. We are taught to think of these complex "ways of seeing" as part of a natural, transparent process.

Such approaches have sometimes under-valued the ways in which the meaning of an image is also determined by the historical and institutional context of its production and reception.[2] More importantly, they may also concentrate solely on the binary opposition of woman/man at the expense of other possible oppositions, notably that of labour/capital. Usually the woman's "symbolic lack" (of the phallus) and her exclusion from the patriarchal order have been stressed; but I would like to ask if the concept of "woman as sign" can also illuminate her place in the "symbolic order" of capitalism? In other words I want to broaden the question of decoding images of woman to take into account not just the symbolic sexual lack, but also the exploitation of women's labour power under capitalism.

In this reformulation it may help to map out some possible approaches.

The personal
As an example, I have examined myself as a system of signification which can be recorded. This makes "me" the *mediator* as well as the *subject* of the information. This work has enabled me to start to deconstruct my own "image", and then start the work of reconstruction within a wider understanding of theories of visual representation. A photographic record of some of this work is available in the Arts Council of Great Britain catalogue for the 1979 show *Three Perspectives on Photography* held at the Hayward Gallery.

The empirical
I monitored representations of women aimed at a broadly "popular" audience, between 1972 and 1978. Thousands of images from women's and family magazines, from popular newspapers, children's books and comics, cartoons, street hoardings, greetings cards, wrappers, film posters, and wherever else they could be found, were put onto 35mm colour slides. These were sorted and categorised on a light box which then made it possible to track ephemeral or random images, as well as trace visual links and study areas of constant repetition and overlap. This way it was possible to arrive at some preliminary conclusions about the very limited "narratives" set up for women, and the ways in which "femininity" was constructed through representation.

The specific
It is possible to discover some of the many differently inflected significations of one basic stereotype by examining in depth particular representations of women. By doing this with the contemporary image of the "secretary" (office worker) it becomes obvious that stereotypes are not *universal* but differ markedly depending on the *context* in which they are used, and the type of (class) audience. For example, the stereotype offered to women in women's magazines is totally different from that offered to, say, business men in trade magazines.

The historical
A comparison with a historical conjuncture (like World War II) in which typical representations of women differ considerably from today's dominant stereotypes, can suggest some of the ways in which images are affected by economic and political changes. It also makes clear that stereotypes are not necessarily *fixed* but emerge – as did the "industrial worker" stereotype illustrated here – and disappear when the news or advertising "agendas" change in response to the needs of industry or the state, or to changed legislation.

It is the historical approach that I concentrate on here, but that work needs to be placed back in the context of the results of the empirical and specific studies which are in *Screen Education* No 29. Hopefully this work will be useful to illuminate the difference in visual representations between

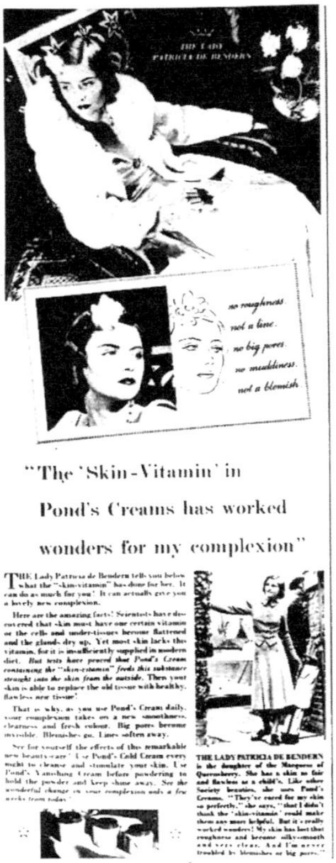

14.6.39

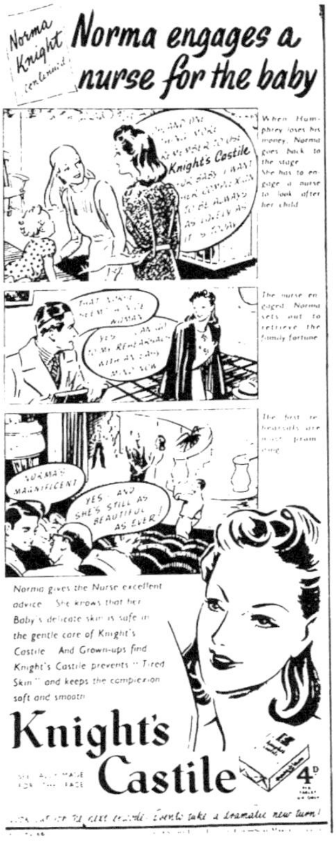

30.09.39

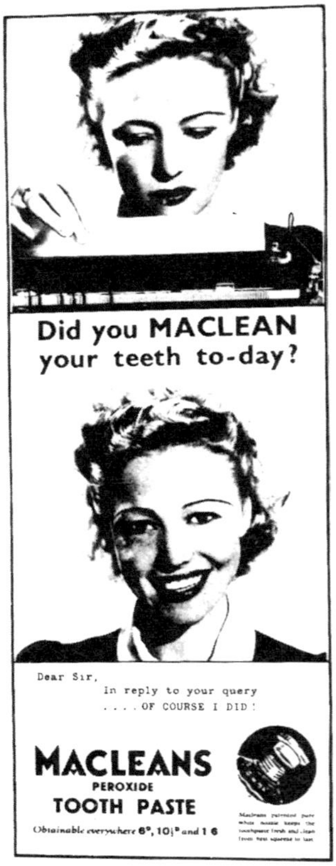

25.11.39

Class differences among women were signalled quite clearly. So were the similarities; of their "need" to look beautiful.

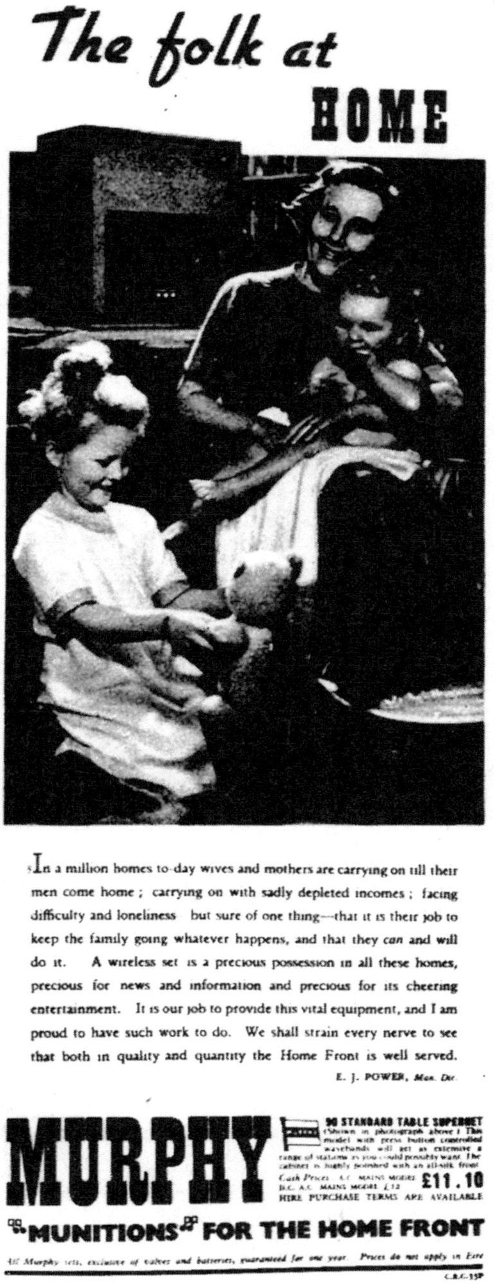

11.5.40

periods when women are needed as labour (as in wartime), and as consumers (as now, in a time of a crisis of capital) and how this shift can be studied for its "ideological effect".

Women, work and war

This case study comes out of some more general research which has included looking at the illustrated news magazine *Picture Post* from its inception in October 1938, through to 1947. This research has revealed some dramatic shifts in the ways

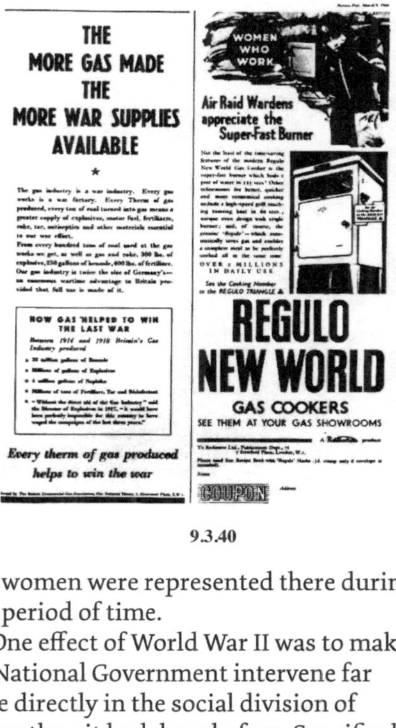

9.3.40

that women were represented there during that period of time.

One effect of World War II was to make the National Government intervene far more directly in the social division of labour than it had done before. Specifically, it had to mobilize large numbers of women into essential war work. This was done through powers given under the *National Service (No 2) Act*, and through the machinery of the *Registration for Employment Order* and the *Essential Work Order*. Emergency training centres were opened, linked to recruiting drives, which were made in most large towns. Additionally there were frequent radio appeals, advertisements in a variety of places (including the cinema), as well as labour recruitment vans and even door-to-door canvassing in some instances. Later a special order was made called the *Employment of Women (Control of Engagement) Order*. As women were continually exhorted to "go to work in the factories" it is hardly surprising to find many visual representations at that time in which the primary signification was that of women as labour. This idea of women as an integral part of

decoration, sewing and knitting, cooking, gardening, ideas for comfort... stressing the words beauty and comfort." The ideas of women as domestic and narcissistic were therefore only displaced from the separate features on women at work. Women's "sexuality" or "glamour" were hived off into other features on the world of fashion, or show business, and these features continued to use the more traditional images of women displaying themselves.

The advertisers in *Picture Post* also took up the theme of "women at war" with

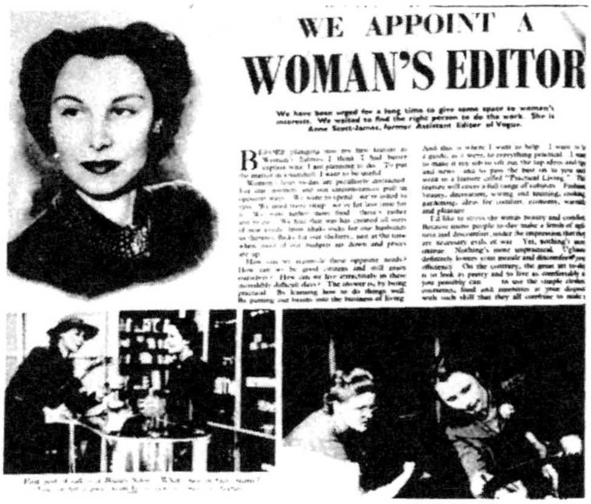
WE APPOINT A
WOMAN'S EDITOR
We have been urged for a long time to give some space to women's interests. We waited to find the right person to do the work. She is Anne Scott-James, former Assistant Editor of Vogue.

8.2.41

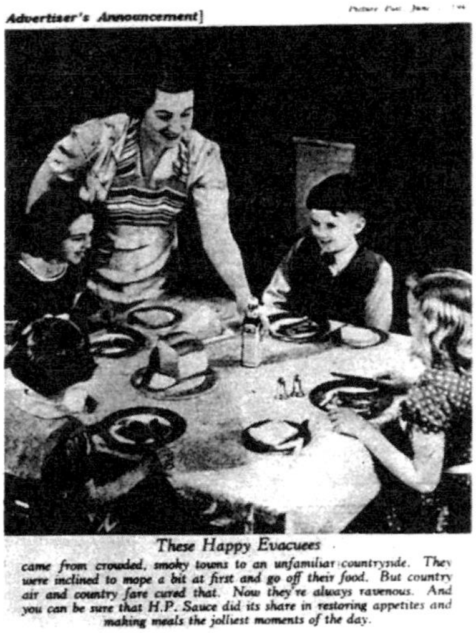

1.6.40

the industrial and agricultural workforce (as well as the armed forces), concurrent with their "jobs" as wives and mothers, was taken up and expanded upon by *Picture Post*. The old ideas about women did not disappear though. The need for "beauty" had been a running thread in early *Picture Post* editorials, and in February 1941 a Woman's Editor, Anne Scott James, was appointed. Her job was to provide articles of "interest to women", dealing with "fashion, beauty,

amazing rapidity, often using news-type photographs or "realist" drawings. Before long specific class stereotypes emerged, e.g. the industrial worker, the land girl, the bus conductress. Advertisements soon showed women doing two jobs, and filled out the little "human details" that were often too trivial for news and feature stories. Products were offered which would enable women to function better as "working mothers", keeping their health,

The need for "beauty" had been a running thread in early editorials, and in February 1941 a woman's editor was appointed... Advertisements soon showed women doing two jobs, and filled out the little human details that were often too trivial for news and feature stories.

safety and strength up to scratch, and to do the washing and cooking more quickly. Women were seen as the mainstay of the family and the home front at a time when everything else was chaos. The products and services offered were usually aimed at very real and immediate needs, rather than at some fantasy future. Particularly of value to me in this research has been Stuart Hall's work on *Picture Post*, in which he comments on the "limitations of the news photograph":

> Its (*Picture Post's*) "social eye" was a clear lens. But its "political" eye was far less decisive. It pinpointed exploitation, misery and social abuse, but always in a language which defined these as "problems" to be tackled and remedied with energy and goodwill: it was instinctively reformist – in both a good (humanist) and bad (humanist) sense. It never found a way... of relating the surface images of these problems to their structural foundations.[3] (my emphasis)

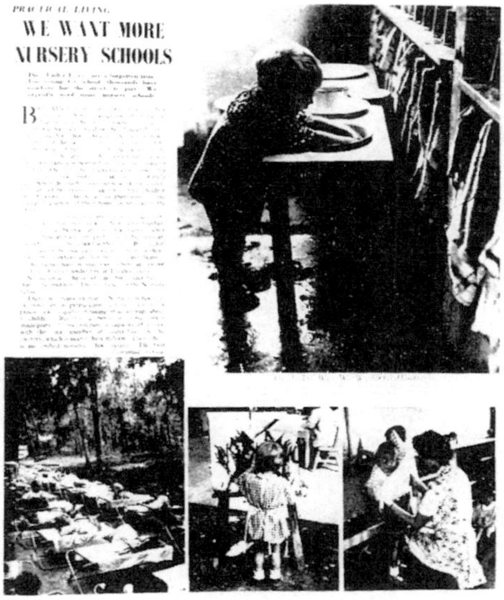

25.10.41

Looking at the illustrations here of the industrial woman worker in the light of this concept of *limitation*, we can perhaps get some idea of how some advertisements have been doubly stripped of their potential range of "meanings" . For instance, news photographs could not reveal that while women were being conscripted and coerced (in the name of patriotism) to enter the labour force, their average pay packet was just half that of men. Nor could photographs show that it was illegal to strike, or that (as an article in May 1944 later reported) nearly 24,000 workers were prosecuted for industrial offences not punishable before the war, and that 1,807 were actually sent to jail. Moving on to look at the advertising which used this news-type photograph (like the ad for *Rinso*) we see a woman at work, doing a man's job, and contributing to the war effort. But, bearing in mind again its "limitations" it is possible to try to read it differently. Not only is the woman producing surplus value for someone else and being encouraged to "buy back" the commodities produced by workers like herself; as a "mother of three" she is assumed to perform unpaid domestic labour and reproduce the future workforce needed for capitalist production.

Another aspect of visual representation which should be mentioned is that with the onset of war the depiction of extremes in social and economic inequality became less pronounced, and in the news, features and advertisements women of all classes were shown working together. This is important to note because the repertoire of signs connoting class (or class power) is far more limited than those connoting gender. Class relations are structured and, therefore, in visual terms, "absent"; they were, in Hall's terms, beyond the scope of *Picture Post's* "political" eye. A class identity is – like sexuality – constructed through a system of representation. In the case of *Picture Post*, the identity produced was social democratic, stressing consensus and co-existence rather than oppression and struggle. Although quite clearly these wartime images of

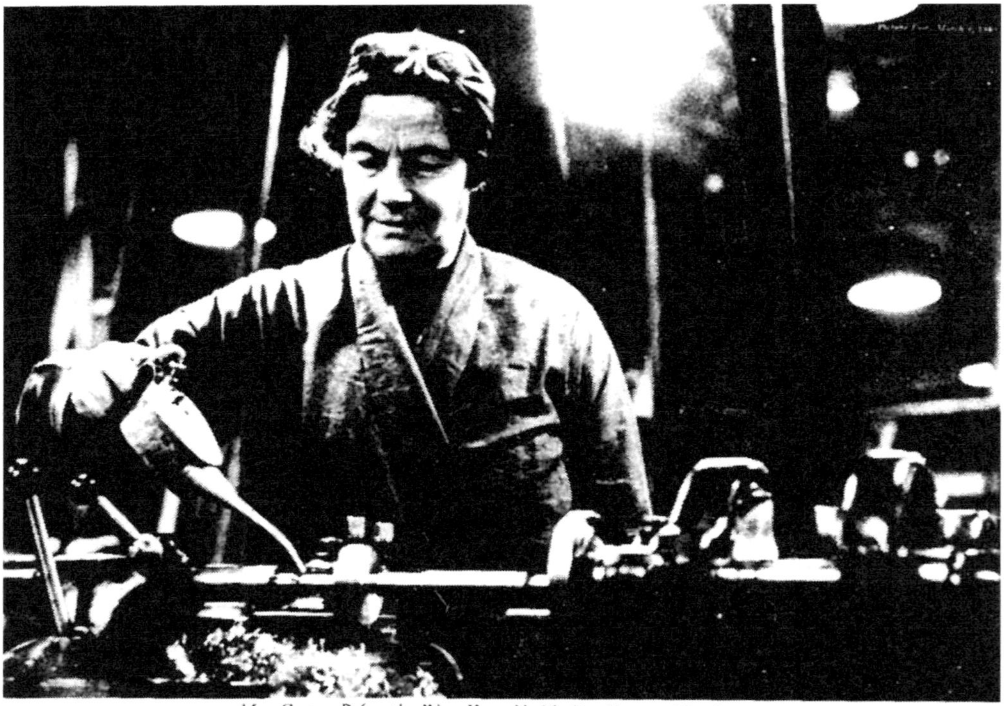

Mrs. Groves, Before the War, Knew No Machine Except a Mangle

"I'd never had anything much to do with machinery before," said Mrs. Groves. "I left all that to men. Even if the mangle went wrong there was usually someone to put it right. But if the men are all being called up it seems we'll have to run the factories ourselves."

9.3.40

1940-42: women as industrial workers. Not only were all women now alike, but also women could now do men's work... The (class) identity produced stressed consensus and co-existence.

women could in no way be considered "sexist", the continual use of the term "woman", with the concentration on gender similarities (i.e. not only were all women now alike, but also women could now do men's work), masked the very real social and economic class differences which existed between women, and which continue to exist.

Although the research from which these examples are drawn is still incomplete, it is possible at this stage to see that there were clear differences between representations of in the social division of labour had some effect on the types of images of women that were produced during the war. This also seems to be borne out by what happened when the war ended. Just as the "new" and "positive" images emerged when women were desperately needed in the labour force, so the idea of "two jobs" soon collapsed back into "one job" when women were encouraged to re-enter the domestic sphere during the massive task of the re-employment of demobbed labour. This is epitomized in the *Milk of Magnesia*

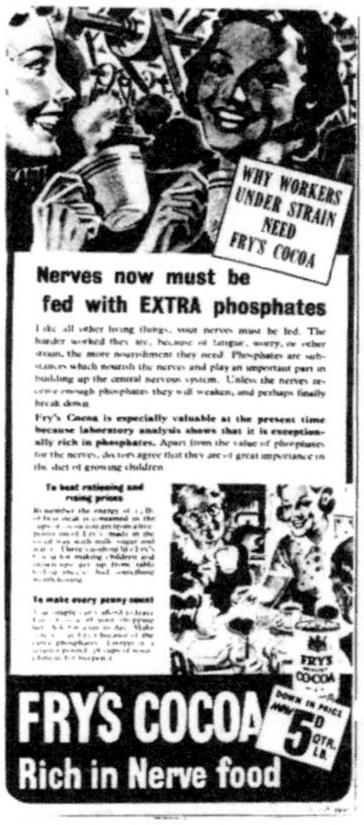

28.9.40

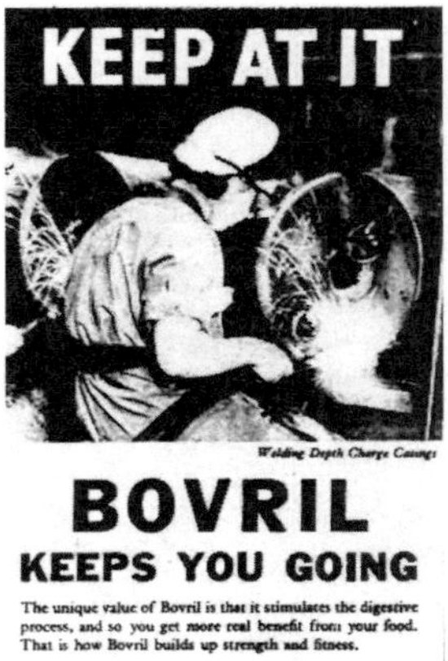

24.1.41

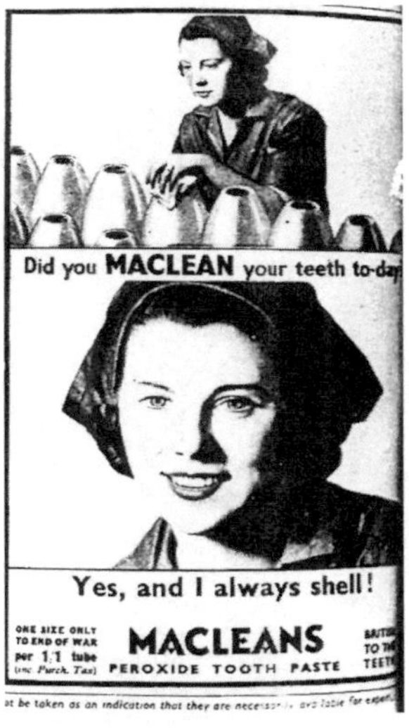

7.3.42

the same stereotype. I would relate this to the general distinction between the point of production (the labour visually represented and written about in the "serious" news and feature articles), and the point of consumption represented by the advertisements. A study of the various images of the industrial worker shown here will give an indication of some of the shifts of visual rhetoric between news and various types of advertisement.

Such images do suggest quite clearly that industrial and state needs for changes advert which shows a mother saying "I'm clocking in at home".

Of course the war was a "special case" – the historical and socio-economic determinants of particular stereotypes are seldom so blatant. But it does underline the potential usefulness of using the binary opposition of labour/capital in analysing images. This "historical" work is offered to indicate an approach to encoding practice, as there is no simple way of understanding the potential range of "readings" available to *Picture Post's* original audience, whose

THE MEN CALL HER "MUSCLE"!

Mother of three saws two-ton gun barrels—then does the washing

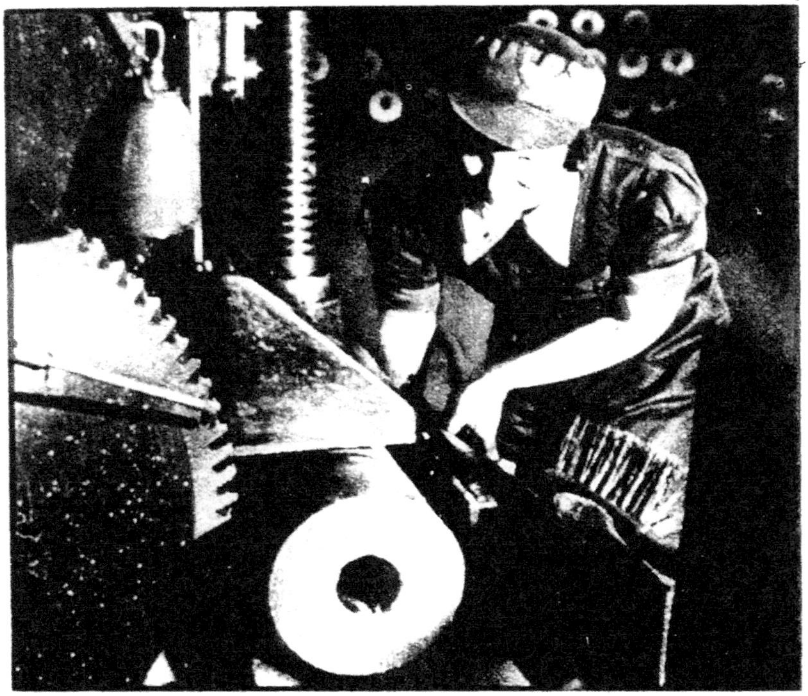

MRS. ELSIE RAMSCAR is known as "Muscle" in the North-Western war factory where she does a man's job sawing gun barrels weighing 2 tons apiece.

"Hard work keeps you young, I reckon," she says. She wants to keep young for the sake of a very nice husband in the Forces!

Mrs. Ramscar lives near the factory, so goes home to get dinner for her three children—all school age. The washing she fits in according to her "shifts."

She does it the Rinso no-boil way—lets the clothes soak for 12 minutes in Rinso and hot water from the tap. Even her dirty overalls come clean without boiling if she smooths a little dry Rinso on the worst places. "This method saves me an hour and a half's hard work," says Mrs. Ramscar.

Hitler *can't* win so long as women like Elsie Ramscar keep a happy home around them while they make the weapons to defend it!

R 3088-151-68

R. S. Hudson Limited

21.2.42

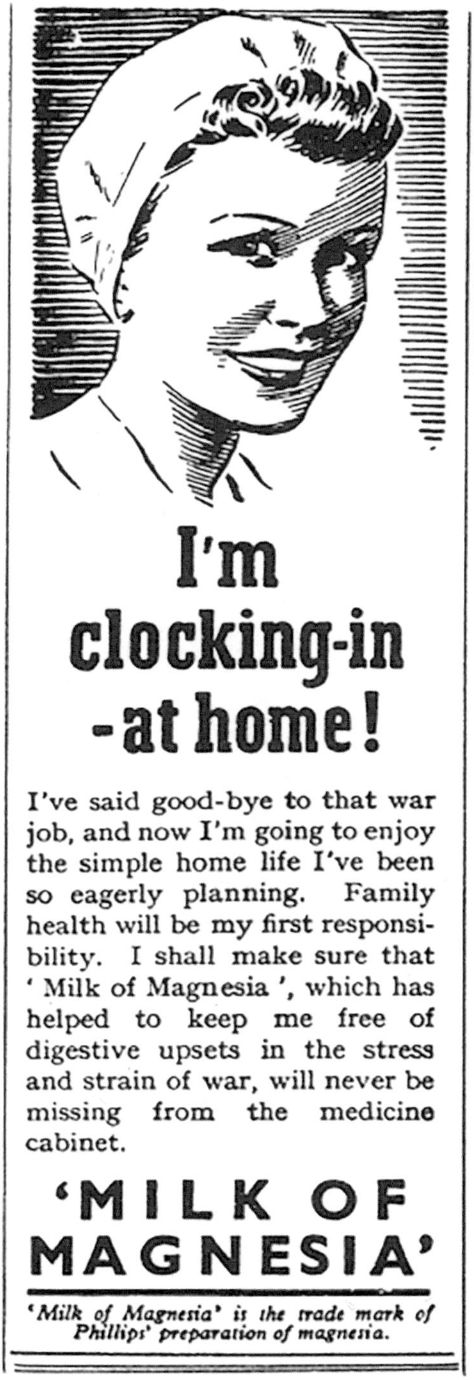

18.8.45

"readings" were informed by their own historically specific class and gender positions. It is important to emphasize that we need to understand the ideological process by which a class identity is constructed, especially as this construction is not necessarily the same as our actual class location in the capitalist relations of production and reproduction. This becomes a crucial issue for working class women who are scarcely visible within visual representation (except in a negative sense) and are continually forced to locate themselves as "women"

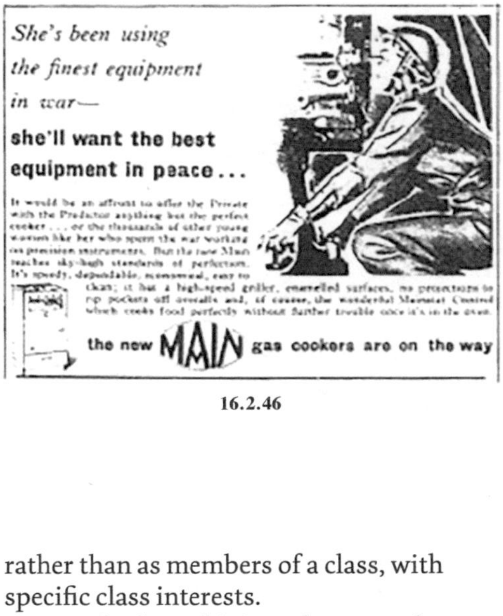

16.2.46

rather than as members of a class, with specific class interests.

As a final word it is perhaps worth mentioning that when Penguin published Tom Hopkinson's anthology *Picture Post 1938-1950* in 1970 (now in reprint) almost all evidence of women's war efforts had disappeared. Perhaps its inclusion no longer seemed so vital and relevant?

This is an abridged version of an article which appeared in *Screen Education* No.29, Winter 1978/79: "What Do People Do All Day? Class and Gender in Images of Women".

We would like to thank the copyright holders and *Picture Post* for the use of illustrations used in this and the preceding article.

Recommended reading
Judith Williamson, *Decoding Advertisements, Ideology and Meaning in Advertising*, London and Boston: Marion Boyars, 1978.
Revolutionary Communist No.5 contains useful information on "Women's Oppression Under Capitalism", especially during wartime.
Janice Winship, "Women at Work Bibliography", Birmingham: *CCCS Stencilled Paper* 54, 1979.
CCCS Women's Studies Group (eds), *Women Take Issue. Aspects of Women's Subordination*. London: Hutchinson, 1978.

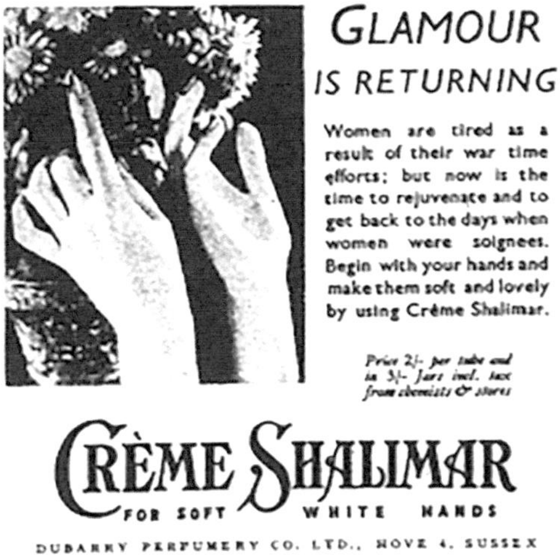

26.1.46

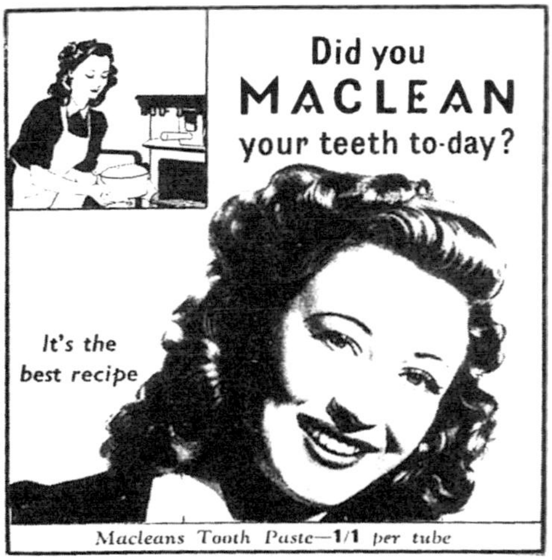

20.4.46

NOTES
1. I am using the term "sign" in its semiotic sense. The sign consists of two interlocking elements: the signifier (what means) and the signified (what is meant). Cf. Jonathan Culler, *Saussure*, Glasgow: Fontana, 1976; especially pp. 18-23.
2. On such determinants of production cf. John Tagg, "The Currency of the Photograph", in: *Screen Education* 28, Autumn 1978; on those of reception, cf. Stuart Hall, "Encoding and Decoding in the TV Discourse", Birmingham: *CCCS Stencilled Paper* 7.
3. Stuart Hall, "The Social Eye of Picture Post", in *Working Papers in Cultural Studies* 2, Birmingham: CCCS.

1945-46: back to "normal" after the war After the war women were encouraged to re-enter the domestic sphere during the massive task of the re-employment of demobbed labour.

Heartfield's Millions Montage: (Attempt at) a Structural Analysis

Eckhard Siepmann

Translated by Sylvia Gohl

1. Aim and method of this investigation

AMONGST THOSE ARTISTS who have produced scripto-visual sign systems with directly relevant political themes in the last two centuries, Goya (1746-1828), Daumier (1808-1879) and Heartfield (1891-1968), occupy a particularly eminent position. The picture/text compositions, with which they reacted to political developments, differ from most of the innumerable other contemporary broadsheets with political content in that they constituted an innovation in the contemporary vocabulary of form and consequently an innovation in the aesthetic appropriation of reality.

According to information theory, an illustration is a codification of signals from the environment.[1] This definition is of importance not only for linguistics and epistemology but can also be applied to pictures which have been painted, photographed or filmed. Coding rests on social conventions; the transmission of the structures of reality – in this case optical

– into structures of signs relies on shared assumptions reached through a multitude of social factors. Within these processes of codification, artistic production has a specific function: aesthetic innovation is the rupture from a traditional code through to the inauguration of a new code which takes account of the changes in social conditions.

> The message with an aesthetic content is an example of an *ambiguous* message, that brings the code into question, and within this context forges such a novel relationship between the signs that from now on our way of comprehending the possibility of the code will have to change... [2]

Thus, the practising artist not only reaches backwards for his codes, but by his work he modifies traditional codifications. He is able to translate his experience of new realities, which have been determined by the development of the social process, into hitherto unknown rules of transmission.

The progress of the Industrial Revolution in the 19th century brought with it a complete change in the relationship between human subjective activity and the technical objective possibilities. In this connection we find that in the 20th century the traditional forms of art are no longer capable of proposing without restriction codes appropriate to new social conditions. The limits of painting, in which the brush is the only instrument mediating between the performing hand and the receiving material, and thereby transmits a maximum amount of personal subjective elements, become increasingly apparent in the attempt to devise systems of signs for an environment whose mode of appearance is determined by semi-automatic and automatic production. [3] The advanced modes of commodity production are characterised by the fact that the human being merely keeps pace with the process of production as an ancillary rather than its principal agent. Productive activity is transferred to scientific processes which precede the material production.

Since the mid- nineteenth century, photography has existed as a medium the application of which is based on the relation between the initiating subjective factor and (chemical) technical automation. The same relation also characterizes the advanced techniques of industrial production. The procedure of photography gives rise to a completely novel system of coding visual and potentially visual signals from the environment, because this system has been developed along a technical path to a hitherto unknown degree.

The following essay investigates the ways in which Heartfield uses photography as picture material, his intentions in using it and the results he achieves with it. In the analysis of one photomontage [4] I shall be examining how artistic means and political intention relate to one another in his production. This montage is not conceived of as a work of art with its own internal frame of reference; the technical and artistic effort which went into its formal completion disappears beside the task of achieving effectivity amongst the masses.

An analysis which took the aesthetic qualities of the montage into account without considering its functionality would therefore go just as wrong as an investigation which – armed with the maxim that in art, too, politics must assume primacy – regarded the form and specific technique of montage as secondary. In opposition to most of the literature on Heartfield the emphasis in this analysis will be on the technical artistic conditions of photomontage. Thus it will be our object to show that precisely with Heartfield, who considered himself a "proletarian artist"[5], socialist agitation and the artistic technical means form a dialectical unity; the consequences of this unity for the psychology of perception is the basis of the argument proposed at the outset: namely that Heartfield's artistic production amounts to a new mode of aesthetic appropriation of reality.

2. The Motivation of the Montage

2.1 Hitler as a "revolutionary socialist"

After WW1 thousands of soldiers didn't find their way back into settled civilian life. Depressed by the outcome of the war and socially uprooted from their class, many of them formed themselves into *Wehrverbände* (defence associations), and *Militias* whose militaristic, nationalistic and anti-democratic attitudes laid the ground for the ideology of the National Socialists. When the economic crises of the post-war era reduced millions of peasants, workers and petty bourgeois to misery, these associations registered a large increase from amongst the masses disillusioned with democracy.

From the failure of his putsch in 1923 Hitler concluded that his movement could only achieve power by legal means. In the years 1924-1928, when *die Dollarsonne schien* (*the dollar-sun shone* – Arthur Rosenberg) in Germany, and the economy was being restabilized, the National Socialists were not able to win any significant influence on the masses. In the 1928 Reichstag elections Hitler's party received a mere 800,000 of the 30.7 million votes cast. Between these elections and the following ones in 1930, in which 6.4 million voted for the NSDAP (Nazi Party – ed.) there was a period of two years during which the world economic crisis effectively created support for the demagogy of the most reactionary political groups, by virtue of the increasing social misery of the lower classes.[6] It was a characteristic of the strategy of National Socialist propaganda to give the different groups in the population exactly those promises which they wanted to hear – irrespective of the fact that in practice it was objectively impossible to keep all these completely contradictory assurances. This strategy was primarily directed at the labour force which was the strongest social class in terms of numbers and at the same time had been exposed to the greatest misery by the economic crisis: the percentage of workers unemployed was: 1928 - 10%; 1929 - 15%; 1930 - 23%; 1931 - 35%; 1932 - 45% (seven million).[7] If the number of workers on short-time is added, we find that in 1932 only every third German worker was fully employed. In 1932, only fourteen out of 100 unemployed still received unemployment benefits; the real wages of those in employment fell by more than a third during the crisis.

In this situation Hitler's party presented itself to the workers as a revolutionary organisation of the proletariat. They called themselves the National Socialist German Workers' Party and assembled under the red flag to declare war on – as they said – international finance capital, stock exchange speculators, usurers in trade and finance. "German socialism," as *Reichsorganistionsleiter* Gregor Strasser proclaimed in 1932, "was the answer to anti-capitalist longing, which today already has perhaps 95% of the German people in its grip without them being aware of it".[8]

> He wrote in the inner-party *NS-Briefe*: "We don't give a damn about national rhetoric which, without the social deed of the liberation of the German working class will have to remain empty words! We don't want a social policy of 'charity'; instead of the exploitative capitalist economic system we want genuine socialism."

The petty bourgeoisie and the peasants were promised the "abolition of interest slavery", the small independent middle class was assured of a fight against monopolies and department stores. With these promises National Socialism was able to secure itself the broad base amongst the masses who had been unsettled by economic crises, which was eventually to lead it to a parliamentary majority.

But by its broad mass base, from 1930 on it also recommended itself as a reliable "servant of the political will" of the bourgeoisie to whom, doubly worried by crisis and communism, the party ideologist Alfred Rosenberg had already explained the central "programme of the movement" in 1923:

> National Socialism regards... Marxist ideology... as its deadly enemy... To overcome this ideology and to destroy it, to render its main protagonists harmless... is one of the most important objectives of the NSDAP.[10]

By distinguishing between "international capital" deemed to be "alien to the people" and national industrial capital which was "linked to the people", Hitler gained the possibility of giving a common denominator to a rhetorical anti-capitalism and the acceptance of private ownership of the means of production.

2.2 Heavy industry as Hitler's protagonist

In the first few years after the world economic crisis, the production of German industry sank to 40% of the previous years. There was an attempt at avoiding a drop in the rate of profit by tightening the conditions of work and wages:

> Article 48 of the Reich constitution which enabled the *Reichspresident* to decree emergency laws without prior agreement of the Reichstag, was used to raise contributions to social insurance and to decrease its benefits. It was used to reduce salaries and wages for the purposes of the state and also to crush the workers' wage struggles[11]

The gradual dismantling of bourgeois parliamentary democracy began in the 1930, with the Brüning cabinet. Right in his first year in office, Brüning presented industry with wage reductions of 20% - 25%[12], but he came into increasing conflict with the "inflationist conceptions and ambitions for political power of German heavy, and export, industry." [13] In October, the National Socialist – Anti-Democratic Front was formed in Bad Harzburg. It was not only directed against Brüning but also against the foundations of the Weimar Republic. In it, civil servants in the economy, industrialists, bankers and big landowners joined forces with Hitler, Hugenberg and Schacht. The latter mediated between Hitler and the banks. Hitler, who up to 1930 had only had limited success in turning industry to his service, could count in 1932 on support from those branches of industry whose stability was damaged: heavy industry, mining and banks. (Economically stable branches of industry like the electrical and chemical industries at first regarded Hitler's plans with a certain scepticism.) On 27th July 1931, the *Wirtschäftliche Vereinigung Frankfurt am Main* (Economic Alliance F.a.M) wrote to Hindenburg:

> It is incompatible with the Constitution that the party which is today by far the strongest, the NSDAP, should be kept out of any position of influence... The national opposition... disciplined and led by men who have proved their importance in the daily struggle against Bolshevism, demands its rights. And we, the leaders of the German economy, who have come to see politically, WE STAND BEHIND IT.[14]

After the elections in November 1932 (the immediate occasion of Heartfield producing the millions montage) representatives of big finance and industry despatched a note to Hindenburg which said:

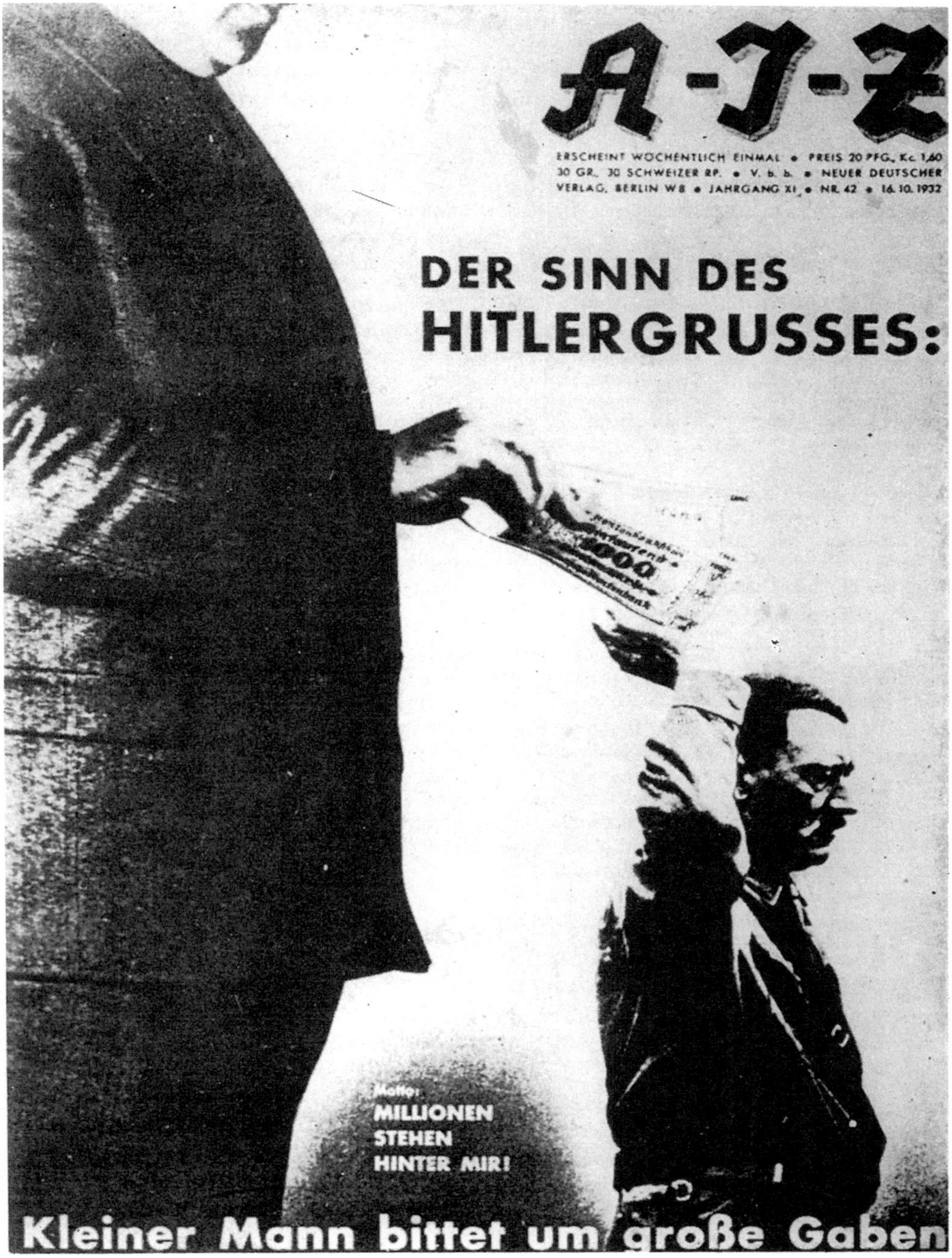

The meaning of the Hitler salute/Motto: Millions stand behind me!/Little man asks for great gifts
Arbeiter-Illustrierte Zeitung, October 16, 1932

> We agree with your Excellency that it is necessary to have a government which is less dependent on the parliamentary party system... It is... evident that every change of the Constitution which is not supported by the broadest trend in the population will cause economic, political and psychological effects which are even worse...
>
> The delegation of the responsible leadership of a... presidential cabinet to the leader of the biggest national group will eliminate the shortcomings and mistakes which are part and parcel of every mass movement, and will fill millions of people who now stand aloof with an affirmative power and enthusiasm.[15]

The first financial donations by industry to Hitler's party at the end of a phase of relative economic stability in 1928 were not yet significant. But they nonetheless made it possible for Hitler's party to force through the setting up of professional associations and factory organisations (NSBO) as well as the development of the SA, the publication of newspapers, etc.[16] In 1929, the party was again able to register an increase in votes for the first time for many years.

The massive donations of money after 1930 became known in the course of the Nuremberg war trials. In the autumn of 1932 finally, after "the coming together of the Hitler and Papen wings of German industry the most pressing financial problems were solved for the moment: a syndicate of industrialists paid part of the debts resulting from the election and made... one million Reichsmark available for financing the SS. On 20th February, Hitler once again received an election fund of at least three million Reichsmark... It was primarily the pressure from these industrialists as well as that from the Reichslandbund which in the end made Hindenburg offer Hitler the post of Reich Chancellor."[17]

2.3 *On the Anti-Fascist Action of 1932*

While the leadership of the SPD (Social Democratic Party – ed.) rejected any joint action with the Communists, from 1930 the KPD (German Communist Party – ed.) increasingly sought to oppose the rapidly growing fascist movement with the help of a "united front of all workers". Thus, in January 1931, a resolution of the plenary of the central committee of the KPD urged the:

> ...radical promotion of propaganda work amongst the masses, multiplication of efforts to convince the Social Democratic workers of the correctness of the revolutionary policy of a united front, and prevention of the National Socialists making a breach in the ranks of the working class. In accordance with its orientation towards the development of a broad people's movement the Central Committee of the Party gave the German Communists the task of driving a wedge between the fascist leaders and those workers, employees and other working people who had been misled by National Socialism.[18]

Propaganda for the "Anti-Fascist Action" was accompanied by an ideological offensive which was supposed to make apparent the class character of National Socialist politics. Heartfield's montage, which had the same aim, appeared at the climax of the election campaign for the Reichstag elections called for November 6. In mid-October numerous "anti-fascist unity" meetings and "people's congresses" took place: on the 12th October in Hamburg, the 14th in Dresden, 15th and 16th in Mannheim, 18th in Bremen, the 23rd in Weinheim. Both here and at the simultaneous mass rallies of the KPD in Berlin, Bremen, Mannheim, Köln, Breslau, Magdeburg and other towns, the effectivity of the montage was multiplied by millions through the sale of AIZ (*Arbeiter Illustrierte Zeitung* – Ed.)

So far only the political motivation and with it the meaning of the contents of the montage have been explained. We must now examine the way in which Heartfield used the possibilities of photomontage to make plain the support Hitler was receiving from representatives of industrial and finance capital and at the same time to expose to ridicule the ritual of the Hitler salute.

3. Photomontage as a sign-system of icons and words

3.1 Icons

3.1.1. Relation of form

Basic dimensions

In both parts of the picture the basic dimensions are repeated: the axes of the bodies are parallel to the vertical edges of the picture, forearm of the financial backer (F) and belt of Hitler (H) are parallel to the horizontal edges of the picture.

The stiffness produced by the vertical axes of the bodies is relieved by the convex curves of the front parts of the bodies of (F) and (H) which also correspond to the vertical borders of the picture. Yet they remain linked to the basic vertical dimension in the same way that the similarly convex line of (H)'s skull remains linked to the horizontal. The right upper corner of the picture is repeated in the right angle created by the arm (H), and the forearm (F), and in the lower part of the bundle of money. The bottom right corner is reiterated in the protruding corner of the jacket (F).

Diagonal

There is a diagonal from the top left to the bottom right which stretches from (F)'s collar and the swelling of his chest via his middle finger to (H)'s hand and nose. The diagonal is supported by the probable direction in which both people are looking. The middle of the diagonal is marked by the bundle of money.

By virtue of the economy of the geometrical construction all the divergences immediately stand out: the corpulence of (F), (H)'s figure which tends towards stoutness. In these emphases is expressed a moment of caricature, although the montage leaves untouched the inner structure of the photographic components.

Level of action

The economy, introduced *by* the repetition of the basic dimensions is continued on the level of action and its axis. Both bodies stand in a plane which is parallel to the picture surface. The axis of the action constructed by the two hands stands vertically on the axis of vision and corresponds to the direction in which the two people (F) and (H) are looking.

Body space relationship

The spatiality claimed by the two bodies and the banknotes is not indicated by any further object; it's not that the background remains empty, but it actually does not exist at all. The bodies, though light falls on them, don't produce any visible shadows. A mantle of light cloaks both figures and changes into a dark patch in the upper and lower regions of the area between the bodies.

The area outside the bodies appears to be "soft" thanks to the soft gradation of lighting; the contours of the bodies appear "hard". The background surface remains undefined as it does not have any objects in it; the inner structure of the bodies is highly defined. Both bodies, by the contrast with their surroundings, are brought into a close relation to each other which is strengthened by the way the bottom corner of the jacket (F) sticks out.

Overlapping

An important detail of the picture's construction is to be seen in the apparently insignificant intersection of the banknotes and Hitler's hand. Without this overlap, the size of (F)'s body almost twice the other would have given the impression that the receiver, the smaller figure, was standing in a plane further away from the picture surface than his patron. As this tiny intersection is in the centre of the composition, it moves the massive body into the same pictorial plane with the smaller figure. It thus makes it possible to suspend the logical-optical development of the picture for one of alienation.

3.1.2. Relation of signification

The financial backer

The ensemble of collar, double chin, suit, diamond ring and bundle of money, has the connotative component: *capitalist, employer, rich man* etc. The distinctive marks are not pursued consistently, however: the tie is missing; the jacket is a bad fit and the crease is poor; the shirt cuff has disappeared into the sleeve. These are indications that Heartfield is not trying to give a stylized image of the industrialist.

The head of the financier is cut off above the mouth by the upper edge of the picture. He remains anonymous. He represents not a certain person, but a specific social class. The movement of the arm with which he hands over the money is discrete; he does not want to attract any special attention.

Hitler

The recipient of the money is identified primarily by the physiognomy of the face with its small black moustache and by the hand opened above the shoulder in a salute. Unlike his hidden backer, Hitler wears a military uniform: brown shirt, shoulder belt and gun belt, together with the trousers of the uniform.

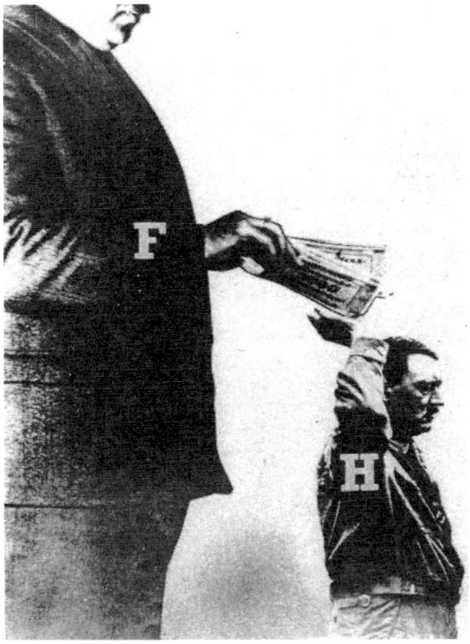

The drooping bit of his neck – an ironical repetition of his backer's double chin – as well as the S-shaped pose of this man who is inclined to stoutness contrast with the militant note of his clothing. This indicates that the wearer's military function is limited to administration, the representation of higher authority and the giving of orders.

Tie and moustache – well-known psychological symbols for penis and pubic hair – appear, but only in order to immediately "disappear" again: the moustache is trimmed in a "spartan" manner to prevent any outgrowth, and the tie disappears under his clothes at the height of the nipples. After the Hitler salute, the best known gesture of the Führer was probably the crossing of his hands before his sexual parts. He exhibits his sexual aura, of whose value he, as supreme training master of the nation, was surely conscious, by consciously pretending to be modest.

Hitler's clothes emphasize action, his gestures contemplation. The raised hand, the bowed head, the downward look not only form part of the salute – they seem to seal a "solemn bond" which has religious implications. The half-closed eye seems to look inward, unwilling to see anything worldly. The forehead is furrowed, the brows are drawn slightly together. Hitler's miming appears to express extreme concentration. But what does the Führer concentrate on? If one isolates the (H) section from its context it becomes clear: Hitler is getting in "touch" with the masses assembled around him, and who the salute is intended for. Seen in context with the (F) section however, the meaning of gestures and mimic art shifts: Hitler is now concentrating on receiving the bundle of money.

For the moment we will be content to state the double meaning, or rather the ambiguity of Hitler's gesture, whose meaning shifts synchronically with the change of the observer's angle of view.

Lighting
The unreality of the room is indicated by the lack of background. It is emphasized by the distribution of light that contradicts logic. The light which falls on Hitler diagonally from above we would expect to strike the financier's front. Instead, it is shrouded in darkness (by retouching). Light falling on the financier however from the direction of the observer in turn does not strike Hitler.

The political meaning of this differentiation is clear: Hitler's forehead is lit up as if he was inspired by and in alliance with some superior power, whereas the financier has to stay in the darkness, especially if seen from the direction of the Führer's invisibly present audience.

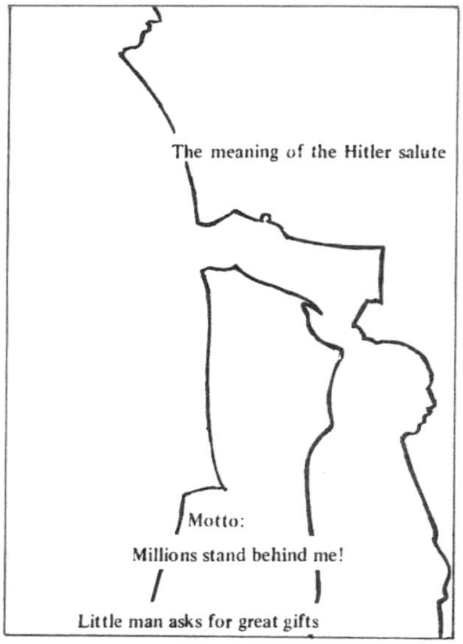

3.2 The verbal part

The verbal components of the montage I will call title, caption and subtitle. The title is composed of two nouns with articles, one in the nominative, one in the genitive. The second noun indicates what the "object" of the montage is: the Hitler salute. The first noun gives the motivation for the examination: to clarify the social meaning of the salute.

The colon accelerates the shift from the first verbal level of reading to the icons and to the word in small print, *Motto*, which itself carries a colon and marks the transition from one speaker to another.

The sentence *Millionen stehen hinter mir* (millions stand behind me) is a phrase which Hitler frequently used in a more or less varied form. It means, in Hitler's sense: " ...support me", " ...are in agreement with my struggle". The metaphor transforms the agreement and the material support of millions to the mass of people who stand "behind" the Führer. Thus they experience every attack on him as an attack on them; they follow the Führer wherever he leads them. The sentence, supported in the text by an exclamation mark, is mainly directed at those who still hesitate to join this army. Its function is to strengthen the followers and to intimidate the doubters. (The photomonteur is after all addressing himself not least to the doubters.)

The subtitle with its ironic tone exposes Hitler's charismatic way of talking to ridicule. Here he is called a little man. Heartfield makes use of a simple opposition in language by having the little man beg for great gifts.

It is now possible to describe precisely the structure of the verbal part: if one reads the caption together with the subtitle, then a process is set in motion which resembles the one in the iconic part: the words *grosse Gaben* (great gifts) change the meaning of the word *Millionen* (millions). Through the subtitle Hitler is made to declare involuntarily that capital stands behind him. Heartfield supports Hitler's reading of *Millionen* by the title, only to rob it of any credibility with his final comment.

It has already become obvious that the three parts of the montage text refer to different speakers: Heartfield and Hitler. Heartfield, visually not present in the montage, figures as a speaker "off-screen" Therefore his comments are not really title and subtitle, but internal elements of the montage. The alternation of speakers in the picture confirms the impression that photomontage is a "static film" (Raoul Hausmann). [19]

3.3. Iconic – verbal intersection

Speaker

Heartfield is invisibly present in the picture – as voice off – whereas the speaker Hitler is visually perceivable – though not as a speaker. The quotation *Millionen stehen hinter mir* is not accompanied by the outward appearance of talk, but by a dumb gesture of salute. In other words: of the two speakers, one remains invisible, while the other one is visible but does not visibly talk.

Ambiguity

For the moment it is sufficient to notice that there is an ambiguity at the centre of the iconic as well as on the verbal part. This ambiguity is based on a ritualized mode of speech, and gesturing. Around it are grouped with differing intentions the various verbal and iconic segments of the montage.

Semantic intersection of word and picture components

Sinn (meaning) refers to the ensemble of the montage. *Hitlergrüss* (Hitler salute) relates to the cod's of recognition of the right-hand figure.

Finally, *Der Sinn des Hitlergrüsses* (the meaning of the Hitler salute) argues that the interpretation of the salute ritual is connected with the left-hand figure.

Motto indicates that the ensemble of the montage is characterized by a well-known and programmatic slogan. *Millionen stehen hinter mir* directs the view to the man behind Hitler as well as to the banknotes with the numerous noughts.

Syntactic intersection of word and picture parts
"Little man" refers to the "little" Hitler, "great gifts" corresponds to the banknotes which are in proportion with the size of the money-giver figure, while the little man is made to look even smaller by them.

A crosswise syntactic intersection is effected by the fact that the figures are ranged beside each other, and the textual parts vertically.

Metaphor and "re-metaphor" [20]
Hitler's sentence *Millionen stehen hinter mir* contains a conventionalized linguistic image which is called metaphor. Heartfield takes Hitler "at his word" i.e. neglects the "transformed" meaning Hitler implies, and shows that there really are millions behind him. These millions, however, are different from what Hitler wants to put across.

Heartfield thereby indirectly employs the rhetorical figure of "re-metaphor": He does not re-metaphorize what Hitler subjectively meant with his metaphor. Instead he takes advantage of the double ambiguity which comes about by Hitler's elliptic (*Millionen*) and metaphoric (*stehen hinter mir*) way of talking, in order to re-metaphorize into a single photo complex (capitalist with bundle of money) precisely that pole of the two ambiguous rhetorical figures which Hitler did not intend.

The *Millionen* montage is built on this complex process which reappears in other montages by Heartfield in a similar form.[21] From it stems the hard-hitting effect of a great part of Heartfield's production.

The same mechanism is repeated in a simpler form within the same montage: if our interpretation of the quasi-religious meaning of the Hitler salute is correct, then the arm raised for the salute can be regarded as another (visual) metaphor. In this case, Hitler's relationship as a metaphoric "mediator" with the "Almighty" – who figures repeatedly in his speeches – is re-metaphorized as the "almighty" capitalist personified. In this indirect re-metaphor too, the ambiguity of a rhetorical element (here of gesture) becomes the point of departure for a change of function. By this change, the real historico-political connections are laid bare, and at the same time, it is made transparent that the intended implications of rite are a manoeuvre.

So far in the analysis of the construction we have abstracted from the different linguistic levels of the montage. The lack of precision which we have thereby accepted disappears in what follows with the location of different linguistic levels of the montage in space (metaphorically speaking).

3.4. Object language and metalanguage
Every communicative act is based on the transmission of information according to rules which are validated by social conventions. Semiotics calls these rules – whether linguistic, visual, mimic or gestural – *codes*. It attempts to reduce "every phenomenon of communication to a dialectic between codes and messages." [22]

Bearers of information or of the component parts of information are the *signs*. Every sign refers to something distinct from itself, to an object or to a relationship between objects. These objects or relationships are the bearers of the meaning of the sign. [23]

The sign, however, is not identical with the signifier, that which "means", which relates to what is "meant", signified. Rather, the sign is the link connecting signifier and signified. [24] For instance: slapping somebody on the shoulder remains empty as a "signified", until I invest it with a certain meaning: solidarity, catching attention, aggression etc. Only together with the signified does the signifier become a sign.

One can imagine the example in the following extended context: a shop-floor meeting has just finished. The employer meets the workers' representative and jovially slaps him on the shoulder. A reporter photographs this scene and publishes the picture in an illustrated magazine. It is obvious that this photo says more than the "literal" news item ("two men getting on with each other"). The hidden information of the photograph says rather: in our society employer and employees form a happy community which keeps its interests in harmony with one another.

Roland Barthes gives an analogous example in his book *Mythologies*:

> I am at the barber's, and a copy of *Paris-Match* is offered to me. On the cover, a young Negro in a French uniform is saluting, with his eyes uplifted, probably fixed on a fold of the tricolour. All this is the meaning of the picture. But, whether naively or not, I see very well what it signifies to me: that France is a great Empire, that all her sons, without any colour discrimination faithfully serve under her flag, and that there is no better answer to the detractors of an alleged colonialism than the zeal shown by this Negro in serving his so-called oppressors.[25]

In this case, Barthes is talking about an extended semiological system whose characteristic it is that the sign of the first system becomes the simple signifier of the second system, which then together with the new extended signified builds a new sign. He calls the first system the object language, the second system the meta-language or the language of myth.[26]

At first this model seems complicated but it proves effective when applied to iconic-verbal sign systems as, for example, to advertising.[27]

Wieland Herzfelde was the first to point out affinities between Heartfield's photomontages and advertising. He writes:

> The joining of photo and text became the preferred means of commercial advertising in the 1920s. And so it has remained, in film and television advertising, too. Such commercial graphics in advertising and Heartfield's works have one thing in common (despite important differences), namely that both of them are totally "aimed". They ask something definite of the viewer: to buy a book or a magazine, to visit a meeting or a rally, to support an action or to fight against unpopular laws and regulations... (Heartfield) learned "pure" as well as commercial painting and drawing in Berlin and Munich.[28]

In 1912, Heartfield had worked as a commercial artist at the publishing house of the Baür brothers in Mannheim. There he had taken part in competitions for commercial advertising posters. He knew the techniques of consumer advertising before he used his artistic talents for political ends. The use of photo-text combinations in his political montages should certainly be taken in connection with these commercial activities. The "decisive differences" Herzfelde talks about can be seen in the altered function he gives to information which works at a subconscious level (on which advertising strategies are based to a great degree). Heartfield cannot transfer to his montages the use which advertising makes of the meta-language, since he wants to convince and not to influence. We shall now examine if and how *metalanguage* is nonetheless present in the *Millionen* montage.

It had already become obvious (cf. paragraph 3.1.2.) that the information from the – isolated – segment (H) does not only consist in the simple fact of "the action of saluting". In order to discover the linguistic level on which the hidden information is transmitted and in order to "decipher" their social meaning, one has to go back to the photograph from which Heartfield cut out the Hitler figure, to get to the reality "captured" in it.

The photograph shows the Führer at a flag ritual. In this context, Hitler's salute is more than just a simple salute; it is precisely what else it is that we must now examine.

the man in the suit could equally well be a white-collar worker, an intellectual or an employer.

The text on the poster says: "In thirteen years Adolf Hitler has brought you together. German workers, mental and manual, German peasants! Don't let anyone divide you again! Vote National Socialist list 1!"

The concept of peace between the classes in the sense referred to here, is explained by the chairman of the *Deutsche Arbeitsfront* (German Labour Front), Robert Ley:

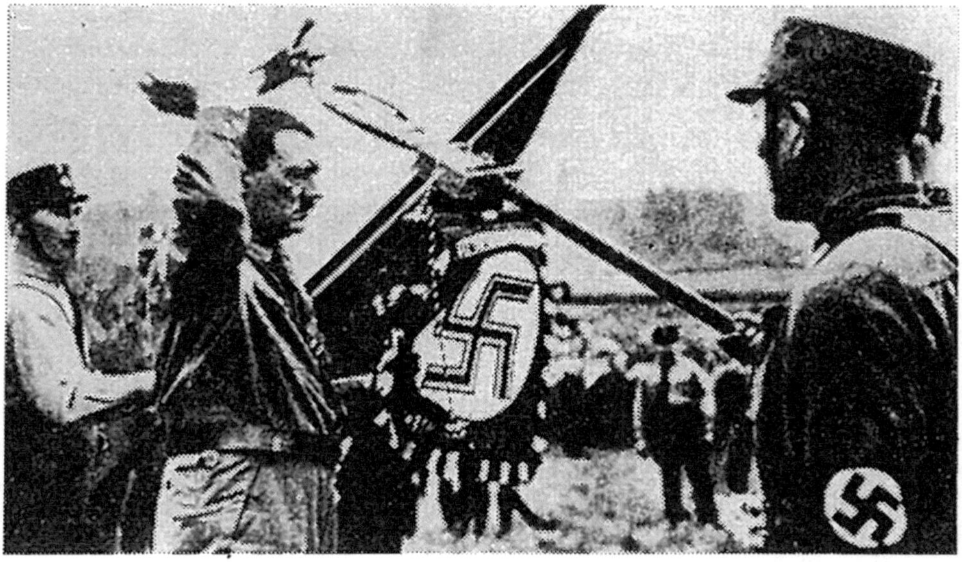

3.4. The information of the meta-language (Digression: the category of wholeness in the ideology and aesthetics of National Socialism.)

A poster of the NSDAP,[29] probably from the year 1933, shows three men standing and looking at each other, holding their right hands. One of them carries a scythe, the second a hammer, the third wears a shirt and tie. Whereas it is easy to recognize the first two as worker and peasant,

> Work... ennobles, whether performed by forehead or fist... There is no distinction within work. The work of a general director has no more intrinsic value and is no better than that of a street cleaner... In the light of this realization everything that till now had been in a state of hostility, that appeared to be an irredeemable contradiction, deadly enmities have now become a meaningless Nothing.[30]

A photograph of the Führer at a flag ritual.
It is this photograph (and the event it represents) which Heartfield "quotes" in the Millions montage.
By changing the context of the "quote" Heartfield achieves a shift of meaning.

The end of the class war, the wholeness of the people was personified by a living symbol:

> ...the past had only chairmen and a pile of other such people: chairmen of the board, of administrative councils, of parties, of unions, of employers' associations, of friendly societies, and of strike committees. Today we have the leader of the whole people... everybody has risen up and now marches behind one Führer. [31]

The march of the millions is connected with a rebellion the description of which sounds like a satirical comment on the *Millionen* montage. As a fighter in the National Socialist "Revolution" describes it:

> Blood rises up against formal understanding, race against the rational pursuit of ends, honour against profit, bonds against the caprice that is called "freedom", organic totality against individualistic dissolution... state against society, folk against the individual and the mass. [32]

The enumerated oppositions can be divided into two groups. The attack in the first group is directed against "formal", "rational" and "calculating" ways of thinking. The side taken is that of the primordial truths which according to National Socialist conceptions precede all thought and on which thought depends.

In the second group, the whole is conjured up as a counter image to that of dissolution and fragmentation.

But it is the starting point of rational thinking to destroy primordial truths and wholes; analysis dissects its objects in order to understand their structural laws and it has not arrived at its goal until no further connection remains closed to it.

This activity however, when referring to the social whole, has to be deemed subversive because the National Socialist strategy of wholeness of the people is based on an insoluble contradiction. It promises the coming of a classless society, "the establishment of a real folk community, which elevates itself above the interests and conflicts of status groups and classes. [33] But it wants to reach this without eliminating that social institution which in the Marxist view is the cause of the division of society into classes, namely the private ownership of the means of production.

The ideologues of National Socialism protect this conflicting strategy by giving the signal for transcending logical thinking and turning towards an archaic and pre-logical world.

"For the very reason", one protagonist writes, "that National Socialism is an *elementary* movement, it cannot be gotten at with 'arguments'. Arguments would be effective only if the movement had gained its power by argumentation... [34]

Accordingly, those of Heartfield's professional colleagues who obeyed the state were instructed:

> An overpowering speech, the spark-giving text of a poster, a captivating poster illustration must overwhelm. Coldly calculating intellect and conscious thought must here be switched off. Here must be trod the direct path to the subconscious, to emotions. The "art" of the psychologist, of the guide of the soul, is to unearth the primeval feelings. [35]

Insofar as art aesthetically transforms and encodes the contradictions of reality, it gains a pre-eminent importance for fascism: its spokesmen themselves feel like artists. Goebbels wrote to Furtwängler in 1933:

> Politics, too, is an art, maybe the highest and most all-embracing there is; and we who are making modern German politics feel like artistic people entrusted with the responsible task of forming the solid shape of the people, from the raw material of the mass.[36]

The preferred vehicle of the religion-oriented aesthetics with which National Socialism celebrates the mystical union of the formerly hostile classes is the highly organised mass rally, such as the night rally on Zeppelin Fields in Nuremberg in 1936, at which (amongst other things) Hitler shouted and whispered the following:

> As we meet here, we are filled by the magic of this get-together. Not every one of you can see me and I cannot see every one of you. But I can feel you and you can feel me! We are now one.
>
> (*Deep emotion of the masses*, the chronicler of the *Niederelbisches Tageblatt* writes at this point.)
>
> Quiet and self-assured are we... (Hitler continues) I am so because I can see you. I am aware of this unique and single movement behind me... All these 140,000 have only one mind and their heart has only one beat, they are all thinking of the same thing.

Hitler crowns this identification ritual with the Hitler salute at the end of his speech, the apotheosis with which he declares himself mediator between the people's community and almighty destiny. The reaction confirms to the craftsman that his work of art has succeeded:

> Hardly has the Führer given his salute to those present when it roars forth, thunderous jubilations, so full of gushing strength and enthusiasm that you are carried along by this powerful experience whether you like it or not.[37]

This is exactly the moment which Heartfield "quotes" in his montage. The message of the sign system (H) transmitted in the *object language* is limited to imparting that the Führer salutes the masses. The message of the *meta-language* can be summed up as follows: National Socialism creates a great community of the people in which there are no more classes, in which the millions stand like a single block behind the Führer as the exponent of their unity. His authority is not socially based. It transcends the realm of history, and is therefore not accessible to any sort of criticism.

Let us recapitulate again the signs which the meta-language uses and on which its interpretation is based: the title and the caption refer to the millions "saluted" by Hitler; the light falling on his forehead from above emphasizes his claims which transcend history; the inward turned view signalizes the mystical empathy with the mass, the contemplation of that whole which "can never be grasped by hands, nor seen with outer eyes. Composure and depth of spirit are necessary in order to behold it with the inner eye."[38]

3.6 The "visual quotation" as a specific means of photomontage

If one takes a picture as a sign for a material object, then the conditions for the constitution of this sign are very different depending on whether it is a painted or a photographed picture. In both cases, the relation rests on syntactic analogies between the picture and the depicted. But in the case of the painted picture these analogies are created by the author of the picture, namely by his attempts to imitate the syntax of the object as closely as possible (as far as the author is concerned with similarity). In the case of photography, on the other hand, the syntactic analogy comes about because the picture is mainly caused by an "automatic activity" – namely the physical presence – of the object which reflects rays of light. The photographer takes on a role which can be exactly determined: he decides at what moment the light reflected from the object changes the chemical surface of the film, and he decides to a degree (which again can be exactly determined) the separate modalities according to which the light enters the camera: direction, duration, intensity.

The Hitler segment of the montage is not a representation of the Führer. The material which makes up this sign is the product of physical and chemical effects of the physical presence of Adolf Hitler at a specific moment in front of a specific camera. These circumstances remain intact through out all the technical manipulations which the film (the negatives) and the first print as well as all further reproductions are subjected to. The segment (H) therefore corresponds to a quotation in direct speech whose unchanged internal structure is brought into a heterogeneous context.

The "literal" visual quotation makes it possible for Heartfield to reproduce the aesthetic appearance of the Fascist ritual from a maximum distance and with the highest possible objectivity – and at the same time unmask it through the confrontation with exactly those social facts which it is supposed to conceal.

Precisely because Heartfield seems to reproduce the (H) segment without manipulations, the photograph projects fragments of the meta-language of the ritual onto the reality of the recipient in the most positive way.

These fragments concentrate on the claim which Hitler associates with his salute. The immediacy of the projection of those quasi-religious implications on which the mechanisms of identification of the ritual are based, is repressed by the photographic medium.[39]

This immediacy is also relativized by the separation of the figure of Hitler from its original context, whose contribution to the definition of the gesture of salute is thereby eliminated. The technique of quotation separates the quote from its given context and thus makes it liable to an arbitrary shift of function of its intended meaning. Heartfield uses this means, as we have shown, in the verbal as well as the iconic part of the montage – and in such a way that the hidden truth of the quotation becomes apparent by its alienation from its context.

4. The dialectics of montage

Commercial advertising and the dominant part of political propaganda use sign systems in which the things communicated are simple communications of the meta-languages. In contrast to this, in Heartfield's production, the language of the montage destroys the *meta-language* of sub-systems by confronting it with semantically opposed *object* languages.[40]

The question about the relationship between political intention and artistic technique in Heartfield's montages can now be answered. Heartfield uses his artistic tools not only to make political facts and processes visible in a picture, or (phrased in another way), to destroy the *contents* of political illusions, but he destroys at the same time the aesthetic superficial form which helps produce and maintain these illusions. The montage not only gives contrasting information but at the same time it makes visible the codes with which the hidden information is transmitted.

Roland Barthes calls these codes on which meta-language is based the language of myth. It is the political function of the myth, he writes, to de historicize social facts and processes. [41]

If Heartfield's photomontages reached an incomparable effectivity as an instrument of anti-fascist struggle, and if Heartfield himself was more hated by the Fascists than virtually any other artist, this was because the mythical transfiguration of the community of "The People" and their Führer, as realities removed from the historical process, was at the centre of National Socialist ideology and propaganda. [42]

As we have shown, in order to call on the idea of "the whole" and present it as free of contradictions, Hitler had to have recourse to aesthetic means, means of concrete illusion, whereas Heartfield uses artistic means to render the dialectical structure of the social totality visible. With scissors and photograph Heartfield demonstrates the dialectical principle for politics and history; the dialectical principle which, according to Hegel, says that:

> ...the consideration of everything that reveals (in itself) that in its identity it is not identical, is contradictory with itself, and in its variety, its contradiction, it is identical with itself, and in itself it is the movement of transition from one of these determinations into the other, and this is because each in itself is the contrary of itself. [43]

Heartfield understood social totality not as the bequest of destiny, but as a product of history and people, that product's appearance being largely determined by the direction of movement of its internal conditions. Heartfield's dialectical procedure attempts to render ineffective the de-historicization, the mythologizing of society by National Socialist ideology and aesthetics. He does so by quoting the world of images which it employs, and by turning them against their authors through the addition of pictorial segments which make the dialectics of appearance and reality obvious.

As was said at the outset, aesthetic innovation is the rupture of traditional modes of perception and coding. Visual perception of the environment is based on codes whose structure the recipient is hardly ever aware of, and whose concealment becomes a means of social control.

Heartfield's aesthetic intention, which was an integral part of his political programme, is directed towards vigilance in the choice and structure of political information. His didactic approach is to make the reception of everyday political life political. One aspect of his production might be termed "the training school of vision". Its curriculum varies with the objects to hand, but it seeks to train and practice the ability not to accept social realities and the dominant modes of their transmission as quasi-natural facts, but instead to recognize the centres of power according to whose frames of reference reality is defined and presented.

[Written in 1972]

* This article appeared in German in: Eckhard Siepmann, *Montage: John Heartfield. Vom Club Dada zur Arbeiter-Illustrierten Zeitung*. Berlin (West): Elefanten Press Galerie, 1977, pp. 240-252. We thank Eckhard Siepmann and the Elefanten Press for permission to translate and reprint this article. We also want to thank Richard Scott of Leeds for his help with the translation and Gertrud Heartfield of East-Berlin for giving us permission to reprint John Heartfield's work.

NOTES

1. See *Philosophisches Wörterbuch*. Eds./ Georg Klaus and Manfred Buhr, vol.1, Leipzig: 1971, p.34.
2. Umberto Eco, "Articulations of Cinematic Code", in: *Cinemantics* 1, January 1, 1970, p.4.
3. See Maruta Schmidt, *Das Verhältnisltnis von Kunst zur Fotografie. Die aesthetische Diskussion in den 60er Jahren des 19. Jahrhunderts in Deutschland*. MA thesis, TU Berlin: 1972.
4. Here I agree with Bodo Uhse who calls the *Millions* montage "the simplest example for pointing out origins, methods and effects of photomontage". (Bodo Uhse, "John Heartfield und seine Fotomontagen", in: *John Heartfield und die Kunst der Fotomontage*, ed. German Academy of Arts, Berlin: 1957, p.18).
5. John Heartfield on his work in photomontage, in: *John Heartfield und die Kunst der Fotomontage*, op.cit.
6. See Arthur Rosenberg, "Der Faschismus als Massenbewegung", in: Otto Beuer *et al.*, *Faschismus und Kapitalismus. Theorien über die sozialen Ursprünge und die Funktionen*

des Faschismus, Frankfurt am Main: 1967, p.133 f.
7. See Joachim Streisand, *Deutsche Geschichte von den Anfängen bis zur Gegenwart*, Cologne: 1972, p.344.
8. Cited by Iring Fetscher, "Zur Kritik des sowjetmarxistischen Faschismusbegriffs", in: *Karl Marx und der Marxismus. Von der Philosophie des Proletariats zur proletarischen Weltanschauung*, Munich: 1967, p.232.
9. Cited by Iring Fetscher, op.cit.
10. Alfred Rosenberg, *Wesen, Grundsätze und Ziele der National sozialistischen Deutschen Arbeiterpartei. Das Programm der Bewegung*. Munich: 1923, p.9.
11. Joachim Streisand, op.cit., p.347.
12. See Heinrich Bruening, *Memoiren 1918-1934*, Stuttgart: 1970, p.480.
13. Manfred Clemenz, *Gesellschaftliche Ursprünge des Faschismus*. Frankfurt am Main: 1972, p.48.
14. Cited by Wolfgang Ruge, *Deutschland von 1917 bis 1933*, Berlin: 1967, p.411 (author's emphasis).
15. Cited in: *Geschichte der deutschen Arbeiterbewegung*, ed. Institute for Marxism-Leninism, Berlin:1966, vol. 4, p.559 f.
16. See H J Bartmuss *et al., Deutsche Geschichte*, vol.3, Berlin:1968, p.109.
17. Manfred Clemenz, op. cit., p.52 f.
18. Wolfgang Ruge, op. cit., p.395.
19. Raoul Hausmann, *Am Anfang war Dada*, Steinbach/Giessen: 1971, p,50.
20. "If a verbally constructed metaphor is reversed visually by translating a verbal image in great detail into the visual, then one talks of a word-image-remetaphor." (F Knilli und E Reiss, *Einführung in die Film – und Fernsehanalyse. Ein ABC für Zuschauer*, Steinbach/Giessen: 1971, p.109.)
21. See Wieland Herzfelde, *John Heartfield, Leben und Werk Presented by his Brother Wieland Herzfelde*, Dresden: 1971, (2nd edition) ;plates 136,141, 145,154,176.
22. Umberto Eco, op. cit., p.4
23. See G Klaus, M Buhr, op. cit., vol.2, p.1175.
24. Roland Barthes, "Myth Today", in: *Mythologies*, St. Albans: 1976, p.112-113.
25. Roland Barthes, "Myth Today", op. cit., p.116.
26. To understand Barthes' scheme of object language and meta-language see Barthes, *Mythologies*, op, cit., p.115.
27. See Roland Barthes, "Rhetoric of the Image", in: *Image-Music-Text*, Glasgow: 1977, pp.32-51.
28. Wieland Herzfelde, "Der Fall Heartfield", in *Sinn und Form*, Berlin: 1964 (16. Jg.), No.3, p.472.
29. Illustration in: Erwin Schockel, *Das politische Plakat. Eine psychologische Betrachtung*. Munich: 1938, p.165.
30. Robert Ley, "Der Führer und der deutsche Arbeier", in: *Adolf Hitler. Bilder aus dem Leben des Führers*, ed. Cigaretten Bilderdienst Hamburg/Bahrenfeld: no date, p.60.
31. Robert Ley, op. cit., p.63.
32. Ernst Krieck, Nationalpolitische Errziehung, 14th-16th impression (1933), p.68; cited by Herbert Marcuse in: "The struggle against liberalism in the totalitarian view of the state", in *Negations. Essays in Critical Theory*, Harmondsworth: 1972, p.3.
33. Koellreutter, *Allgemeine Staatslehre*, pp. 184-185; cited by Herbert Marcuse, op. cit., p.21.
34.Wilhelm Stapel, *Nationalsozialismus und Christentum*, cited by Wilhelm Reich in: "The Authoritarian Ideology of the Family in the Mass Psychology of Fascism", in *The Mass Psychology of Fascism*, Harmondsworth: 1972, p.68.
35. Erwin Schockel, op. cit,. p.168.
36. Cited by Hildegard Brenner, *Die Kunstpolitik des Nationalsozialismus*, Reinbek nr. Hamburg: 1963, p.178.
37. Cited in *Niederelbisches Tageblatt*, September 9, 1939.
38. Othmar Spann, Gesellschaftslehre, (3rd ed., 1930), p.98; cited by Herbert Marcuse, op. cit., p.7.
39. For the relationship between ritual, painting and photography see Walter Benjamin, "The Work of Art in the Age of Mechanical Reproduction", in: *Illuminations*, London and Glasgow: 1973.
40. See also Roland Barthes: "Myth, as we know, is a value: it is enough to modify its circumstances, the general (and precarious) system in which it occurs, in order to regulate its scope with great accuracy". (*Mythologies*. p.145.)
41. See Roland Barthes, *Mythologies*, op. cit., p.142 ff.
42. See Herbert Marcuse. op. cit., p.23 ff.
43. Georg Friedrich Wilhelm Hegel, *Wissenschaft der Logik*, vol.2, ed by G Lasson, Lelpzig: 1951, p.26 (translation S G.)

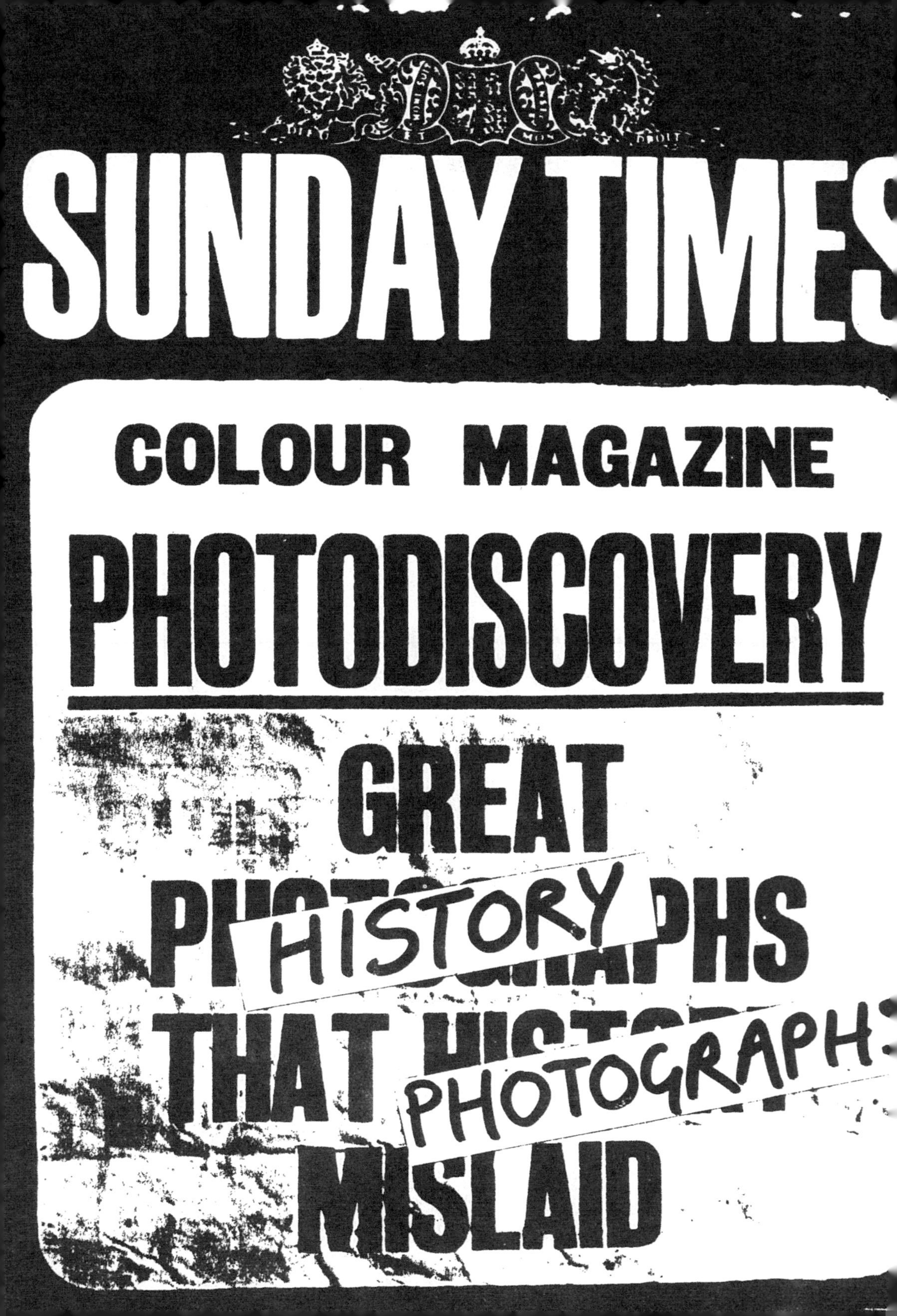
SUNDAY TIMES
COLOUR MAGAZINE
PHOTODISCOVERY
GREAT
HISTORY
THAT
PHOTOGRAPH
MISLAID

The History That Photography Mislaid

Judith Williamson

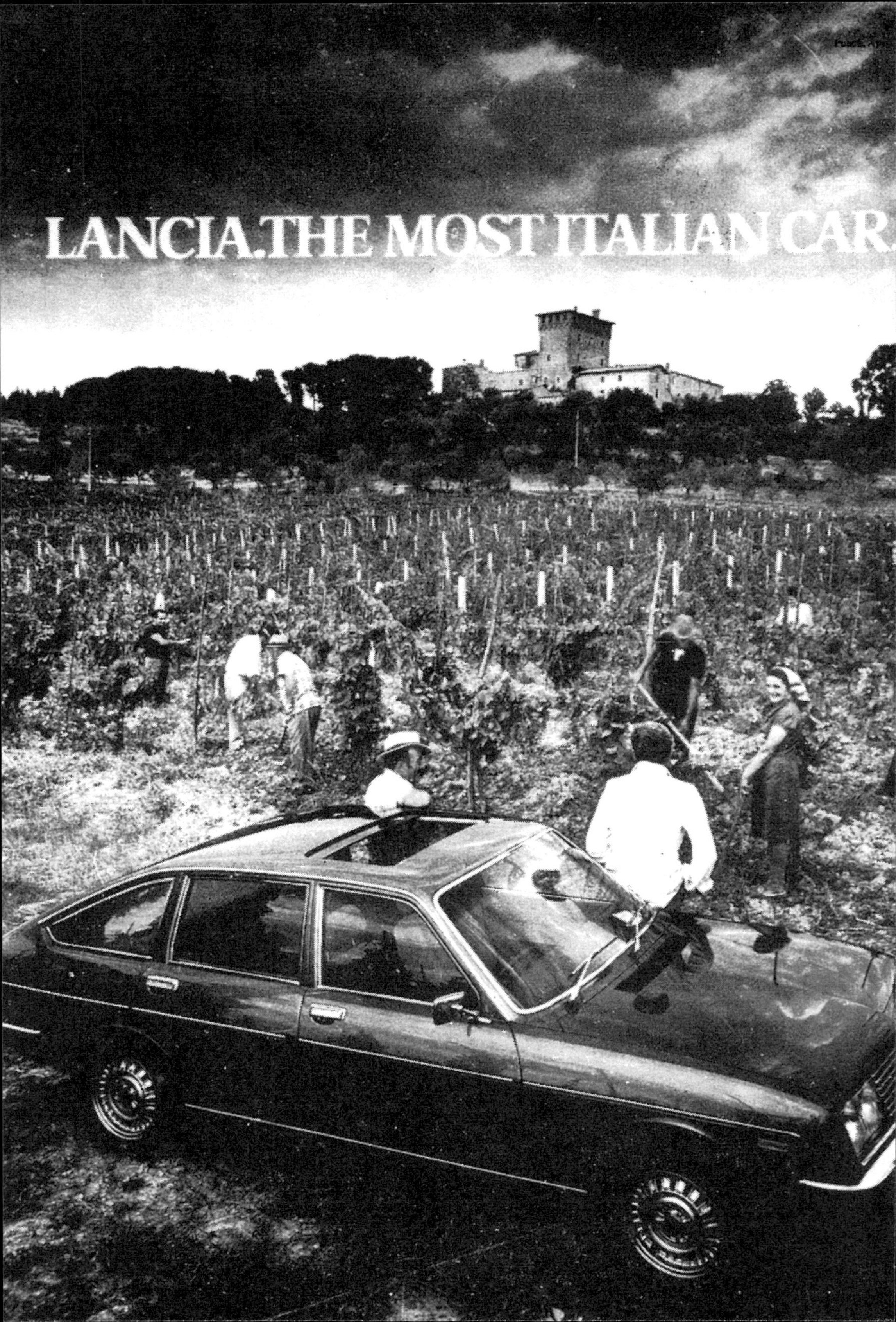
LANCIA. THE MOST ITALIAN CAR.

Has it just emerged new and gleaming from the soil,
its finished form as much a product of nature as the grapes on the vines?

Has it grown freely out of nothing, an organic and priceless gift of nature's abundance?

Nobody makes the grapes, but the land they grow on in the photograph is owned – how can they have any social place except through possession?

The car, the vines, the field, are not *produced* but they can be owned, and therefore *exchanged*. The grapes or the wine will be sold. Everything is owned by the man leaning against the Most Italian Car, as he surveys his land, his fruit, his castle – and his peasants.

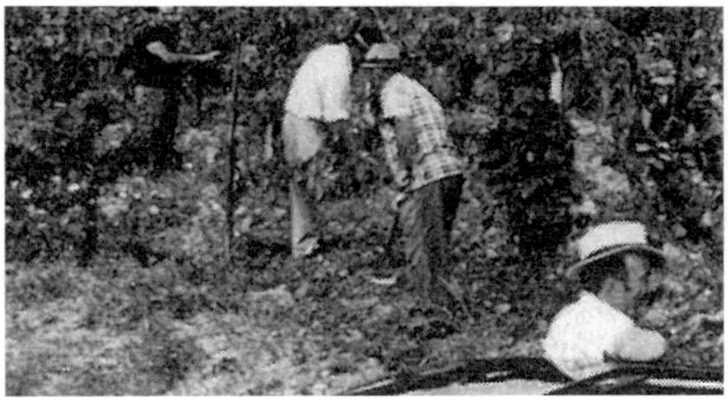

What mode of production is this? How can a car even exist in these feudal relations, how can such a contradiction be carried off? If the car is not the product of this kind of labour, what is it doing here? – bearing traces of the happy, feudal scene on its shiny surface, almost like film: carrying in the form of an object an image of reality which is simultaneously a denial of its own production.

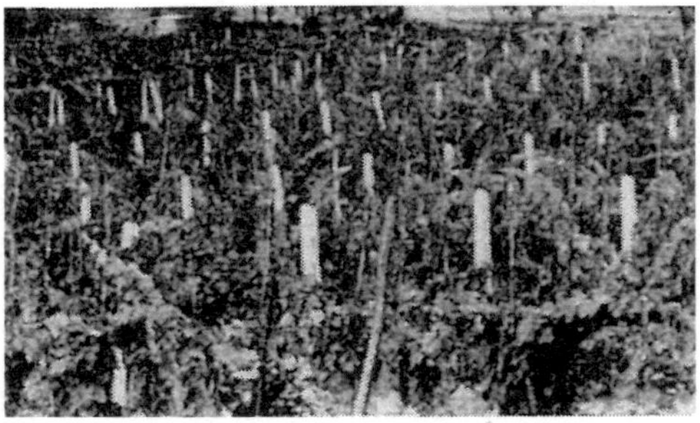

Who are these peasants? Have they made the car, out in this Most Italian field?

Have they nurtured its growth as they hoe the earth, tending it as they tend the vineyard, so that one of them in his checked t-shirt and straw hat leans affectionately on the roof as on familiar handiwork?

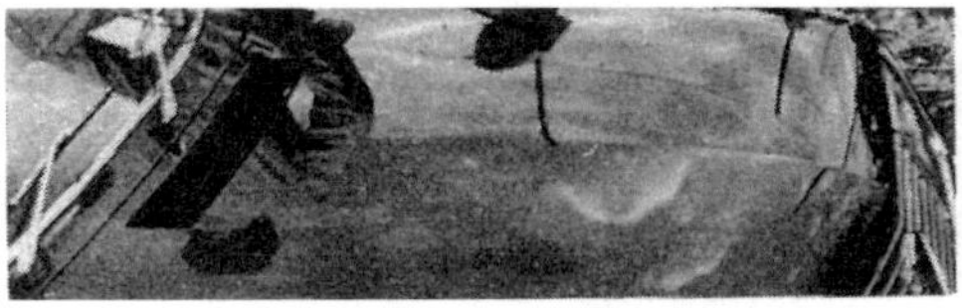

Because what is this, if not a complete slipping over of the capitalist mode of production, as we survey a set of feudal class relations, represented by the surveying gaze of possession, the look of the land lord with his back to us?

The angle of his head shows he is looking across the peasants – a class who labour, but not the class who made the car, providing a feudal substitute, a sort of rustic translation of the working class – to his castle (surrounded by uncultivated nature – "pure" nature which can only be possessed) – which again represents class, but a ruling class of old nobility, a class whose relation to those it exploits is paternal, familial. Although the men in the field are busy, the woman peasant has time to look up and smile at her superior.

What is to be gained by seeing essential "Italianness" as lying in feudal relations? At what cost is the representation of Italianness made? History becomes simply a view to be looked at. What does the Most Italian mean in terms of twentieth century history and specific social formations – like fascism? How is this real history excluded from the photograph?

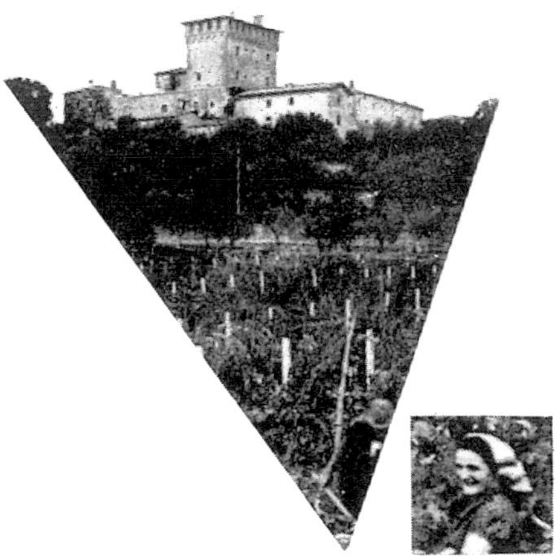

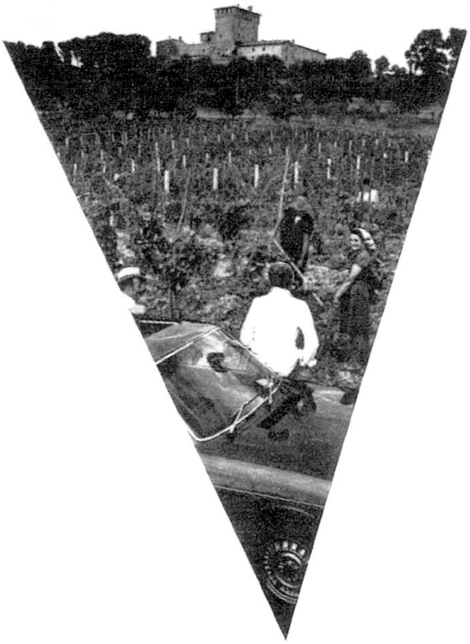

But why is it that the owner's gaze, encompassing peasants, land and castle, does not include the Most Italian Car? It is our view which encompasses both the car *and* the field of vision of the owner himself: the product of modern capitalism and the relations of Italian feudalism. And just as the owner's look is one which links all the objects within its compass through *possession*, so, our look implies, we can possess the car and with it the image of *Most Italian* feudal labour in which (the photo suggests) the car sprang up, but which, literally, is seen as reflected in it and which the car therefore seems to contain. It can be shown as embodying labour – but not the capitalist labour that produced it.

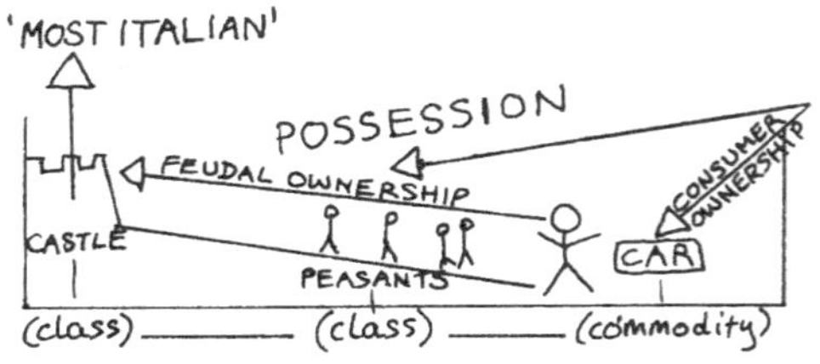

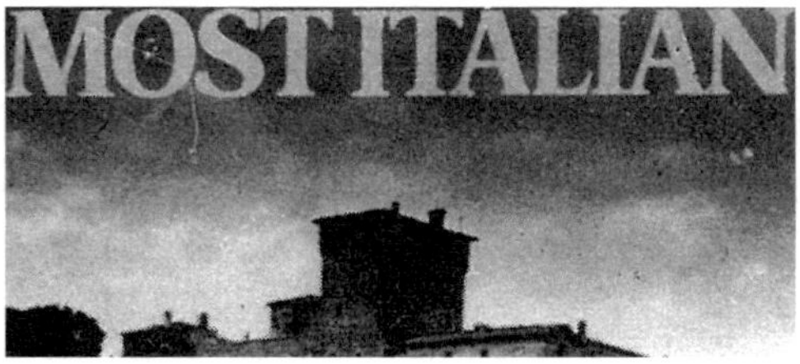

The *Most Italian* – the statement, the caption itself – emerges above the castle, the apex of the whole movement that traverses the car – the twentieth century commodity – the owner, and his possession of the peasants, who are *looked over* to the castle, the pinnacle of the whole Italian scene, the end of the view. Who is the most Italian, the peasants or the owner of the peasants?

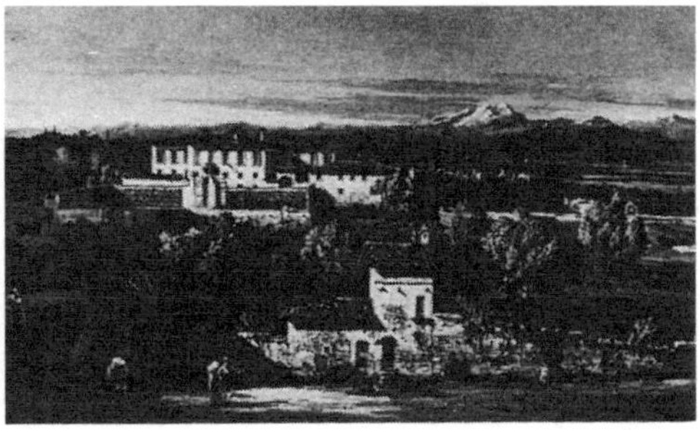

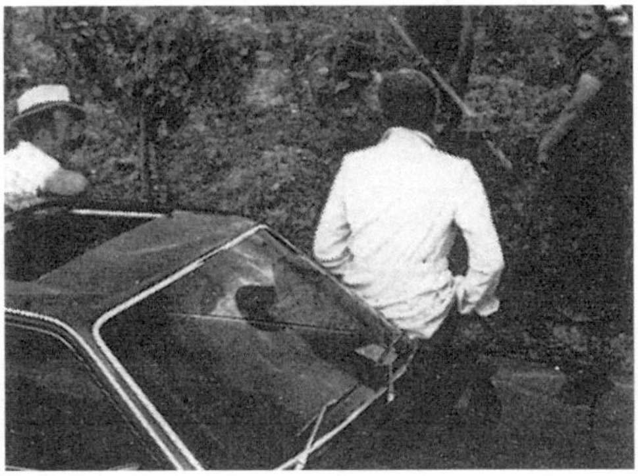

But although the man in the white jacket owns the car – isn't it being held out to *us* as ownable? Part of the reason the man's back is turned is so the car can appeal to us all on its own, almost privately – the show-room effect of the camera angle emphasises "carness", just as the classical art perspective of the view reads "Italianness". The look of the car can be read in terms of a kind of "grammar" of car adverts which here intersects with the representation of Italianicity. However, the social relations of Italianicity must exist when the car is driven off, we must feel they are not just an effect of the car being there: it has to represent these relations after it has left the field. Looking at the photo in this light, perhaps the man in the jacket is not the landowner? Perhaps not even Italian? But has simply driven the Lancia into the field and stopped to chat to the peasants, who assume an attractive openness and familiarity with the tourist or traveller.

The whole scene could be merely a chance encounter. After all, cars are for driving, not planting – it is a maxim of advertising that the product must be shown *in use* – and the ad suggests that the Most Italian Car will *get* you nearest the most Italian places and people.

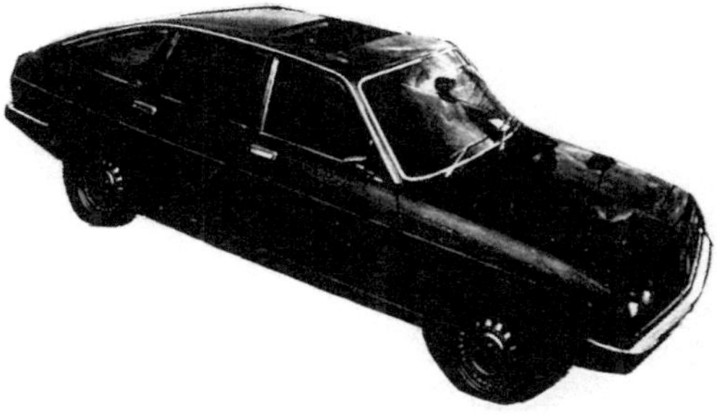

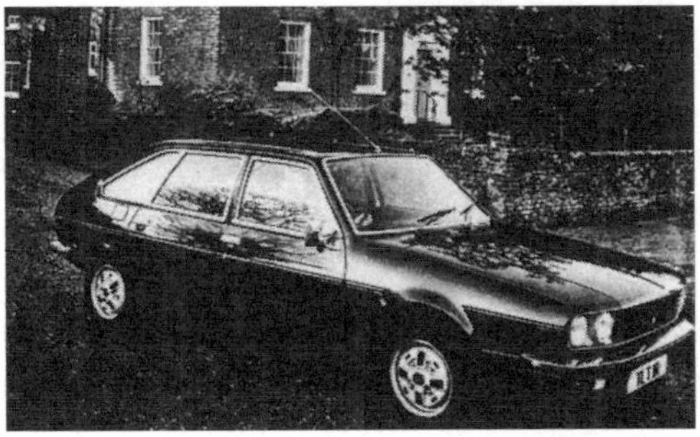

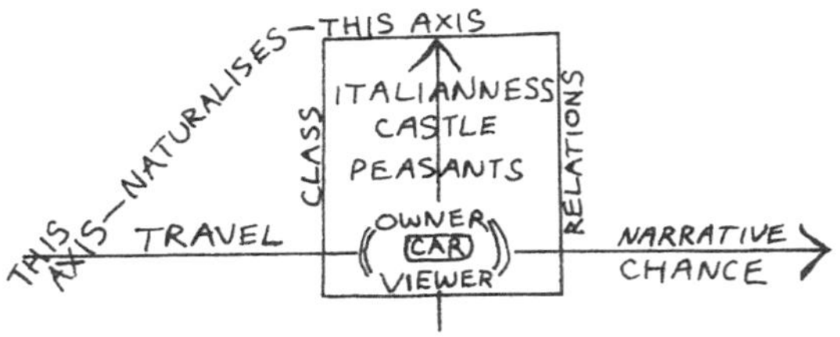

But why is it that what seems so casual, so momentary, is also so static, so unquestionable? What is it about the *photograph* that allows these two shifting readings? One, a narrative of chance events – the photograph which could be a high-class snapshot, where the owner is a transient yet welcomed figure; the other, a monolithic, "painterly" embodiment of a past era, a fixed scene under a cloudy neoclassical Italian sky? What is *our* position in relation to this scene? We *can* own a Lancia; we cannot be Italian landowners. But the photo allows a double reading: either the man is like us (potentially), owning just a Lancia, or he's a landowner with a Lancia – pictured surveying his wealth like the landowners in eighteenth century oil paintings. And although for us these possibilities are mutually exclusive, the photo contains the contradiction. The car is naturally forever embedded by chance in the field momentarily. This doubling is carried into the picture itself: there is the angle from which the photo is taken, multiplying the viewpoints available, ours and the landowners; *two* of the peasants look at him, the woman's look reinforcing the "friendly traveller" story, while the man leaning on the car serves to anchor, physically, the permanent presence of the car and the man's status as landowner (this peasant is a sort of foreman); finally, there is the way the man is reflected twice in the surface of the Lancia, a double image on the windscreen and the bonnet. The ad is simultaneously a "composition" of classic perspective, and an event, part of a story.

The photograph can always evade the kind of internal analysis which questions the relations it represents by the implied narrative in which photos are "just" taken, produced as naturally as the commodity itself.

For in the absence of any representation of the real labour that produced the car, isn't what is needed an alternative explanation of how the car came to be here? Doesn't this photographic narrative help supply that explanation?

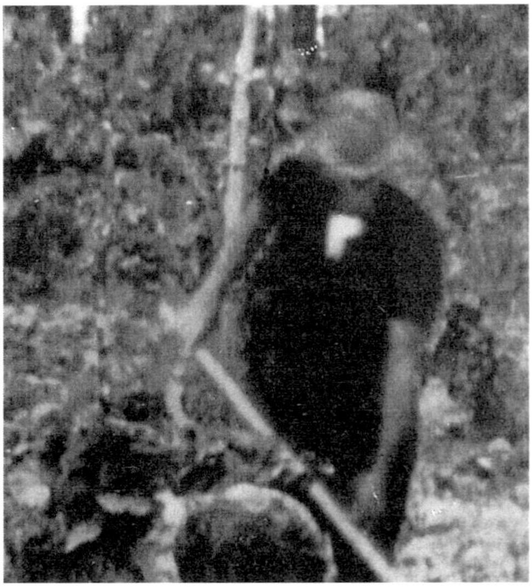

This is a representation of social relations which cannot have produced the car, but in which the car emerges – in the photograph, in which it is enshrined.

Aren't we supposed to see the car gilded with the image of these relations in the absence of its own production – *where labour becomes the blurring of the image of one peasant who has gone on working during the time the photo was taken* – doesn't the man's gaze string together peasants, castle, most ltalianness and doesn't our gaze take possession of these through the car?

But what structures all this? Simply the photograph, which can deny the whole reading with its alibi of chance – which although it ha apparently stopped time forever in the golden twilight of pre-capitalist production, has eternal recourse to a mythical present in which the photo is taken. The components of the photo, which all together in their stasis provide a map of social relations, are perhaps only connected through a narrative that slips sideways through the picture and denies any meaning other than in contingency. With this simple explanation for the complex set of relations in the picture, the car acquires its meaning of *Most Italianness*, naturally – as naturally as it seems to have acquired its very existence.

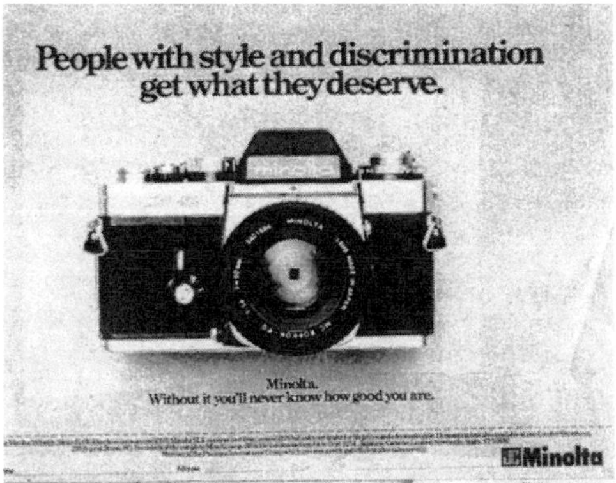

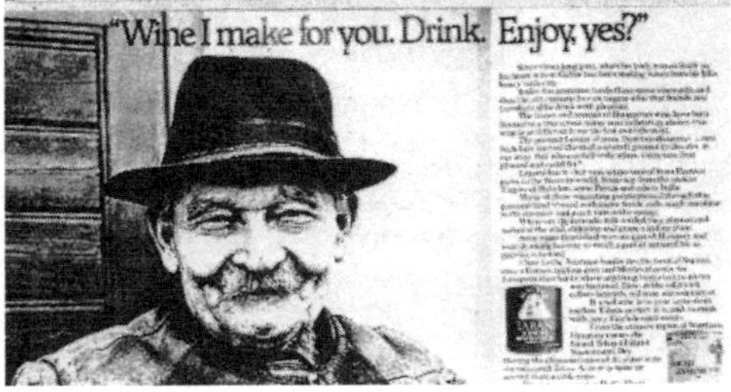

And how did it get made – by whom – under what conditions?

The forms which stamp products as commodities and which are therefore the preliminary requirements for the circulation of commodities, already possess the fixed quality of natural forms of social life before man seeks to give an account, not of their historical character, for in his eyes they are immutable, but of their content and meaning... It is precisely this finished form of the world of commodities... which conceals the social character of private labour and the social relations between the individual workers, by making those relations appear as relations between material objects, instead of revealing them plainly.

...Value, therefore, does not have its description branded on its forehead; it rather transforms every product of labour into a social hieroglyphic. Later on, men (and women) try to decipher the hieroglyphic, to get behind the secret of their own social product: for the characteristic which objects of utility have of being values is as much men's social product as is their language.
– Marx, *Capital*, Chapter 1

...a photography which is able to relate a tin of canned food to the universe, yet cannot grasp a single one of the human connections in which that tin exists; a photography which even in its most dreamlike compositions is more concerned with eventual saleability than with understanding... the true face of this photographic creativity is the advertisement...
– Walter Benjamin, *A Short History of Photography*

Advertisements are the main form in which commodities, the products of social labour, are represented to us in terms of value. They are also commodities themselves, the most ubiquitous form in which we encounter commercial photography. While advertising cannot in itself affect the actual exchange-value of a commodity, it can intervene on the level of use-value and plays a role as part of the "hieroglyphic" which collapses those values into one another and separates the product from the relations of its production.

It is important to outline the social and economic relations *in which* advertising as an apparatus functions, before going on to discuss the way they are misrepresented, excluded or obscured *within* advertisements, because it is these real relations which have to be changed – not advertisements. There is a current tendency to confuse the "work" of the "text" with the work that goes on inside factories, the "production" of meaning with the production of commodities, so that by a convenient metaphorical doubling of language it is possible to discuss politics and perform political actions without ever leaving the comfortable and fascinating field of signification. This field is politically relevant in as far as it helps or prevents an understanding of social reality which might lead to changing that reality: a perspective that is rapidly slipping out of "radical" theories of film and photography and being replaced by a perspective whose farthest horizon is merely the change of those media. I am stressing this because the confusion between representation and the object of representation – of the sign and its referent (the thing represented) – is precisely the mechanism of bourgeois ideology, employed, for example, in classical representation and in advertising itself. It emerges in theory as a type of idealism which can replace revolution with revelation. The dominant forms of media invite us to take their representation as an adequate reproduction of social reality: and to imply that political change can be brought about by engaging with those forms alone is to accept that invitation. The systematic misrepresentation and denial of production in advertisements cannot be understood in isolation from the actual system of production outside advertisements.

The specific economic function of advertising is to fulfil a competitive need within the sphere of circulation. The necessity for manufacturers to compete over a particular margin created by the disparity between the actual cost of labour and the value produced by labour appears as the "freedom" of those from whom this surplus value has been extracted, to choose between different brands of products in the shops. The flip-side of competition, ideologically, is "choice": but this competition is bounded by the limits of profitability, which itself only exists through paying labour less than the value it produces. The real *effects* of advertising in purely economic terms are very hard to measure: although they are not nil, they are clearly marginal to the system as a whole and are hardly an essential component of capitalism. This makes advertising, even in *capitalist* terms, a tremendous waste of labour and resources; although in itself it is a flourishing and highly profitable industry, apparently invulnerable to the economic crisis.

Ideologically, however, advertisements contribute to the feature of capitalism which Marx calls commodity fetishism. Marx distinguishes between the use-value of a commodity, defined by its ability to fulfil a specific human need, and its exchange-value, which is determined by the amount of socially necessary labour put into it (Example 1), and which is represented by money – its price. This appears a "natural" and "objective" form of representation, determined by a "free" play of supply and demand, and seems detached from the social relations of production. Similarly (though it is not *the same*) advertisements represent commodities as having an apparently inherent value which involves not only an equation of use and exchange values but an attempt to add value to the commodity by uprooting it from the context of its production and re-presenting it in another social context from which it then *seems* to derive its value and which, ideologically, it then seems like a currency for. "Martini" people seen *consuming* Martini give it a certain social value which then appears buyable along with the commodity itself: as though commodities had the power to bestow value on people and create social relations, when in fact it is people's labour which gives *commodities* value.

In the sense that use-value incorporates non-material needs, this linking of a commodity with people or scenes that have particular connotations is clearly a way in which real use-value *is* added to commodities: they come to represent things which we need – which we desire – which we desire to be. Use-values can be socially determined – as with perfume and make-up for example, which are certainly not necessary for human survival but which for some people fulfil a social need; one which, however, is also *perpetuated* by advertisements.

However, while advertising can develop use-values in this way, it cannot, as I have said, affect exchange value, which is created by labour. What advertisements do is to conflate use-value and exchange-value so that they seem mutually explanatory: the price, the *representation* of exchange- value, is also apparently a natural equivalent for the use-value, and is in fact naturalised by this association with use value (Example 2). Bourgeois economics recognises only one value for the commodity and this one value conceals its origins by being embedded "in" the commodity as though an objective quality it *contained*.

Two points are crucial here. One is the denial of production. What matters about the equation of use and exchange-values is not simply that it is a *mistake*, a theoretical error: in order to maintain the illusion that value is determined "naturally" the commodity must lose its own history, and therefore, in effect, the *exploitation* which takes place in the manufacture of a product is translated as natural, *invisible*, through this misrepresentation of the origin of value. The other point concerns representation itself. Money *represents* exchange-value but it never actually *is* value. The idea that money is value in itself, and that value is created in exchange, is a central part of commodity fetishism: it denies that value is created by labour and only *realised* in exchange. This mistaking of representation for the thing represented, of currency for value, functions at every level of bourgeois ideology, politics and economics: it provides, in fact, a good example of the way these areas, far from being autonomous, are completely welded together in the actual fabric of social life (Example 3).

Even without advertising, relations between people under capitalism come to be represented as relations between objects: but the peculiar suitability of photography in this representation is its ability to *naturalise* relations between objects, providing a form which is almost custom-made for commodity fetishism. The photograph can show any configuration of people and commodities, trapped in an immutable form which is itself an object; it can render static and eternal any arrangement of things. In this sense the photograph is always a denial of history: it can never capture change (except as a blur); the time it represents in thousandths of a second is frozen into an object which lasts. Yet the photograph always suggests an element of chance about its own existence – chance being the ultimate guarantee of truth in a culture where economic laws are as "natural" as good or bad weather, and freedom means the enjoyment of fortuity and chance, no matter how violent. The random nature of suffering suggests that it is inevitable, the competitive chaos of capitalism suggests that it is natural, not historical. It is the accidental quality of photographs that gives credibility to the events depicted in them: the *composition* of a photograph appears natural through the implicit reference to the *practice* of photography, to the photograph as an event. This event, by being clearly deliberate, gives a priority of innocence to the pro-photographic event, i.e. what is photographed. Although static itself, the photo suggests a continuous time in which the event it shows "naturally" happened. Any photograph has a paradigmatic relationship with other imaginary photos which could have been taken instead. It just "happened" to be this one – yet it always is just this one.

If its "natural" stopping of time allows the photograph to evade history, *what* it naturalises, in advertisements, is the removal of a commodity from the actual sphere of production and its re-placing in another social context (Example 4). This is usually the context of consumption, sometimes a mythical context of production. But real production is (almost) always absent: what apparently replaces it, and magically "produces" the commodity out of nowhere is the photograph. And in the case of *advertising*, the photograph itself is a commodity, with an exchange value: its own production is made invisible, as with all commodities. On the other hand, family photos, for example, are without exchange-value: they are not commodities and their production is in no way denied – they are always represented in ads as photos, with frames and a necessary process of production (Example 5). It is well known that work done in the home is "not *really* work" – it doesn't produce exchange values: similarly home photography is demarcated from the kind of photography that brings us these ads in that one produces commodities, the other does not.

Both these types of photography share, however, an element of "tourism" in the sense of the "chance"aspect already described – the photographer is always just "passing through". Geographical travel provides an "explanation" for the photograph just as the photograph provides an "explanation" for the commodity – even if this travel is merely a visit to the other side of town. The point of interest is *where* you go, not *when*. "Then" and "now" are collapsed together, and the historical aspect of the photograph's content is cut out. The holiday snapshot is the acceptable face of imperialism: there are ads for travel to "natural" places like *Ireland*, where"time is slower", "life moves at a different pace" etc. etc. Spain, Italy, Greece, are populated by peasants in these representations: no mention of the particular manifestations of capitalism in *those* countries.

For production in "foreign" countries, in advertising, is always represented by peasants (Example 6). Class becomes a family affair (Example 7). While at home (in both senses) the family as a unit of *consumption* cuts across class differences, abroad the family is represented as the unit of production – suggesting a quite different historical social formation. The family was a productive unit in pre-capitalist society – whereas now, nothing it produces, as was seen with photos, is exchangeable. On a family holiday time doesn't just stop, apparently it goes backwards.

These areas – travel, the family, photography – form a complex nexus of social and economic interaction; photographic firms like Kodak aim vast amounts of advertising at the family as consumer and literally take over the work of production (at a price) – "you push the button, we do the rest". There are the camera ads – *Ken Russell's Pentax* – where the emphasis is on the marks of *possession* on the equipment, not on what it does. The whole subject of technology, the family, amateurism, and so on, is a vast area which can really only be touched on here in relation to the points already made, about production and about representation. What is relevant here is that outside the commercial sphere, photography is very largely a family institution and that the family plays a major role, ideologically, in the denial of class. This is shown in the representational pyramid that links the "Royal" Family with the working class family with the *Family of Man* and so on. However, a Royal family photo *is* a commodity, unlike any other family snaps – and the *Family of Man* photographic exhibition was also a commodity. "History" is constructed through photos as commodities – photos of figures who must themselves be "representative". Family "memory" in snapshots is set apart from "history": this has a direct effect on the photographic institution of *what* you photograph. A holiday in Spain provides you with images of children on the beach but never of police arresting strikers in Bilbao (Example 8).

The family is the major cross-class social unit and is used in every way (by the State, especially e.g. the projected Ministry of Marriage) to negate class divisions – economically and politically, not only "ideologically"; another example of these "instances" being inseparable. And in advertising, the constant emphasis on families, eating, buying, consuming in every way, provides a means of identification with the bourgeoisie which would be impossible if the class basis of production were apparent. Private snapshots of those two non-historical phenomena, the family and foreign places, are the B-side of advertising photos which show the family consuming, "foreigners" and peasants producing – but never the class basis of the production which actually produced the commodities on show all around us.

There is one exception to this rule. Only in advertisements aimed at employers, at capitalists, do we see a representation of the working class and working conditions which immediately reveals what is *absent* in all other types of advertising: the social relations of *capitalist production* (Example 9). This finally makes totally explicit the class nature of the advertising audience. Adverts seem to be aiming at anyone in general, this in itself gives the impression that there is no class, only consumers: until we see the ads in the Sunday supplements aimed at factory owners who wish to increase "their" productivity, "in which case there also vanishes the semblance that the ruling ideas were not the ideas of the ruling class and had a power distinct from the power of this class." (Marx, *The German Ideology*)

EXAMPLE: 1

This is an example of socially un-necessary labour: the only kind of labour regularly represented in advertisements. *Socially necessary labour* is whatever requires the least time and cost to manufacture a product under given social conditions – these include, for example, the state of technology at a particular time, the lowest "acceptable" wage, etc. Under present conditions the socially necessary form of producing nearly all goods involves a division of labour – the cheapest way of exploiting people's labour power.

What this Hovis ad shows, however, like a photo-story, is *one* individual – whom it is essential to name and locate, *Reg Mansbridge of Hemel Hempstead*, performing a *variety* of tasks throughout the day; instead of many different people each monotonously performing the *same* task – alienated labour, the reality of most production. This reality is denied through the ideological effect of "personalising" work: we are told in the first line of small print that "Reg" is a *family* baker (what exactly is this supposed to mean?) and Reg's continuous relationship to the bread he makes, controlling each stage of its production is clearly an idealised, individualistic myth which bears no relation to modern conditions of production, including the production of bread. Only socially *un*necessary labour – which usually means crafts etc. – is so attractive.

The combination of diversity and continuity that marks this form of labour is brought out by the format of the ad, like six frames from a film: as a sequence it shows continuity in time, yet diversity of action – the link being provided, not by the product, as would actually be the case in factory production, but by *Reg*, whose story this is. The photographic style also contributes to the attractive aura of this kind of work – the soft focus, the golden and brown tones, almost like an old tinted photograph, all connote *olde-worlde* (history is hardly the appropriate word) and natural: the two go together. This outdated form of labour appears as natural and good.

Moreover, it appears as the form of all labour; this is what work *is*, or can be. It is crucial to the ideology of this ad that the *reason* for this fulfilling labour is apparently an effect of Reg himself: one caption is *While you've still got muscles, who needs a conveyor belt?* – as though the form of production one is involved in were a simple matter of personal choice and physique. And what creates Reg's tremendous "stamina" that enables him personally to by-pass the stranglehold of modern capitalist production is Hovis itself. Reg is shown as a *consumer* of Hovis: in all the other frames except the first, we *watch* him working, but it is the final frame where he looks *at* us, and addresses us as a consumer, turning to face the reader as he eats his Hovis sandwiches. This is the culminating image where the product is validated by its consumption – in symmetry with the first frame where the lighted window signifies Reg's presence inside the house, while in the last frame the Hovis is inside Reg. This is not such a far-fetched point as it sounds, because in fact most of the images of "production" of Hovis are in some way involved with consumption, "putting in" – into mixer, into oven, into van.

So, as in most ads, value is attributed to this commodity not on the basis of who produces it but on the basis of who *consumes* it: the formula is simply given a twist by the fact that the consumer is

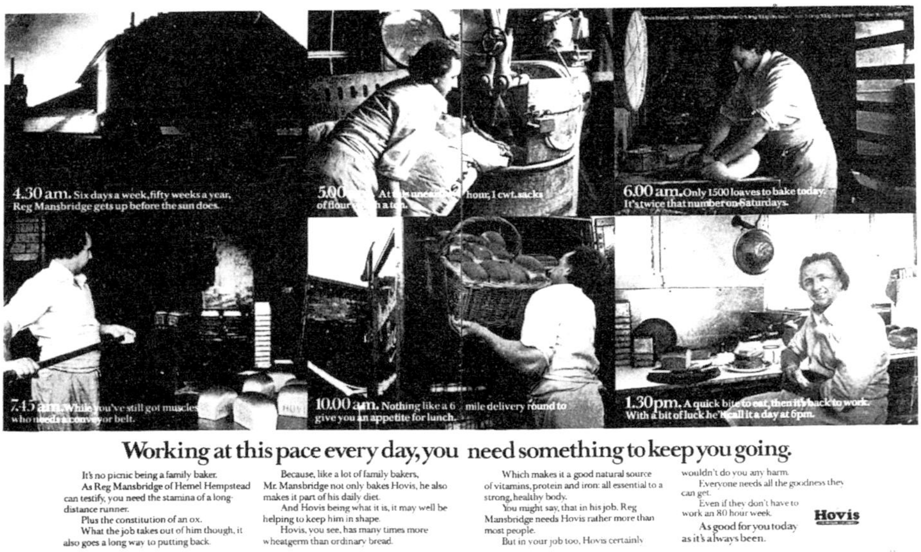

also the baker. But even as the baker, it is not so much that he gives Hovis its value – rather that Hovis (and the photograph) give a golden, healthy aura to the whole work process. Connected with this is the emphasis on how *hard* Reg works. The captions for each frame, the small print beneath, all emphasise the long hours and heavy physical strain of this labour – but also the wholesome goodness of it all. The corollary of this is that such hard work is a good thing. The last four lines of the ad are:

> But in your job too, Hovis certainly wouldn't do you any harm.
>
> Everyone needs all the goodness they can get. Even if they don't have to work an 80 hour week.
>
> As good for you today as it's always been.

And the last (baker's) dozen words are: *an 80 hour week… as good for you today as it's always been.*

EXAMPLE 2

This is a particularly explicit example of the way use value is seen in terms of price; it also shares some aspects of the Lancia advert. As with the Lancia, by a clever doubling of perspective we are able simultaneously to look down on the car and up to the horizon; our look suggests possession despite the caption, as it incorporates such a large quantity of car, yet the apparent horizon also forces the look upwards, "forwards" as it were. With its completely barren setting this ad, unlike the Lancia one, contains no representation of

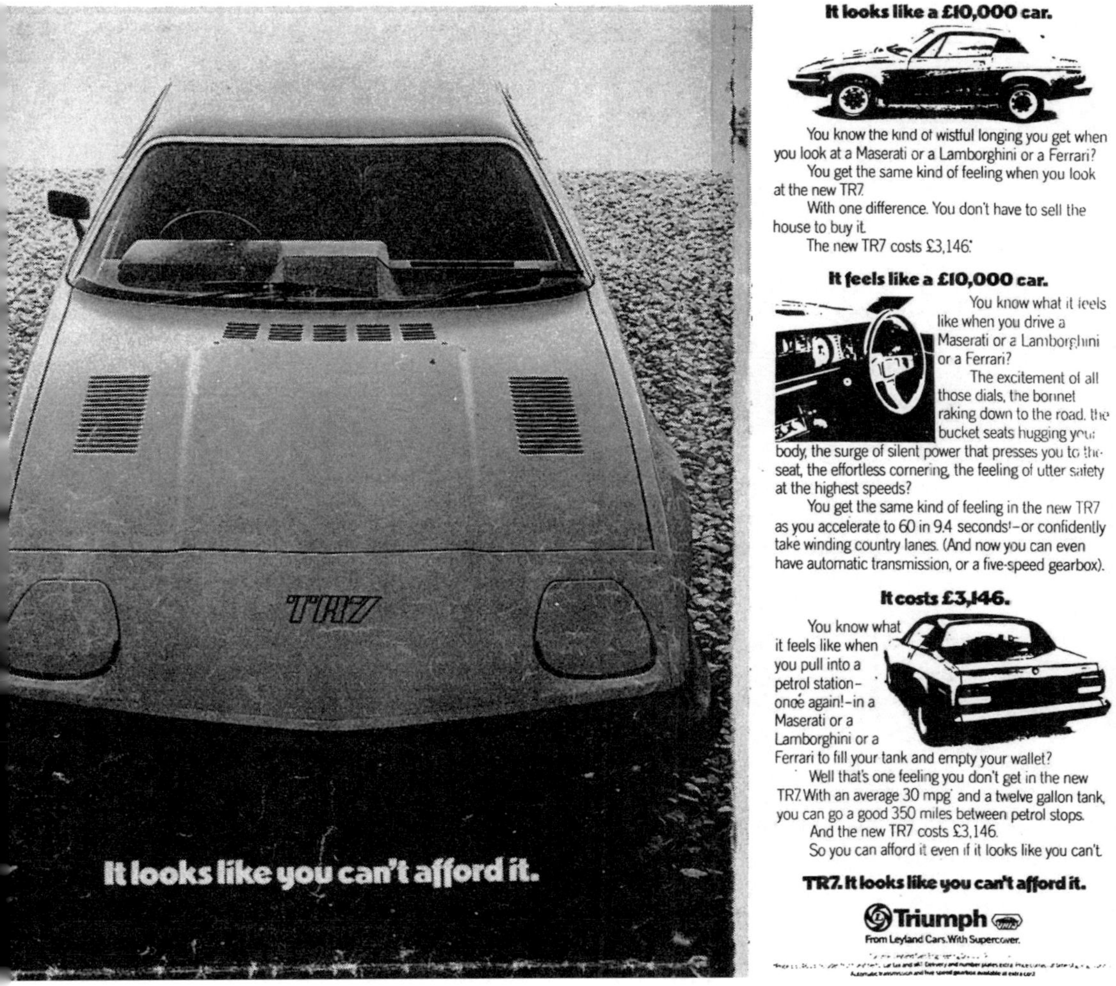

labour of any sort, we are presented with pure "carness".

In the absence of any suggestion of *labour* which could give value to the car, the strip of writing and inset photos down the right-hand side of the ad attempt to describe its value in quite different terms. The car has a real exchange-value: *It costs £3,146*. But this actual price is supposed to be surprising: it is the punchline to the first two captions, *It looks like a £10,000 car* and *It feels like a £10,000 car*. The point about these two captions is that they imply that there actually is a use-value, a material quality, which is naturally equatable with £10,000 so that this price becomes descriptive, like a quality in itself, and a quality bound up in the physical attributes of the car: it "*Looks* like you can't afford it." So although you are supposed to be able to buy it, the car actually seems to contain the quality of un-affordableness: this is really having cake and eating it, because if prices and physical qualities *are* mutually expressive then the car should look *like* a £3,146 car, or, seeing quality in terms of the hypothetical £10,000 price, it should presumably *cost* more. Only by grasping that *£10,000* is being used like a use-value can this contradiction be explained. This is very explicit commodity fetishism in precisely the form Marx describes it: use-values, from "the excitement of all those dials" to "safety at the highest speeds" and a "five-speed gear box" are seen in terms of an exchange-value, £10,000; and so paradoxically a car whose actual exchange-value is £3,146 appears to contain this £10,000 exchange-value as a sort of natural use-value. This contributes to the naturalisation of exchange-values as though they were born in commodities, and not created through labour.

EXAMPLE 3

In these two ads, the relationships between historical figures are represented through sherry and port: at first sight a very straightforward example of relations between people appearing as relations between commodities. Nelson and Napoleon are two barrels of sherry, identical except for the different names: "Arch-enemies though they were, Nelson and Napoleon at least saw eye-to-eye on one thing: the quality of Domecq sherry". On the other hand, "it would hardly have been fitting for the Great Duke of Wellington to partake of Napoleon brandy." One ad is using the commodity to resolve the "difference" between Nelson and Napoleon, the other draws on precisely the same historical event, the Napoleonic wars, to stress the "difference" of the commodity, its specific Englishness. These examples show not only how commodities are used to represent people and history, but precisely how arbitrary this representation is, since it can be made to signify completely opposite things. In one ad Napoleon is "our old chum", in the other he is all that is un-British. These contradictory significations show that history is being used merely as a formal structure in which to place the products; it provides as it were a set of counters that can be arranged in any way. However, there is another kind of representation implicit in the very subject matter of these ads, in their using Nelson, Napoleon and Wellington at all – as though a lengthy war had been fought by these men alone and had been merely an effect of their own personalities. Representation is a word used in two different spheres, one "political", in elections and so on, the other in the sense of pictures and language as representational. In each case, however, something stands for something or someone else which it or they can never wholly or satisfactorily replace. Thus the state is supposed to be in some way representative of civil society. "Freedom" is represented by the struggle of one Russian scientist to carry out research, rather than the freedom of millions not to starve. Workers in the baking industry are represented by Reg Mansbridge rather than a production line of Sunblest packers.

The way this phenomenon of representation functions at all levels facilitates the work of ads, which seek representationally to link commodities with particular people or images or scenes. In these two ads it is significant that this "personalising" effect of friendly: "*your local merchant* will be delighted to supply you... we hope you'll prove a better customer than *our old chum, Napoleon*" – thus putting you on a level with Napoleon, simply as two consumers of the same product, though Napoleon has the privilege that "he still hasn't paid his bills". Yet this personal touch still manages to carry the full weight of "History" – a history created apparently by and for a few individuals, just

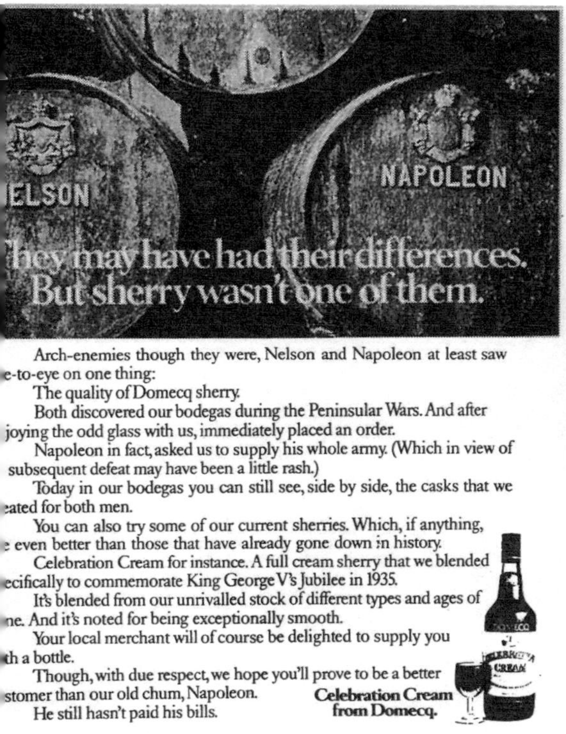

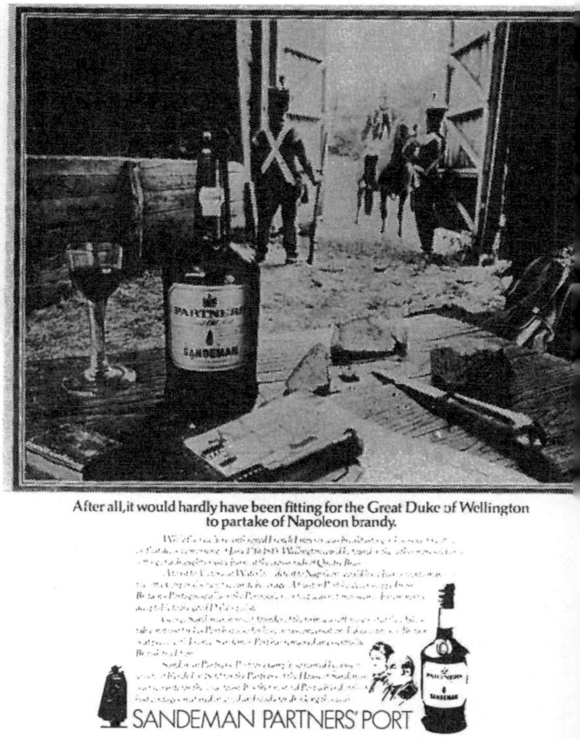

social representation – as though one person were more human than six million – is what is used to link the historic event to the commodity: the former represented by military leaders, the latter through the individual manufacturers – not the workers but the owners of the companies involved. The Domecq ad is written in the first person plural, *we*: "the casks we created for both men" (*who* created??). All is individual and like the sherry. History is a commodity you buy with the present day commodity, Domecq.

A similar emphasis on the personal, individual characters of the *manufacturers* is found in the Sandeman ad. "George Sandeman himself, founder of the firm, was often a guest at the Duke's table, not just for his Port but also for his conversation..." The name of the Port, *The Partners* (shown on the two inset engraved busts) involves precisely the many layers of "representation": *The Partners: these two characters represent the felicitous combination of Conservatism and Enterprise* (the capital letters even give these abstractions the status of "characters") *that has controlled the House of Sandeman since 1790.*

There is thus a pyramid of representation in these ads, as history is seen through leaders, and they in turn are used purely to signify the "value" of modern commodities. The photographic presentation of these ads is different, in accordance with their different uses of social representation. Domecq, which is drawing on a connection between Nelson and Napoleon, uses a first person address to talk about the two names that are shown on the two barrels – so the reader, looking at the picture, provides the link, and is also linked to it as another potential customer. Sandeman, however, is stressing the difference and individual British quality of the Port, only using one side of the situation that Domecq draws on. Instead of providing a *connecting* look between two "historic" consumers, here the viewer is positioned by the photograph *as* the consumer – almost as Wellington himself, looking over the shoulder of history. History becomes a place, a position, carefully composed in the photograph by a collection of "historic" objects, one of which is the product. The photo signifies a particular time purely through our recognition of a set of objects that are placed in a particular way. Our reading of this arrangement draws us into it inevitably, and the story is told here in the third person, unlike the other ad, so that the reader can be inserted into it.

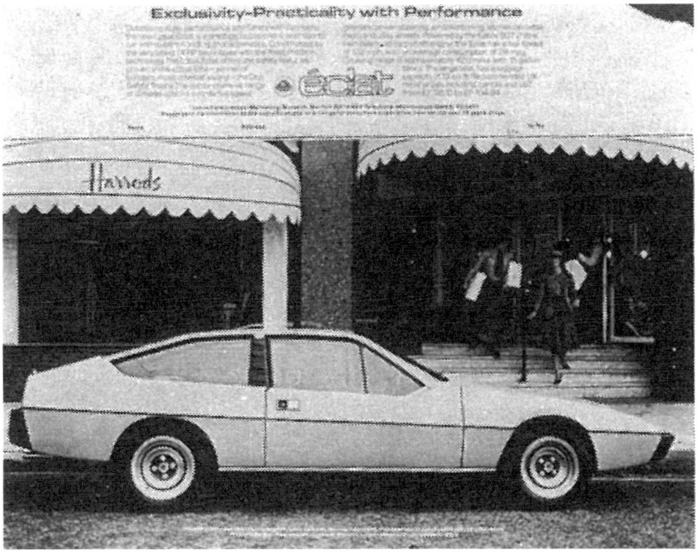

EXAMPLE 4

This car appears to derive its value purely from its surroundings: the upper class connotations of Harrods needs no explanation. However, there are several important elements of advertising brought out by this photo. Most ads work by visual juxtapositions of some sort, bringing about a transference of meaning. As in the Lancia example, this ad presents a particular scene, a shop which connotes "class" (and "*expensive*") – and a car, which simply by being placed here seems to pick up the same connotations. What the *photograph* contributes to this process is the combination of chance and inevitability which guarantees the exchange of meaning between Harrods and the car. There it is, fixed in one of the smartest locations in London; but because this is a photograph, the connection can be seen not as a structural, formal one but as a natural event. A man and woman are coming down the steps, carrying parcels: they scene, and a sort of connoted exchange-value, since once photographed *on* the scene it seems almost like a commodity Harrods might offer, gaining an "expensive" image from the notoriously overpriced department store. The two "axes" discussed in relation to Lancia are here almost visibly part of the picture: horizontal, the street, the actual driving of the car, soon to zoom out right of frame – a story which naturalises the vertical, the building "Harrods", the connotations of class and consumption. The horizontal here corresponds to use-

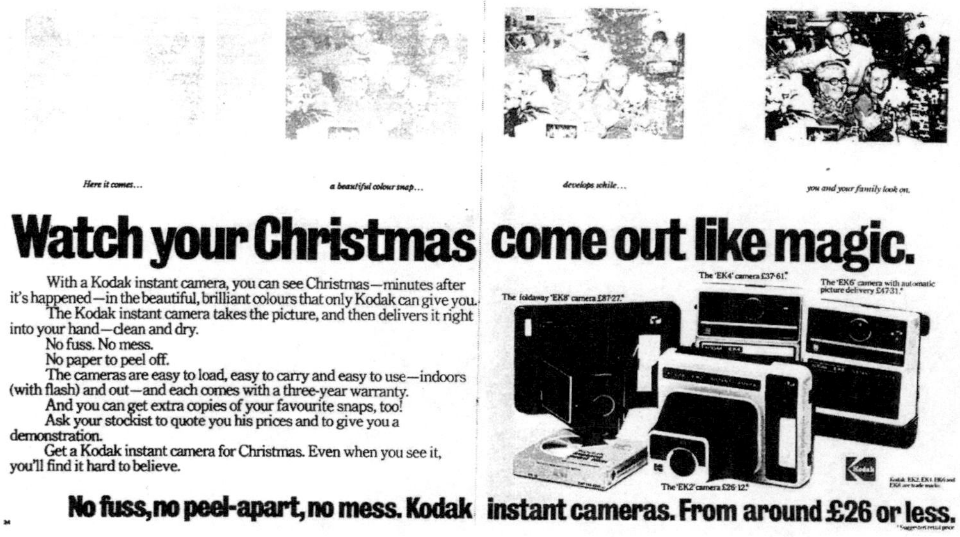

have driven up, parked their car and gone shopping, and are now about to get in and drive away again. But the photo has stopped time just at the point where the elements of the photograph form a web of social connotations to enhance the value of the car.

Unlike in the Lancia example, this value is suggested not by an image of production, but an image of *consumption*: an expensive shop, and people whose social position is indicated simply by the fact that they shop there. The car therefore picks up both a use-value, since it is used to get *to* this

value and the vertical to exchange-value: through the car and the photograph they merge. And all this is achieved entirely within the context of consumption: production is absent altogether.

EXAMPLE 5

Here, the photograph actually "appears", in the ad, before our eyes; and if it is the ad which brings us the finished photo, what the photo presents us with is The Family – 'your' family. The family snapshot is a mirror where not only can you and your family watch yourselves – "Watch your Christmas come out like magic" – it is also a mirror looked into by the reader of the ad, who also "looks on" at the developing snap. These photos are certainly shown, framed, *as* photos: not being *commodities* they provide a direct link between families, between viewer and viewed, between anyone watching the ad and someone watching their own family snapshots. They provide a direct link precisely because they are outside commodity production and can therefore bypass the social relations of that production. To Kodak, the world is a collection of families. Of course, the *camera* is a commodity, but that is another story. We don't see *it* made – only *what* it makes.

EXAMPLE 6

Here again production is represented by an individual, and not only a peasant but a woman – she could easily be the female peasant from the Lancia vineyard. She offers a description of her labour – "much hot, much work" (much exploitation) and she also appears to be offering the commodity itself, "my wine. Drink" – as if she could give you the wine without you having to buy it. This speech is circumscribed by the other discourse of the ad, which although in smaller print is like a voice speaking around the woman, introducing "knowledge", geography and history, and illustrated with wine labels: producing an experience closer to being in an off-licence than a Hungarian field.

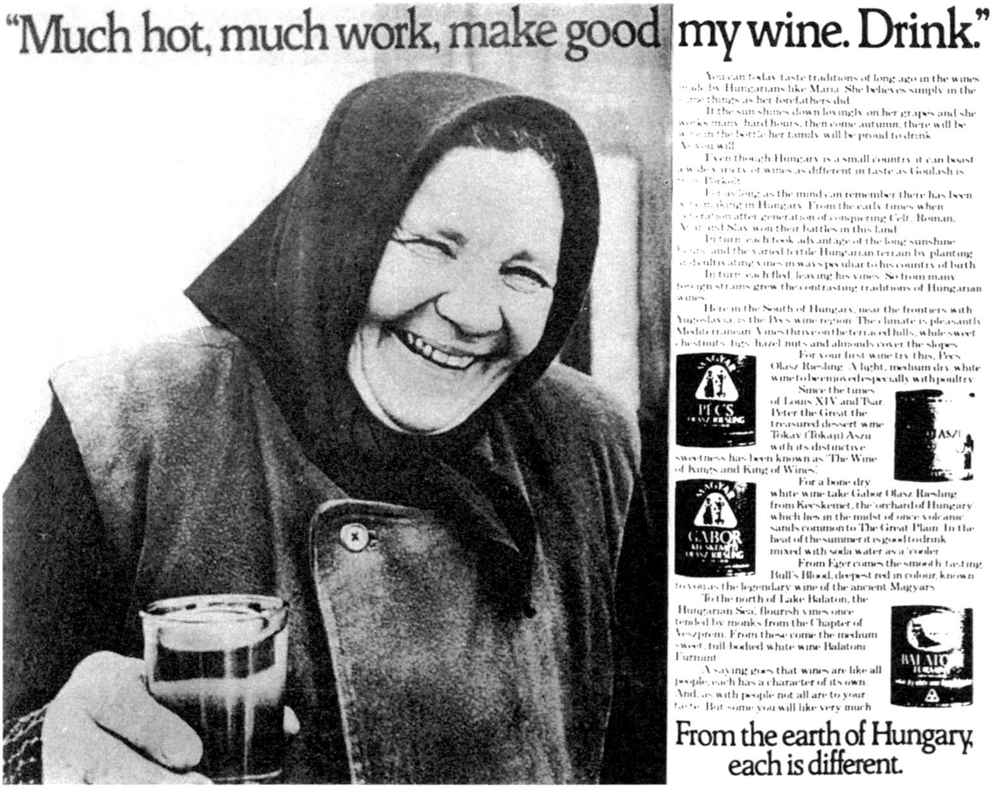

The woman appears to represent the labour which has gone into the wine, direct "from the earth", but as with the Hovis example she does not really stand for labour on its own because she is holding a glass of the wine she makes: it is unclear whether she is about to drink it ("much hot" work requires refreshment) or whether *she* is holding it out to the tourist that the reader of the ad has inevitably become: "Drink". Either way the emphasis is on consumption; and the choice between watching the woman from a detached position, and participating, accepting the wine, outlines for us precisely the place of the tourist. This tourism is reinforced by the documentary realism style of the grainy, black-and-white photograph, part of a whole representational convention which adds the connotation of healthy, and especially *foreign* poverty to the already chauvinistic use of the peasant woman. Suggesting a "nitty-gritty" reality and down-to-earthness about this kind of labour, the photographic style is in itself as patronising as the actual text: "You can today *taste traditions of long ago* in the wines made by Hungarians like Maria. She believes simply in the same things as her forefathers did. If the sun shines down lovingly on her grapes and she works *many, hard hours*, then come autumn, there will be wine in the bottle *her family will be proud to drink*". And so on. In some way her ignorance is historic ("she believes simply in the same things her forefathers did") and she and her family directly contribute to the "tradition" we are to taste in the wine in proportion as they are made to appear "primitive".

After this personal history of Maria's family and forefathers, the informative voice moves on to a history of "historic" figures: Louis XIV and Tsar Peter the Great. Again, value appears to come either from peasants, who are seen as almost like part of the earth, or from the semi-feudal ruling class of aristocracy: the classes of modern capitalism, working class and bourgeoisie, are always absent. We then move back still further to "legendary" time – history is like one long myth centred around the commodity – which even becomes the "*legendary wine* of the ancient magyars" – "legendary" being presumably even more historic than "historic".

The representation of "class" through feudal classes and "representative" individuals, combined with commodity fetishism of a very crude kind, (a combination discussed in Example 3) can be seen in the way one wine is described as "The wine of Kings and the King of wines". Identified simply (and metonymically) by *labels*, different Hungarian wines are described as "characters" in themselves, while also being connected with characters like Kings, Magyars and monks. We are told at the end that "wines are like all people, each has a character of its own. And, as with people not all are to your taste. But some you will like very much". *Your* consumption is referred to throughout: the wines come to represent the history of your own consumption of them "for your first wine try this..." etc. It is a voyage through consumption of Hungarian wines just as the information is like a coach trip through fictional history, and the photo makes us tourists in another class, almost another era. Centuries of history are spanned as we can somehow skip straight from this antiquated peasant production to the modern context of *consumption*. The link is that both are separated from modern *production*: which is why the woman can offer the wine direct (you have driven into the field) while the text offers knowledge and choice (you are in a wine shop). What is missing from the text with the labels – literally, the wine itself – is supplied by the photograph – the glass held out; while what is missing from the photograph and caption – "knowledge" – (Maria is made to be inarticulate and ignorant) is supplied by the text, like a voice-over to the image in a documentary film. So you can actually have (buy) the product of apparently feudal labour relations but in the context of present-day consumption – no labour problems and all the advantages of modern distribution and packaging.

château. There is the family that works for the Martells – clearly of a much lower class, as is shown by the tattooed arm of "Marcel Duguet's grandson" – and there is the family that has made pot-stills for the Martells since 1818. In other words, employers, workers and subsidiary businesses

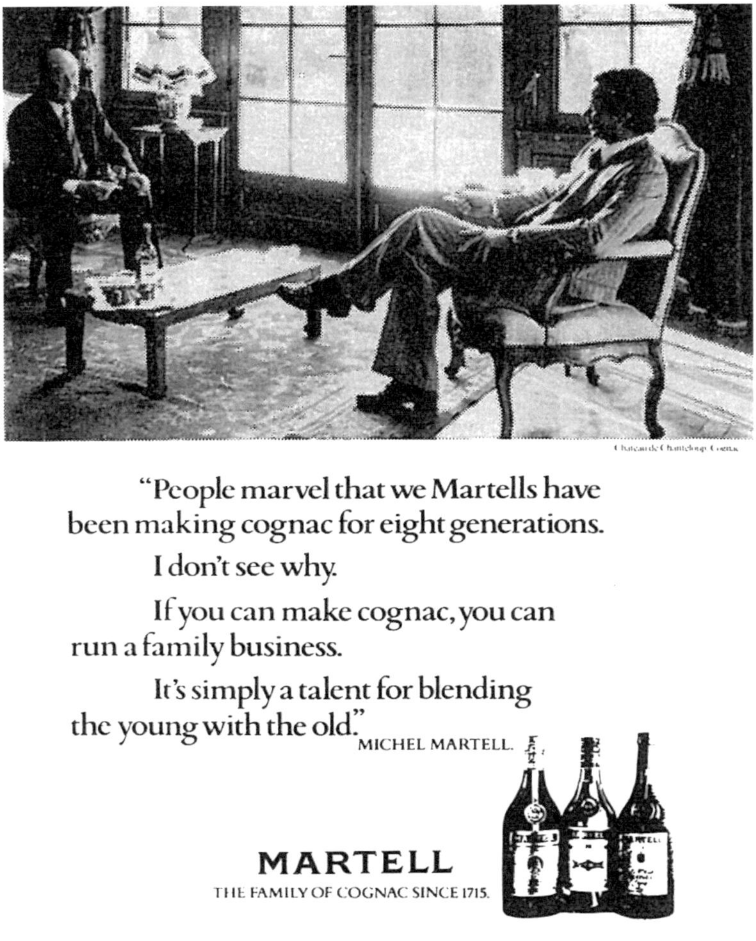

EXAMPLE 7

In these three ads we are shown all possible relations of production as familial relations. There is the Martell family itself, running a "family business" – represented by father and son in the drawing room at their

apparently add up to a social structure consisting entirely of *families*. Every different class involved in this cognac production is just another family, like the Martells: who themselves have a paternalistic relationship to these other families.

For this network of families is not a symmetrical one; the Martells are the family the family other families work for, and “The Family of Cognac since 1715”. They are the representative family; it is their family “tradition” that sets the (slow) pace of history. The emphasis in the ad showing Martell father and son is on the length of time, measured in generations, they have been producing cognac for. The emphasis in the other two ads is on how fussy the Martells are, and the length of time it takes performing tasks for them: “As Marcel Duguet used to tell his grandson: ‘When you are making casks for the Martells, it doesn’t pay (doesn’t pay whom?) to rush things. Seven years over one cask is quite fast enough.’ And, “My family has been making pot-stills for the Martells ever since 1818. Believe me, they’re so fussy, it feels like a lot longer”. Thus the family replaces both class and class history, and reduces production to a selection of “secrets” passed on from generation to generation. The history of production of Martell cognac, and of exploitation by the Martell family of those who work for them, is completely obscured by the apparently *parallel* position of the different families involved, oppressed and oppressing. And time appears to have been slowed down in this familial set-up almost to a standstill, preserving French rural relations of 1715 in the mellow, golden tinted photography of 1978.

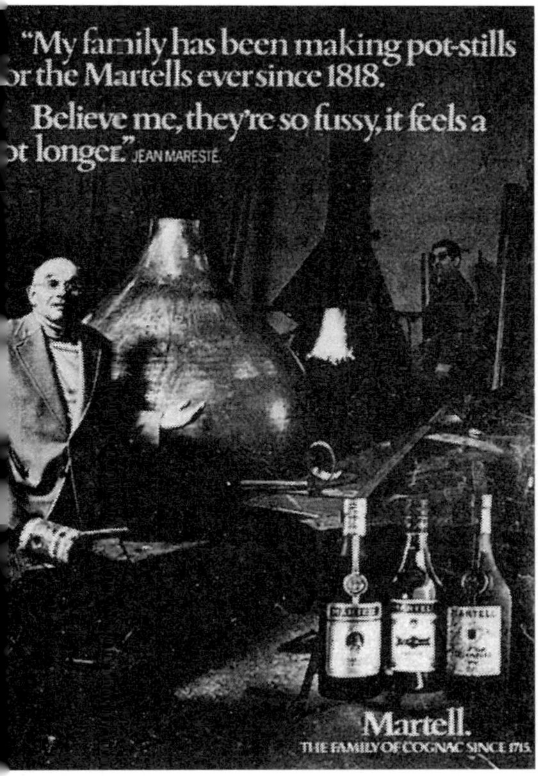

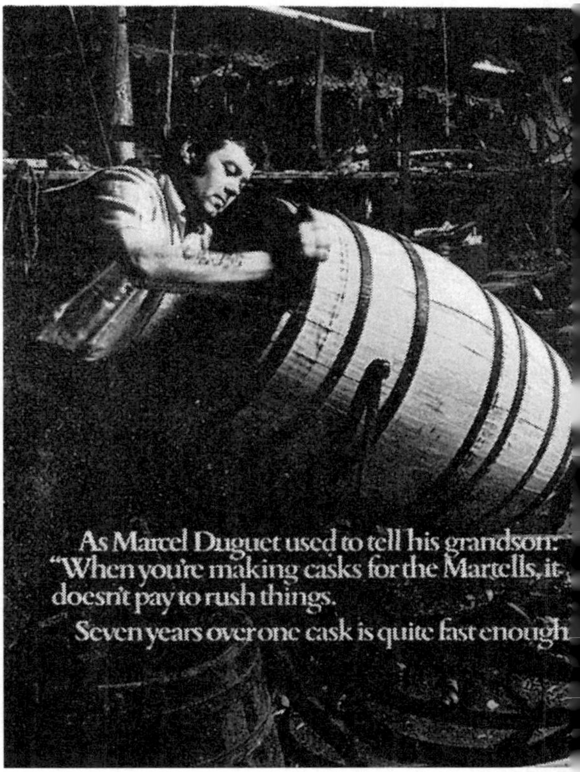

EXAMPLE 8
Here, a travel ad provides standard examples of holiday snapshots: "your" holiday is represented through photographs as photo- graphs, their status as subjective snaps is guaranteed by the frames and the way they overlap, as though just flung down. Personal photos that are outside commodity production make up the commodity which is the advertisement – this latter, of course, bears no marks of its production and is completely transparent, simply bringing you direct the trophies of your as yet hypothetical holiday in Canada.

As a photograph of photographs, it provides a good illustration of the conventions of holiday photography, but in every other respect it is like any other advertising photo: a naturalised grouping of apparently casually placed objects – here they just happen to be photos themselves. Of course, the ad is not intended to bring you Canada direct, as it were, e.g., in the form of a full-scale, unframed photographic spread – because this is precisely what *travel*, the commodity advertised, is supposed to do. The small glimpses of Canada we see in the snapshots make Canada viewable *only* through travel; we are only brought any image of it through a form that suggests taking the holiday advertised. This shows not only the way in which photography and travel are connected ideologically, but also the way they are in some aspects mutually replaceable.

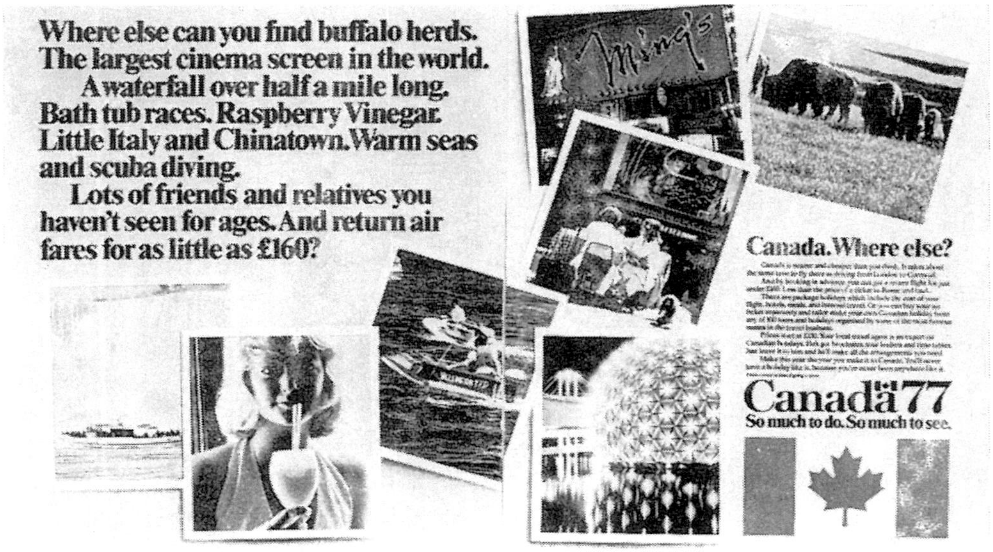

EXAMPLE 9
Finally, an advertisement that appears to defy nearly all the conclusions that have arisen from other examples. It shows an *advertisement*, on the left hand side, *as* an advertisement: "This advertisement appeared in the *Financial Times* on May 4, 1971"; thereby assuming an awareness of advertising as an apparatus, and also recognising that this apparatus exists in history, since the date and location of the ad are named. Here, unemployment figures are quoted directly, production, real, capitalist production is the subject matter of the ad; bad factory conditions are discussed, "static markets", general industrial problems.

So in every respect this ad seems to break the general "rule" of denying production which has been borne out in all the other ads. But who is it for? The text has no problem in referring to "those of *us* who are employers". It describes how "productivity is affected by working conditions" – the basis of this argument for Colt factory conditions being that it is "in *your own interests*". After all, "on the productivity of the workers still on *your payroll* depends *your competitiveness* in static markets". There can be no doubt about the class

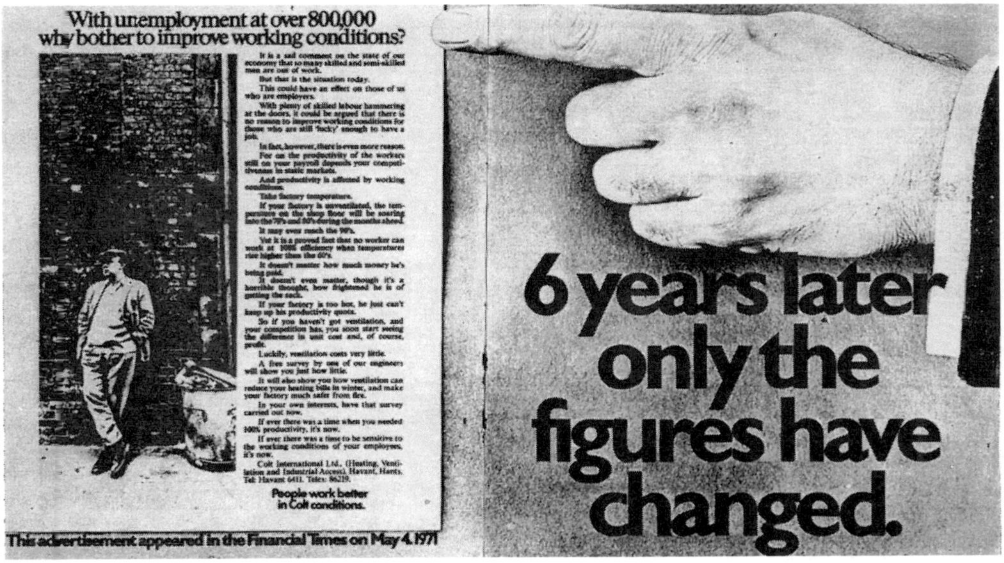

nature of this "you". And the photograph itself shows that the ad cannot be directed at those workers themselves who are talked about here purely as exploitable labour power: it is an *image* of labour, an image shared by the bourgeois Right and Left alike, equally patronising. This clichéd photo of a man in a cloth cap by a bulging dustbin bears a very strong resemblance to the photo of the peasant woman in Example 6. It is a photograph by a class tourist for class tourists: the man is as foreign to those who will "recognise" this style as if he too were from the Hungarian plains, like that woman. Grainy black-and-white "realism" turns this worker into an object, the repository of a bourgeois style, a bourgeois vision, in which he will never be a person, only an unemployment statistic or a work of documentary art.

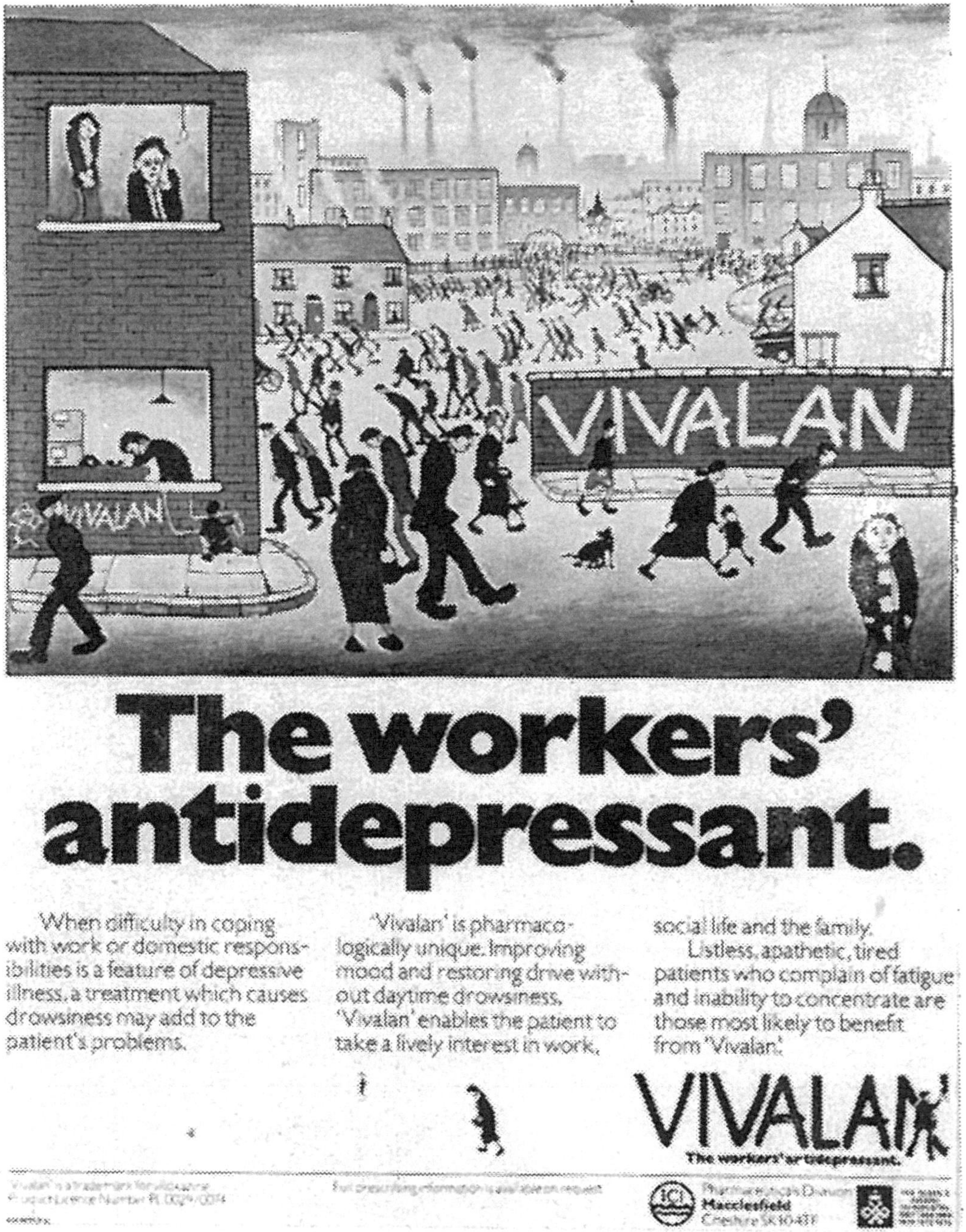
VIVALAN
VIVALAN
The workers' antidepressant.
When difficulty in coping with work or domestic responsibilities is a feature of depressive illness, a treatment which causes drowsiness may add to the patient's problems.
'Vivalan' is pharmacologically unique. Improving mood and restoring drive without daytime drowsiness, 'Vivalan' enables the patient to take a lively interest in work, social life and the family.
Listless, apathetic, tired patients who complain of fatigue and inability to concentrate are those most likely to benefit from 'Vivalan.'
VIVALAN
The workers' antidepressant.
ICI
Macclesfield
Cheshire SK10 4TF

Who built Thebes of the seven gates?
In the books you will find the names of kings.
Did the kings haul up the lumps of rock?
And Babylon, many times demolished
Who raised it up so many times? In what houses
Of gold-glittering Lima did the builders live?
Where, the evening that the Wall of China
was finished
Did the masons go? Great Rome
Is full of triumphal arches. Who erected them?
Over whom
Did the Caesars triumph?
Had Byzantium, much praised in song
Only palaces for its inhabitants?
Even in fabled Atlantis
The night the ocean engulfed it
The drowning still bawled for their slaves.
The young Alexander conquered India.
Was he alone?
Caesar beat the Gauls.
Did he not have even a cook with him?
Philip of Spain wept when his armada
Went down. Was he the only one to weep?
Frederick the Second won the Seven Years' War.
Who Else won it?
Every page a victory.
Who cooked the feast for the victors?
Every ten years a great man.
Who paid the bill?

So many reports.
So many questions.

Bertolt Brecht
A Worker Reads History

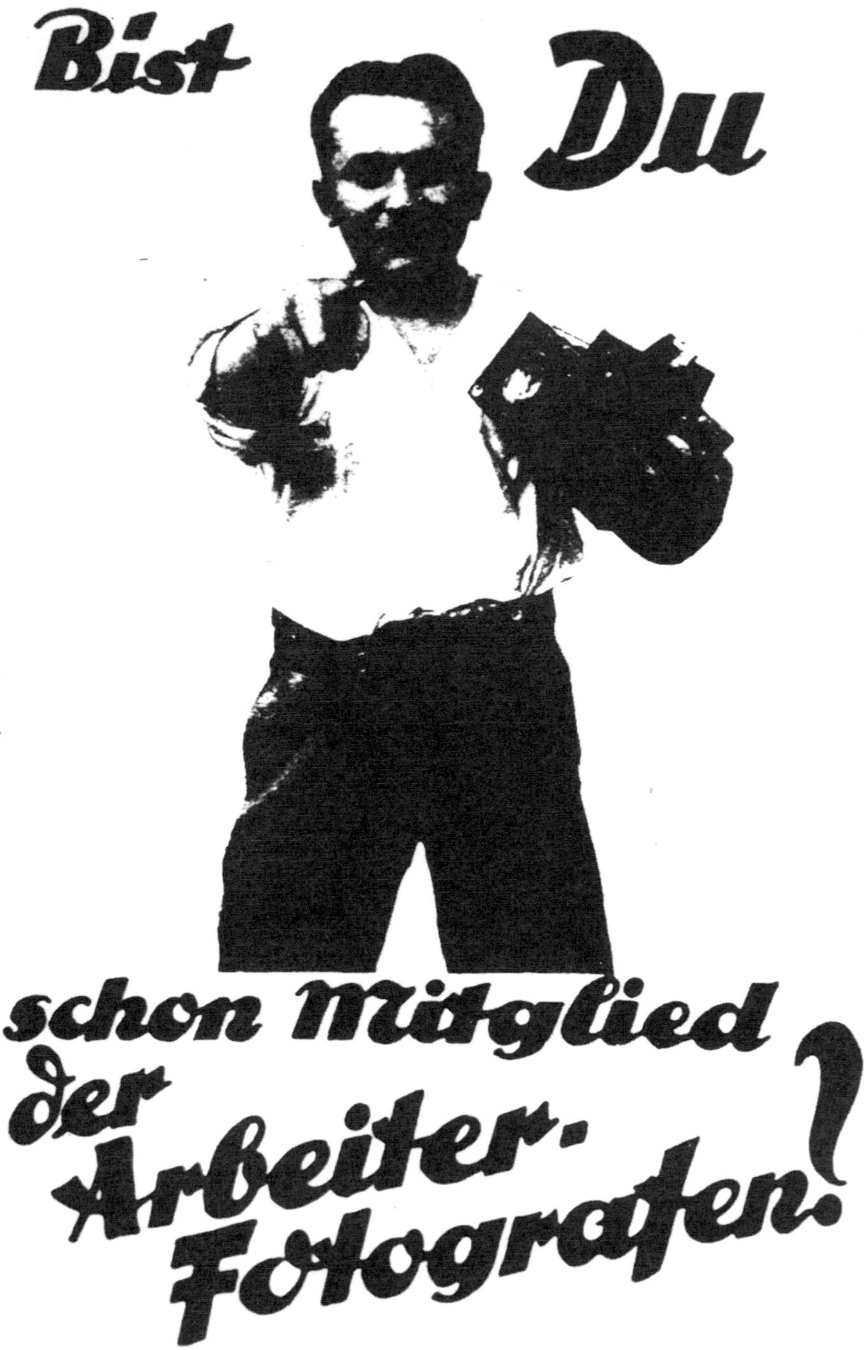

Are you a member of the Worker Photographers yet?
(Propaganda postcard, Germany, 1928.)

LEFT PHOTOGRAPHY BETWEEN THE WARS

The International Worker Photographer Movement

The worker photographer movement mainly existed in the interwar period, related to the various national communist parties, under the leadership of the Third International. This is the first extensive presentation in any language of some of its activities. There are gaps – we have little or, as yet, no information on established groups in, for example, Austria, Czechoslovakia, France, Japan, Romania, Scandinavia, Switzerland and the USSR! But we hope to publish more material on them in future annuals.

Tasks and Aims

Thirty or forty years ago, the bourgeoisie already understood that a photograph has a very special effect on the viewer. For an illustrated book is easier to read and more likely to be bought, and an illustrated paper is a more entertaining read than the lead article of a political daily. Photography works on the human eye; what is seen is reflected in the brain without forcing the viewer into complicated thought. In this way the bourgeoisie caters for the mental laziness of the masses and also makes a lot of money, for the illustrated magazines often achieve a circulation of millions.

That's not all, however. Much more important, in the end, is the political effect which is achieved by the juxtaposition of several pictures – by captions and accompanying texts. That is the decisive point. In this way a skilful editor can falsify every photograph into its opposite, and can influence the politically naive reader in any way he chooses.

The revolutionary workers of all countries have to realize these facts very clearly. They have to fight the class enemy with all means, have to beat him on all fronts. Just as the workers of the Soviet Union have learnt to make their own machine-tools, to invent things themselves to be put into the service of peaceful socialist construction, and just as workers in capitalist countries have learnt to write their own newspapers, so the proletarian amateur photographers have to learn to master the camera and to use it correctly in the international class struggle.

Willi Münzenberg,
Der Arbeiter-Fotograf, 1931

Germany: Arbeiter-Fotografie

W Körner and J Stüber

Translated by David Evans and Sylvia Gohl

On March 25, 1926, the AIZ[1] called for a photo competition:

> The illustrated magazine is the paper of the future... today the biggest bourgeois publishers announce that in a few months time there will be no German newspapers without illustrations, that the illustrated papers will soon achieve the circulation of existing dailies.
>
> A whole organisation of press agencies for photographers has already appeared. Just as the capitalist news agencies shower the dailies with tendentious news about the world, so the bourgeois press photographic agencies create a wealth of pictures to influence the masses with capitalist and bourgeois viewpoints. Pictures from the life of the proletariat are unknown and aren't produced...
>
> This gap has to be filled. The workers have to keep abreast of new developments. The big expansion of the *Arbeiter-Illustrierte Zeitung* shows the importance of reporting political, social and cultural life with text and pictures.
>
> But we openly admit that the AIZ has not always been able to achieve its self-imposed aim, because we found it impossible to obtain the necessary picture material. The *Neuer Deutscher Verlag* (the publishers of AIZ) has therefore decided to call upon its readership, the whole of the working population, to help it achieve this aim.[2]

Besides this appeal, the AIZ gave its readers – its future contributors – clear guidelines for the content of their photographs:

> The following points must guide the choice of subject:
> 1. Photographs that typify the revolutionary movement amongst the workers;
> 2. Photographs that typify the social conditions of the workers;
> 3. So-called "genre pictures" which give a good impression of the daily life of the workers in all its phases;
> 4. Photographs of the workplace which clearly reveal the working conditions;
> 5. Photographs which show modern technology and its modes of labour, industrial buildings and their construction.
>
> This task certainly isn't easy and nobody should underestimate it. You have to keep your eyes open and see what until now counted as old and uninteresting in everyday life, yet is of interest to thousands. You must courageously capture the beauty of your own work and workplace, but also the horrors of social misery...[3]

To clarify their political concept – guiding workers towards photographing their own lives and struggle – the editorial board put four photographs on the same page which they considered exemplary in terms of their contents, form and technique.

AIZ's appeal was successful. Already in the next issue they published two photographs that were taken according to the proposed guidelines: "We received an unexpectedly large number of entries for our competition. With this, the workers have proved that they realized the importance of photography for reporting political, social and cultural life" the editorial board wrote,[4] and designed in the same issue for the first time full page spreads of workers' photographs.

Most of the photographs were still feature pictures – the news photograph was still rare – but a process had started of slowly educating workers who were taking photographs into class-conscious, aesthetically skilled photo journalists, able to solve even complex problems of photo journalism.

At the same time as the AIZ competition, workers with cameras in some of the bigger cities had already freed themselves from the ideological influence of the bourgeois amateur photographer clubs, and were starting to organise independently. By mid-1926, a local group had already been founded in Hamburg.

The worker photographers organise

To consolidate the developing movement and to make their contribution a constant feature of the magazine, the AIZ appealed to the worker photographers again, asking for their addresses. Two weeks later, the editorial board wrote:

> In Berlin, a central agency of worker photographers has formed. This agency aims at a closer union of all the worker photographers in the German speaking areas, and the creation of a common newsletter to exchange experiences and to hand out photo commissions for the entire workers press.[5]
>
> The agency also aims at helping the worker photographers with their work through a collective purchase of materials, equipment, etc., and at making possible a further exchange of news items.[6]

This statement, as well as the subsequent constant publication of workers' photographs in the AIZ, encouraged the creation of more local groups, e.g. in Berlin, Frankfurt, Dresden, Stuttgart, Leipzig and Halle. The publication of the newsletter, out as early as August 1926, also encouraged communication and organisation amongst worker photographers. This rapid development cannot be imagined without the intensive organisational support of the KPD (German Communist Party) and their agitprop work; but it was also due to the new worker photographer groups catering for a latent need felt by many amateur photographers, previously unorganised or in bourgeois photographers' clubs: the need for a realist photography.

On September 16, 1926, a provisional National Committee of the Worker Photographers of Germany was formed in Berlin.

The first conference of the delegates of the *Vereinigung der Arbeiterfotografen Deutschlands* (VdAFD – Association of Worker Photographers in Germany) on April 17, 1927 in the Volkshaus in Erfurt may be regarded as the end of the formative phase. Twenty-five local groups sent eighteen delegates; five foreign guests (from the Soviet Union, Czechoslovakia, Great Britain and Belgium) were present, as well as representatives of the communist and social democratic press. Unlike the KPD (Communist Party), the SPD (Social Democratic Party) had not sent an official representative.

The first programme

Membership was not dependent on belonging to a particular political party; anybody who professed socialist views could join. An important task was to supply the entire workers' press. Here one can see the attempt to create the unity of working class action on the level of photographic creativity and photo correspondence. The aim was technical and political cooperation between communist, social democratic and non-party member workers, as demanded by the KPD at its Tenth Party Congress.

However, the leadership on Reich, district and local group levels was in the hands of KPD members, and about 60% of the VdAFD members were also in the KPD. Nevertheless, the foundation of the Association of Worker Photographers, as well as its concrete practice, have to be seen as a step towards the cultural and political cooperation of the split labour movement (despite the later SPD attempt to break up the association). This shows particularly in the local collective work as well as in the friendly relations to the photographic clubs of the *Naturfreunde* (nature friends).[7]

A new photography develops

Despite financial problems, darkrooms were rapidly set up by all the local groups and photographic materials and equipment were collectively bought, soon after the first Reich Conference. Soon the groups reached the public with numerous small exhibitions which were avidly received by their bourgeois "colleagues". The first photographic exhibition in Berlin on January 21 and 22, 1928, was wildly discussed in the bourgeois press. The worker photographers' own evaluation and critique was found in the movement's magazine *Arbeiter Fotograf* (Worker Photographer):

> ...Technically good throughout, some things excellent, but we didn't like the tendency. Too many portraits, landscapes, mood pictures; pictures valuable for the individual but not appropriate for the general public. Where was the material from the working class, where the wide coverage of social conditions?
>
> Apart from pictures of miserable housing and women on sewing machines – nothing! This gap, Berlin comrades, has to be filled. Seriously, we are not just any photographic club, we are worker correspondents! [8]

This short self-criticism indicates one of the major problems of the worker photographers' movement. The influence of bourgeois photography was immense in the beginning, which is not surprising since most workers who took pictures had previously been organised in bourgeois amateur photographer clubs. Their work had largely been informed by the conventional photo magazines which then already were mainly financed and determined by the German photographic industry. Here the petty-bourgeois idyll, the "sweet" portrait, the "romantic" landscape were dominant. The frantic search for technical refinement and *raffinesse* in negative and positive technique, bromoil printing and offset printing were triumphant and real life was retouched to the same extent as the photographs.

Bourgeois art photography, as it was still cultivated around the turn of the century, was the teacher and ideal of amateur photographers. Thus spoke the *Arbeiter-Fotograf* about a Kodak photo competition:

> In the Kodak contest a photograph won the first prize of DM 63,000 which must represent the highpoint of kitsch and sentimentality. In the foreground of the picture, a young maiden is sitting in a meadow; in the background a gigantic mountain of clouds, or something like that, is piling up, on which the last sunbeams seem to fall. The prize winning photograph made its round through the bourgeois illustrated papers and was praised as the most beautiful picture in the world...[9]

The *Arbeiter-Fotograf* continued to dedicate itself to this debate for a long time. Training, in particular picture criticism in the local groups, only slowly repressed the "mood picture". If one thinks of the gigantic task of the worker photographers' movement to educate the worker to a new way of seeing, to a new aesthetic consciousness within a world visually determined by the bourgeois mass media, then the long-term nature of the project (and its limitations) becomes clear.

Working for the press

In the meantime, a great number of local groups had begun regularly to send photographs to the AIZ, the *Rote Fahne* (Red Flag), also to an important degree to the district organs of the KPD and SPD, furthermore to papers and magazines of the unions, the *Arbeitersport* (workers' sports) organisations and the *Naturfreunde* (nature friends). For example, the local group in Leipzig, one of the biggest and most active, reported after a two year existence that "up to now about 150 picture reports for the most diverse newspapers of the working class have been produced." [10]

The Leipzig group also was the one that began workers' film production with short documentaries on the life and struggle of the Leipzig working class. Photographs by the worker photographers appeared regularly in newspaper sections like *From the Worker's Life, From the Labour Movement, Pictures of the Week, From the Whole World.* The pages of AIZ concerned with the labour movement in Germany became the proper domain of the worker photographers.

But these new picture sources were not only available for the national press of the communists and a section of the social democratic press. It's even correct to say that with the growth of the worker photographers' movement, the emphasis of proletarian picture journalism shifted more and more to the local workers' press. That is consistent with the VdAFD's line:

> Pictures which because of their local value were only of importance for the district press are now used. The task of the worker photographers must be... more than occasionally sending in pictures when a picture magazine announces a competition. Local groups... must seriously start getting into contact with the editorial board of their district and must play their part in making the paper more vivid. [1]

The Second National Conference

At the second meeting of national delegates in Dresden (March 30-31, 1929), as many as 45 delegates and guests from 24 local groups took part. Quite a few of the local groups, because of financial difficulties, were unable to provide the travelling expenses for a delegate.

At the conference it was stated that the association had 1,480 members, and that one had to assume a large number of sympathisers (suggested by the AF's printing run of 7,000). Therefore the conference decided, amongst other things, that one task was the organisation of an extensive propaganda campaign and the creation of new local groups.

Most of the initial two years after the foundation of the VdAFD was taken up with organising a core of worker photographer groups and their gradual introduction to the tasks of a proletarian photography, as formulated by the AIZ in its first appeal.

Only a few local groups, mainly in the large cities, were sufficiently advanced with their experience and qualification to supply the workers' press in the required manner. For photographs to be powerful, effective agit-prop material, both politically and aesthetically trained eyes were needed. The basis for this had been created within the two years of the VdAFD's existence.

New tasks for the worker photographers

The period from 1929 to 1933, marked by a general growth of internal contradictions in Germany, brought new tasks for the worker photographers, too. The beginnings of the world economic crisis, creating a radical deterioration in the living standards of the working class as well as of the petty bourgeois strata, a rapid succession of emergency laws and increasing provocation from fascist groups, also directed the worker photographers towards a struggle against the rise of fascism and for the creation of a united front of all democratic and antifascist forces.

Their photographs now showed the working class victims of Nazi assaults and became a kind of accusation of the troops of SA thugs; also the pictures became legal evidence. In this situation, the political and moral responsibilities of the worker photographers grew, but so did the dangers involved in their work. Despite this intensification of the class struggle, the number of worker photographers rose and their political and ideological force consolidated. Under the new social circumstances, both the content and the method of production of workers' photographs changed. More and more, forms of collective work were developed.

The amateur photographers and pioneers of proletarian photography had developed into organised workers' collectives, so-called *Kampfaktive* (literally: struggle action groups). These were broad networks of proletarian journalists who had matured technically and formally, i.e. they had become more political in the sense that they catered for the need for pictures within the proletarian mass press in a more comprehensive and concrete manner.

Facing increasing difficulties through police interference etc. the groups switched to collective production for particularly difficult tasks. Some groups then consisted of:

> Group 1: a 'flying squad' which had to be positioned for the coverage of, for example, a demonstration from the beginning to end.
> Group 2: will be positioned in key place in corner houses, ideally on the ground floor.
> Group 3: darkrooms
> Group 4: a bicycle courier service, delivering messages, bringing plates to dark rooms, then immediately passing on the prints to the press. [12]

With these *Kampfaktive* working with a division of labour and collectively, it was possible for the worker photographers to compete with the professional news agencies and networks of reporters of the bourgeois and National Socialist press, opposing them

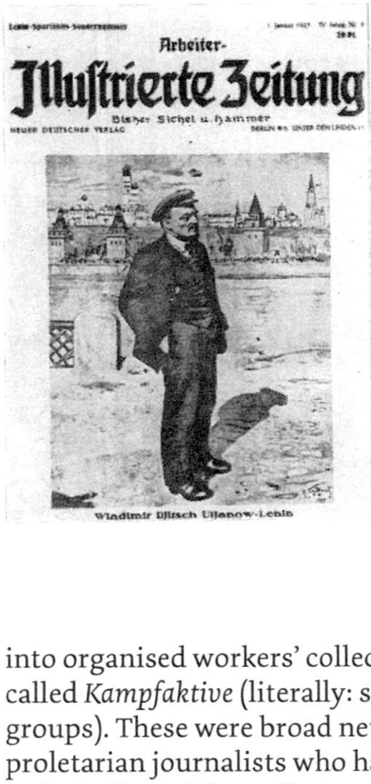

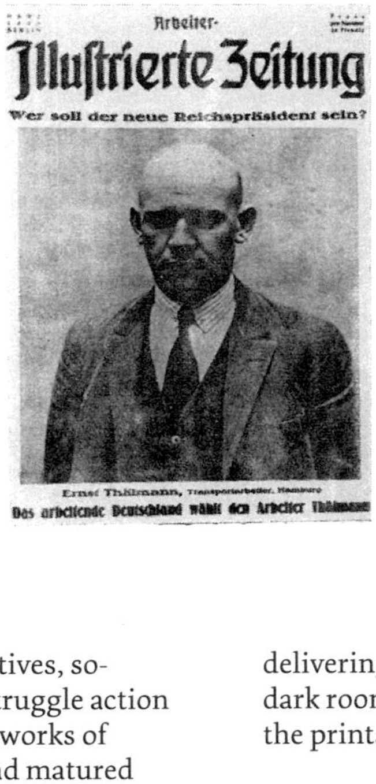

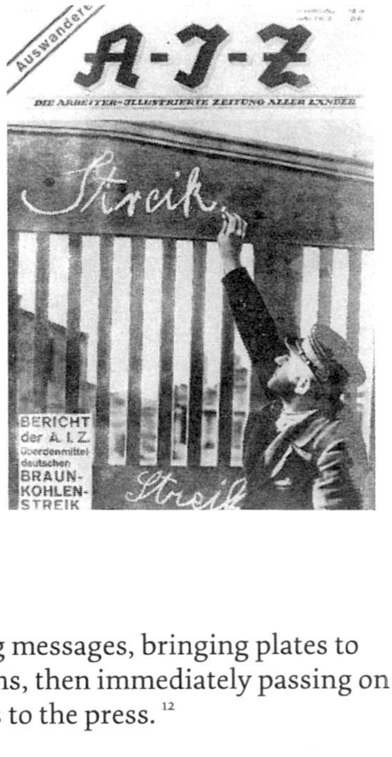

1. Lenin. AIZ, January 1925.
2. Who ought to be the new Reich President? Ernst Thälmann, transport worker, Hamburg. Working Germany votes for the worker Thälmann. AIZ, March 1925.
3. Strike. AIZ report on the brown coal strike in Central Germany. AIZ, November 1927.

with a photo journalism geared towards the publishing interest of the labour movement.

Reporting
Not only the methods of working advanced, but the journalistic quality of the photographic news was also improved. Worker photographers were facing up to the task of revealing complex social processes through the form and content of their genre – in the form of the picture report.

With this the importance of the accompanying text also increased. The worker photographer had to be in a position to lead debates with objective arguments to convince the victims of bad conditions. He had to collect information on the photographed event to provide a basis for the complementary written story. In a report on a news story to reveal housing conditions in Berlin, it was written:

> Obviously we did not confine ourselves to taking pictures in the flats. We also noted down exact information on the living conditions of the tenants, etc.

The worker photographers realised, "that the agitational picture receives a special kind· of political acuteness when underpinned by text. The... well photographed news story is very effective for accusing the capitalist system if the written explanation is informed by the methods of Marxist criticism." [13]

News photo reports from the factories
The Communist Party and mass press gave particular attention to reports from factories. They thus put into practice the guidelines laid down by the Third World Congress of the Communist International about the party press, for example:

> Everything that is of social or economic interest, from the industrial accident to the shop floor meeting, from the mistreatment of apprentices to the

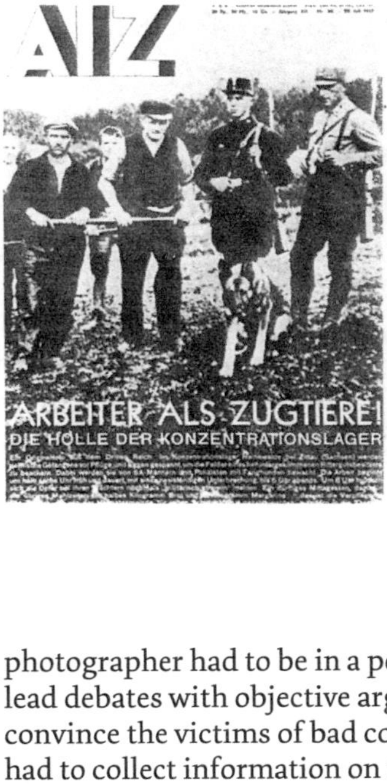

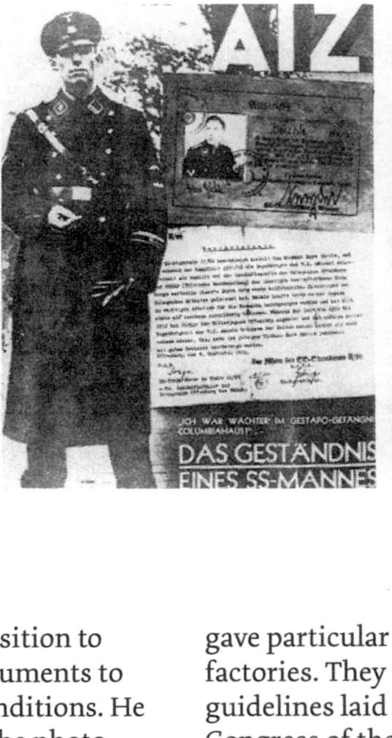

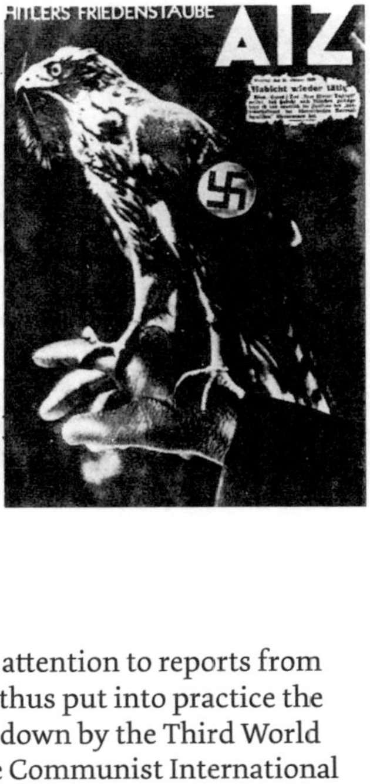

4. Workers as beasts of burden! The hell of the concentration camp. AIZ, July 1933.
5. The confessions of an SS man. "I was a guard in the gestapo prison Columbiahaus!" AIZ, May 1935.
6. Hitler's Peacedove. After having finished with the Saar happily, I can now let my hawk advance to the South. AIZ, January 1935.

employer's business report, must be reported as quickly as possible from the factory cell to the press. [14]

To the same degree as the distinctive role of the worker photographers' movement as a special organisation within the class struggle of the proletariat crystallised, so resistance from the bourgeois side grew. Slander, defamation, legal measures of all kinds, censorship, and finally open police terror, were all used against the young movement.

Thus, for example, a few reactionary photographers, these *Schwarzkünstler* (underground artists) aren't averse to a little industrial espionage, as is well known.[16]

The fears of unpleasant surprises probably stemmed much more from the fact that the often catastrophic hygienic and social conditions of many factories were being revealed to the light of day. For the exposure of such social conditions was one of the most important aims of the worker photographers.

This employers' campaign later led to a ban on photography in many capitalist

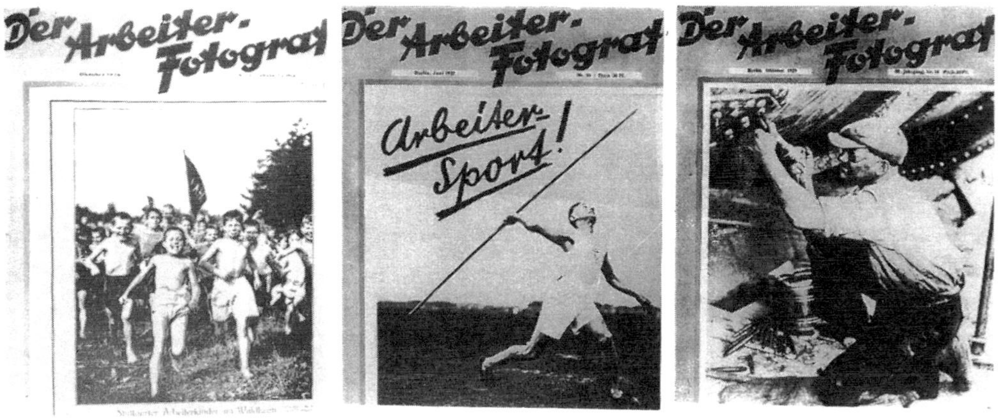

groups and newspapers demanded the dissolution of the association "since the worker photographers' movement merely serves the purpose of spying on the economy and trade for the benefit of Russia." [15]

Employers were urged to immediately react with lay-offs "if a worker is snooping around the factory with a camera. Otherwise, the board of directors could one day have a very unpleasant surprise, and so could the German national economy. For the worker factories, and to the creation of black-lists, i.e. a list of workers who, once fired, would not be able to get work in any other factory.

As a result of rationalisation, thousands of workers were laid off, particularly communists. Rationalisation, piece work on the conveyor belt, shift-work, etc. inevitably led to a fragmentation of the factory labour force. This made solidarity more difficult, which of course had consequences for the reporting activities of the worker photogra-

1. Working class children from Stuttgart at a holiday camp in the forest. AF, October 1926.
2. Workers' sport! Javelin thrower. AF, June 1927.
3. No caption. AF, October 1929.

pher, too, who was dependent on maximum cooperation from his work colleagues.

It was particularly difficult to get news photo stories from the large scale enterprises, as the percentage of communists within the labour force decreased with the increasing size of the factory. In addition, these larger enterprises had factory police and spies amongst the workers, so that the majority of photographs from there showed façades or the insides of machines rather than the actual working conditions, etc.

These factors also explain the extraordinary difficulties experienced in getting news photo stories out of plants. Photographs from capitalist factories and workshops weren't able to appear in the AIZ and the other organs of the working class in the quantities, and with the concreteness, the magazines themselves both wanted and demanded.

From about 1929, police harassment of worker photographers intensified:

> On May 1, 1929, a great number of worker amateur photographers in Berlin were randomly kicked, beaten and arrested by the police. As well, their cameras were seized, destroyed with truncheons, cassettes broken, plates smashed. All these actions were illegal... On behalf of 2,000 organised worker photographers we strongly protest against these unlawful, terroristic, arbitrary acts of the Berlin police.[17]

Continuously, the editorial board of the *Arbeiter-Fotograf* published articles which endorsed the legitimacy of the activities of the worker photographers. But censorship, police interference, and bending of the civil law were not the only methods for fighting the worker photographers' movement: the industrial associations and the bourgeois photographers' associations tried to put economic pressure on the VdAFD. They called upon the photographic dealers to boycott the *Arbeiter-Fotograf* magazine by not submitting advertisements. However, the campaign remained unsuccessful, as the worker photographers could win over

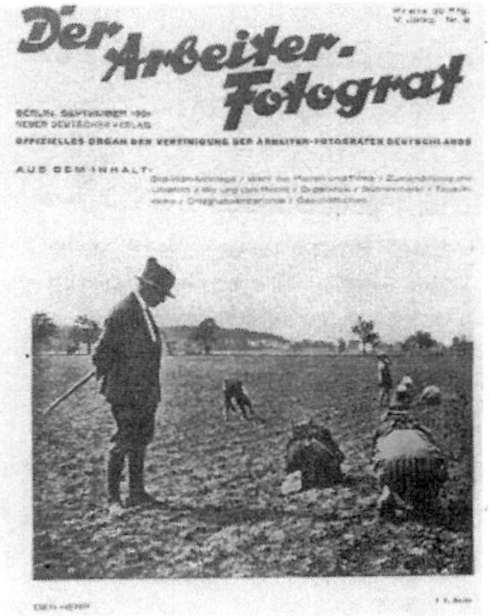

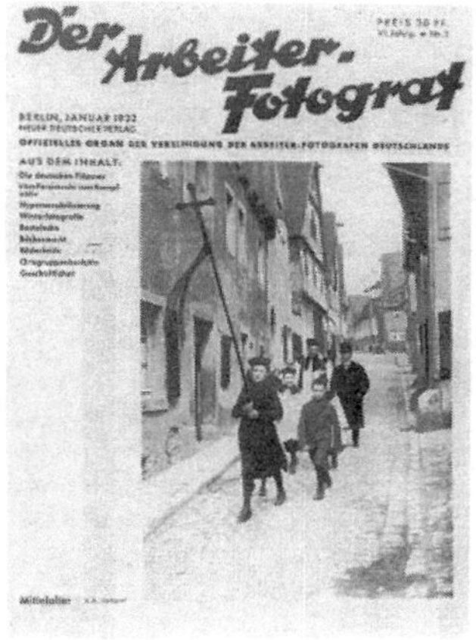

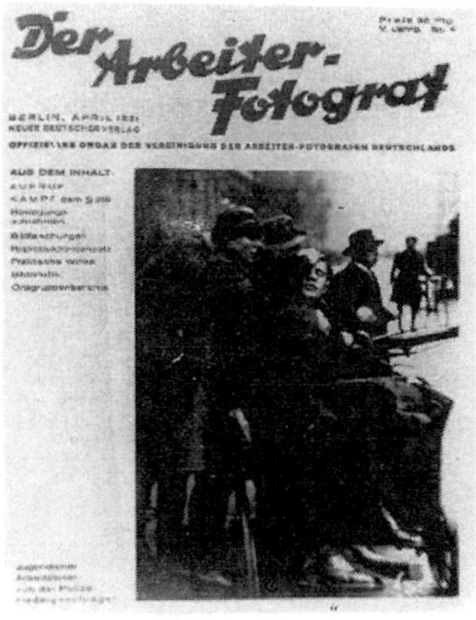

4. The Lord. AF, September 1931.
5. Middle Ages. AF, January 1932.
6. Unemployed youth beaten down by the police. AF, April 1931.

the small photo dealers who depended on the workers as customers and who were themselves under economic pressure from the photographic industry.

The SPD's attempt to split the movement
A particularly dangerous move against the increasingly powerful worker photographers' movement was the attempt by the right-wing leadership of the SPD and the *Naturfreunde* to influence it ideologically and to split it organisationally. As mentioned earlier, from 1930 the SPD started to build their own photographic organisations in Berlin and other cities. From April 10, 1930, they edited their own news paper *Das Neue Bild* (The New Picture) and, referring to strict neutrality in party politics, forbade any contact between the photographers' group of the *Naturfreunde* and the worker photographers. This was also intended to render ineffective a new tendency amongst the *Naturfreunde* photographers to abandon the usual landscape and still life pictures in favour of showing the condition of the smallholders and agricultural labourers whom they discovered on their "social hikes".

The Reich leadership of the *Naturfreunde* opposition addressed the *Arbeiter-Fotograf* with a letter that attacked this attempt at a split, which probably expressed the opinions of the majority of *Naturfreunde* photographers:

> We think it is right that the *Naturfreunde* are obligatorily associated with the worker photographers' association because we, as worker sportsmen, can only join the ranks of the cultural front of the revolutionary proletariat and not those of the ALB (*Arbeiter Lichtbild-Bund Deutschlands* – the Worker Picture-League of Germany) which was forcibly and artificially created as the result of a lot of trickery, and into which the Reich leadership of the TVDA wants to press all photographers.[18]

The worker photographers started a propaganda campaign against this splitting attempt, and were successful. Sixteen new local groups and eight sub-groups in Berlin were formed within a few months. Altogether they recruited 588 new members. The SPD groups did not last long.

The Third National Conference
At the Third National Conference, held on October 10 and 11, 1931, the VdAFD had 100 local groups and 2,412 registered members. Besides the discussion of new tasks in the struggle, they also passed a new action programme. The precise definition of the main task of worker photography is striking: "an indispensable means of propaganda and enlightenment in the proletarian class struggle".

The offensive political thrust of the worker photographer movement is emphasised, in contrast to the first action programme which tended to be a defensive reaction against bourgeois manipulations. However, this new emphasis must not be exaggerated since the role of workers' photography in Marxist propaganda was also stressed in the first paragraphs of the original programme in the *Arbeiter-Fotograf*. For the first time this new version speaks of the tasks of cooperation with proletarian cultural organisations! This is a reference to KPD initiatives, operative since 1927, which culminated in the foundation of the *IFA* (*Interessengemeinschaft für Arbeiterkultur* – the Association for those interested in Workers' Culture). At the Third National Conference the worker photographer movement linked itself to the national activities of the IFA. Without going into detail, one denotes lessons learnt in this new revised action programme. Some of the initial absurdities, resulting from lack of practical experience, are corrected and replaced with a clearer conception of aims and expanded tasks.

Meanwhile, sophisticated forms of photo journalism had developed as a result of the many kinds of collective modes of working of the worker photographers, as a result of even closer cooperation with the workers' press (the photographic "special squads" of the *AIZ* being the most eminent example), as a result of courses and, particularly, as a result of constant practice.

The International Office of Worker Photographers

Two days after the start of the Third National Conference, on October 12, a conference of the International Office of the Worker Photographers of the World took place in Berlin. Delegates from France, Switzerland, Austria, Czechoslovakia, Holland, USA and Germany were present; the seven delegates from the USSR were not given an entry permit. The conference revealed the ideological and organisational growth of the worker photographers' movement and their cooperation on an international scale.

Of particular importance was the close relationship between the Soviet and the German worker photographers. It was marked by an intensive exchange of experience, ranging from the swapping of hiking maps to what almost amounted to regular journeys of delegates and sponsorships. The close, friendly relationship between the Soviet and German worker photographers was a regular feature of the coverage in the *Arbeiter-Fotograf*. Many issues carried pictures by Soviet amateur photographers and, conversely, the Soviet magazines *Raboshaya Gaseta* and *Sovetskoe Foto* published pictures by German worker photographers.

> The cooperation between German and Soviet worker photographers reached a higher stage with the creation of the photo agency *Union Foto GmbH* in Berlin. This first international socialist photo agency was collectively organised and financed by Russ-Foto, the biggest photo agency in the USSR, by the general secretariat of the All-Russian Worker Photographers' Clubs and some Soviet publishing houses.
>
> Union-Foto, later called Union-Bild (Union Pictures), began its activities on May 1, 1930. It took care of the world wide distribution of Soviet press photographs, amassed all of the material from worker photographers in capitalist countries that could be used by the press, and sold it to those interested.[19]

It was also the German and Soviet worker photographers, the most progressive national organisations, who – relying on the steadily growing international significance of the movement – decided to form an international headquarters for organisation and guidance to coincide with the celebration of the 13th anniversary of the October Revolution in Moscow. A *Proclamation to the Worker Photographers of the World* stated:

> In the coming struggle between the capitalist and socialist worlds, the political photograph will play an important role as a convincing visual means of propaganda. The workers of the world have to fight for control of this means of propaganda, to then turn it into a weapon in class struggle...[20]

The foundation of the International Office of Worker Photographers of the World was the first step. From here, important impulses were sent out to many European and overseas countries, resulting in the foundation of small photo circles, based particularly on the example of the German local groups.

Prohibition and illegal work

At the beginning of the thirties, the fascist terror increased and the work of the worker photographers became both more difficult and more dangerous. Also, the ideological tensions between them and the SPD grew.

In this worsening situation, a tighter organisation became necessary. Erich Rinka[21] was appointed full-time secretary of the VdAFD, responsible for politics, organisation and finances. He writes on the difficulties:

> There were good examples of up-to-date reporting and increased activity, especially because of the greater leisure time created by unemployment. But a few local groups stayed on a club basis, got into financial trouble, became passive. Getting the cash was difficult here. It was not always recognised that the worker's photograph fulfilled an operative function in the proletarian press and in the daily political struggle.[22]

To improve their ideological and political formation, the local groups held special meetings, to which they also invited foreign speakers. To educate members, the Marxist Workers' School in Berlin and Leipzig introduced courses on the "basic knowledge of worker photographers".

Until the end, worker photographers fought against bourgeois agitation and fascist terror, against war and fascism, and for a united front of the workers' movement. With the seizure of the *Arbeiter-Fotograf*, the Nazis dissolved the VdAFD. Despite this, many worker photographers continued to operate illegally, risking their own lives in the process. The illegal leadership continued publishing the *Reporter* in a 6cm x 9cm format, until November 1933. The November edition still said:

> Worker Photographers! Never before has your work been more important and bearing a greater responsibility than today. Never before has your task been so great, difficult and meaningful for the struggle of the German working class as now, under the fascist dictatorship. You have the historic task of showing the whole world through visual documents and factual reports the real situation in the Third Reich.[23]

The worker photographers were, however, unable to fulfil this task. Quite a few of them were arrested and some later interned in concentration camps.

This is an extract from an article which first appeared in German as W Körner and J Stüber, "Die Arbeiterfotogragen Bewegung 1926-33", in *Arbeiterfotografie*, Berlin (West): Elefanten Press Verlag (GmbH, 1978, pp.25-66. We thank W Körner, J Stüber, the Verband Arbeiterfotografie and Elefanten Press Verlag GmbH for permission to translate and reprint the article.

NOTES

1. AIZ *(Arbeiter Illustrierte Zeitung*, Workers' Illustrated Paper) was founded in late 1924 and came to an end in 1938. It evolved out of *Sowjet-Russland im Bild* (Soviet Russia in Pictures) founded in 1921, which became *Hammer und Sichel* (Hammer and Sickle) in 1922-23. All three are associated with the name of Willi Münzenberg. He originally founded *Sowjet-Russland im Bild* as an organ for The Workers International Relief (WIR), an organisation to inform the international labour movement of famine in Russia and to mobilise their support. For further information on, and for reprints of, AIZ see Heinz Willmann, *Geschichte der Arbeiter-Illustrierte Zeitung 1921-1938*, Berlin (East): Dietz Verlag, 1975 (2nd edition).
2. *AIZ*, vol. V. March 25. 1926.
3. *AIZ*, ibid.
4. *AIZ*, vol. V. April 1926.
5. *AIZ*, vol. V. No.14.
6. *AIZ*, ibid.
7. The *Naturfreunde* (literally nature friends) were a hiking organisation which developed out of the youth movements around the turn of the century. It was part of the general "back to nature" movement and basically of a social democratic orientation. There was a proletarianisation in the twenties which resulted in a split.
8. *Arbeiter-Fotograf (AF)*, vol II, No. 6.
9. *AF*, vol. VI, No. 3.
10. *AF*, vol. II, No. 15.
11. *AF*, vol. II, No. 3.
12. *AF*, vol. III, No. 8.
13. *AF*, vol. VI, No. 2.
14. From the decisions of the Third World Congress of the Communist International of June-July 1921. Quoted from: Lehrmaterial XI zum Fernstudium der Journalistik, Reihe (*Geschichte der deutschen Presse*, Leipzig: 1956.
15. *AF*, vol. I, No. 5.
16. *Die Deutsche Arbeiter-Zeitung*, Zentralblatt der deutschen Arbeitgeber (German Employers' Paper), Berlin, vol. XXVI, No. 46 of November 13, 1927.
17. *AF*, vol. III, No. 6.
18. *AF*, vol. V, No. 1.
19. G. Danner, "Eine Organisation von Kampfern mit der Kamera", in: B Beiler (ed) *Berichte, Erinnerungen, Gedanken, Zur Geschichte der deutschen Arbeiterfotografie 1926-1933*, exhibition catalogue, Berlin.
20. *AF, vol. V., No.5.*
21. A lengthy interview with Erich Rinka is partly printed in the same book as this article. "Aus dem Alltag der Arbeiter-fotografen", pp.69-87.
22. E. Rinka, "Die Arbeiterfotografen – Was sie waren und was sie wollten", in: B Beiler, op.cit.
23. *Der Reporter*, illegal paper of the worker photographers, November 1933, the only remaining copy.

Holland: Veneenigiung van Arbeiders-Fotografen

Bert Hogenkamp

THE FOLLOWING ARTICLE is a modest attempt to reconstruct the history of the worker photography movement in the Netherlands in the 1930s. Very little has been written about this subject,[1] a fate that it shares with other left-wing cultural movements in the 1930s, such as theatre, film, music, literature, sport, etc. I have researched various contemporary sources and interviewed some of those involved. However, the scope of this article has to remain rather limited, because I have not been able to trace any primary sources, like minutes, personal notes or even a stills-collection and because the Dutch worker photographers never had an organ of their own (as for example the Germans had with *Der Arbeiter Fotograf*). Moreover, Cas Oorthuys, the leading photographer in the Dutch movement, is no longer with us and it seems that during his lifetime (he died in 1975) no one ever bothered to record his reminiscences of that period. I am grateful to Joop Huisken, Joris Ivens, Leo van Lakerveld and Emiel van Moerkerken for providing me with some useful insights into the worker photography movement.

Holland: the beginnings

The *Vereeniging voor VolksCultuur* (VVVC), the Association for Popular Culture, was founded in 1928 in order to show Soviet films to working class audiences without interference of the censor. In 1930 the VVVC extended the range of its activities enormously. With the assistance of Joris Ivens the VVVC film collective started to produce a number of newsreels that were made partly of re-edited old newsreel footage and partly of material shot by the members of the collective. Under the aegis of the VVVC a number of agit-prop theatre groups staged short plays.

In July 1930 the VVVC announced a course in photography: "The purpose is to train a number of VVVC members to become Photo-Workers' Correspondents."[2] The course was to take place in Amsterdam, while courses in other cities were to start later on. It must have taken some time to organise the course, but according to *De Tribune* it started on November 1, 1930.[3] The VVVC claimed that it had found "an excellent technical guide."[4] This must have been Joris Ivens, who was also involved in the film (and theatre) activities of the VVVC. Ivens recalls that he staged special events for a group of worker photographers that they had to catch with their cameras. For example, they went to one of the Amsterdam workers' districts, where Ivens arranged a quarrel between two fishwives. The results were, according to Ivens, rather disappointing.[5] This VVVC photo collective became on February 13, 1931 the Association of Worker Photographers, *Vereeniging van Arbeiders-Fotografen* (VAF). The VAF was affiliated to the VVVC. In the VVVC organ, *De Sovjet Vriend*, a call for new members was published:

> ...photography can be used as a weapon in the class struggle. For with the aid of photography revolutionary events can be perpetuated; the pictures can exercise a profound influence on the masses and therefore serve the cause of the proletariat in its struggle against capitalism. Our German comrades have attained already very good results in this area; one only has to cast a glance at the AIZ to judge how far photography has developed among the German revolutionary proletariat. This example serves for a model. Our Russian comrades too (...) have achieved very much in this area. We must not stay behind. For we are fighting the same fight as the workers everywhere else; their enemies are our enemies. That's why it has been decided to transform the photo collective into an independent organisation – an organisation that will point towards a new direction in photo-amateurism.[6]

In a programmatic statement in *De Tribune* the VAF announced its plan of action for 1931:

> The members will join as much as possible all kind of propaganda tours, demonstrations, meetings, etc., which will be organised by the WIR, the ILD, the RILU, the Unemployed Councils and other revolutionary organisations, in order to photograph moments which are of importance. Furthermore it is a matter of importance that the photographing comrades on the street or in the factory take those pictures, that are connected with our struggle against capitalism and its excrescences.[7]

In practice the making of pictures of demonstrations proved much more difficult for the worker photographers: "By various demonstrators the members of our association (the VAF, BH) were prevented from doing their work, abused or even threatened. Members that identified themselves, were told: *That's none of our business.*[8] In a comment *De Tribune* explained the fear of the demonstrators for plain-clothes policemen with cameras and stressed the need to arrange matters like these beforehand with the organisers of the demonstration. It is clear that worker photographers were as yet an uncommon sight in Amsterdam. From March 1931 onwards the CPH daily *De Tribune* the monthly VWC journal *De Sovjet Vriend* and the ILD organ *De Roode Hulp* published photos with the caption *Photo by the VAF*. One of these was a still of the newly formed agit-prop theatre group *Ontwaakt* (Wake Up).

In a series of four articles, *The photography in the class struggle* in *De Tribune* [9] the work of the VAF was analysed. The existence of an International Bureau of Worker Photographers, headed by Willy Münzenberg, with headquarters in Berlin, was mentioned. The German and Soviet sister organisations were referred to with a mixture of pride and envy. The establishment of local sections in Rotterdam and Leiden was mentioned. The prevailing attitude of the VAF towards photography in that period is best characterised by the following sentence: "Every picture of fighting against police club and sword is a

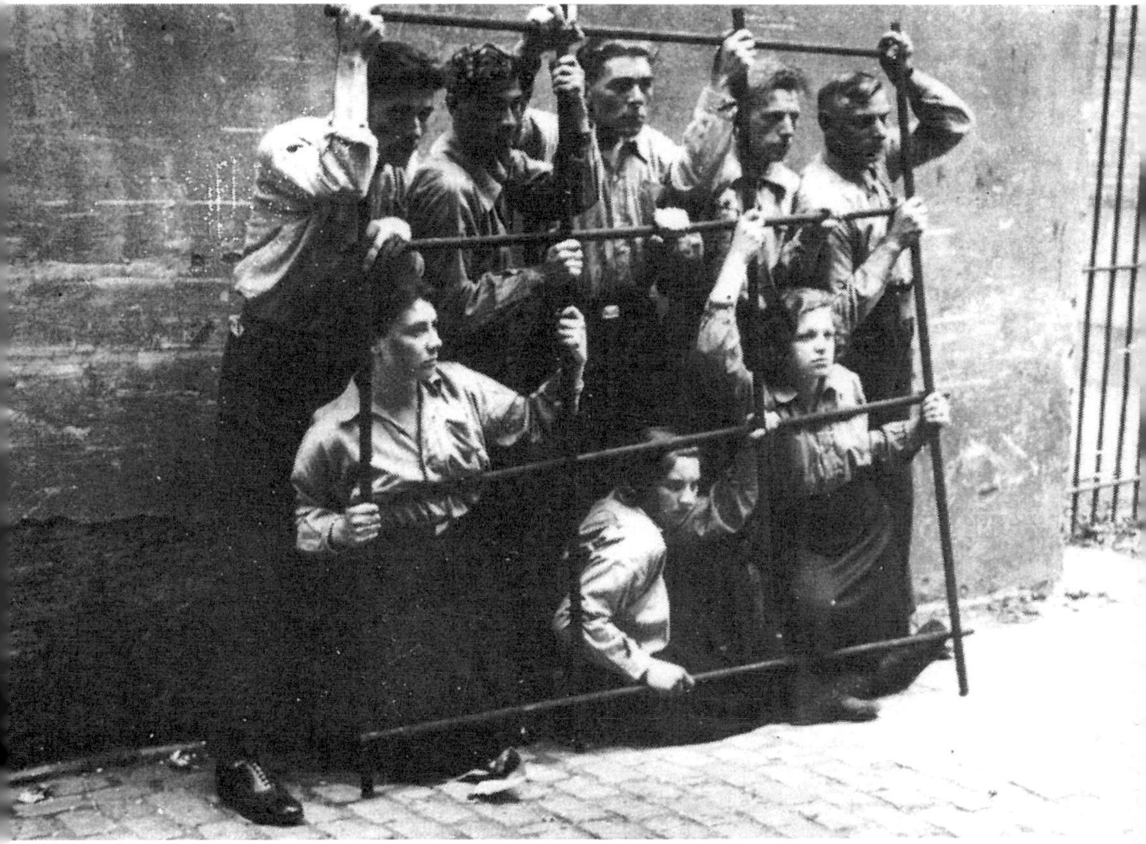

Agit-prop theatre group *Ontwaakt* (Wake Up), Amsterdam 1931.
Still by Vereeniging van Arbeidersfotografen (VAF)
from the Joris Ivens archive, Netherlands Filmmuseum, Amsterdam.

document in our struggle, and promotes the determination and fighting spirit of the workers in other cities and countries." [10]

Extending the movement

This rather simplistic view of photography changed after a reorganisation of the VAF late in 1931. The VAF had lost the services of Joris Ivens who went to the Soviet Union to make his film *KOMSOMOL*. It had published a call for donations in September 1931, so that a VAF delegation could be sent to the International Congress of Worker Photographers in October 1931 in Berlin.[11] The congress must have stimulated the VAF to extend the range of its activities.

In January 1932 the VAF presented itself with renewed vigour as "a New Brigade on the Red Front". [12] From now onwards the worker photographers were to become photo-worker correspondents (*Arfots* in Dutch). Their slogan was, *Our own life by our own photographers in our own press!* In *De Tribune* the VAF published a series of articles in which it explained examples of its work, for example on housing conditions in a slum tenement or in a caravan. Although more primitive, these articles resemble the articles published by the AIZ: informing the reader through a written text, but with the use of stills. An even better opportunity to publish this kind of work was offered by the newly founded illustrated monthly *A(fweer) F(ront)* (Defence Front). This was meant to be the Dutch equivalent of the AIZ. Leo van Lakerveld recalls that they did not have enough money to print it in rotograph. They decided that it should resemble as much as possible AIZ, and therefore printed it in a kind of copper colour. The first issue of AF appeared late January/early February 1932. Only a few issues have survived. It seems however that the AIZ-like design had to be dropped in late 1932 due to lack of money. A good example of the cooperation between AF and the VAF can be found in no.6. A two-page article on the murder of a communist by the police in a small Dutch village is illustrated by a series of twelve photos, provided by the VAF. They show the class contradictions in the village, the widow with her two children, the funeral and the ILD demonstration against the murder. The accompanying article was written by Maurits Dekker, a very popular left-wing writer at that time. Leo van Lakerveld recalls that Cas Oorthuys was the VAF's more or less full-time photographer at that time. Oorthuys probably took the stills for the photo series in AF. Oorthuys was an unemployed building-designer. Through his work in AF and other periodicals he gained much experience in photography, which helped him later in his career to become one of the most famous photographers in the Netherlands.

Photo-montage was a magic word. Through the AIZ the work of John Heartfield was well-known in Holland. Pamphlets were beginning to be sold with photo-montages on their cover. This was something new. At the beginning these photo-montages were rather primitive, as for example on a RILU pamphlet *Hundreds of thousands without work* (November 1931). In fact the photo-montage was to remain an area for professional photographers; the VAF never propagated the use of it by its members. An example of a photo-montage made by a professional was the front cover of *Links Richten*, the monthly magazine of the Dutch worker writers, designed by Paul Schuitema. Schuitema was a member of the Rotterdam section of the VAF. Under his pen-name S. Palsma, Schuitema published an article on *Photography as weapon in the class struggle*[13] in which he stresses the necessity for subjectivity of the photo-worker correspondents. Schuitema was a well-known designer. Joop Huisken still regrets the dominance of bourgeois people like Schuitema in the policies of the VAF. He confirms that the VAF had working class members, but that in the end it was the bourgeois supporters who "stole the show".

Anti-fascist action

On Christmas and Boxing Day 1932 the very active Rotterdam section of the VAF organised, in cooperation with the worker writers collective *Links Richten*, an exhibition on worker photography. The aforementioned Paul Schuitema was one of the organisers. The critic of *De Tribune* called the exhibition a success, but complained about the

The Rotterdam exhibition was the first of a long series to follow. It marked a new area for the Dutch worker photographers. The loss of AF – which had become a small printed sheet – meant the death of the "Photo-Worker Correspondents" idea. *De Tribune* by now hardly published any stills of the Arfots – as the worker photographers were called now. The VVVC had changed itself into an Association of Friends of the Soviet Union (VVSU) and relied completely on Soviet sources. There were some exceptions – the *Links Richten* magazine with its

Wat willen de Foto-arcors?

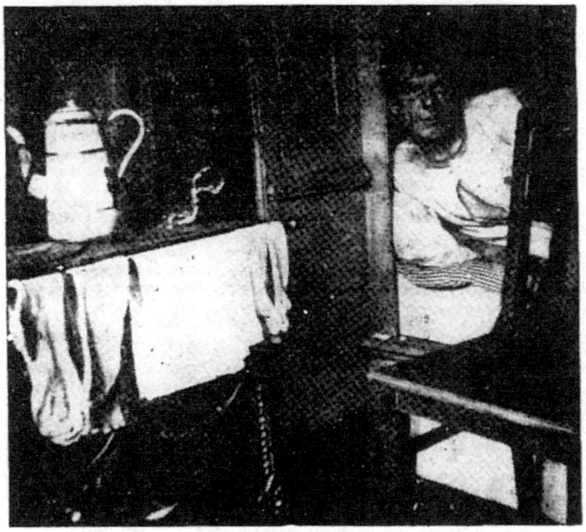

photo-montages: "...the montage has to be comprehensible to the working class, in no way must they degenerate into puzzles or be so complicated, that they can't be understood." [14] These criticisms were undoubtedly directed against the work of Schuitema and his colleague Piet Zwart, who were very active in the Rotterdam section of the VAF. Schuitema and Zwart were quite famous in Holland for their original designs (booksleeves, publicity material, posters, etc.), in which they applied the possibilities of the photo-montage.

front covers designed by people like Cas Oorthuys. Or an occasional pamphlet, like one issued by the Fighting League against Fascism – but generally speaking the Arfots had lost their place in the left-wing press. Instead they organised exhibitions of their work. This might have been the result of the dominance of bourgeois people, as Huisken complains; the exact reasons still remain obscure.

The next exhibition of the Arfots took place in the respectable city of The Hague. It was again organised by the VAF and *Links*

What do the Photo-workers' correspondents want? Self-presentation in *De Tribune* January 5, 1932, by the Dutch worker photographers.

Richten, the worker writers collective. It comprised worker photographs from Holland, Germany and the Soviet Union. The captions that accompanied the photographs were taken from the magazine *Links Richten*. The police intervened on Sunday February 5, 1933, the second day of the exhibition. It took offence at some of the captions and gave orders to cover them with pieces of paper. “Everybody wanted to know what these pieces of paper were hiding. They were soon torn off...” [15] On the last day the exhibition was closed altogether by the police. For *De Tribune*, this provided a good occasion to rail at “the cultural fascism of the Dutch bourgeoisie”.[16] At Whitsun 1933 another exhibition was held in Amsterdam. Without police intervention, apparently. The theme of this exhibition was *Against War and Fascism* (Hitler had just taken power).

In March 1933 the release of the Nazi film *MORGENROT* in Amsterdam and other cities had provoked a mass protest movement among the Dutch left, and the worker writers collective *Links Richten* took the lead and organised a protest movement against the exhibition of the film. One of the means used was letting loose mice in the cinema. Joris Ivens recalls that this was good fun: screaming women, lights on, film show interrupted etc. The boycott of *MORGENROT* [17] united a large section of left-wing artists and intellectuals. Among them were the worker photographers. They were organised in the *Comite van Kunstenaars en Intellectueelen* (Committee for Artists and Intellectuals), which was responsible for the Dutch version of the *Brownbook* on the Hitler-terror in Germany. In 1935 the left-wing *Bond van Kunstenaars ter Verdediging van de Kultuur* (Association of Artists for the Defence of Culture) was founded. It had an important photography section with Carel Blazer, Cas Oorthuys, Eva Besnyo (an exiled Hungarian) and Emiel van Moerkerken. It was within this framework of anti-fascist action that the other exhibitions of the Dutch Arfots took place.

These exhibitions were no longer exclusively photo exhibitions. The exhibits of the Arfots at *Two Worlds* which took place in January 1934 in Rotterdam, were criticised by *De Tribune*:

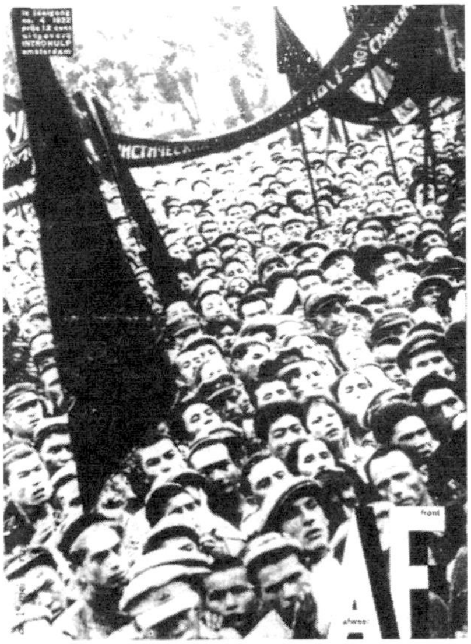

AF (Defence Front), May 1932. Published by the Dutch section of the ILD.

> If we compare this to a photoseries of our own Arfots on Drenthe, it strikes us that the anecdotal prevails and the impression of poverty, which is certainly no less (compared to poverty shown in other photos, B.H.), is weaker. A woman posing next to her little house distracts the attention from the real subject, bad housing conditions. On the other hand we have respect for the Arfot who succeeded in taking an excellent picture in the middle of a riot of policemen and a struck down man, and another one of a policeman with sword drawn, etc. Technically the photos are good enough, but something is missing...[18]

But what is missing? In March 1934 the Amsterdam police forbade an anti-fascist exhibition, organised by the Dutch section of the WIR.[19] In the same month a new version of the *Two Worlds* exhibition was held in Rotterdam. A band of Dutch national-socialists tried to disrupt the exhibition, but had to retreat when some muscled visitors threatened to go into action. After this incident the Fighting League against Fascism organised a permanent defence of the exhibition.[20]

The most important exhibition of its kind took place in Amsterdam in 1936. It was part of a protest movement against the 1936 Olympiad in Berlin. The exhibition was called *De Olympiade Onder Dictatuur* (DOOD – which is the Dutch word for death – The Olympiad Under Dictatorship. Cas Oorthuys and Jo Voskuil designed a famous poster for the exhibition, which comprised exhibits from all over the world. Dutch left-wing photographers exhibited their work too, but as individuals, no longer as members of the VAF or as Arfots.

When exactly the VAF was dissolved, is unknown. However, in its second period (from 1933 onwards) it slowly started to lose its original function. The trend was towards cultural recognition through exhibitions, something the early VAF had never thought of (nor aspired to). By organising exhibitions the VAF lost the mass circulation of its work through left newspapers and magazines, and was more vulnerable to police intervention.

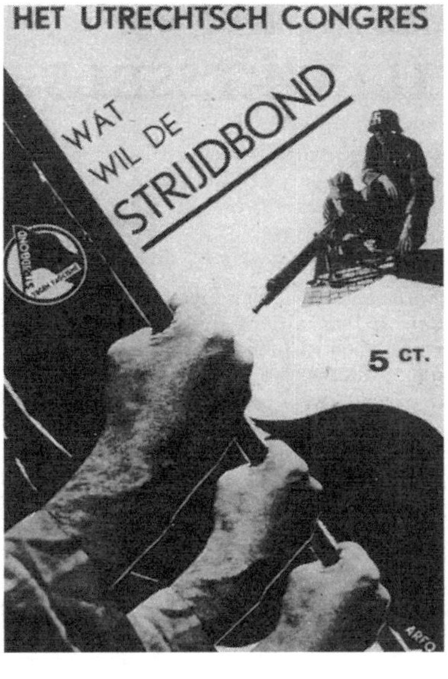

The Utrecht Congress, *What does the Fightng League against Fascism want*, 1933. By the ARFOTS.

One wonders who the visitors to such exhibitions were: those who were already convinced of the cause and just came to seek the company of those who had the same political view? One is inclined to believe this, on the basis of the evidence provided by those who were actually involved. In the 1930s the Netherlands were neatly divided into so-called "families" (for example, the socialist family, the roman-catholic family, etc., etc.) There were little changes in the political relations (even the rise of the Dutch national-socialist ebbed quite soon). This made a political cultural work on a mass base almost an impossibility. Changes in the political line of the Dutch CP led towards the inclusion of "important" bourgeois artists and intellect- uals in the movement. It meant the end of a real proletarian culture which the CPs in Western Europe, the US and Japan had aspired to establish in the early thirties. Still the big question remains: was the disappearance of the Dutch VAF caused by internal weaknesses or by political changes within the CP?

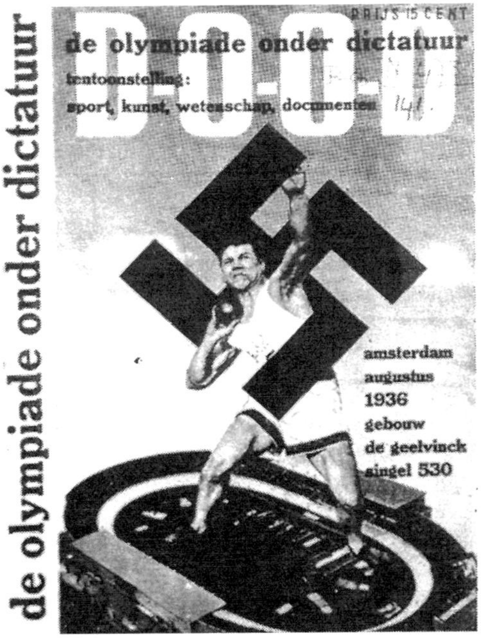

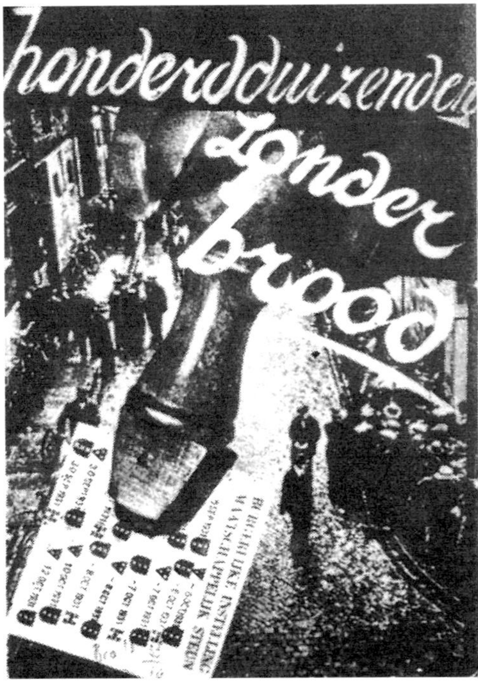

NOTES
1. A supplement to the weekly Vrij Nederland, No.20, May 15 1976 was devoted to left-wing photography in the 1930s.
2. De Tribune, July 24, 1930. p.4.
3. De Tribune, October 13, 1930. p.4.
4. De Sovjet Vriend, No 2-3, March 1931, p.3.
5. Cf. supplement Vrij Nederland, op.cit., p.17; confirmed by Ivens in a talk to the author (July 1978).
6. De Sovjet Vriend, op.cit.
7. De Tribune, March 4, 1931. p.4.
8. De Tribune, March 9, 1931. p.4.
9. De Tribune, March 25, 1932, p.4; April 1 1931, p.3; April 13 1931, p.3; May 13, 1931, p.3.
10. De Tribune, May 13, 1931, p.3.
11. De Tribune, September 24, 1931, p.3.
12. De Tribune, January 5, 1932, p.4.
13. S. Palsma (Paul Schuitema). "Foto als wapen in de klassestrijd", in: Links Richten. No.5-6, February 1, 1933, pp.21-22.
14. De Tribune, January 2, 1933, p.4.
15. De Tribune, February 7, 1933, p.2.
16. De Tribune, February 8, 1933, p.2.
17. Projektgroep "Literatuursociologie" 1. Links Richten tussen partij en arbeiders-strijd. Nijmegen: 1975, pp.397-404.
18. De Tribune, January 15. 1934, p.4.
19. De Tribune, March 1934. p.4.
20. De Tribune, March 12, 1934, p.4; March 13, 1934, p.4.

All photographs (unless otherwise stated) are from the International Instituut Soc. Geschiedenis, Amsterdam, Netherlands.

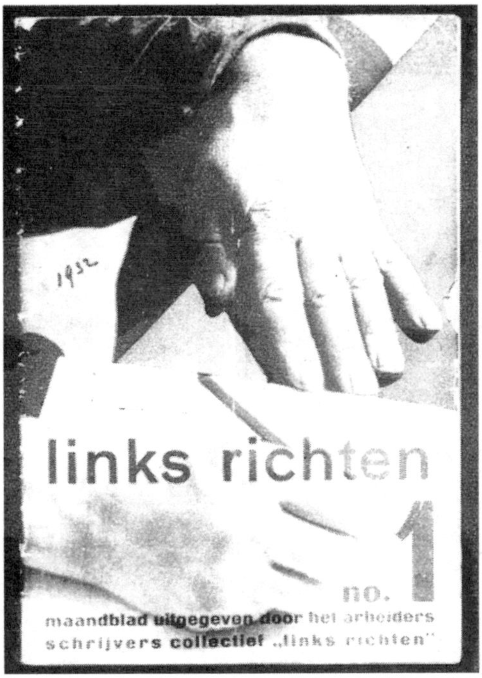

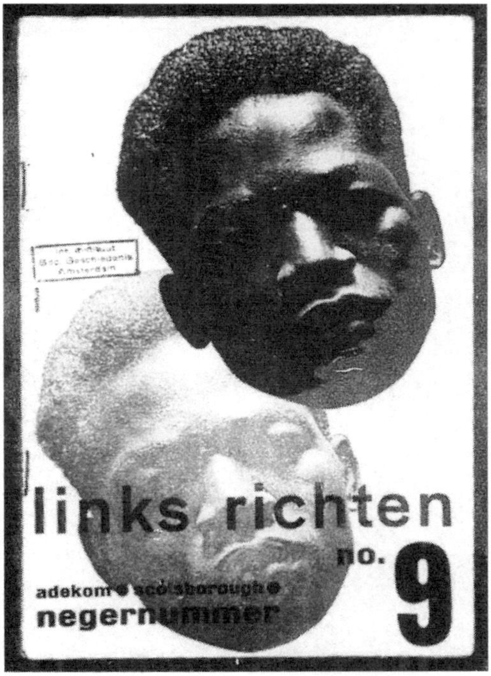

Opposite, top: D-O-O-D (The Olympiad under Dictatorship).
Designed by Cas Oorthuys and J.J. Voskil, for an exhibition against the 1936 Berlin Olympiad.

Opposite, below: Hundred thousands without Bread, 1931. Pamphlet published by Dutch SEction of the RILU.

Above, left: *Links Richten* No.1, 1932. Cover of the monthly magazine, published by the Dutch worker-writers, designed by Paul Schuitema.

Above, right: *Links Richten* No. 9, 1933. Special issue devoted to negroes, designed by Cas Oorthuys.

138

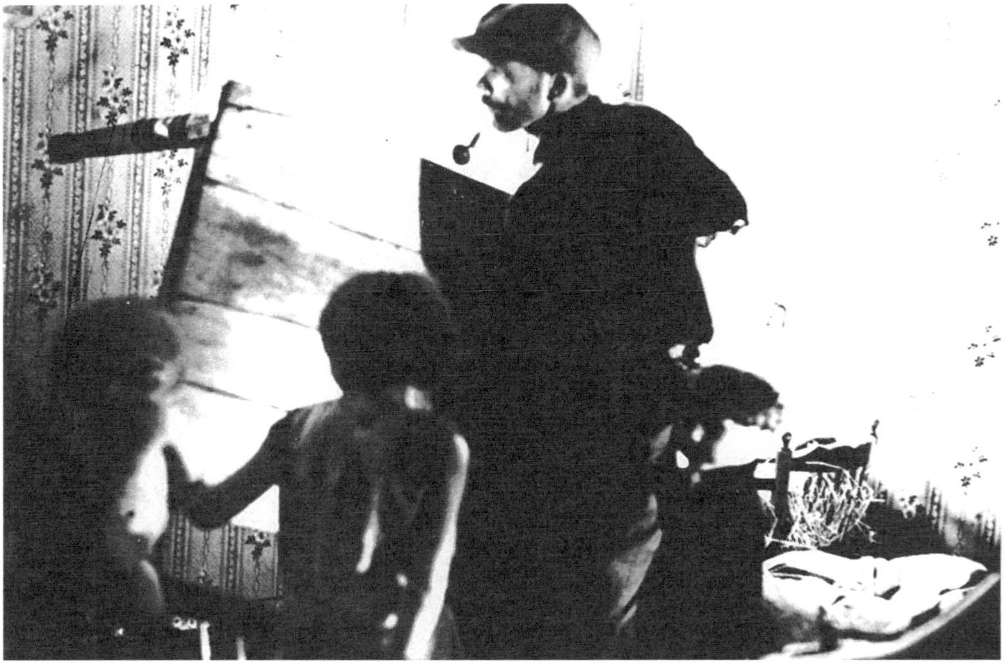

The table serves as a bed for the young ones to sleep in.

Belgium: Willy Kessels and the Borinage Film

Bert Hogenkamp

THE BORINAGE IS A MINING AREA in the south-west of Belgium. It has a long record of working class militancy. When in June 1932 the mining companies announced another wage cut, the miners decided to strike. Their work was hard and dangerous (the number of casualties was rising every year), and still they were hardly paid enough to feed themselves and their families. Another wage cut was too much. The strike spread quickly to other mining areas in Belgium and workers in other industries were prepared to join the strike in sympathy with the miners. This situation alarmed the ruling class. Brutal measures were taken to stop the strike: state of siege was declared in the most militant mining villages, as a result of which the police and military forces killed some miners. The Belgian Social-Democratic Party which had a large following among the miners decided to open negotiations. The result was a disaster: the strike was called off without sufficient guarantees for the miners to get back their jobs. They were betrayed by what was once a working class party, but now a reformist parliamentary body. Of the thousands of miners who had joined the strike, very few were allowed to come back. With huge stocks of coal waiting to be sold, the mine owners were in a good position to get rid of the more militant miners. As the mining companies also owned the houses, in which the miners lived, those who were blacklisted saw themselves evicted and were forced to live in shanty towns. The miners who had produced the coal with their own force, did not even have fuel to warm their homes and had to go and climb the slag heaps hoping to find some coal.

Keeping up its tradition of helping distressed workers all over the world, the Workers' International Relief (WIR) – the workers' Red Cross – tried to help the most urgent cases with medical aid, food and clothing. Another left-wing organisation was active in the Borinage too: the International Labour Defence (ILD). On the 9th July 1933, the ILD organised a demonstration in the Borinage to commemorate the anniversary of the death of Louis Tayenne, a miner shot by the police during the strike. More than 10,000 joined the demonstration, which included the unveiling of Tayenne's tombstone and speeches by various ILD and CPB (Communist Party of Belgium – ed.) representatives. Two members of the ILD, Albert Van Ommeslaghe and Jean Fonteyne, shot footage of the demonstration with their own cameras (they were lawyers and could afford to have one) and made a film of it, called *Manifestation pour Tayenne* (Demonstration for Tayenne). It was undoubtedly as a result of this film experience that representatives of the WIR, ILD and a Brussels film society *Club de l'Ecran* came together and decided to produce a film that would expose the situation in the Borinage.

Henri Storck, film director and prominent member of the *Club de l'Ecran*, was asked to direct the film. Storck came to the conclusion that it would be a good idea to ask his Dutch colleague, Joris Ivens – recently returned from the Soviet Union where he had shot a film in Magnitogorsk – to co-direct the film. Ivens accepted immediately. François Rents was asked to do the camera work, while the production stills were made by Willy Kessels, a photographer from Brussels, and Sacha Stone, a refugee from Nazi Germany. They were accompanied by representatives from the WIR, like Doctor Paul Hennebert from the ILD, like Jean Fonteyne (present with his own

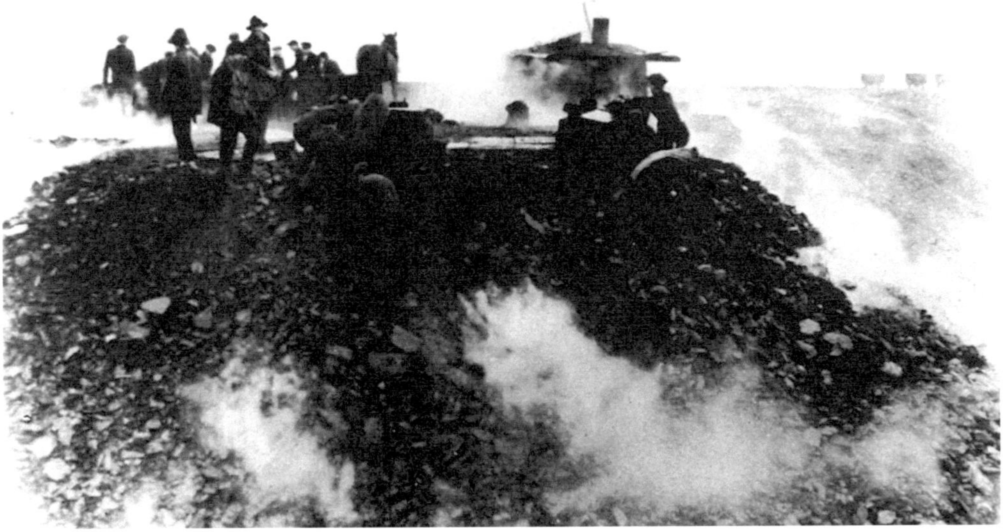

Looking for coal on the slag heaps.

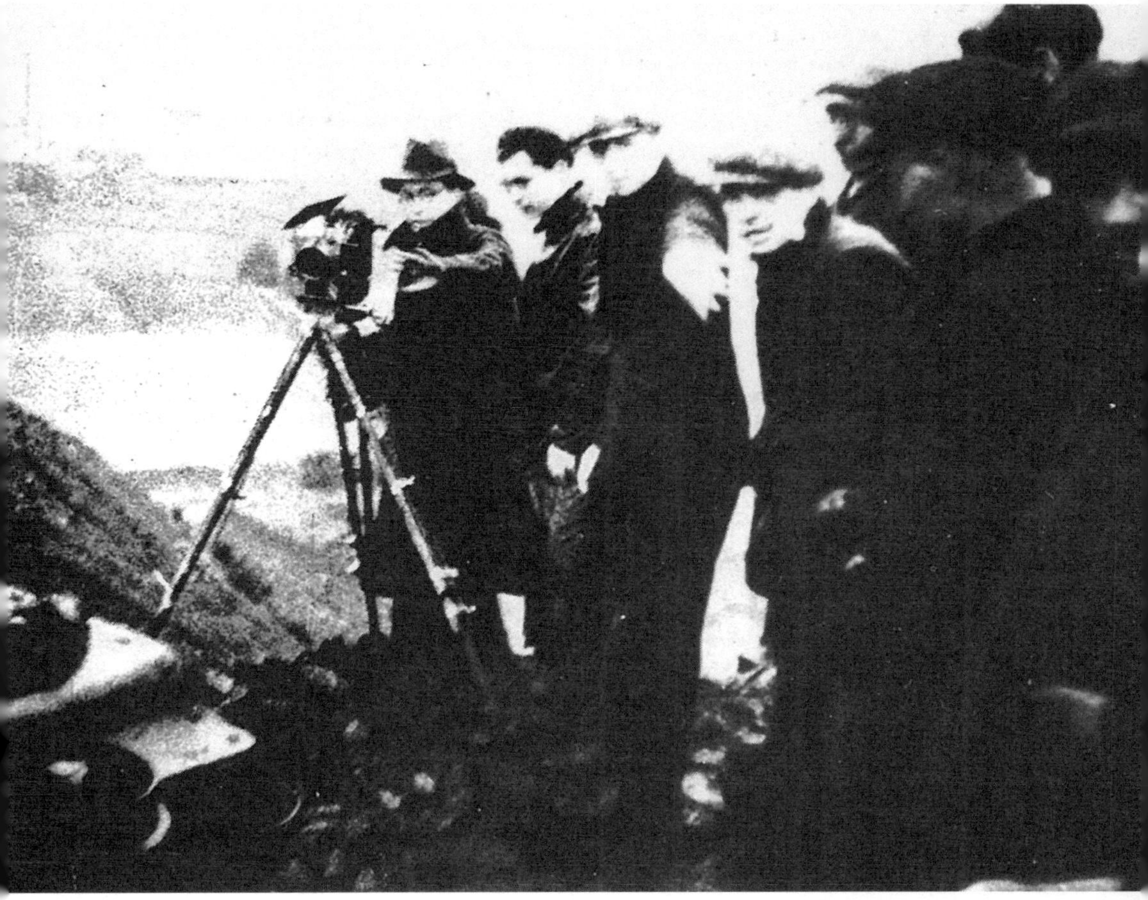

Henri Storck and Joris Ivens near the camera.

film camera most of the time), Van Ommeslaghe or Pierre Vermeylen, and/or local CPB members. With this crew "we connected our film work with our political work," said Joris Ivens.

Recently Henri Storck after many years of persistence got hold of the complete collection of stills that Willy Kessels took during the production of the film. We are publishing here a number of these stills, which deserve attention both within the framework of the Borinage film and on their own as evidence of the history of the working class movement in the Borinage. As far as Henri Storck remembers, Kessels used a kind of Leica miniature camera for most of the stills and an old-fashioned plate camera for the rest. A general feature of the stills taken with the miniature camera is that they are (slightly) blurred in some parts, while most of the plates that have survived are remarkably sharp and bright. Obviously the plate photographs needed some kind of posing, while the Leica-type stills were taken on the spot. The collection can roughly be divided into two parts: on the one hand production stills properly speaking, i.e. stills showing (members of) the crew at work, portraits of crew-members and a series of stills on police intervention; on the other hand stills that have enough expression of their own and seem to have no direct relationship with the film in production.

In a 1934 interview, Joris Ivens explains the role of the photographer within the crew shooting the Borinage film:

> At the same time as we shot the film, in many cases photographs were taken, for example of workers looking for coal on the slag heaps. Those stills were ready in a couple of days and our comrades used them for political agitation. Thus the film did its work in organising the workers, before it actually was ready.[1]

Recalling Kessels now, Ivens remembers him as a humanitarian and Storck as a *convaincu* or devotee. Undoubtedly the guidance of experienced people like Storck and Ivens must have helped Kessels a lot. He probably was not as politically experienced as they were. Pictorially some of his stills have a long tradition, however. In his autobiography *The Camera and I* Joris Ivens refers to this tradition: Emile Zola with his novel *Germinal*, and especially Vincent Van Gogh ("I could understand why after living in the Borinage... (he) stopped preaching and began to paint.")[2] Indeed some of Kessels' stills show remarkable resemblance to late 19th century drawings.

Willy Kessels' later record is a rather sad one. A couple of years after the Borinage film he joined the Rexists, a Belgian fascist group. Ironically, it was Henri Storck who helped to defeat the Rexist leader Leon Degrelle in a Brussels by-election, by making the anti-fascist propaganda film *La Belgique Nouvelle* (The New Belgium) in 1937.

Misère au Borinage is now considered as one of the most important militant films ever made. Ivens himself, author of a considerable amount of left-wing films, considers it as the film that changed his career completely. The most important feature of the film now seems, apart from the political analysis of the economic crisis, the political work of the team as a whole: directors, cameramen, assistants, photographers and political consultants. Within this political work photography had an importance that was unheard of. Of course, situations nowadays have changed, but one can imagine the importance of left-wing photography supporting materially and politically left-wing film collectives.

NOTES
1. *De Tribune*, March 9, 1934, p.6.
2. Joris Ivens, *The Camera and I*, Berlin: Seven Seas, 1969, p.83.

We would like to thank Henri Storck for providing copies of the Willy Kessels stills.

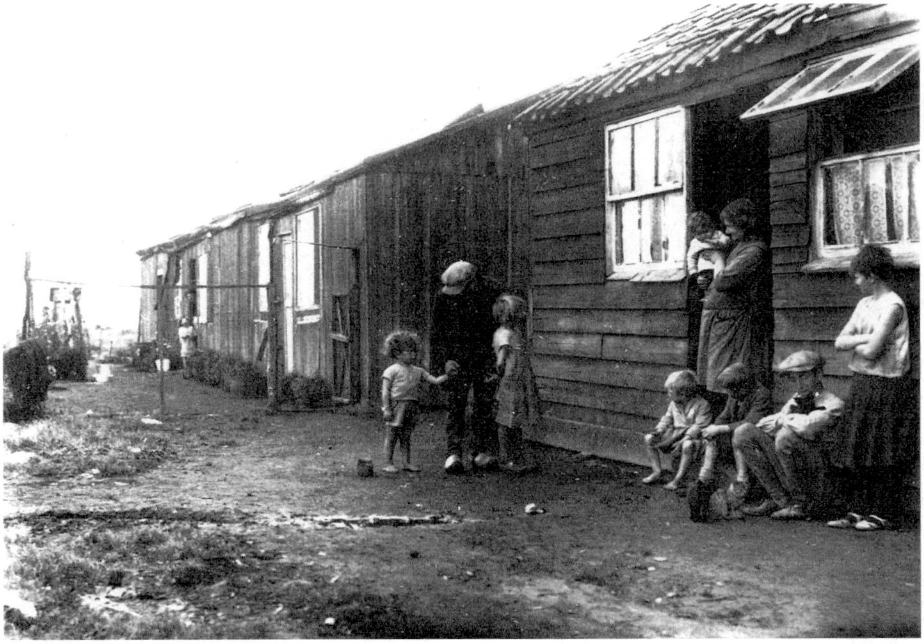

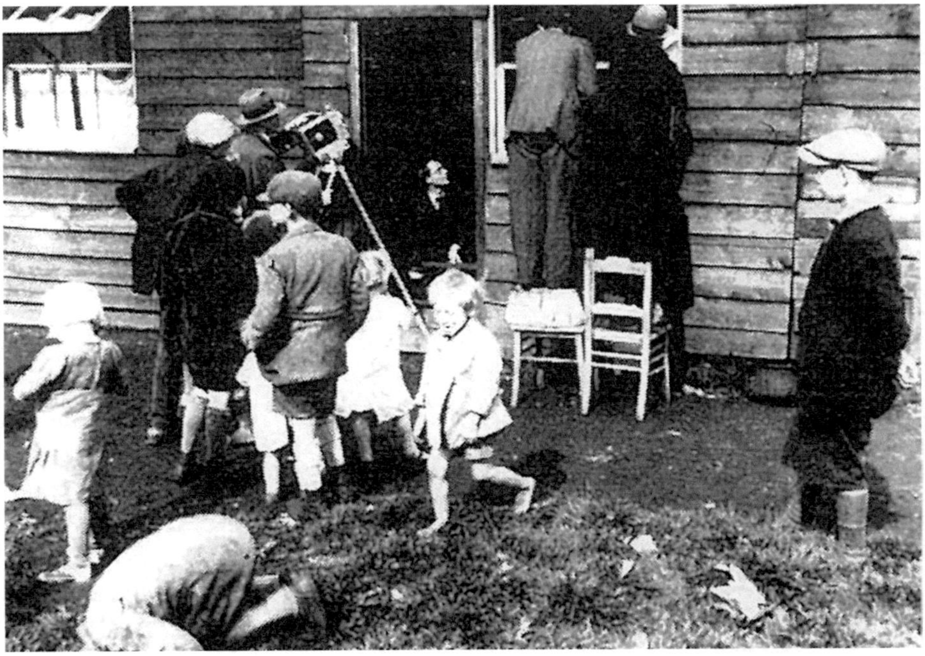

Posing outside the hovels.

Shooting in hovels. The film crew had extra difficulties, while the kids were enjoying themselves.

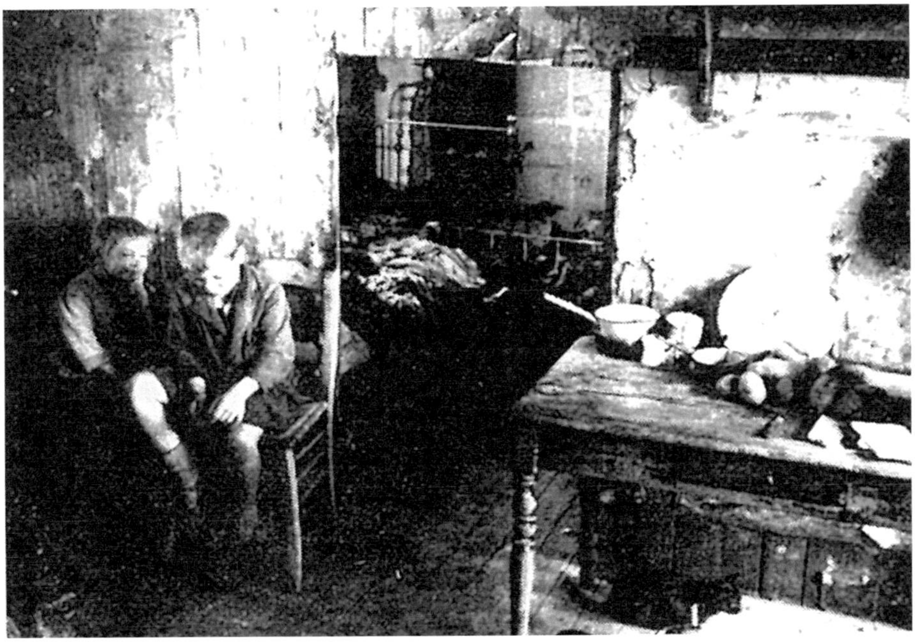

144

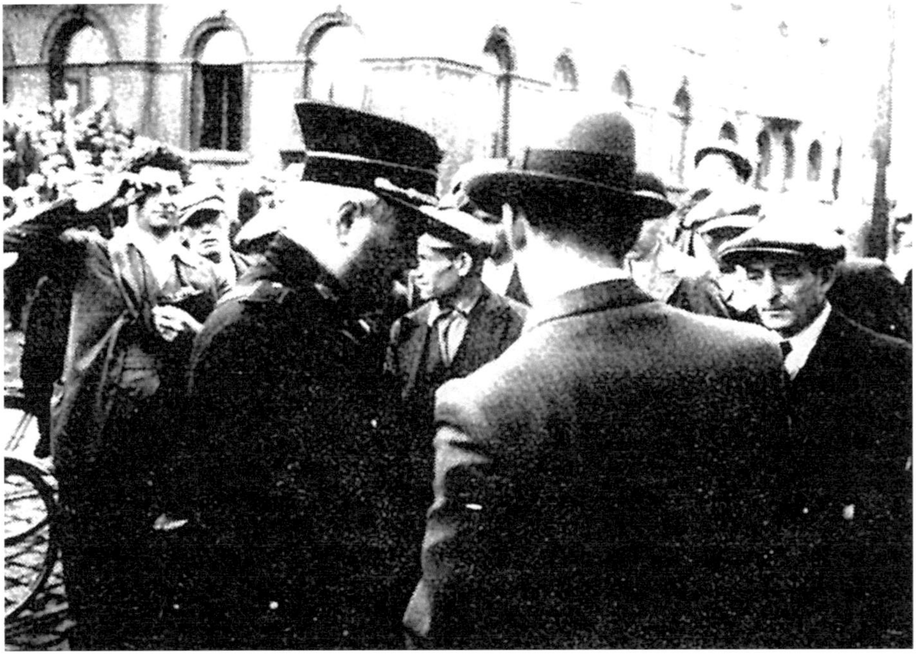

The victimised miners were often forced after the strike to live in hovels. Using the deep focus process Kessels presented the hovel in a poetic way. Notwithstanding the presence of the two kids the photo resembles a still life. Joris Ivens warned against the danger of aestheticising poverty.

A policeman asks cameraman François Rents for his papers. Jean Fonteyne adjusts his spectacles. The party organiser awaits the results.

America: The Workers' Film & Photography League

Russell Campbell

THE WORKERS' FILM and Photo League (WFPL) in the United States, known as the Film and Photo League (FPL) after 1933, was part of the cultural movement sponsored by the Communist International and its affiliated national parties in the inter-war period. Specifically, it was a section of the Workers' International Relief (WIR), American chapter of the Comintern-linked *Internationale Arbeiterhilfe* (IAH) which had been founded at Lenin's instigation in Berlin in 1921.

The WIR's main function was providing food, clothing and shelter for strikers and their families, but like its parent body it engaged also in cultural work. Among left-wing artistic groups supported by the WIR in the early thirties, chiefly in New York, were the Workers' Laboratory Theatre, the Red Dancers, symphony and mandolin orchestras, bands, choirs, art workshops, etc. Film and photography formed part of this cultural spectrum, but because of their potential in reaching mass audiences they were accorded special attention by Communist propaganda theorists such as Willi Münzenberg, head of the IAH.

Münzenberg's commitment to an alternative, working class cinema was expressed in his 1925 pamphlet *Erobert den Film!* (Capture the Film!) and concretely in the extensive activity in film production, distribution and exhibition under taken by IAH organizations in Germany and the Soviet Union during the twenties and early thirties. Priority was also accorded to the sponsorship of worker photographer groups, principally for the purpose of providing visual coverage of the class struggle for the left-wing press; Münzenberg claimed that there were 102 local branches of the *Vereinigung der Arbeiterfotografen* operating in Germany alone in 1931.[2]

In the United States, a New York group known variously as the Workers' Camera League, the Japanese Workers' Camera League, the Workers' Camera Club and the Nippon Camera Club had established ties with the WIR at some point in the late twenties. A report in the *New Masses* of February 1930 described the League as having "about 52 members", holding meetings once a week and exhibitions twice a year. The story continued:

> Only one of the members is a professional photographer. All the other photographers earn their living as food workers, in restaurants, and housework. They have all learned the art of photography in this country. Their spacious headquarters is fully equipped with a dark room, filming room and enlarging room, and all the materials used in the different processes of photography. The club also owns a moving picture projector and screen.
>
> The club was started five years ago by a group of eight people who were interested in photography as an art medium and decided to work together to develop it. When later they found they also had a mutual interest in the revolutionary labour movement, their activities were reorganized to include class struggle propaganda, through the work they were engaged in.

The Workers' Camera League was said to be "particularly interested in photographs of industrial and farm life, natural scenes,

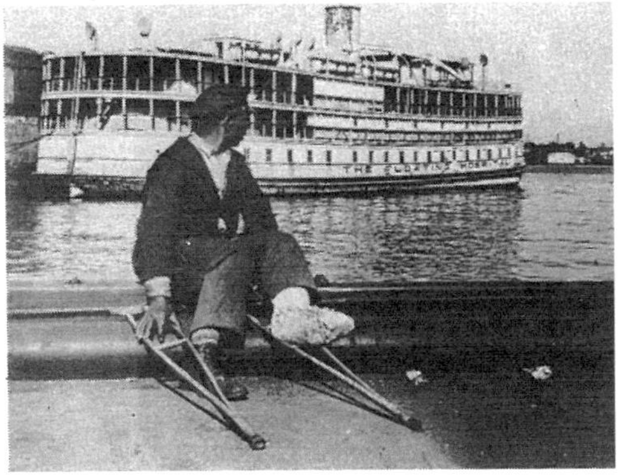

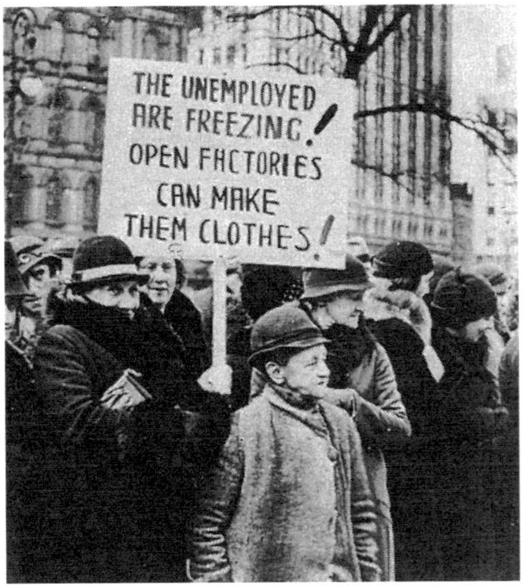

"Floating Hospital", East River Dock, New York City, 1932. Photo: Leo Seltzer.

Unemployed women demonstrate at City Hall, New York City, 1932. Photo: Leo Seltzer.

workers' homes, labour sports, machines, engines, and pictures of individual workers at their tasks". At its Fourth Annual Photo Exhibition, held from December 1929 to January 1930, it displayed photographs "mainly concerned with proletarian life and the class struggle", including "scenes of May Day, demonstrations of food workers, labourers at construction work, a factory, fishermen, etc." It was observed that "class consciousness is the theme of pictures bearing the titles: Sabotage, Movement, Workers, Speed-Up, Exploitation, Red Day, Mobilization to Work, etc." [3]

In the spring of 1930 the Workers' Camera League combined forces with the International Labour Defence, the Communist legal-aid organization parallel to the Workers' International Relief, to form the Labor Defender Photo Group. The purpose of this new association was "to get pictures of the class struggle for use in working-class papers and magazines", particularly the ILD's *Labor Defender*. The secretary announced in July: "Our members are ready with their cameras on the picket line, demonstrations, street meetings, in factories, unemployment lines, and in the homes of workers". A spokesperson for the ILD projected "a network of worker-photo groups throughout the country" with which "we will be able to create a powerful pictorial expression of our struggles which can be used very effectively in building our organization". The group reportedly possessed two motion-picture cameras and was very likely responsible for a small number of workers' newsreels which appeared during 1930.[4]

Both the Defender group and its progenitor were still active late in the autumn. The Workers' Camera League announced an International Photo Exhibition and Dance for November 15, and the issue of *New Masses* for that month reported that the Labor Defender Photo Group had twenty active members, enjoyed the facilities of a studio and darkroom, and conducted a regular photo exchange abroad. The address given for the Defender group was 7, E 14th Street, New York, where the premises (described above) of the Workers' Camera League were formerly located.

In December 1930 the Workers' Camera League was reorganized under the auspices of

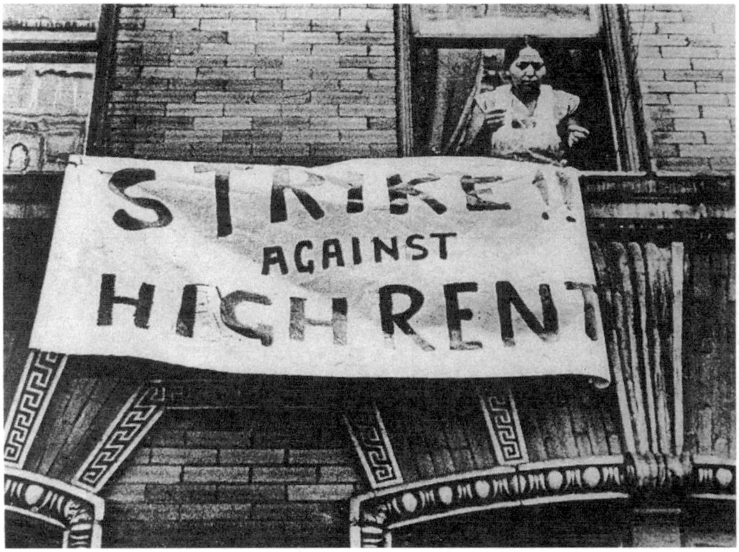

Rent strike, Upper East side, New York City, 1933. Photo: Leo Seltzer.

the WIR and renamed the Workers' Film and Photo League. Apparently the Labor Defender Photo Group was also absorbed into the new body, since nothing more was heard of it. The consolidation resulted in an organisation which, as the economic crisis deepened, could sustain political film making and photography on a permanent, ongoing basis.

League membership, which fluctuated between 75 and 100, consisted of a small core of enthusiasts who spent much of their time (unpaid) at headquarters, and a larger number who appeared at regular meetings and participated on a spare-time basis. According to WFPL organizer Sam Brody, the members were "mainly working-class with a sprinkling of middle-class intellectuals and technicians sympathetic to our progressive goals.[5] Funds came from a variety of sources including membership dues, contributions from the WIR (which usually paid for motion-picture raw stock and processing), donations from sympathizers, benefits (such as costume balls), public film screenings (chiefly of European and Soviet classics), and the sale of stills. New York remained the main centre of activity, but as the decade progressed local League chapters sprang up in most major cities (and some small towns) of the US.

Though film and photo sections of the League usually met separately, their activities were complementary, and there was some overlap of personnel. The (W)FPL's chief work in film was the production of newsreels and documentaries of the class struggle; these were then exhibited by members to workers on picket lines, at communist functions, in union halls, or at meetings of fraternal societies or nationality groups. In addition, the League conducted militant campaigns against fascist and reactionary films and against bourgeois censorship, stimulated and sponsored the writing of radical film criticism, held series screenings of movies significant from a political or aesthetic point of view and offered classes in film history, criticism, and technique.[6]

The goals of the photo section were to provide militant workers (and the unemployed) with the skills to create photographic records of the class struggle, to assure a flow of illustrations for radical publications, to

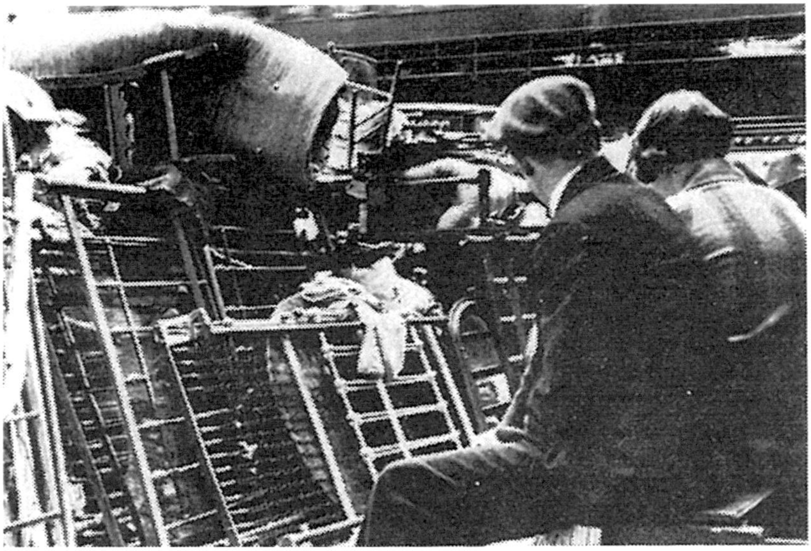

Eviction, Midtown, East Side, New York City, 1933. Photo: Leo Seltzer.

orient established professional photographers more to the left, and to help publicize the work of the WIR, the ILD, and other communist-led organizations. To achieve these objectives, the section provided darkroom facilities, sponsored lectures, ran training courses, held exhibitions, and created channels for the supply of photographs to publishers. In carrying out this programme, the (W)FPL gave a powerful impetus to the growth of both photo-journalism and documentary photography, neither of which was at the time greatly developed.

services. We were able to supply only an average of about 60 photos per month.

The demand is so great that we feel that we could easily place three times as many pictures. This we were not able to do in the past due to the local nature of our photos. Publications soon become glutted with local material. Our photos have appeared in the *Daily Worker*, *Freiheit*, *Der Arbeiter*, *Labor Unity*, *Labor Defender*, *Retter Times Magazine*, *Fortune Magazine*, *Jewish Daily Bulletin*, *Survey Graphic*, and other publications too numerous to mention.[7]

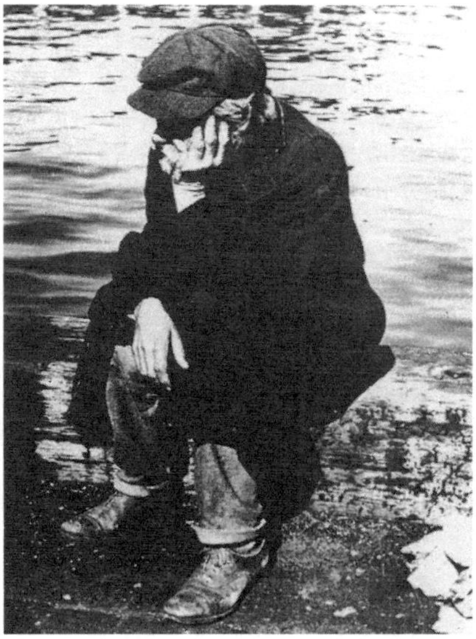

The League photographers discovered a demand for pictures of the class struggle not only from leftist publications, but also from a range of liberal and mainstream journals. Several months after the formation, in September 1934, of a National Photo Exchange as a central clearing house for FPL photographs, it was reported:

> During the past year the New York League has had an unprecedented call for photos from the workers' press, from magazines and book publishers, and from picture

The supply of stills to the commercial press in fact provided a much-needed source of income for League members. One of the more active photographers, Leo Seltzer, recalls:

> Motion-picture film couldn't be sold, no one would want to buy it, the newsreels had their own crews going out. But we could sell photographs, because very often we could get things the commercial news photographers couldn't get. So I took quite a lot of photographs as well as movies, and these could be sold to the newspapers to get a

Unemployed, East River Dock, New York City, 1932, Photo: Leo Seltzer.

few bucks. A lot of times we'd know about a picket line or something that was going to happen, we could scoop the press, and that's what made our photos valuable.[8]

In July 1931 the Workers' Film and Photo League announced a class in photography, to be conducted by Howard D Lester, "a member of the executive board and one of the leading American photographers". This was to be the first of a number of such courses held throughout the League's existence. Advertised as being given "to enable workers to use their knowledge

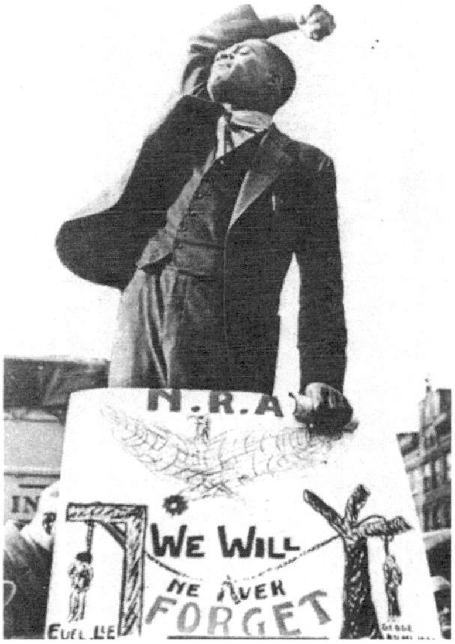

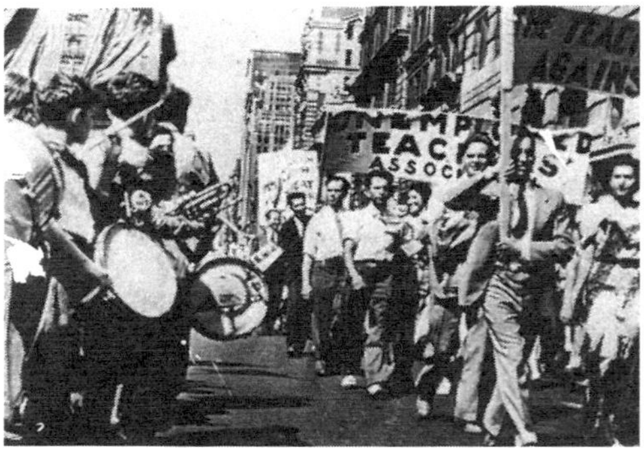

of photography to further the interests of the working-class" or "to meet the pressing need for photo correspondents (for the labour press)", they covered topics such as "camera construction, developing, printing, enlarging, copying, portraiture, press work, etc." At the time instruction in photography was scarcely available at all through other channels.[9]

(W)FPL members were in the forefront of a struggle over what constituted the most vital subject matter of photography. They rejected, of course, the romantic scenes of the Pictorialists and the glamourised products and fashion models of the commercial photographers; they also had little time for the details of nature pictured by "straight" photographers such as Alfred Stieglitz, Paul Strand, and Edward Weston. In 1931 a *Proletarian Photo* exhibition was planned (as an American contribution to a conference to be held in conjunction with the tenth IAH congress in Germany), and it was pointed out:

> It is to be understood that worker photographers intending to exhibit... are to concentrate on the photo of class struggle and proletarian life. No bourgeois portraiture, nudes, landscapes, still lifes, will be exhibited.[10]

In 1933, the scope of (W)FPL work expanded to include pictorial commentary, from a leftist perspective, on Roosevelt's New Deal policies. For a major exhibition in the autumn, the League assembled a collection of photographs intended to portray "*America Today* and all the social and economic transformations it has undergone during the last four years." Subjects which would be covered included unemployment,

Speaker at demonstration in Harlem, New York City, 1933. Photo: Leo Seltzer

May Day Demonstration, 1934. Photo: Leo Seltzer.

housing conditions, militarism, and child misery; and a later appeal for entries was even more explicit, calling for "pictures from North, South, and West, pictures of industry, of farming, of unemployment, misery, stagnation, reforestation camps, child labour, political speakers, the "New Deal", pictures of struggle, strikes, picket lines, demonstrations, etc." Sam Brody, at the opening of the exhibition in November, exulted: "[it] breathes with the fire of workers' struggles and makes the pink-ribbon photographic salon displays look like the last stage of pernicious anaemia."[11]

The extent to which such subjects remained of priority importance to the League is indicated by several published calls for photographs and reports of work from around the country in 1935. In January of that year, the National Photo Exchange stipulated the nature of the material it wished members to submit:

> One – General Photos of Social and Economic Implication. For example: unemployed workers, child misery, bread lines, prostitution, housing conditions, destruction of crops, man power replacing machinery.
> Two – Labour actions. For example: strikes, demonstrations, protest meetings.
> Three – Demonstrations Against War and Fascism.[12]

In the same month the New York FPL announced some forthcoming photo exhibitions. *The City Child* – "undoubtedly the most important photographic document the New York League has made" – was designed to show the "home, school and recreational background of the New York City child" and would be accompanied by statistical charts. *City Streets* was scheduled for April and was envisaged as "a comparative photo exhibit on this subject" in which five photographic organizations of the Metropolitan area would be invited to participate.[13]

The Chicago FPL undertook a photographic survey of living conditions on the South Side, while the Detroit group held a photo display on the subject of the *Forgotten Man*. At the same time, the San Francisco League published an intriguing "proposed plan of work" which outlined a scheme to expand from scenes of proletarian life to embrace a complete pictorial class analysis of American society:

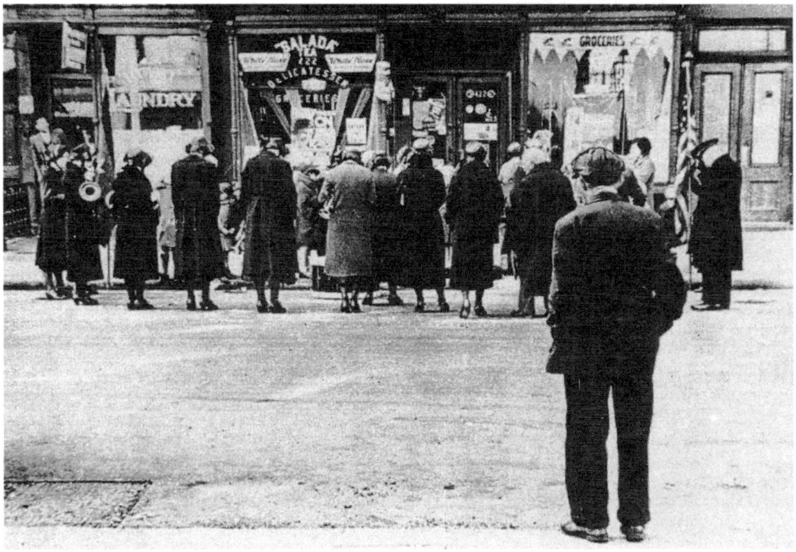

Salvation Army street scene, East Side, New York City, 1932. Photo: Leo Seltzer.

> We want to seek subjects that are powerful and representative factors in the present struggle of social forces. We want bankers, workers, farmers (rich and poor), white-collar workers, policemen, politicians, soldiers, strikers, scabs, wandering youth, stockbrokers, and so on and so on. We want to see them in relation to those things they do, where they live, how they work, how they play, what they read, and what they think. In other words we want to see them as they are in their most significant aspects. This means seeing them in relation to each other. We want this most of all because in this period of economic crisis the whole population is shifting into groups with equally uniform demands. In this shaking down of people into more and more clearly defined classes lies the prospect of vast social change.

Subjects which were specifically suggested included: *l. Waterfront, San Francisco; 2. S.E.R.A. Work Relief; 3. White Collars; 4. The New Legislature; 5. Cold; 6. Disarmament or the Next War; 7. Section 7A (of the National Industrial Recovery Act)*. How successful the project was is not known.[14]

By 1936 the Film and Photo League had been weakened by several splits and the slow demise of the Workers' International Relief. In June of that year the film section of the League moved to its own headquarters, and thereafter little more was heard of it. The photo section, however, seems to have benefited from the break, and, after reorganization, it emerged in strength as the Photo League in 1937. Under the guidance of figures such as Sid Grossman, Aaron Siskind, Sol Libsohn, and Walter Rosenblum, the Photo League sustained the FPL's commitment to documentary photography and left-wing politics for many years to come. Placed on the Attorney General's Subversive List in 1947, it did not finally succumb to witch-hunting pressure until 1951.[15]

This article is based on sections of the author's PhD dissertation, *Radical Cinema in the United States, 1930-1942: The Work of the Film and Photo League, Nykino and Frontier Films*, Ann Arbor, Michigan: University Microfilms. Thanks are due to Jump Cut for permission to reproduce material which previously appeared in the author's articles "Film and Photo League: Radical Cinema in the 30s" and "A Total and Realistic Experience: Interview with Leo Seltzer", *Jump Cut* No. 14, 1977.

2. Willi Münzenberg, *Solidaritat: Zehn Jahre Internationale Arbeiterhilfe, 1921-1931*. Berlin: Neuer Deutscher Verlag, 1931, p.87.
3. *New Masses* V, No.8, January 1930, p.20; and *New Masses* V, No.9. February 1930, *p.20*.
4. *New Masses* VI, No.2, July 1930, p.22; *Labor Defender*, April 1930, p.76.
5. Samuel Brody, in: Tony Safford, "The Camera as a Weapon in the Class Struggle: Interview with Samuel Brody", *Jump Cut* No.14, 1977, p.28.
6. For further information on the film activities of the League cf. the author's dissertation and articles cited above.
7. "Send Photos to the National Exchange!", in: *Filmfront* 1, No.2, January 7, 1935, p.12.
8. Leo Seltzer, in: Russell Campbell, "A Total and Realistic Experience: Interview with Leo Seltzer", op.cit., p.26.
9. *New Masses* VII, No.2, July 1931, p.21; *Daily Worker*, October 12, 1934, p 5, and April 4, 1935, p.5.
10. *New Masses* VII, No.1, June 1931, p.22.
11. *Daily Worker*, August 15, 1933, p.5; October 21, 1933, p.7; and November 13, 1933, p.5.
12. "Send Photos to the National Exchange!", op.cit.
13. "New York Photo Activities" in: *Filmfront* 1, No.3, January 28, 1935, p.14.
14. *Filmfront* 1, No.2, January 7, 1935, p.13; and 1, No.5, March 15, 1935, p.9.
15. On the Photo League see its publication *Photo Notes* (reprinted in one volume by the Visual Studies Workshop, Rochester, N.Y.) Anne Tucker, "Photographic Crossroads: The Photo League" in: *Journal of the National Gallery of Canada*, No.25, April 6, 1978; and Anne Tucker's forthcoming book *Photographic Crossroads: The Photo League* (Knopf).

Scotland: Workers' Photography

Douglas Allen

LATELY WE'VE SEEN the emergence of a fair amount of material that points to Scotland as major centre of workers' culture in the first half of this century. Recent "rediscoveries" of the heritage left by the Glasgow Workers' Theatre Group (1937-40), Glasgow Unity Theatre (1941-48) and the Kino Film Group (1936-39) – and especially the outstanding political films made for the latter by Helen Biggar and Norman McLaren – have helped shift our view of Scottish political culture. Where previously the Orpheus Choir stood alone as representing the "acceptable face" of socialism, we now find beneath it a wealth of more radical, hard-hitting, socialist cultural activities.[1]

What kind of place did photography have in this culture? One must admit that the first glance is not encouraging, with only the very odd newspaper item giving a hint of what might have taken place. An advert in *Forward* for 7 November 1931, for example, tells us that the Friends of the Soviet Union *Russian Revolution Celebrations* the next night were to include – along with a performance by the Glasgow Workers' Theatre Movement – "a poster display and photographs". From this one can assume that there must have been some interest in the visual aspects of politics in the local Communist Party circles in the early 30s. For the later 30s – Glasgow's most prolific cultural period – and from the surviving documentary evidence the following picture of worker photography emerges.

There would appear to be no distinct "branch" of the Workers' Film and Photo League (FPL) in Scotland. Certainly Helen Biggar supplied film of the 1936 Scottish hunger marchers for the FPL compilation *March Against Starvation*; she and Norman McLaren may even have dabbled in photographic experiments at their Glasgow School of Art base (from which emerged their Kino films like *Hell Unlimited*); and another Kino member, Jimmy Fenton, had an amateur interest in photography that developed into a full-time post-war business. But there is no evidence of any commitment of Kino to develop an aesthetic of photography or to use it as a political weapon, in the same imaginative manner as their films – only at best as an adjunct, to supply the raw material or as publicity.

Working on a similar "independent" basis were two figures from the grassroots of the labour movement, who created the unlikely-sounding photographic team of Tarr and Trott. Bert Trott remembers his interest in photography growing from the self-help, self-education, self-expression ethos of the Glasgow working-class movement that was to create such a wealth of cultural activism. The buying of a second-hand camera, the learning from sympathetic fellow amateurs, the experimentation in all techniques, the commissions from clubs, co-ops and political parties – it was all part of the challenge, the struggle for self expression. Again there was no notion of photography as a means of intervention in the contemporary political struggles – of recording them or influencing their outcome. Nevertheless the material that Trott leaves us is itself of major value – a record of the activities of the Glasgow Workers' Theatre Group, with whom he acted.

Those who were documenting the numerous struggles of the day were, of course, the professional newspaper photographers. Some were sympathetic to the labour movement. Jack Gibson for example, who worked for *Scottish Daily Express*, acted with some of the socialist drama groups and became the main photographic chronicler of *Glasgow Unity's* progress in the 40s. But as he himself admits, it was for arch bourgeois and reactionary bodies that they worked (when there was employment, that is), and the official Scottish labour movement seemed to take little interest in countering them. Only occasionally in the pages of the *Daily Worker* could the Scottish working class see the photographic record of its struggle; for the major local paper *Forward* was almost totally lacking in photographic coverage, whether for reasons of finance or philistinism.

Where workers' photography did develop, it was – as with most of the other cultural activities – from the grass-roots, and unofficially. In Scotland though, it never reached the same maturity as the film and theatre side of the movement, so promising beginnings were unfulfilled when the cultural milieu that had inspired it died in the post-war world. How to move beyond the stage it had reached – from photography as self-expression to photography as means of intervention – is the task facing activists today. How to achieve that without the strong cultural base that inspired that initial movement, is the main problem to be overcome.

1 See Douglas Allen, editor, "A Political Scottish Culture?" *New Edinburgh Review* 40, Spring 1978, for articles on GWTG, Unity, Biggar and McLaren; also John Hill, "Towards a Scottish People's Theatre: The Rise and Fall of Glasgow Unity", *Theatre Quarterly* 27, Autumn 1977. There have been showings of British political films of the thirties from the National Film Archive at the NFT, and at the Edinburgh Film Festival, 1977. Note that the Workers' Theatre Group is a distinctive popular front era body, unconnected with the earlier CP Workers' Theatre Movement.

Thanks for information to Bert Trott, Jack Gibson, Norman and Mamie Thomson.

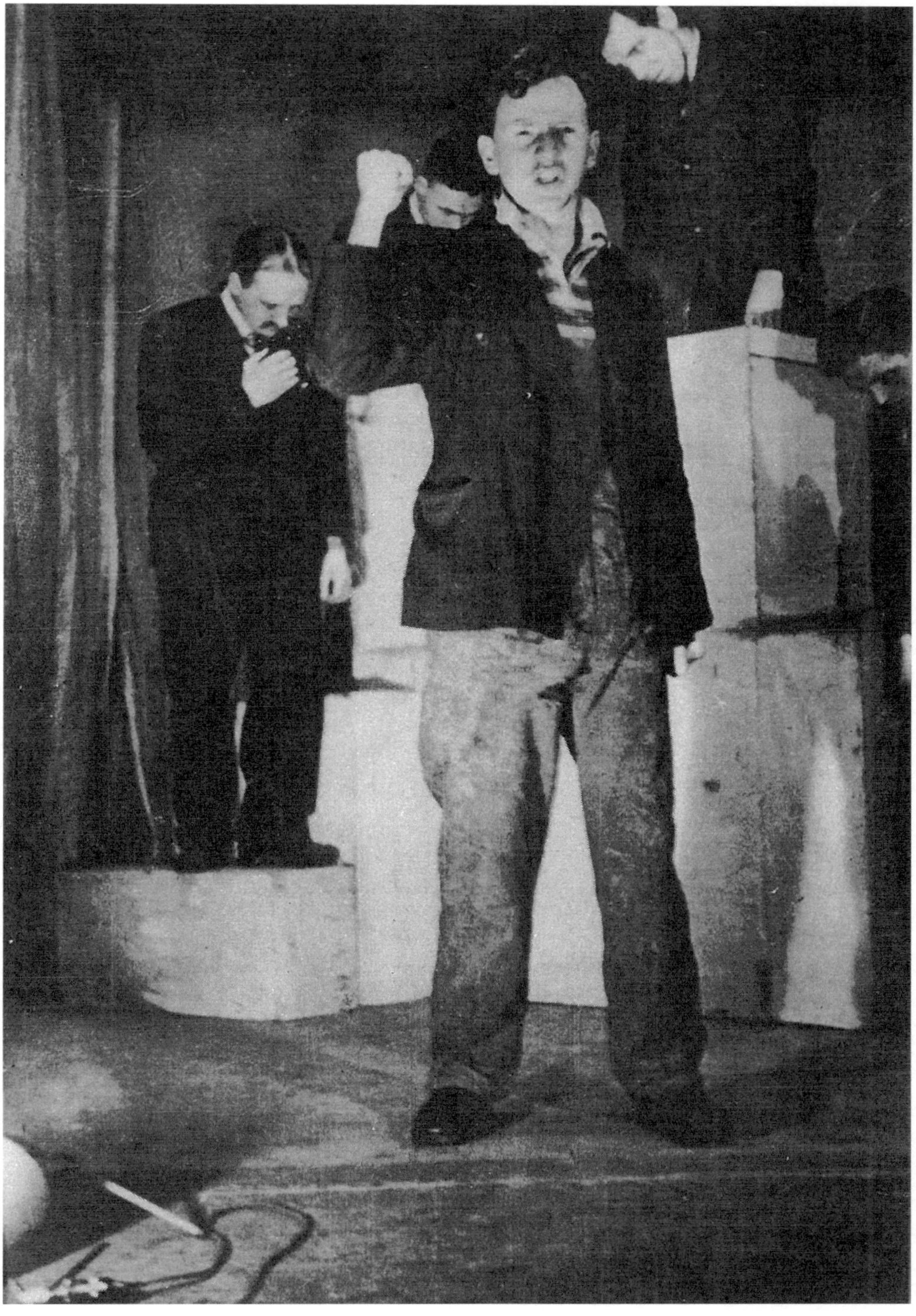

Albert Maltby, *Rehearsal*, Glasgow Workers' Theatre Group, c.1938. Photo: Bert Trott.

England: The Workers' Film and Photo League

Terry Dennett

THE PRESENT ARTICLE is part of a more extended study of the cultural politics of the interwar period being carried out by Photography Workshop, a study which covers not only film and photography but also agitprop art and the independent socialist educational movement *Proletcult*.

Many of the details given below, particularly the various developments leading up to the foundation of the Workers' Film and Photo League, were gathered during two of our earlier projects on photography: *The 1926 General Strike* (1975–6) and *The Thirties and Today* (1976–7). Material relating to the League itself has been derived partly from a study of the archive of films and documents recently discovered by Jonathan Lewis and Elizabeth Taylor Mead of Metropolis Pictures,[1] and partly from conversations with surviving League members who have now been traced.[2]

The work of earlier investigators has also proved invaluable, particularly the pioneering research of Bert Hogenkamp[3] and the excellent film analysis of Vicky Wegg-Prosser.[4] Both their efforts have provided a firm foundation for any future work in this area.

Several other projects and publications related to the work of the League and to left film in the twenties and thirties are also in progress: Ms Wegg-Prosser has made a compilation of the League's films, presented in the next article; Photography Workshop is preparing a master set of negatives and prints of League documents and surviving photographs, (which will also include frame stills made from the original films); an exhibition will also be available shortly.[5] Finally, several books are now scheduled for publication.[6]

A great deal has been achieved in the short period since the rediscovery of the League films but much still remains to be done, especially in relation to the movement's international use of still photographs. More in-depth research is also required into the work of the Russian, Japanese and French Worker Photographer groups, and into the very important *Proletcult* movement headed by A A Bogdanov, a photographer and cultural theoretician whose work is deserving of far more attention than it has hitherto received.

The recent rediscovery of the archives of the Film and Photo League (FPL) brings to light once again a whole period of left-wing cultural politics and grassroots activism which has largely been ignored as a route for socialist agitation by today's dogmatic seekers after parliamentary socialism. It highlights in particular the very real successes of the cultural policies of the Communist International (Comintern) around the time of its "left turn" from 1928-1935, a period which saw the development of a whole host of experiments in working class culture,[7] carried out by the various national communist parties under the umbrella of two Comintern linked organisations: the Workers' International Relief (WIR) and the *Mezhdunarodnaya Organisaziya Pomoschchi Bortsam Revolyutsion* (MOPR).[8] These organizations and others associated with them, such as the International Labour Defence (ILD), were avidly internationalist in character and similarly structured in each country. This fact enabled a more or less unified body of socialist cultural theory and practice to be developed and spread very rapidly to most countries with an organized labour movement.

The guiding political principle behind such activity was the stratagem of the "united front

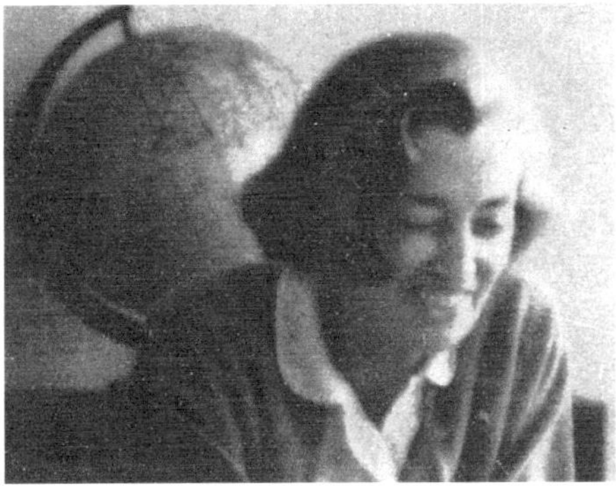

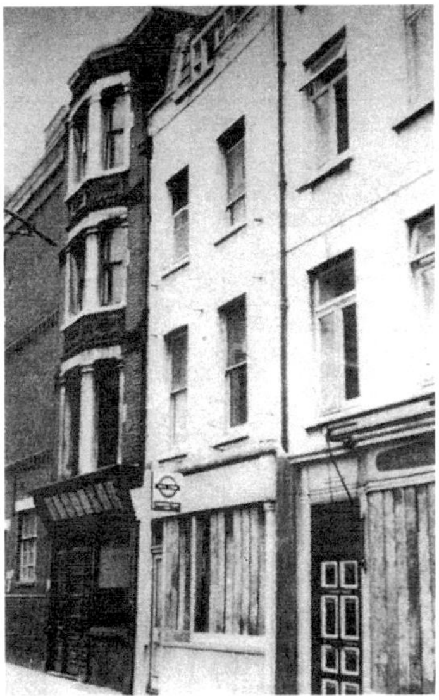

from below" [9] and the policy of "class against class", which sought to mobilize and politicize the broadest possible sections of the working class by appealing to them directly as a class, irrespective of the political parties to which they belonged.

For this purpose a number of broad national and international organizations came into being: the Class War Prisoners' Aid Society, the National Unemployed Workers' Movement, as well as those mentioned above. These created a very favourable atmosphere for agitational socialist art and culture raised on a popular basis the notion of autonomous working class organization and direct action as a means of struggle.[10]

The Film and Photo Leagues [11] were seen as part of this broad agitational movement, being constituted in some countries as a branch of the WIR, and in others as part of either the ILD or the MOPR.

The internationalism of all these organizations exerted a profound effect on the left movement in Britain, especially at grass roots level where the existence of local WIR and ILD branches served as a means of passing on news and ideas from other countries and establishing direct links between workers in various trades and industries. Thus the miners in Belgium were aware of the struggle in the Durham coalfields and the Durham miners were aware of and contributed to the struggles of the German miners.[12] Such links, especially when they resulted in personal contact, through attendances at conferences or by exchange of correspondence, promoted activity and discussion around political and cultural issues which went far beyond anything which previously existed in Britain. This helped to develop a completely fresh approach to political and social agitation and resulted in the formulation of new methods of organizing campaigns, based on the use of contemporary media (graphic arts, music, theatre, film and photography). Most important in this respect was the introduction of an illustrated socialist literature, in particular the development of the WIR monthly illustrated bulletin which is said to have had a world wide circulation of a quarter of a million copies.[13] In Britain this was called *Soviet Russia Pictorial* (1923-24) and then *Workers' International Pictorial* (1924-25). In Germany, the most important centre for its production, it was called *Sowjet-Russland im Bild* (1921-22), which became *Sichel und Hammer* (1922-25), the precursor of the mass circulation pictorial *Arbeiter Illustrierte Zeitung* (AIZ) (1925-33),[14] a publication which fostered two important developments in Britain. These were the agitational illustrations of the *Sunday Worker*,[15] and the attempt to start a British illustrated workers' magazine, the short-lived *Workers' Illustrated News* (WIN).

Film, photography and the Workers' International Relief

From its inception the WIR paid great attention to the development of its own mass media, especially to the use of film which it saw as an important means of reaching a mass audience. Early in its development an international film department was set up, both to produce and distribute WIR films and to encourage the various national sections to use them as part of their work. Each section was urged to develop a simple system of distribution suited to its own conditions: "The French Committee purchased a motor van with cinema apparatus and toured France from town to town...", the "German national section purchased a cinema situated in the heart of the working class quarter of Berlin." [16] In Britain films were shown at meetings, mostly in private halls, though some discussion apparently took place about the purchase of a van for use as a mobile cinema in the same manner as the French section.[17]

Opposite, left: Jean Ross, Secretary of the Workers' Film and Photo League. Photo: courtesy of Mrs. Bernel.

Opposite, right: Darkroom and meeting place of the League's Central London group, at 4 Parton Street, WC2. (Photography Workshop collection.)

Vigorous efforts were also made to encourage the use of still photography, both as a means of documenting the work of the WIR and in order to build up a central collection of photographs depicting working class struggles and activity of use in appeals, the left press etc. Copies of these photographs were apparently sent to the headquarters in Berlin.[18]

In Bethnal Green in East London an attempt was made within the WIR to start a film group.[19] This was apparently in response to a talk given by WIR secretary Edgar T Whitehead on the need for film in the organization's work. Four members met and decided to constitute themselves into a production unit but due to lack of funds were unable to secure enough reliable equipment and film stock to put this into effect; instead they voted to make propaganda lantern slide shows. The first of these was entitled *How the workers live* and depicted poor housing conditions in Bethnal Green, Whitechapel and surrounding districts and urged the formation of tenants' action groups and the setting up of a workers' communal kitchen. The negatives from which these slides were made were later passed onto the *Sunday Worker* and may possibly have been among those used on its pictorial back page.[20] Nothing more is known about this venture in East London, but the value of the lantern slide was recognized by many at the time, especially by organizations like the Plebs League and individuals such as William Paul (editor of the *Sunday Worker*) who developed independently a number of slide lectures on socialist themes and later was credited with making a slide set on the Paris Commune, copied from original photos of the event which he found in Paris.[21] An important development in this field was the announcement in 1928 by the International Red Aid of the lantern film (the film strip), a method which they hoped to adopt throughout their organization as a simple way of giving illustrated talks.[22]

These experiments, although they were to shape the thinking of those who came later, did not in themselves constitute an attempt

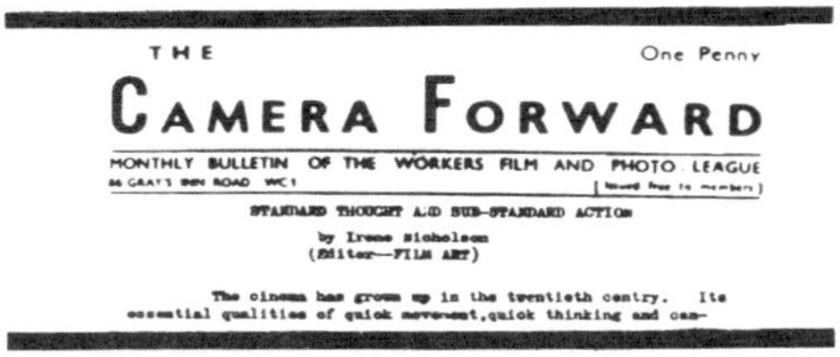

THE — One Penny

CAMERA FORWARD

MONTHLY BULLETIN OF THE WORKERS FILM AND PHOTO LEAGUE

STANDARD THOUGHT AND SUB-STANDARD ACTION

by Irene Nicholson
(Editor—FILM ART)

The cinema has grown up in the twentieth centry. Its essential qualities of quick movement, quick thinking and con-

Front page of the first issue of The Workers' Film and Photo League Bulletin, *The Camera Forward*, 1935/6? (Hugh Cuthbertson collection.)

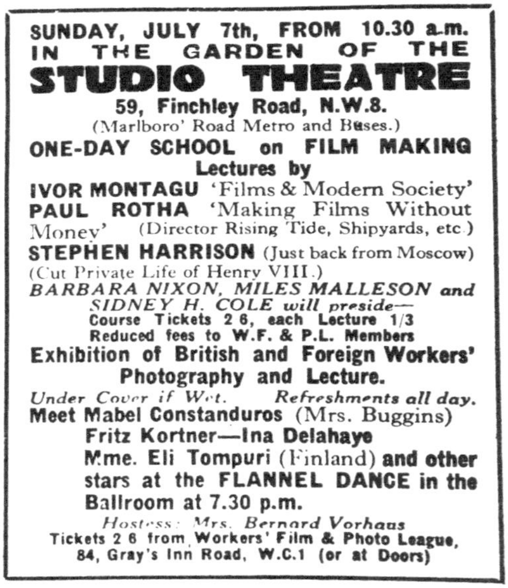

SUNDAY, JULY 7th, FROM 10.30 a.m.
IN THE GARDEN OF THE
STUDIO THEATRE
59, Finchley Road, N.W.8.
('Marlboro' Road Metro and Buses.)
ONE-DAY SCHOOL on FILM MAKING
Lectures by
IVOR MONTAGU 'Films & Modern Society'
PAUL ROTHA 'Making Films Without Money' (Director Rising Tide, Shipyards, etc.)
STEPHEN HARRISON (Just back from Moscow) (Cut Private Life of Henry VIII.)
BARBARA NIXON, MILES MALLESON and SIDNEY H. COLE will preside—
Course Tickets 2/6, each Lecture 1/3
Reduced fees to W.F. & P.L. Members
Exhibition of British and Foreign Workers' Photography and Lecture.
Under Cover if Wet. *Refreshments all day.*
Meet Mabel Constanduros (Mrs. Buggins)
Fritz Kortner—Ina Delahaye
Mme. Eli Tompuri (Finland) and other stars at the FLANNEL DANCE in the Ballroom at 7.30 p.m.
Hostess: Mrs. Bernard Vorhaus
Tickets 2/6 from Workers' Film & Photo League, 84, Gray's Inn Road, W.C.1 (or at Doors)

Announcement of an early Film School, run by the League. (Hugh Cuthbertson collection.)

to initiate a film and photography movement in Britain. This didn't occur until much later, not in fact until after the main centres of the workers' photography movement in Germany had been destroyed, following Hitler's rise to power in 1933.[23]

The Foundation of the Kino Production Group and the Workers' Film and Photo League

Following this defeat, the Soviet Union became the main centre for left cultural initiatives and provided the stimulus for the formation of a Film and Photo League in Britain. This took place as a result of a meeting of the International Workers' Theatre Movement Olympiad which was held in Moscow in May 1933.[24] Among the events at this meeting was a film conference organized by the Cinema Bureau of the Moscow-based International Union of Revolutionary Theatres (IURT). The main focus of this conference was the discussion of the poor state of workers' film organizations in many countries, and the possibilities for its restructuring. The conference decided that under the prevailing conditions only the Workers' Theatre Movement (WTM), which was already well developed in many countries, was likely to be able to provide the necessary degree of co-ordination and expertise which would bring about viable developments in workers' film. The theatre movements were therefore instructed to start Film and Photo Leagues in their respective countries, based apparently on the then successful American Film and Photo League.[25]

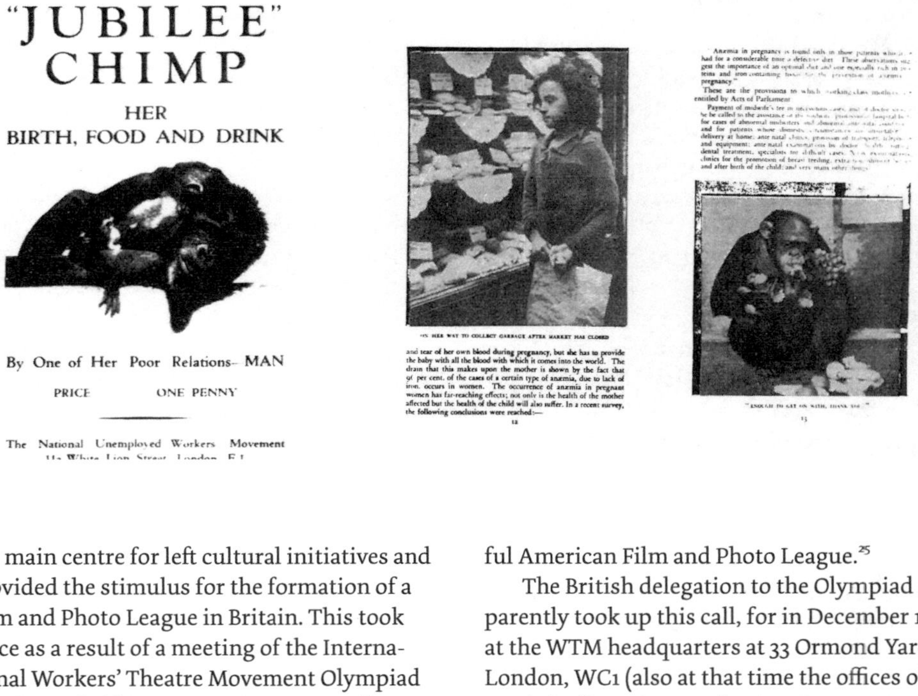

National Unemployed Workers' Movement (NUWM) agitational pamphlet with photos by WFPL member John Maltby (left and right; centre by Edith Tudor-Hart – Ed.)

The British delegation to the Olympiad apparently took up this call, for in December 1933 at the WTM headquarters at 33 Ormond Yard, London, WC1 (also at that time the offices of the WIR) the first Kino Production Group meetings were held.[26] Discussions took place regularly thereafter, especially around the possibilities of film production and the organization of showings of a newly acquired Russian film

Battleship Potemkin.[27] Audiences were enthusiastic everywhere, despite the group's general lack of experience and the technical limitations of their equipment. An enormous amount of ingenuity was often required to show films during this period both because of the frequent police raids and because of the poor facilities available in the unlicensed halls and rooms which had to be used in order to show films without a censor's certificate. Often the group would turn up to show a film and find the building had only gas lighting. Electricity then had to be "borrowed" (often illegally) from a nearby building. In one case this involved stretching a cable high across a busy main road.Spurred on by these initial successes they acquired another film, *The General Line*, early in 1934 and commenced an intensive series of showings, giving 120 presentations in the first six months of operation. These sessions took the form not simply of film shows but of film meetings with a speaker, a relatively new departure which served to further increase the already intensive police harassment and interference which the group encountered.[28]

In the summer of 1934, the group set up its first operational production unit, making two one-reel films, *Hunger March* and *Bread*, and the first of its Workers' Newsreels.[29] In November 1934 the production unit held talks with members of the Workers' Camera Club[30] and the two agreed to merge and form the Workers' Film and Photo League.[31] The remaining members not directly concerned with making films constituted themselves into a distribution group, later to become Kino Films (1935) Limited.[32]

The Workers' Film and Photo League (1934-35)

The newly formed League, apparently inspired by examples of the American, Japanese and German movements, and probably taking its name from the former[33] moved into a room at 84 Grays Inn Road, London, WC1[34] and set about producing and popularizing "films and photos of working class interest."[35] During its first few meetings future policy was formulated and codified into a constitution and manifesto. The organization also applied for registration under the Business Names Act, the League's first secretary, Jean Ross,[36] being named as the applicant. Its first public statement *The Manifesto of the Workers' Film and Photo League* proclaimed the League's aims in a forthright manner:

> ...up to now the making of films in this country has been almost entirely monopolised by the capitalist class. What have they done with this monopoly? They have used it to give us a capitalist view of life; to show us life from a distorted angle. They have used it to glorify and justify their own parasite existence. Above all, they have used it to make us forget our own lives.
>
> Obviously, most people go to films to be entertained or to learn something. But there is nothing entertaining or instructive in the empty, hysterical love affairs of decadent society women and their gangster or gigolo lovers – the subject of most commercial films. We have only to compare any of the great Russian films like *Potemkin* or *The General Line* with any English or American commercial film to prove that there is more real heroism and real drama in the daily lives of our class – in the class which is making history – than in anything the capitalist class can show us.
>
> Workers' Film and Photo League thinks the time has come for workers to produce films and photos of their own. Films and photos showing their own lives, their own problems, their own organized efforts to solve these problems.
>
> ...Workers' Film and Photo League exists to provide this co-ordination.

The membership fee, which was apparently the sole source of funds, apart from donations from members' wages, was the princely sum of 2/6d per annum, including the subscription to a "monthly bulletin" which evidently only appeared twice.[37]

Film activities were also outlined in the *Manifesto*:

> The League will produce its own films giving a true picture of life today, recording the industrial and living conditions of the British workers and the struggle of the employed and unemployed to improve their conditions.
>
> It will popularize the great Russian films and endeavour to exhibit them to the widest possible audiences.
>
> It will carry out criticism of current commercial films in the press and its own literature and expose films of a militarist, fascist or anti-working class nature.

During 1935 League members, putting some of these aims into practice, were jointly involved in a number of activities of current political concern, utilizing both still and movie cameras. This centred especially around events organized against the pomp and ceremony of the jubilee, which many considered to be an insult to the conditions suffered by the unemployed. Walter Holmes,[38] a *Daily Worker* columnist, recalls one such incident which League members were asked to film:

> A number of people associated with the Party (CPGB) thought up an ingenious way to demonstrate against the jubilee and to draw attention to the existence of working class poverty. They constructed a "two-faced" "banner" consisting of two canvas sheets laced together at the corners. The outer surfaces were printed with a typical royal slogan *God save the King*; this covered the inner banner which contained a more suitable comment which would be revealed when the corner strings attached to the banner were released. The banner was hung from a hired office window adjacent to the law courts in Fleet Street and caused a big stir when the outer cover was pulled away, right in front of the royal coach, revealing the proclamation *workers of the world unite*, and *twenty-five years of hunger and want*. Film was successfully taken by members of the League who were stationed under the banner.

League photographer John Maltby recalls a still photography project of the period:[39]

> I was asked by Jean Ross to provide illustrations for a pamphlet being produced by the National Unemployed Workers' Movement. This was to contrast the great concern shown for animal welfare with the utter disregard for the health of working people. At that time a new baby chimp, Jubilee, had been born at the zoo; this was front page news and a lot of trouble was taken to ensure its well-being. I was smuggled into the animal quarters by a sympathetic zoo official and managed to get pictures of mother and baby tucking into the daily ration of grapes, oranges and other goodies. These pictures were published in the pamphlet with great effect.

The Film and Photo League 1935-39

In October 1935 the organization underwent the first of its many internal "reorganizations" when a proposal was put to the members to drop the word *workers* from its title. This proposal was carried and the organization became simply the Film and Photo League, and Jean Ross its first secretary stepped down to allow Albert Pizer (apparently the proposer of the change of name) to occupy the position. Several interesting "coincidences" point to this being more than simply a change of

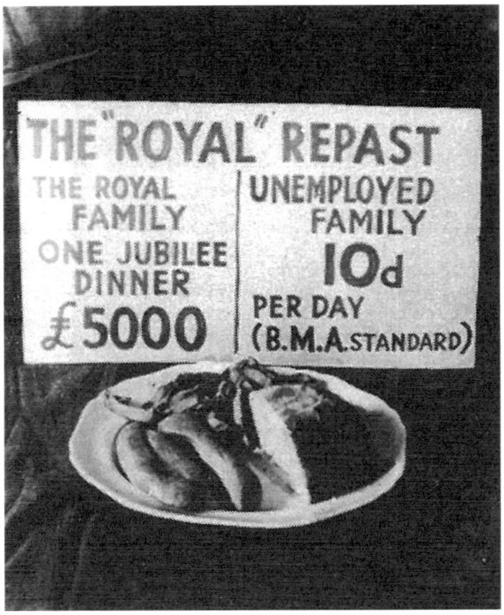

1

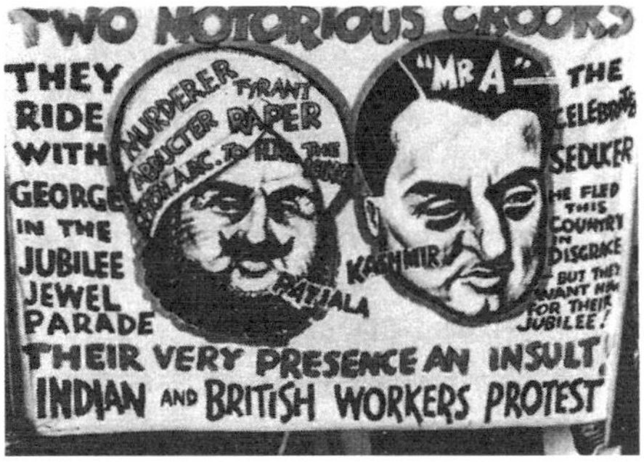

2

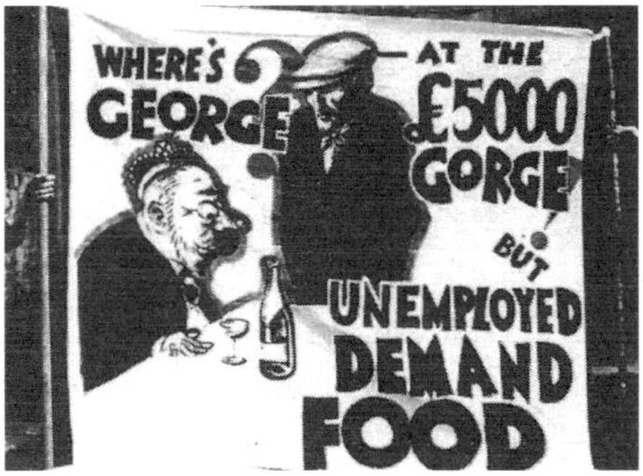

3

name. Most probably it was an attempt to bring the League into line with the changes in policy within the Communist left, following the decision of the Seventh Congress of the Communist International (July 1935) to abandon its previous policy of "class against class" and institute the tactics of a multi-class "popular front",[40] in which the word "workers" would obviously be unacceptable. The League's manifesto was also completely redrafted into a much blander statement of intent, devoid of all previous phrases of proletarian fervour.

During those early days a great deal of still photography was carried out, probably because the strongest contingent of the League were former members of the Workers' Camera Club. Documents from the archives that have survived indicate that a number of groups existed in different parts of the country; one in Manchester styling itself The Manchester Film and Photo League, and a very active group in Hull (part of the Hull Workers' Film Society, an early affiliate of the London League) which was said to be making "copies of the American Film and Photo League photos." [41] It is clear that at this time also many individuals who were employed in film, photography and other media, gave their services freely to the League. Two such people were professional photographers – John Maltby (London) and Helen Musgrove (Oxford); another apparently was Edith Tudor-Hart (sister of the noted animal photographer Suschitzky).

From secondary documentary evidence it is also clear that extensive stills coverage was carried out by various groups between 1934 and 1938. Unfortunately none of this archive appears to have survived or has not yet come to light, though there is some indication that at least part of it may be in the possession of a former League member who is yet to be traced.[42] During the present investigation, however, a number of stills and a few negatives have been discovered. These enable us at least to have a glimpse of the type of photography carried out by the League. Various documents

Part of the WFPL "celebration" of the 1935 Jubilee: 1. Agitational "still life" set up by Jean Ross. 2 and 3 Anti-jubilee pictorial banners. Photos: John Maltby.

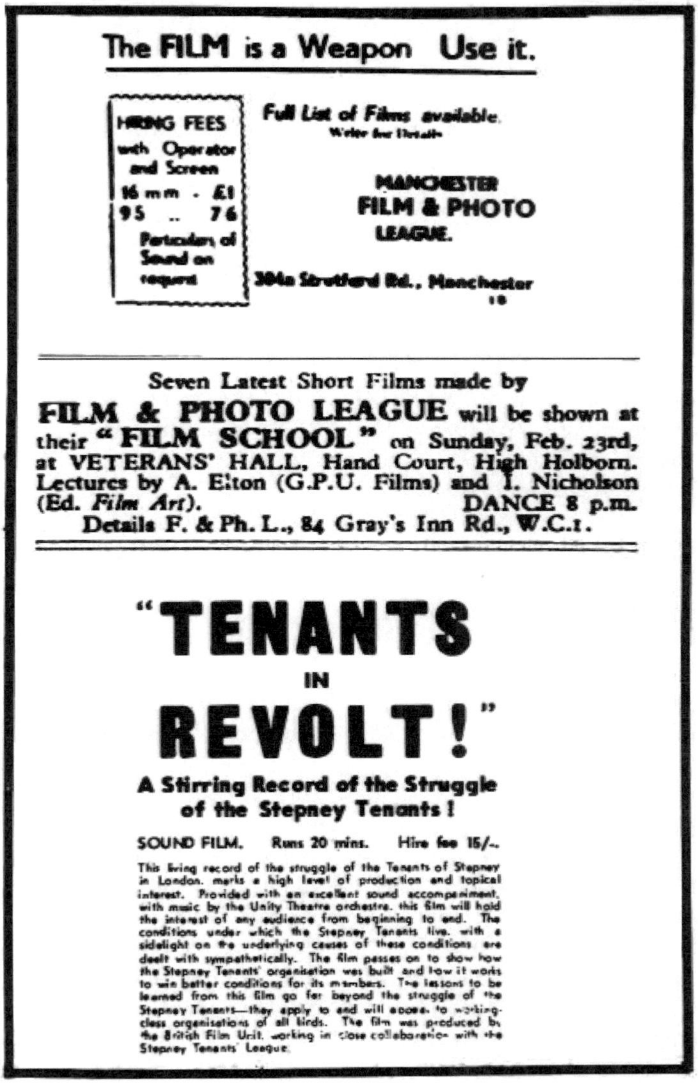

The FILM is a Weapon Use it.

HIRING FEES with Operator and Screen
16 mm - £1
9.5 .. 7/6
Particulars of Sound on request

Full List of Films available.
Write for Details

MANCHESTER FILM & PHOTO LEAGUE.

304a Stretford Rd., Manchester 16

Seven Latest Short Films made by FILM & PHOTO LEAGUE will be shown at their "FILM SCHOOL" on Sunday, Feb. 23rd, at VETERANS' HALL, Hand Court, High Holborn. Lectures by A. Elton (G.P.U. Films) and I. Nicholson (Ed. *Film Art*). DANCE 8 p.m.
Details F. & Ph. L., 84 Gray's Inn Rd., W.C.1.

"TENANTS IN REVOLT!"

A Stirring Record of the Struggle of the Stepney Tenants!

SOUND FILM. Runs 20 mins. Hire fee 15/-.

This living record of the struggle of the Tenants of Stepney in London, marks a high level of production and topical interest. Provided with an excellent sound accompaniment, with music by the Unity Theatre orchestra, this film will hold the interest of any audience from beginning to end. The conditions under which the Stepney Tenants live, with a sidelight on the underlying causes of these conditions are dealt with sympathetically. The film passes on to show how the Stepney Tenants' organisation was built and how it works to win better conditions for its members. The lessons to be learned from this film go far beyond the struggle of the Stepney Tenants—they apply to and will appeal to working-class organisations of all kinds. The film was produced by the British Film Unit, working in close collaboration with the Stepney Tenants' League.

Three of the documents found in the Hugh Cuthbertson collection.

also give some indication of the nature of worker photography as seen within the League. Of particular importance are the statements in the WFPL *Manifesto* issued in 1935 by Jean Ross which read:

> The League will hold exhibitions of photographs all over the country. It will invite exhibits from workers of other countries and arrange for British workers' photographs also to be exhibited and published abroad.
>
> It will organize competitions of photographs of working class interest which will be judged as much on their social value as on their technical merit.
>
> It will arrange for shop window displays of news photographs and endeavour to distribute these to the widest possible sections of the press both in this country and abroad.
>
> It will arrange popular lectures both on films and photography to working class organizations and societies.
>
> It will assist local production groups to obtain film and photo apparatus and technical instruction.

This was apparently to be carried out by collecting and taking photographs which could be used by the left press and in pamphlets and exhibitions. Central to this was the importance placed upon photographs of typical conditions taken by the workers themselves:

> There are thousands of workers in this country who own cameras, but who only use them for taking an occasional snapshot. If even a number of them were to photograph the conditions around them – in the factories, workshops, dockyards, railways and country side, in their streets – we should have an invaluable record of working class life, which would enable workers in different branches of industry to understand each other's problems. This vivid understanding of the problems of other workers will help to bring the workers in different branches of industry and in different districts closer together. It will thus actually become a weapon in the struggle of the whole working class.

The draft constitution of the League was also phrased in similar terms:

> Objects are to provide and popularize film and photos of working class interest, giving a true picture of the industrial and social conditions of the workers today and of their organized struggle to improve their conditions.

Notes on still photography within the League

The League's East London still photo section established at 74 Anthony Street, London, E1 appears to have been the first and major photography group in London, though references also exist in the archives to a "North London stills group". Details of the activities of the East London group are sketchy at present but the members seem to have engaged in two forms of work. Firstly, in the making of production stills during the League's filming sessions, and secondly as visual propagandists for the left movement, producing documentary illustration for pamphlets, propaganda exhibitions and visual displays. Some theoretical discussions also apparently took place,[43] but for the most part there does not seem to have been any great concern to elaborate a Marxist critique of photography or to engage in extended polemics against the photographic establishment. Among the group's projects was photographing for local East End organizations such as the International Labour Defence (ILD) and, during 1934-36, the National Unemployed Workers' Movement (NUWM) and a number of Jewish anti-fascist organizations. Some members also took photographs on a freelance basis for the *Daily Workers*. [44] Others, like Eli Silver, who was also an actor (later to work with Unity Theatre), took photographs of cultural events, theatre groups etc. The group's darkroom and premises in Anthony Street served both as a meeting place and as a photographic resource for the left. Its position in the East End made it eminently suitable for this purpose, especially during demonstrations when it could serve as a rapid printing and processing station. Pictures of the big mass action against Mosley in 1936 are said to have been processed there.[45]

A number of exhibitions were prepared by the group, the earliest apparently in 1935. It is clear from the references to these shows in the League's archive that they were either agitational displays of specific political issues, or exhibitions designed to promote the concept of workers' photography. In this context they were used at various conferences and in conjunction with lectures and discussions. Plans were also in hand to set up a system of touring exhibitions, and an ambitious "recruiting exhibition of workers' photographs, collected from all parts of the world." [46] During this period there appears to have been a fairly regular liaison between the League and similar groups and interested individuals in other countries, especially the American FPL, and also apparently the Film Foto Group of the left front in Prague, a note naming this organization being amongst material belonging to the FPL member H A Green.

Regular contact was also established between the British Communist Party and the exiled Münzenberg group in Paris through joint membership of the so-called Western Bureau of the WIR. The party's delegate, Isabell Brown, attended meetings once each month in Paris, facilitating a regular flow of information and ideas between continental communists and those in Britain.[47]

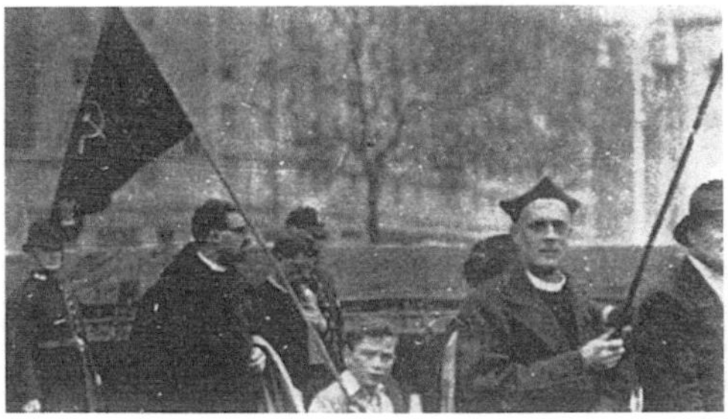

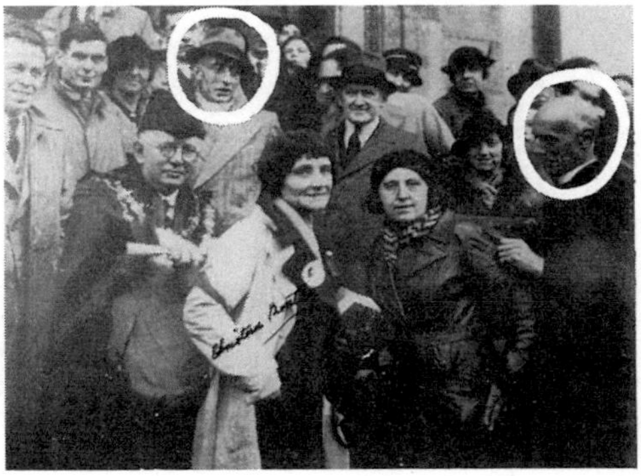

The Rev. Iredell the "Red Vicar of Islington" and colleagues, May Day, 1937.
Photo: Islington Film and Photo League. Courtesy of Mrs. Gwen Iredell.

Reception for the Women's contingent of the 1937 Hunger March, outside Islington Town Hall.
Included are H A Green, producer of the film *Jubilee* and the Rev. Iredell (both ringed).

The League's minute book records some of the results of this contact:

> JOHN HEARTFIELD Duncan asked if any steps had been taken to arrange for the exhibition of photo montages at present on exhibition in Paris to be shown in London. This had not been done. HC (Hugh Cuthbertson) asked to write to Paris asking for (a) particulars of the exhibition, (b) to ask if John Heartfield could come with the exhibition and give a series of lectures...
>
> STILL GROUP Mr. Duncan reported that the exhibition was ready except for three boards to be used for foreign material.

These references and many others in the League's literature give us a picture of a small but very active still group which accomplished a great deal despite the fact that all activities were carried out as a spare-time activity during evenings and weekends. An analysis of the League's address lists and conversations with some of its surviving members indicate that the still group averaged about eight people, and the film group from between twelve to fifteen, with a very active caucus of about ten regulars.

The Islington Group

In addition to a Central and East London group there were at least two (possibly more?) others in London; one in Hackney, E8 about which no information has yet come to light, and another in Islington in North London. Research has been successful in the later case, following the investigation of a number of references discovered in the League documents.

This group [48] formed some time in 1936 and met at the St. Clements Occupation Centre, Liverpool Road, London, N1, a voluntary self-help workshop centre and meeting place set up for the unemployed by the Rev. Elliot Iredell. This remarkable vicar, who was a revolutionary Christian Socialist, later became more directly associated with the League through his friendship with its last secretary the Rev. Hugh Cuthbertson, and another Christian Socialist who was also a League member, Father Archer. Although the Islington group was apparently very active, very few details of its projects have so far been discovered. It is known to have prepared several exhibitions of photographs, some of which were displayed during Spain Week in May 1937 at the Labour Party headquarters at 295 Upper Street, N1; also on show were "some 'snaps' taken by Father Iredell during his visit to Spain."49 A few original photographs have come to light during the research of this group, among which is a rare picture of Iredell with his colleagues on May Day which gives an indication of the attitude that the Christian Socialists group had towards convention.

Film production

As the League's membership grew, regular film production took place. A document from the FPL archive gives the following impressive list of films, together with personnel involved and methods of finance:

> *Newsreel 3:* an attempt to make a film of more than newsreel interest, with permanent value.
>
> *4th Newsreel* J Harris, J Maltby, J Turner, A Pizer. Financed by organizations featured in film. Made principally because organizations such as ILP, Pioneers, etc., wanted their camps filmed. Certain sections shot for other films, but never used.
>
> *February 24th* J Maltby, F Cox, P Davis, J Turner, A Pizer. Private loan (this was crossed out and *Film and Photo League* written in its place).
>
> *Transport* F Jackson, P Davis plus various people on scenario. Loan and advance royalties. Made by a production group set up for the purpose. Group after dissolved.
> *Jubilee* Green, S Handel, A Pizer. NLFS (North London Film Society), financed by.

Brought by secretary of the North London Film Society to Kino for release. Recut with the help of members of the League, with additional material shot for another newsreel.

Holiday from Unemployment E Stich, J Turner, S Handel, H Green, A Pizer, P Leacock, P Rhodes. Camp Committee financed by. Made at the request of the Camp Committee. At first as a private matter, later with the official aid of the League.

Defence of Britain Production group set up specifically for the film. Half the unit continues as a group for future films. *Fight*: H Vorhaus, R Burke, F Cox, N Boddington, S N Serter. Group raised finance itself. Made by the Feature Film Group of the League, but not yet passed by the Committee of the League. (Later entry states) Completed to satisfaction of the League.

Construction W McGarry, Garrard, A Pizer, H Campbell. Loan and builders themselves. Shot by a builder on the job. His group asked the League for help with finance and cutting, scenario etc. Cutting done by a League member, with the aid of the builders.

Winter R Bond, I Nicholson, J Goldman, P David, A Pizer, S Handel, F Jackson, McNaughton Financed by WFPL.

This list is apparently not complete, for a report read at the League's first AGM, by acting secretary Sime Seruya, stated, "During the past few months fourteen films have been made or adapted by the FPL and are touring the country." In contrast to this activity the report noted also that "the attendance (at the AGM) was so small and unrepresentative that it was decided that the main resolution could not be voted upon." The membership is given at this time as about "80 paid up members". An examination of the minutes reveals that only twelve people were in fact present at the AGM.

The main item on the agenda at this meeting was a proposal by Albert Pizer (who had previously successfully negotiated the change of name to the FPL) to amalgamate the League with Kina, a proposal which had been put to the committee earlier in the year and held over to the AGM. This was now referred back to a small sub-committee who put it to the members a few days later, only to find that there was quite a large opposition from members who declared that they would continue to function as the FPL, come what may. The committee's report on this matter sent to members concluded that if this was the case then the following distinct organizational groups would henceforth operate:

> The Film and Photo League (offices: 4 Parton Street, London, WC1) which will appeal mainly to photographers and to those members whose interest in films is mainly general (film discussions, lectures, etc.) although it is also planned for the production of films of a definite social value to supplement those made by Kina Production Group.
>
> Kina Production Group (offices: 84 Gray's Inn Road, London, WC1) which will appeal to those members who wish to concentrate on the production of films. (NB. Kina Production Group has already completed one film and scenarios for other films are now being prepared.) This group's primary and immediate aim is to enlist the co-operation of professional technicians and amateurs with some experience of film production to produce films and to act as an advisory body on production to film groups throughout the country.[51]
>
> Kina Films (1935) Ltd (who) wish us to emphasize that the existence of a special

production group will in no way affect their readiness to distribute such films as may be produced by the League. Their main reason for forming their own production group is that the League has in the past not been able to provide Kina with a sufficient number of good films to meet the demand from working-class and other organizations.

Following the decision to continue in its own right, on the 9th April 1936 the League issued a letter to its supporters which read:

> The League goes on! We are functioning at the hands of a very live provisional committee. The following groups are meeting at our new premises every week: Feature Film Group... Still Photo Group. Now preparing a *Portfolio for Peace* and doing practical work, enlarging etc. in their own darkrooms...[52]

The decision to continue as the FPL does not appear, however, to have been an entirely helpful one for the organization, for the Committee which was elected was apparently not very good at organizational matters and never met on a regular basis or kept minutes. Part of the reason for this may well have been the absence of a number of members who went to Spain. During this time a number of differences arose between members, both over the loyalty to the League and the use of funds for non-League activities.[53] These disagreements led to discussions to vacate the premises they had occupied at 5 Great Ormond Street, London, WC1 and temporarily store the property of the organization with members of the committee.

The minutes noted that the darkroom "sink had to be left, needing plumber to disconnect". From this date effective responsibility and control for the FPL passed to the Rev. Hugh Cuthbertson at whose flat at 3 Somerset Terrace, London, WC1 meetings were henceforth held. In order to pull the organization into shape again Cuthbertson and his new committee sought to involve the League in a broader range of left-wing activity and concentrate more on the co-ordina-

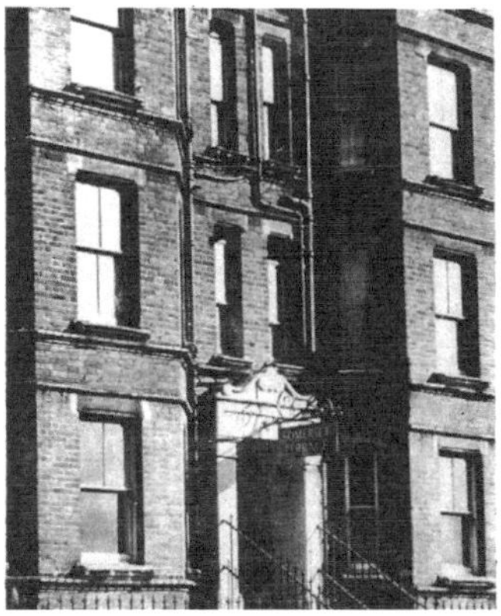

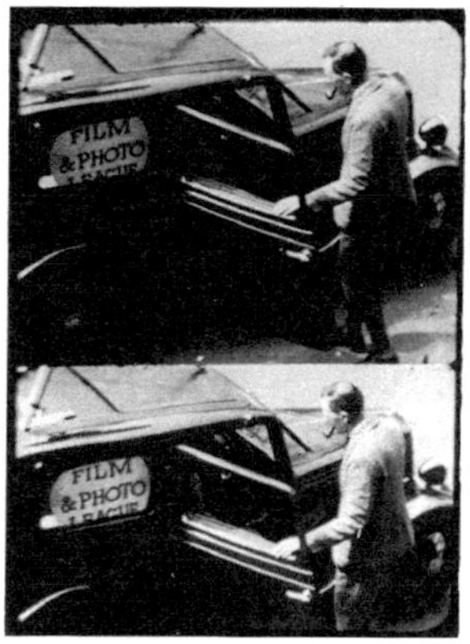

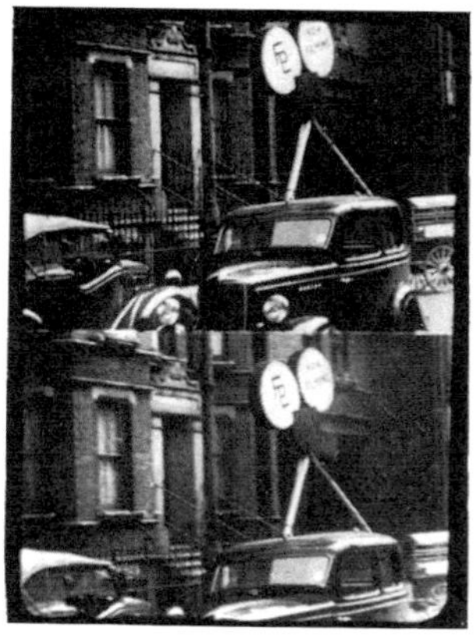

Somerset Terrace, home of the Rev. Hugh Cuthbertson, meeting place of the Film and Photo League during his period as Secretary. About 1937. (Photography Workshop collection.)

tion of film and photography. A move which had been made inevitable in the case of still photography because of the virtual collapse of that side of the League's activities. As a first step a joint initiative was embarked on with Kino and important fraternal links were established with the Left Book Club, an enterprise set up by publisher Victor Gollancz, and one which would have significantly assisted the League had its structure been in a better shape. As it was, only Kino with its more business-like organization was able to take full advantage of the potential offered by this collaboration with the Gollancz organization.

The Left Book Club groups

After a number of discussions, early in 1937 Kino and the Left Book Club agreed to cooperate by extending the use of Kino's films throughout the Club readers' groups. *Left News*, the Club's bulletin published an appeal for "district organizers for Kino" [54] which produced an enthusiastic response from Club members. By June 1937 Kino's films could be hired through Left Book Club agents established in Belfast, Birmingham, Blackpool, Bradford, Cardiff, Doncaster, Durham and Glasgow. Many groups also began to enquire about the activities of the Film and Photo League following a note on its activities which appeared in the April issue of *Left News*. [55] This issue also contained the suggestion that Club members interested in film and photography "should come together in the near future". In May, members of the League visited the offices of the Club and held a lightning demonstration of their films. The editor of *Left News*, obviously impressed, commented: "The League invaded my office a few days ago with their apparatus, and in less than five minutes were projecting on the wall an excellent film on 9.5cm of (but against) the coronation, and on the street activities in East London, in colour." [56]

On the 7th June the Left Book Club convened a special conference to discuss the coordination of film for left propaganda and to work out practical details for the formation of film units within the Left Book Club. Michael Burke from the FPL opened the conference by outlining the history and development of progressive film organizations and called for the production of "films with a purpose". This was followed by a talk given by Dr John Lewis on the value of film in supplementing the printed word and bringing concepts to life, in particular the presentation of such material as statistics. He went on to discuss the importance of documentary work by land and factory workers who, seeing things from their own angle, could contribute more for our purposes than most expert professional artists approaching the subject lyrically and from the outside. The conference ended with the showing of two Film and Photo League productions, one of them dealing with the public events of May 1937 and "employing new techniques in colour." [57]

During July and August both Kino and FPL participated in the Left Book Club Summer School at Digswell Park, Welwyn Garden City. Kino organized a programme of films and gave talks on how to arrange film shows, and the FPL demonstrated their methods of working with small films and equipment and helped in the arrangement of a photographic exhibition put on by the "distressed areas group". (A film was also made called *Red, Right and Bloo*.) The August issue of *Left News* published the details of the scheme for joint co-operation which were finally worked out at the-July conference, plus a list of the League's films and details of its activities. The main points were:

- Formation of amateur units collateral with political and cultural groups.
- Showing and making films illustrative of the left movement.
- Short films (10-15 minutes) to be a frequent feature of ordinary group meetings.
- Units to be coordinated with the League as control body and liaison with the Central Committee.
- Lectures and practical instructions in the use of camera projector and technique,

advice in subjects and treatment. • Pooling of facilities in use and economic purchase of equipment and film stock.
• A centre for editing and studio work in London for the mutual use of various units and common meeting place.
• League and distribution centre for sub-standard (9.5/16mm) films, suitable for small audiences, to be rented at the most economic rates possible.
• All units to co-operate on subjects of national scope (as for example the 1937 Hunger March).
• A monthly bulletin to be issued dealing with film group activities, problems involved, films available.
• Membership of units to involve membership of the League and receipt of all central publications.
• Type of films to be made: local conditions, working class life and cultural problems, story and documentary films, also subjects suitable for children.
• Exchange of films, for material from foreign countries.
• Acquisition of useful film material from other societies and amateur workers. [58]

The scheme apparently got a good response and also led to an appeal for "the formation of a collection of still photographs of England of left-wing interest which could be used to make lantern slides and illustrate books." [59] Members were urged to send in prints and look around for suitable subjects to photograph. By November the Left Book Club, Kino and the League had agreed on a subscription scheme giving affiliated groups the right to hire films and call on them for assistance. The success of this arrangement was commented on in the December issue of *Left News* which reported the results of one group:[60]

> Ipswich tried an interesting experiment last month. They asked the Film and Photo League to come and demonstrate the value of affiliating to the League, hiring thew YMCA hall for a special show. They were shown the League's development in film technique, seeing the first brave efforts in the early *Newsreels*, then *Jubilee* and *Bread*... When the demonstrator asked whether they would like to see the coloured film satire on the *Coronation*, they answered with an enthusiastic affirmative. At the end of this showing, the Ipswich LBC wished to affiliate at once, and a spontaneous collection among the audience showed that they appreciated what they had seen.

This response was apparently typical, for letters in the League's archive show that many LBC-affiliated and a number of joint LBC/FPL ventures were developed, particularly during 1938 and the early part of 1939. During this time League members were "cooperating in a scheme for the production of left film and slides with LBC units in Manchester, Reading, Sutton, Wembley and Pontypridd. [61]

These activities were, however, becoming too widely scattered for the central group in London to successfully coordinate. In particular, membership losses amongst the committee and regular activists increasingly prevented continuous organizational work from taking place. Meetings became less and less frequent until eventually the organization ceased to be a functioning entity, though individual members met on an informal basis and a number of regional groups carried on.

The League's educational activities

In addition to making and showing films and photographs the League initiated a number of film schools and debates, activities which if they had continued would have undoubtedly produced the first attempt at a theoretical analysis of photography in Britain from a Marxist perspective. However, in the event, these attempts were both too infrequent and finally too over-shadowed by the problems of the approach ing World War to extend beyond these initial stages.

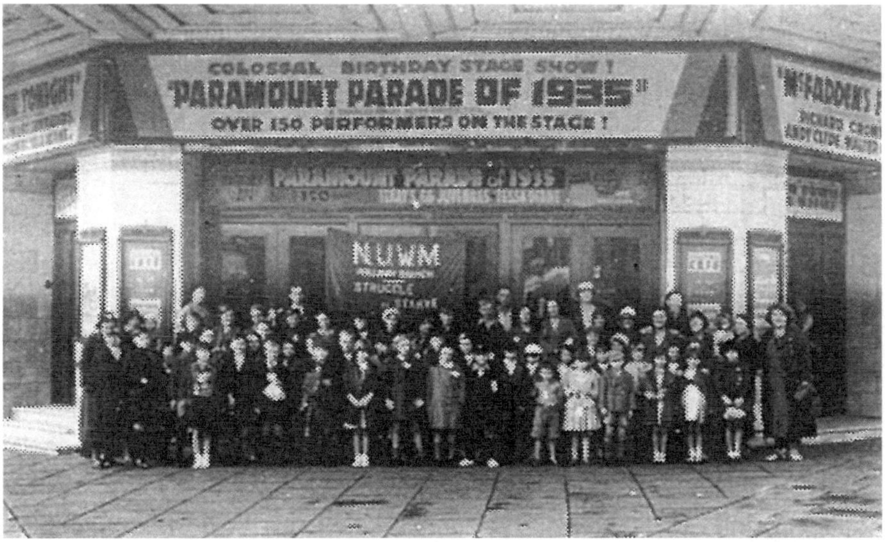

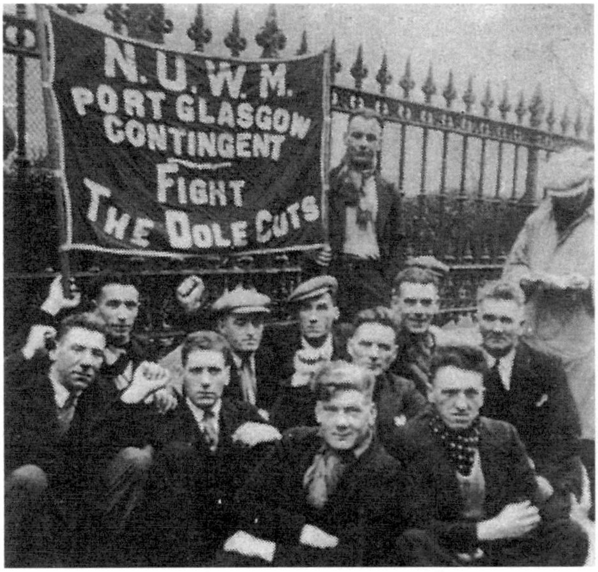

Demonstration and picket by children and members of the National Unemployed Workers' Movement, North London.
Photo: John Maltby.

Hunger Marchers: one of a series of pictures by FPL member Norman King.

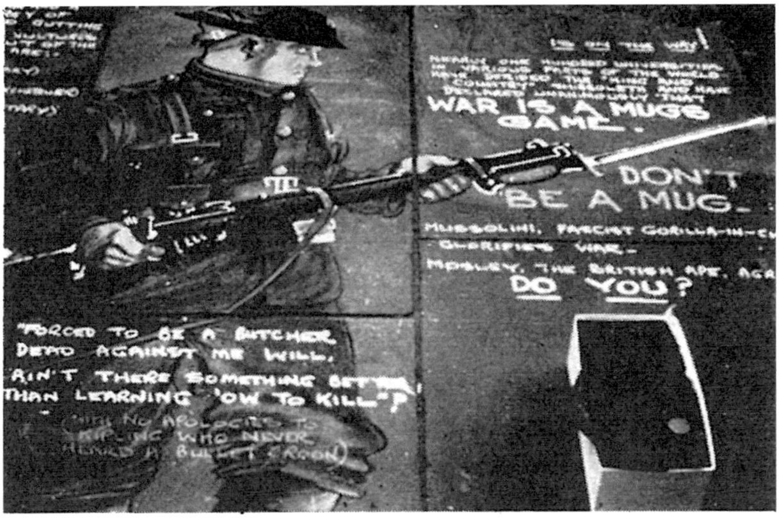

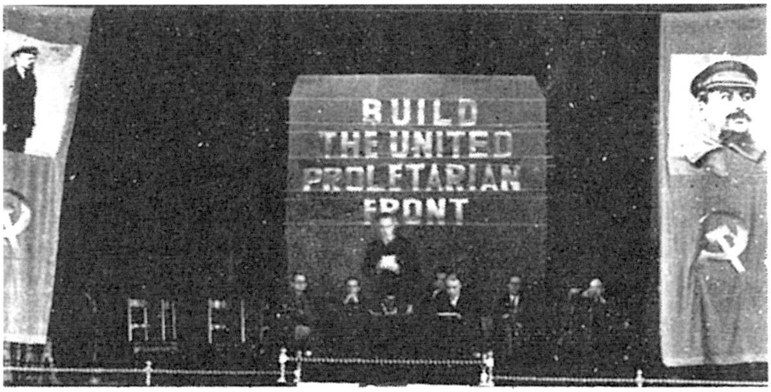

Anti-Fascist pavement art.

Communist Party meeting.

This aspect of the League's work is nonetheless useful, both as an insight into how a socialist photographic education was envisaged during the period and because it was undoubtedly the first attempt to carry out such a project in Britain. Three schools were apparently held, the largest and most important of these lasting four days and forming part of the League's AGM for 1938. These sessions were under the chairmanship of Herbert Marshall, a former student of Eisenstein, in Moscow. Topics ranged across *Film Consciousness*, *The Practical Task*, *Production*, *Techniques of Propaganda*, *The Static Film* and *Practical Work*. Of particular interest in the two latter sections was the emphasis on what is now called slide-tape, then referred to as "film slide talkies". These were a combination of still images and sound disc-records which was thought to have great potential for the production of short programmes with minimal outlay of time and money. If the League had continued it would undoubtedly have developed this medium and produced sets of slides for political campaigns. Undoubtedly also they were becoming critical of the pervasive and dominant Hollywood cinema and film news coverage, and

Programme of the FLP four-day school 1938. (Photography Workshop collection)

ay, January 21st

ion One: Film Consciousness

p.m. Exhibition of films
Opening of School,
H. Marshall
"The critical approach to the commercial cinema"
Olga Venn
"The Socialist alternative"
Basil Burton
0 Discussion "What we can do"

rday, January 22nd

2 noon Practical work

ion two: The Practical Task

p.m. "At the work bench"
Geoffrey Innes
Demonstration of new apparatus
"Projection. How, When and Where"
H. Cuthbertson.
"Experiences as camera-man in Spain."
Pete Davies

12 midnight GRAND SOCIAL AND DANCE
ets The highspot of the rally!
at Bring all your friends!!
Any costume...carnival & fun.

.m. Workers Ballet in "OUR 30 YEARS"
Walter Badham, BBC Entertainer
Character by Handwriting, by an experienced graphologist!!!!
Film projected. Film taken!!!!!
DON'T MISS THIS EVENT!!!!!!

ay January 23rd

ion Three: Production

0 a.m. "The use of the Cine Camera"
Vivian Braun
0 "Script and Direction"
Michael Burke
0 Visit by Unity New Theatre conducted by John Allen of Unity Theatre Guild, with picnic lunch in the stalls.

p.m. F.P.L. ANNUAL GENERAL MEETING
(members only may speak or vote on business. Others in school are invited to be present)

Agenda: Minutes of previous A.G.M.
Secretary's report.
Treasurer's report
Election of officers
Other business to include discussion of future work.

Session Four: Technique of Propaganda

6.30 p.m. Projection "Gaiety of Nations" and a new housing film
7.00 "Mass Observation with the camera" David Stein
8.00 "The psychological Angle"
Jim Gordon
9.00 "Getting the message over"
John Fothergill

Projection and Discussion.

Monday. January 24th

Session Five: The Static Film

6.30 p.m. Film-pictures of Palestine and U.S.S.R. etc
7.00 Demonstration of film-slide talkies. Leslie Daiken
8.00 "The Camera in Political Education" Dr. John Lewis
9.00 Film-pictures of Distress Areas Mrs. Helen Dunn

Discussion.

Tuesday. January 25th

10 a.m. to 4 p.m. Practical Work

Session Six: The Place of Sound

6.20 p.m. Disc-records to be made by members.
7.30 "Sound". E.D. Swann
8.30 "Plans for the Future"
The Chairman.
9.30 Discussion
11.00 Close of School

PLEASE SUPPORT BY MAKING THIS SCHOOL A SUCCESS.
COME AS OFTEN AS YOU CAN. BRING YOUR FRIENDS.
THERE IS PLENTY OF ROOM AT THE HALL.

Programme of the FLP four-day school, 1938. (Photography Workshop collection.)

saw this criticism as an integral part of any work programme.

Other schools were less ambitious but offered important speakers such as Paul Rotha, Ivor Montague, Arthur Elton and Irene Nicholson. Sessions included *Making Films Without Money*, *What's Wrong with the Cinema?* and *The Film in Relation to Modern Society*. In addition to questions of film, more emphasis was placed in these shorter schools on photography, with talks being linked to the exhibition shown. In one case this was of *English and Foreign Worker Photographers* with a lecture entitled *Still photography and social criticism*, details of which unfortunately do not appear to have survived.

The existence of an active Workers' Film and Photo League in Britain in the 1930s has come as a shock to many people, especially those who believe in the comprehensiveness and impartiality of reference works on cultural history. For not one mention of this movement, or indeed any of the parallel developments of the period in workers' sport, music, literature and theatre, have ever appeared, even as footnotes, in the scholarly works of the experts. We don't have to

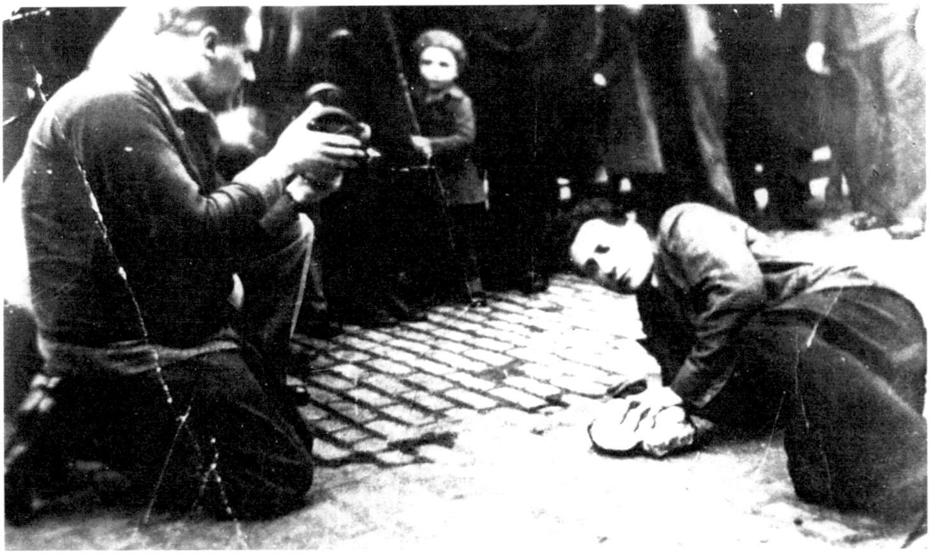

look very far for a reason for this "omission", for all these movements arose in opposition to the dominant culture, as agitation against it... then (as now) not considered by status quo opinion as "art". On the contrary, it must be argued, that whatever the merit of the work, the fact that it attempted to give visual and dramatic emphasis to capitalism's social and political ills placed it immediately outside the framework of "culture" and into the category of political "propaganda".

Its makers, likewise, were not considered as "artists". Rather they were "agitators" and "disturbers of the peace", fit only to be persecuted and harried whilst they were alive, and lied about and used out of context when they were dead. In a recent book, *Germany, the New Photography 1927-33*, this has already happened to some of the work of the German *Arbeiter Fotografie* movement which is now sandwiched without comment or analysis between a

Taken during the making of the film *Bread*. This production still shows Sam Serter (FPL producer), with camera.
Sam Serter comments, "In 1929 I attended an ad hoc lecture given to ten people at the Marx Memorial Library by the Soviet director Eisenstein. His methods had a profound influence on me and were used during the making of this film".
Photo: courtesy of Sam Serter.

number of the bourgeois trends which it fought against in its life. This unlikely mixture, collectively called *New Photography* – a title calculated to make it into a cult, is undoubtedly seen as a worthy successor to the now well-worn Farm Security Administration (FSA) project which has hitherto provided handsome profits for the producers and salesmen of glossy duo-toned images of working class life and poverty. Just as a number of the FSA pictures have become ikons, repeatedly used in various contexts far removed from their historical origin, so undoubtedly will images from the

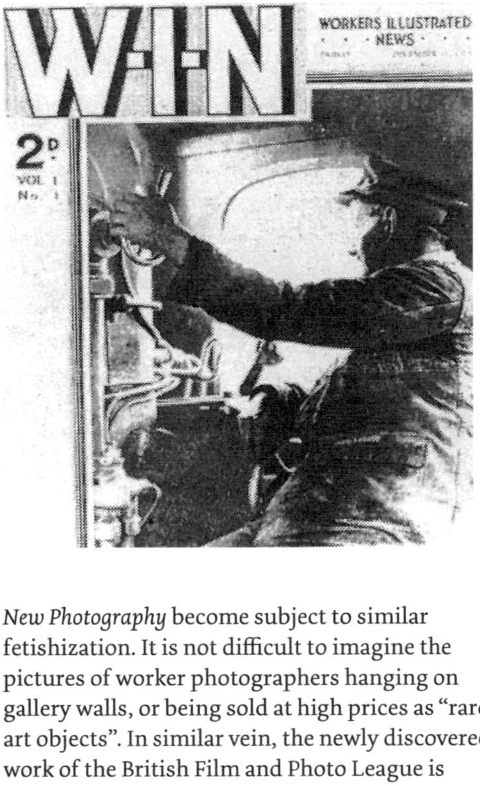

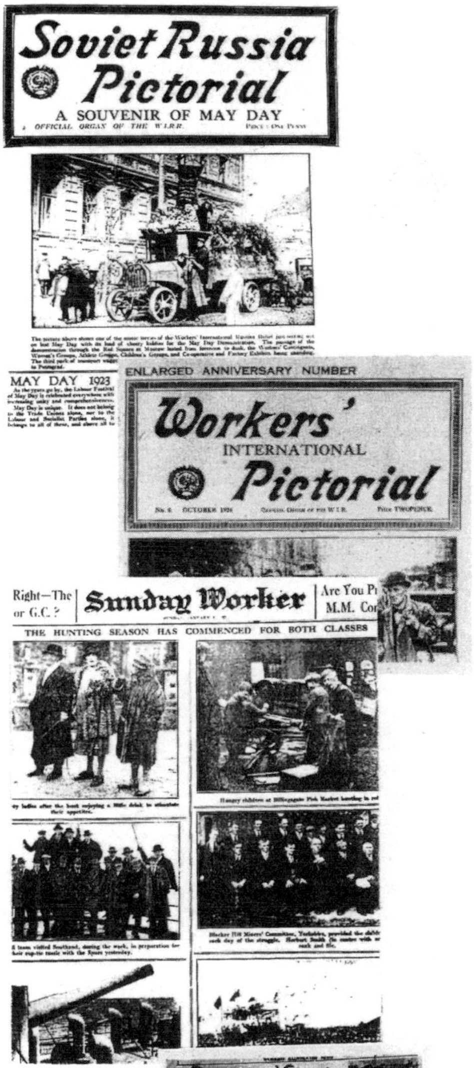

New Photography become subject to similar fetishization. It is not difficult to imagine the pictures of worker photographers hanging on gallery walls, or being sold at high prices as "rare art objects". In similar vein, the newly discovered work of the British Film and Photo League is undoubtedly on the agenda for incorporation as another strand of the bourgeois "documentary" tradition. Indeed, already one can almost hear the clink of sherry glasses when the name Film and Photo League is mentioned in art photography circles. Fortunately, the recent developments in socialist photography in various countries are

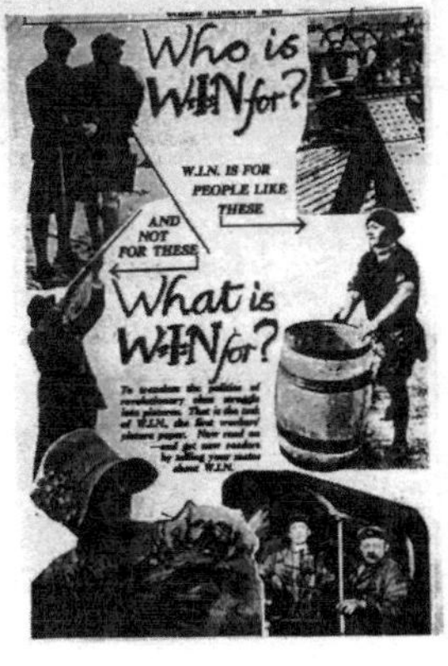

Panels from the Photography Workshop exhibition *The British Film and Photo League.*

leading to the re-emergence of a new Worker Photographer movement, a situation which will guarantee that the distorted and vulgarized "histories" of socialist photography now being cobbled together by bourgeois academics in search of fresh fields in which to shine, will not go unopposed.

The evolution of an illustrated workers' literature

The earliest successful attempts at a mass circulation pictorial literature with a working class message and Socialist orientation were carried out as part of the activities of the Workers' Inter national Relief (WIR). This international organization was popularly known as the *Workers' Red Cross*, and was originally formed at the suggestion of Lenin to help co-ordinate aid to Russia during the famine of the early 1920s. After 1924 the organization broadened its scope and provided aid to all workers in need, such as the families of strikers and the unemployed. It also engaged in grass-roots Socialist agitation on a world scale.

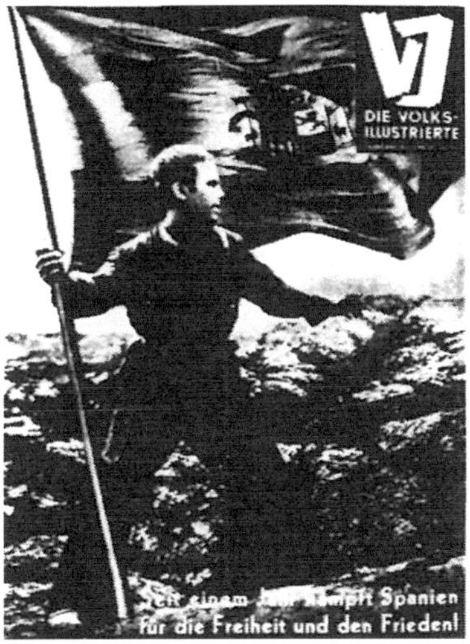

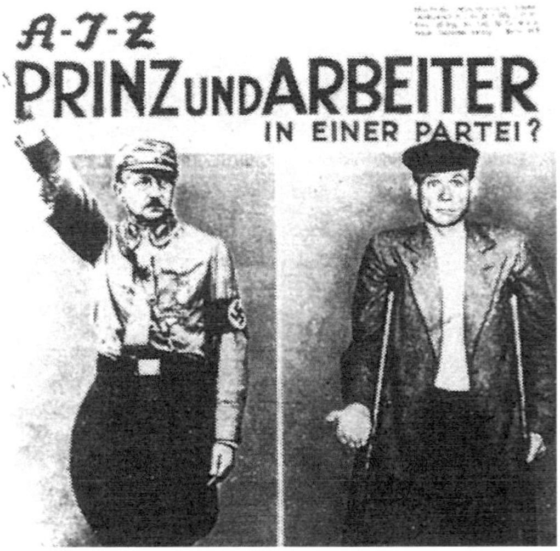

This activity was organized and directed by the remarkable Communist entrepreneur Willi Miinzenberg, whose efforts brought into being a giant Red Trust which was involved in a wide range of cultural activity, especially publishing.

The WIR, which had its headquarters in Berlin, employed a staff of 40 people and had branches in almost every country of the world. Its journals, which were published in several languages, had a formative influence, with total sales of more than a quarter of a million per issue. In Germany, the main centre of their production, they published *Sowjet Russland im Bild* (1921-1922), which later became *Sichel und Hammer* (1922-25), the precursor of the unique and important mass-circulation *Arbeiter Illustrierte Zeitung* (AIZ) (1925-36), which continued in Prague and became *Die Volks Illustrierte* (1936-38).

These publications fostered similar experiments in Britain such as *The Workers' International Pictorial*, *The Workers' Pictorial*, *The Sunday Worker*, and the short-lived *Workers' International News* (WIN).

During the period of the Russian famine in the 1920s the WIR published an important illustrated journal, *Soviet Russia Pictorial* (1923-4), which attempted to develop a visual emphasis and style similar to that of its German counterpart *Sowjet Russland*. It also attempted to develop the use of films and photography in left agitation, appealing to its readers for photographs "illustrative of British working class life and struggle."

This was a prelude to the attempt to provide "a good workers, illustrated paper" from within the WIR: the *Workers' International Pictorial* (1924-25), a journal which (had it continued) would have undoubtedly provided the first lively coverage of life in Britain from a Socialist viewpoint. In the event this was carried out not by the WIR, but through the medium of the *Sunday Worker* (1925-29), a left-wing newspaper greatly influenced by the early work of the WIR and having as its editor a photographic enthusiast and socialist lantern slide lecturer, William Paul.

This publication, which developed a unique agitational display of photographs on its back page, led directly to an attempt similar to the successful German publication AIZ: this was the short-lived *Workers' Illustrated News* (WIN), 1929.

All these experiments had a big influence on the emerging workers' photography movement in Britain and were especially important as they helped in the development of a completely fresh approach to visual presentation within the left. This approach for the first time was influenced by Marxist rather than bourgeois styles of pictorial journalism.

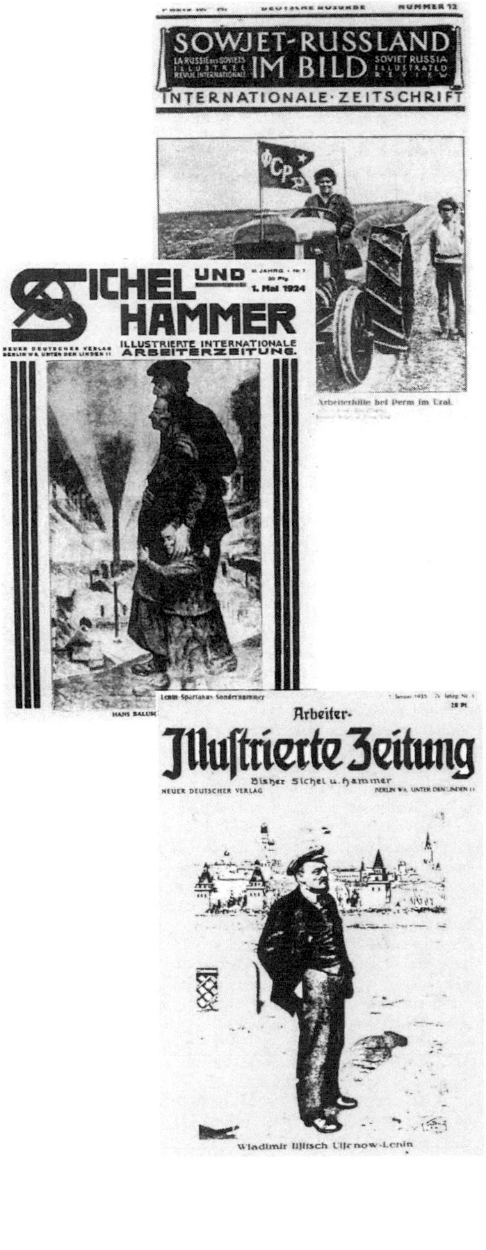

Opposite and above: Panels from the Photography Workshop exhibition *The British Film and Photo League*.

NOTES

1. For details of this discovery and an outline of the work of the League, see Victoria Wegg-Prosser, "The Archive of the Film and Photo League", *Sight and Sound* (Autumn 1977). See also *Before Hindsight* (Metropolis Pictures) for some examples of the League's film work.
2. Norman King, John Maltby, Sam Serter, Mrs. Hetty Vorhans , Ivan Seruya, Charles Cooper, Joe Arloff, David Brotmacher, whose help is gratefully acknowledged.
3. Mr. Hogenkamp is currently working on a book based upon his research. Other references accessible to English readers are: "Film and the Workers' Movement in Britain, 1929-39", *Sight and Sound* (Spring 1976); *Workers' Newsreels in the 1920s and 1930s*, Our History pamphlet 68, Communist Party of Great Britain, available from Central Books, 37 Grays Inn Road, London WC1.
4. Unpublished notes on a study of the League's film.
5. All enquiries about these projects to Photography Workshop, 152 Upper Street, London, Nl.
6. Don Macpherson (ed.), *Traditions of Independent Cinema in Britain: The Thirties.* London: British Film Institute, 1979. John Clark (*et al*), *Culture and crisis in Britain in the 1930s*. London: Lawrence and Wishart, 1979.
7. In England the Workers' Theatre Movement (WTM), the Workers' Music Association, the Propaganda Art Group, the British Workers' Sports Association, to mention only a few. In Germany and the Soviet Union there were also active worker correspondents and workers' radio groups which sought to utilize the hobby interests and talents of workers for political agitation and activity.
8. The Russian version of the WIR, founded in 1924 to carry on broadly similar activities, but which often worked in opposition to its Berlin based counterpart.
9. The policy of "the United Front from below" (that is organization by the rank and file) was adopted by the Communist International up to the time of its seventh Congress (1935). It aimed both to oppose the bourgeois structures and leaderships of the reformist socialist parties and develop working class political consciousness and organisational self-reliance. Tactically this was achieved by encouraging the militant autonomous actions of the working class over the heads of and despite the more legally minded leaderships. Such activity often cut across party lines by uniting those involved as members of the working class, rather than as labour or liberal party members. Organization "from below" also encouraged the development of flourishing and often irreverent agitprop art and culture. A culture not to the liking of some sections of society – "capitalist" and "socialist" alike.
10. The principle of political education and control, by means of mass action and organizational involvement of the working class, underlies both the concept of the Workers' Council (or Soviet) as the form of proletarian government and the artistic equivalent of Agitprop as a rudimentary form of proletarian culture. It was the fundamental concept behind much of the Comintern's work prior to the multi-class (Popular Front) policy put forward in 1935.
11. Comintern-linked film and photo groups existed in the Soviet Union, Germany, Switzerland, Czechoslovakia, Austria, Holland, France, USA, Japan and Britain. A note in a contemporary English anti-communist publication lists both Kino and the Film and Photo League as organizations affiliated to the Communist Party of Great Britain. See J Barker White, *The Reel Network*, London: 1937.
12. *The Sunday Worker*, "The WJR helps the miners." August 29, 1926, p.7.
13. *Soviet Russia Pictorial*, organ of the Workers' International Russian Relief, No. 1, 1923, p. 10.
14. See Heinz Willmann, *Geschichte der Arbeiter-Illustrierte Zeitung*, Berlin (East): Dietz Verlag, 1975 (German language only).
15. *The Sunday Worker* was the most successful communist orientated publication ever produced in Britain, both in terms of the broad base of its readership and in the way it was able to integrate a visual style of agitation (then developing in Germany) into the British tabloid newspaper format via its polemically juxtaposed back page photographs.
16. *Soviet Russia Pictorial*, September 1923, p.16.
17. Conversation with Walter Holmes, *Daily Worker* and *Morning Star* columnist.
18. Walter Holmes.
19. George Sinfield, Secretary of the British Workers' Sports Federation.
20. Walter Holmes.
21. The Plebs League advertised a number of slide sets on socialist themes; these could be hired, together with a portable slide lantern, or purchased outright. See *The Plebs* magazine: "How to make a lantern lecture", August 1927, pp.273-4; "The slide film method" (advert), November-December 1928, p.263; "Revolution in lecturing", January 1932, pp.9-10; and a back page advert for the "unit portable lantern", January 1934. A reference to William Paul's Paris Commune slides appears in *Left News*, March 1937, p.260.
22. *Red Aid Activist*, No.1, November 1928.
23. This destruction was observed at first hand by Jean Ross, first secretary of the Workers' Film and Photo League, who lived in Germany during 1932 and the early part of 1933 (conversation with her daughter Ms S C Cockburn).
24vInternational Union of Revolutionary Theatre, see "Film Conf erence", in: *New Theatre*, September-October 1933, pp.24-5. *New Theatre* called itself the "Organ of the Workers' Theatre, Film and Photo Leagues, and the Workers' Dance Leagues".
25. Sam Serter, FPL member who attended the Olympiad as a delegate from the Workers' Theatre Movement.
26. *Daily Worker*, December 3, 1933: "What's On" column.
27. Banned from general distribution in many places but could still be shown (due to anomalies in the law relating to film) if it was on 16mm non-inflammable stock and exhibited in a hall or meeting room not licensed for public exhibition but operating in the context of a private club; a loophole still used today by the purveyors of pornographic films.
28. From a *History of Kino*, issued at the organization's first AGM in 1936.
29. Interview with Mrs. Hetty Vorhans, Kino Production Group member and co-producer of the film *Bread*. Some scenes from these films were shot in an attic studio set up in Mrs. Vorhans' home at 88 Albert Road, London NW8.
30. Little is known at present about the origin and membership of this group; it was apparently amongst the earliest organizations of its kind in England and seems to have been modelled upon the American worker photographer groups, such as the Nippon Camera Club, and the Photo Defender Group, reports of which appeared in the widely-read left cultural magazine *New Masses*. The group appears to have later formed the basis of the WFPL East End still photographers group, run from 74 Anthony Street, London E1. One member is said to have been the (then) left-wing photographer J Allan Cash (recollection of FPL member Norman King.) An analysis of the early membership lists carried out with the help of WFPL members suggests that the active caucus of the Workers' Camera Club consisted of the following people: A Oliver, Fred Duncan, E Silver, J A Cash and C Calnan. Eli Silver was also the organizer of a small film unit in the East End (see letter in *Red Stage* No5 April/May 1932, p.6.)
31. *Daily Worker*, November 27, 1934, p.4.
32. "History of Kino", op.cit.
33. Walter Holmes.
34. Conversation with Peggy Ross, sister of the late Jean Ross, first secretary of the League.
35. *Manifesto of the Workers' Film and Photo League*, London, 1935.
36. Jean Ross played a formative role in the early policy development of the League. Her contact with revolutionary communist cultural movements in Germany gave her a more developed theoretical background than many other members.
37. Two bulletins issued by the League have so far been discovered: *The Camera Forward*, probably published in 1936, and *Left Film Front* which was produced some time in 1937.
38. Conversation with the author.
39. Mr. Maltby worked with the League from 1934 until its demise in 1939. Involving himself in both still and cine work, his archive contains a number of negatives made for the League and a

film produced in 1934 for the Merseyside Workers' Film Society, previously thought to be lost: *Liverpool, Gateway to Empire*.
40. The "Popular Front" tactic demanded a complete reorientation not only of policy but also of organizational structure. This involved the deliberate closure of several successful international organizations such as the WIR, ILD, CWPAS, and the running down of many national organizations with "class against class" policies, especially those whose agitprop structures were not amenable to multi-class propaganda.
Tom Thomas discusses the closure of the WTM (Workers' Theatre Movement) in *History Workshop Journal* No. 4, 1977 p.125: "I was very surprised when it was put to me in 1935 or 1936 that as the organizer of the WTM and as author of so many lampoons upon the Labour Party, my continued leadership might be considered in some quarters a minor obstacle to the development of a popular front. If my resignation would remove even a minor obstacle I could not allow my personal regret to stand in the way. So I resigned after nearly ten years of hard but extremely interesting work. I then took up activities in the Communist Party in Welwyn Garden City and was soon busy getting signatures for the peace petition."
Joe Jacobs recalls the end of the ILD (International Labour Defence) in Stepney in his excellent book *Out of the Ghetto*, p.152: "George Allison called a meeting of the members of the party faction of the National Committee of the ILD. I don't know who had discussed our organization or how a decision was arrived at without any prior consultation with us, but George simply said that the Party required us to liquidate the ILD."
41. Note in the League's minute book.
42. A separate research project has been initiated by Photography Workshop to examine the activities of the Workers' Camera Club, and a similar organization, the Progressive Photographic Group. It is hoped that this will lead to the recovery of the League's still photography archive and exhibitions.
43. Conversation with Peggy Ross.
44. Conversation with Walter Holmes.
45. Walter Holmes.
46. Note in the League's minute book.
47. Conversation with Isabel Brown, last secretary of the WIR.
48. Members included Reg and Herbert Green, producers of the film *Jubilee*.
49. Islington Gazette, April 30, 1937, p.4.
50. Collection of Mrs. Gwen Iredell.
51. See also *Left Review*, May 1936, p.415.
52. Letter to members in the FPL archive.
53. Two events in particular are constantly referred to in the League's minute book: the unauthorized transfer of funds to a new venture started by one of the members, International Sound Films, and the interesting saga of Fleet Films which the minute book records in the following manner: "From enquiries made by various members of the committee it appeared that the personnel of this organization consisted only of Mary Robson, a Mr Wurzel and our treasurer Cox... A propos of this Burke raised the question of the Fleet Films advertisement which must have been handed in to the DW (*Daily Worker*) before the film had actually been shot. He complained that as no film whatever had been made, Fleet Films were injuring the whole Workers' Film Movement in eulogizing a film which did not exist and in further adding the suggestive words "Fleet Films never let you down". It was further reported that Kina had lodged a similar complaint with the DW for accepting the ad."
54. *Left News*, January 1937, p.196.
55. *Left News*, April 1937, p.309.
56. *Left News*, June 1937, p.392-3.
57. *Left News*, August 1937, p.479-80.
58. Report of the Left Book conference in *Left News*, August 1937, p.497-8.
59. *Left News*, October 1937, p.542.
60. *Left News*, December 1937, p.623.
61. *Left News*, July 1938, p.906.

ACKNOWLEDGEMENTS
Apart from all the people mentioned in the text, especially the members of the FPC, I would like to acknowledge the assistance of the following people:
Joe Arloff
Bert Hogenkamp
Jonathan Lewis, Metropolis Pictures
John Maltby
Elizabeth Taylor-Mead, Metropolis Pictures
Victoria Wegg-Prosser
Ralph Bond
Charles Cooper, Contemporary Films
Stanley Foreman, ETV Films
Margaret Kentfield
Seona Robertson
Sam Serter
Ivan Seruya
Michelle Snapes, Film Archive, BFI
Nick Wetton
J M Alexander
Bram Bootman, custodian of the Unity Theatre archive
Isabel Brown, Secretary of the Workers' International Relief
Vi Crowther
Ms S C Cockburn (daughter of Jean Ross)
Mrs Angela Green
Kathy and Norman King
Leo Kruks, formerly of Unity Studios
Mrs Gwen Iredell
Bill MacGarry
Peggy Ross
Joe Stern
Mrs Hetty Vorhans
W S Walter, former secretary of the Rebel Players Theatre Group

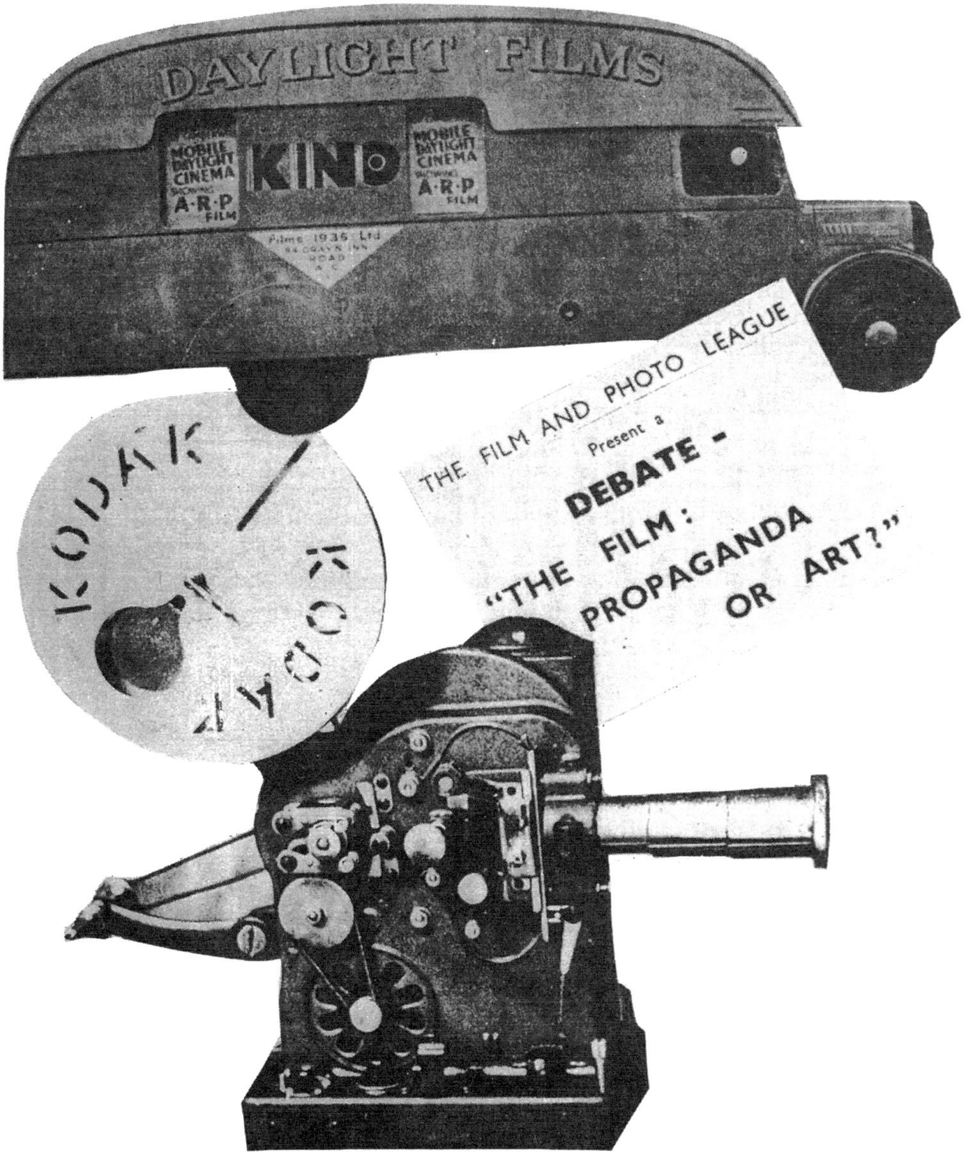
DAYLIGHT FILMS
MOBILE DAYLIGHT CINEMA
A·R·P FILM
KIND
MOBILE DAYLIGHT CINEMA
A·R·P FILM
Films 1936 Ltd
KODAK
KODAK
THE FILM AND PHOTO LEAGUE
Present a
DEBATE -
"THE FILM:
PROPAGANDA
OR ART?"

England: The Hugh Cuthbertson Collection

Victoria Wegg-Prosser

THE REVEREND Hugh Cuthbertson was Secretary of the Film and Photo League from 1936 to 1939. In that position he assumed responsibility for films made by various political groups in the early 1930s, and became custodian of all the films made by the Film and Photo League before its demise in 1939. The collection which has survived his death in 1976 is now in the care of the National Film Archive. This division of the British Film Institute, together with the Film Availability Services department, have financed the copying to sound speed of a number of the films (asterisked in the following list).

These films will shortly be available for hire through Film Availability Services, 127 Charing Cross Road, WC2H OEA

The films are listed in chronological order under putative owner. The given date is the year of production, not the release date of the version in the Cuthbertson Collection. The use of brackets denotes a made-up title.

Further information is available from Victoria Wegg-Prosser, 22 Kildare Terrace, London W2 SLX.

Federation of Workers' Film Societies | London Workers' Film Society | Atlas Films
* AGAINST IMPERIALIST WAR – MAY DAY 1932. 16mm b/w st. c.15 mins. Incomplete. This is almost certainly a fourth WORKERS' TOPICAL NEWS, mentioned in the *Daily Worker*, February 24th 1932, p.3.

? Kino Production Group, London?
* LONDON MAY 7th 1933
16mm b/w st. c.9 mins. Incomplete and part unedited. There is no evidence to confirm that this film was ever released. The note in the can

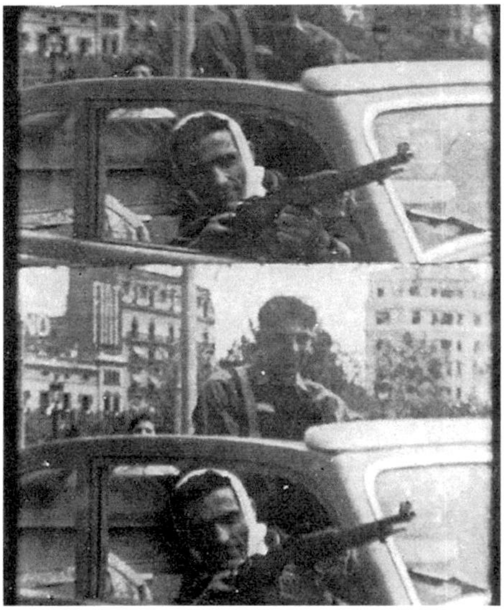

with the original film – "all demonstrations, walking, Hyde Park" – suggests the film was to be used to provide stock shot material.

Kino Production Group | Workers' Film & Photo League
* WORKERS' NEWSREEL No.1 1934
16mm b/w st. c.11 mins. Incomplete.
Daily Worker Gala in Co-op Woods, Plumstead; "The Workers Create": building of new LCS store; "Capitalism Destroys": Hendon Air Pageant; Youth Anti-War Congress, Sheffield; Anti-War Demonstration, Hyde Park, August 1934.

* WORKERS' NEWSREEL No.2 1934
16mm b/w st. c.15 mins. Complete.
"Release Thaelmann" banner in the Strand; International Anti-Fascist sports rally, Paris; Hyde Park Anti-Fascist rally September 9th 1934; Wrexham Colliery Disaster; ad. for *Daily Worker*.

* NATIONAL HUNGER MARCH 1934
16mm b/w st. c.15 mins. Complete.

* (AGAINST FASCISM 1934)
16mm b/w st. c.5 mins. Sections.
Re-edit of parts of the above three films, plus new footage outside Olympia Stadium, June 1934.

* BREAD 1934
16mm b/w st. c.11 mins. Abridged version with logo LEFT FILM FRONT. Story documentary ending with footage from 1934 Hunger March.

Film and Photo League
(most titles also distributed by Kino)
* U.A.B. (WORKERS' NEWSREEL No.3) 1935
16mm b/w st. c.13 mins. Incomplete. The February 24th 1935 mass demonstration to "bury" the Unemployment Assistance Boards.

* JUBILEE 1935
16mm b/w st. c.9 mins. Abridged version with logo LEFT FILM FRONT. Green brothers' satirical attack on 25 years of progress.

* CONSTRUCTION 1935
16mm b/w st. c.11 mins. Complete.
Re-enactment by builders involved in strike for union recognition.

* REVOLT OF THE FISHERMEN 1935
16mm b/w st. c.13 mins. Complete.
Easter 1935 strike by fishermen for union recognition, shot mainly in Hull.

* STRIFE 1935
16mm b/w st. c.22 mins. Complete.
Story documentary re. struggle for union recognition in factory.

* WINTER 1935-36
16mm b/w st. 13 mins. Complete.
London street scenes, contrasted with winter "fun for the rich".

* DOCKWORKERS 1935-36
16mm b/w st. c.11 mins. Complete.
"Social disgrace of casual labour" in London's docks.

* MARCH AGAINST STARVATION 1936
16mm b/w st. c.30 mins. Complete.
"The national protest 1936" organised by the NUWM.

* MAY THE FIRST 1937
16mm b/w st. c.13 mins. Complete.
May Day Parade and Trailer for 1938 May Day film (never made).
* The MERRY MONTH OF MAY 1937
16mm Kodachrome st. c.13 mins. Incomplete.
"A satire and document" on the Coronation of George VI.

* SPIRIT OF MAY DAY 1937
9.5mm b/w st. c.13 mins.
May Day as "part of historic process".

* RED RIGHT AND BLOO 1937
16mm b/w st. c.35 mins. Complete.
Story documentary made at the Left Book Club Summer School, August 1937.

* (SPAIN – BARCELONA) 1936-37
16mm b/w and Kodachrome st. c.13 mins.
Incomplete. Republican scenes in Barcelona; Arms for Spain demonstration in Trafalgar Square.

* INTERNATIONAL NEWSREELS (bought in from Eugene Castle, USA) 1937-38:
3x16mm b/w st. c.11 mins. each. Invasion of China, Austria etc.

* (SOCIALIST YOUTH CAMP AT HERNE BAY) 1937. 16mm b/w st. (neg. only) c.15 mins.
Incomplete.

* (FPL MIXED NEG 1938)
16mm b/w st. c.11 mins. Sections.
Unity Theatre rehearsals; Medical Aid to China demonstration.

* (FPL PRODUCTION TRIMS) 1935-38
16mm b/w st. c.15 mins. Sections.
Offcuts from JUBILEE, rushes of Cable Street clashes, and anti-war demonstration on Embankment, 1937.

Four 16mm films made by Cuthbertson for his own use, and some 80 16mm reels between

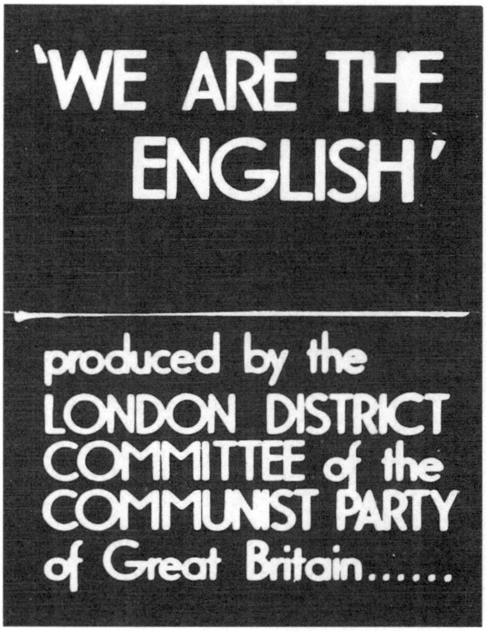

50' and 100' in length of trims, offcuts etc. from FPL and private productions.

London District Committee of the Communist Party of Great Britain
* WE ARE THE ENGLISH 1936
16mm b/w st. c.11 mins. Complete.
People's March through London, September 20th 1936.

LEFT PHOTOGRAPHY TODAY

For financial and technical reasons
we have had to limit the length of this book to 208 pages.
This has meant that a number of articles
originally prepared for this section cannot now be included.
We hope to present a more comprehensive review of current work
in Photography/Politics: Two.

THE EDITORS

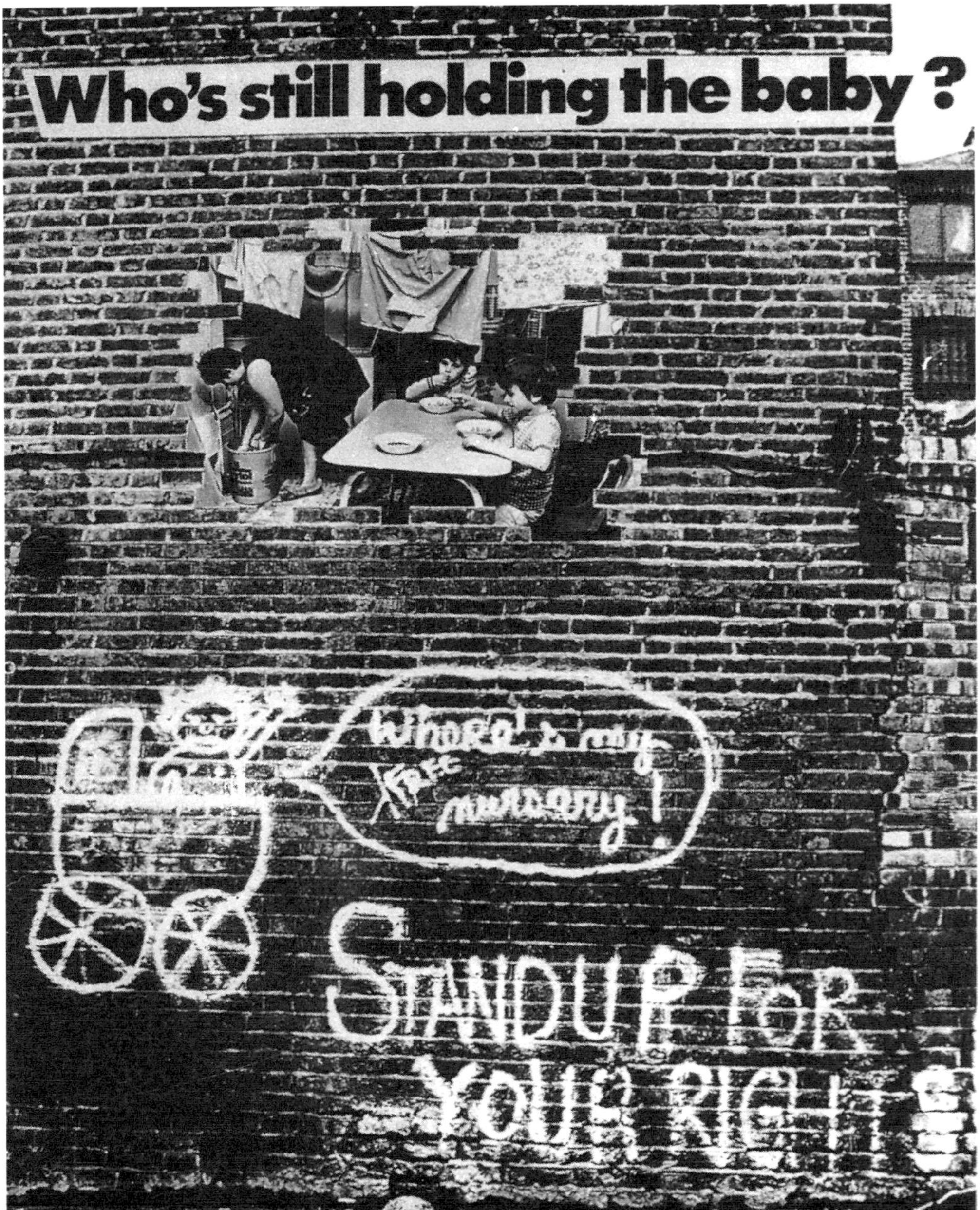

This image was entirely constructed.
The wall was graffitied by us, then photographed; another photograph was taken of the mother and children, then a print laid underneath the hole which we cut in the print of the wall.
Thus the link could be made between the WHY of struggles for childcare facilities, and the HOW.

Hackney Flashers Collective: Who's still holding the camera?

Liz Heron

THE HACKNEY FLASHERS is a collective of ten women who, although they do not share a unified political line, would all define themselves as socialists and feminists. All of them work either in education or the media and some combine teaching and freelance work. The work of the collective has until now been centred in Hackney because most people live in or near the borough and also because, like many other working-class inner city areas with a high immigrant population, its hospital, housing and other services are coming increasingly under attack through the cuts in public spending.

In 1975 the collective produced *Women and Work* – an exhibition of around 100 photographs. It opened at Hackney Town Hall and since then has been in constant demand all over the country and was also shown at the Paris Socialist Feminist International Conference in 1977. Slide shows using *Women and Work* photographs and other images have also been developed and used at a wide range of discussions and events within the women's movement, trade unions and community organisations. Hackney Flasher photographs are used widely in the left and feminist press and are credited not to individual photographers but to Hackney Flashers Collective.

Unlike the original group, the Hackney Flashers is no longer made up exclusively of photographers and photography is only one aspect of the recent *Who's Holding the Baby?* exhibition which opened in July 1978 at Centerprise Community Project in Hackney. It uses cartoons, collage, montage and graphics with photographs and text, and consists of 36 laminated 20" x 30" panels. It is available for hire from: 152 Upper Street, London, N1 1RA.

Collectives get off the ground when people with some political or social purpose in common look for a space to work together. Theatre collectives, film collectives, magazine and book collectives are by now familiar cultural phenomena. But all those fields are more than one-person enterprises anyway and the collective is the democratisation of what is more usually a hierarchical structure. Not so photography – photographers generally work alone, a factor which contributes to the dominant ideology of photographers, professional and political: the lone photographer stalking the decisive moment, showing the bits that no one else sees and which we then recognise as the familiar – the humanist. Whether as "artist" or free-lance photojournalist, the photographer works alone, perceiving himself or herself on the margins of media production.

When a group of North London photographers got together with the aim of organising a joint project because they felt that their work was isolated from any social or political context, it was a new step to take. Certainly exhibition projects have been carried out by two or three photographers together, but with only that specific purpose in mind; and of course there are those who express their politics through the work they do for the left and alternative press. The aim of this group was to develop an ongoing activity in the area where they lived and worked, which probably could define it as what has become known as "community photography" – or rather one of its many varieties. That definition is certainly more applicable to the collective as it was then – four years ago – than now.

Once the group was consolidated it was then a question of what issues to focus on and what form the project would take. The majority – not all at that stage – were women, and wanted to photograph women in the local area, illuminating some of the inequalities faced outside and in the home. But whether it was to be "art", information, or agit-prop, an exhibition, posters, or published in book-form were still questions – so was the eventual audience. An opportune solution came along when Hackney Trades Council offered a project: an exhibition of photographs on women at work in the borough as part of their 75th anniversary celebrations *75 Years of Brotherhood*, (the sisterhood was an afterthought).

Hackney is a predominantly working class borough in East London. The clothing trade, once its major industry, has declined over the last few years as factories have closed and moved north or further east (Hong Kong!). Sweat shops still offer work for women, with poor pay and often in conditions that must pre-date the first Factory Acts. There's a toy factory and the usual range of shop and service jobs – typifying a female labour force in what is usually low-paid and unskilled work. Photographs taken included women in the professions as well as office and manual jobs and were accompanied with statistics and other information. To publicly exhibit so many images of women working was an indisputable achievement – such images were rare. The exhibition was well received and has been in constant demand ever since. However there were also inadequacies and in retrospect it seemed to do no more than make a strong statement in favour of equal pay – necessary, but not enough.

Self-criticism wasn't lacking though, for in the process of preparing the exhibition, sharing skills and ideas, the politics of our feminism had become clearer. There was disparate political experience. Some had been active in left groups and trade unions,

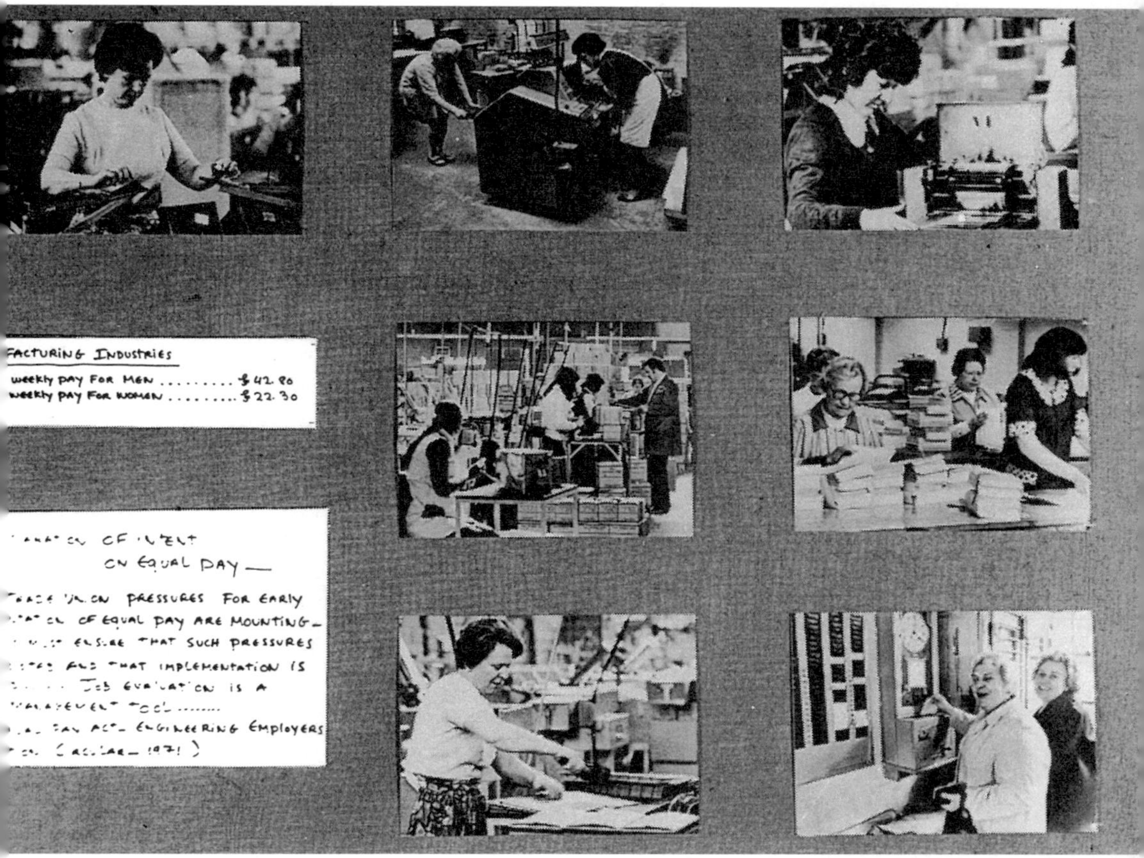

A panel from the exhibition *Women: Work in Hackney*.
The collective's original aim was to document women in Hackney, at work inside and outside the home.
The intention was to make visible the invisible, thereby validating women's experience
and demonstrating their unrecognized contribution to the economy.
The limitations of documentary photography became apparent with the completion of this exhibition.
The pictures were based on the assumption that the camera was a "window on the world",
and did not question the idea that reality is rooted in appearances.

some in community politics and some in the women's movement; the group's cohesion was its feminism, even though not everyone agreed on what that was. There were other differences – in levels of practical and technical knowledge. I joined about two years ago because I wanted to learn about taking pictures and at the same time have a reason for taking them – to work in a group and explore ideas about how pictures were used. My lack of technical knowledge presented no problems. "Professionalism" was never an issue. In principle everyone had something to contribute and those with practical

That was instructive – for what it *didn't* show. The photographs of nurseries and playgroups were useful enough, but the real issue was the long list of children waiting for nursery places, and unlikely to get them. Hackney, for example, has 1,000 children on its top-priority waiting list for day care, to say nothing of all the other under-fives who weren't considered to be in desperate need.

It was only when the decision was made to under take a long-term project on childcare that the difficulty of making it a single issue became clear. The urgency of more childcare

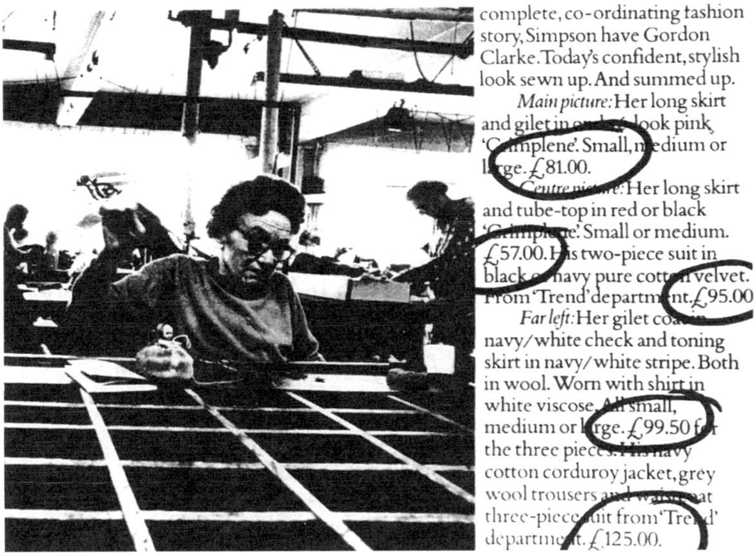

skills were willing to give help and encouragement to the others – there were workshops on darkroom techniques, design and layout. By the time *Women and Work* was completed, a graphic designer and an illustrator were also involved. By then, too, there was a group identity, we had become *The Hackney Flashers*.

One comment made by some other women about the exhibition was taken to heart – there wasn't enough on the difficulties childcare presents for women. A small exhibition on childcare facilities was subsequently produced for the Under-Fives Campaign in the borough.

provision was undeniable but it was recognised that we had to go beyond just supporting the campaign for more nursery places. We had endless meetings where we argued – for keeping things simple, for not alienating anyone, for showing what was desperately needed, and what could be done, and for an overall analysis of motherhood and childcare. Of course we had general agreement on what the problems were, but different emphases – whether to focus on the positive aspects of a local community nursery or concentrate on an analysis of women's oppression in the family and on the ideological role of the media.

We began to juxtapose our naturalistic photographs of women working with information from adverts about the products they were making. We also began to use montage. This way we felt we could better indicate the contradiction between women's experience and its representation in the media. We also wanted to raise the question of class, so much obscured in the idea of women's experience as universal.

That's why it took us over two years to complete the exhibition. I think it's evident

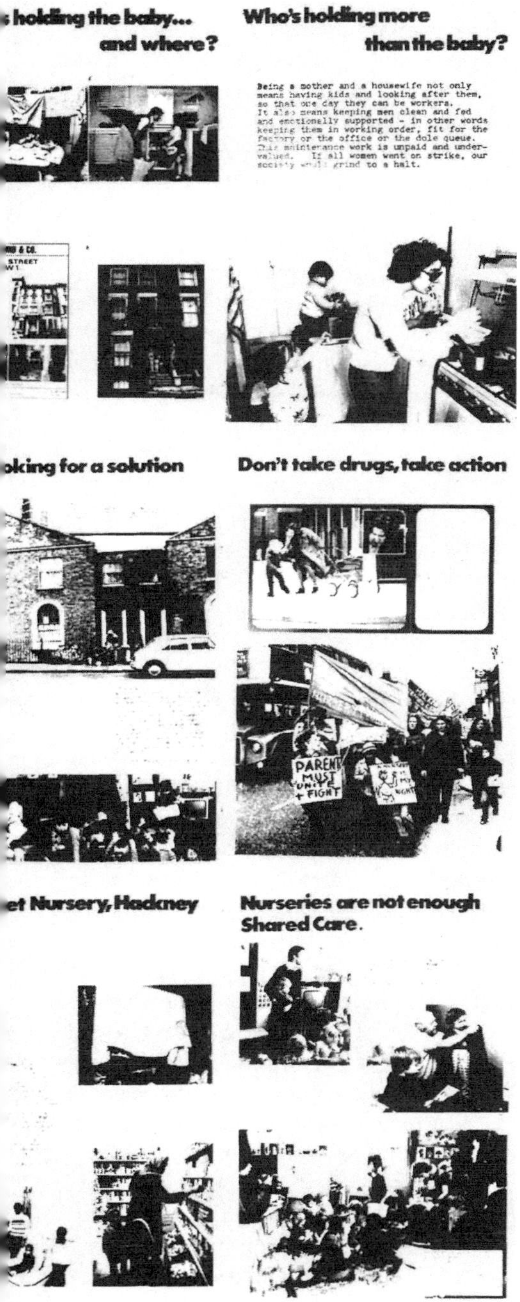

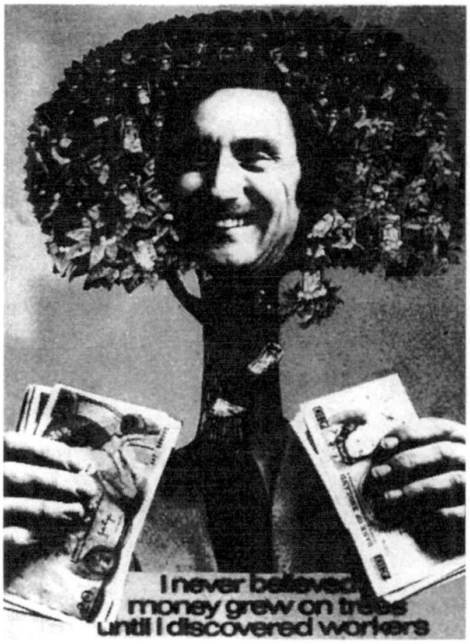

that we tried to do all of those things and more – which may weaken the overall impact, but is proving to be an asset because it can be used by different people in different ways and is even big enough to be split into two separate small exhibitions.

A comparison of *Women and Work* and *Who's Holding the Baby?* demonstrates how much the work of the group has changed. Class is an issue – of course it generally is for middle class photographers with a "socialconscience";

Panels from *Who's Holding the Baby?* Women's "problems" are usually seen as individual, requiring individual solutions. They are represented as passive, suffering, victims, unable to find their own solutions. We wanted to show people taking *collective action*.

the "poor" and the "disadvantaged" have been camera fodder almost throughout the history of photography – but we've moved away from just doing documentary exposes of the "real conditions" (which is not to say that they aren't useful in campaigns for better housing, social services etc.) What we've been more explicit about is the necessity for fighting class oppression as well as women's oppression and showing the two as mutually reinforcing.

We are oppressed by structures that are both capitalist and patriarchal. Patriarchy predates capitalism and women's oppression will not automatically disappear with the end of the capitalist system, but the sexual division of labour has specific forms in capitalist society. The family is not "natural" but is a unit within a set of specific economic and social relations. It is also one of the institutions that has the ideological role of forming our consciousness – giving us an explanation for reality and constructing us within that reality. This consciousness is not simply "false" – its structures are too deeply embedded in our reality for us to simply see right through it once we become aware that it is a construct, but we can understand how ideology works and challenge it.

Women's position in the family is central. Women have the subordinate role of servicing the wage labourer and reproducing the future labour-force. But as well as being domestic labourers women themselves are also wage labourers. Capitalism attempts to deal with this contradiction by continuing to treat women as economically dependent on men and as having the primary role of wives and mothers, and (despite legislation) managing to conveniently maintain women as the cut-price section of the labour force, concentrated in low-paid and unskilled jobs. Women's struggles around equal pay, childcare, abortion, contraception and other issues are of crucial importance in undermining the ideologies of femininity and domesticity. By challenging their subordinate roles not only in the family, but also in the hierarchy of labour, women are also attacking the class structures of capitalist society.

It is possible that capitalism could incorporate other forms of the family, but it is the ideology that supports it in its present form that we have to challenge. As women, we learn about ourselves through the family and the education system, and also through the images of ourselves that society holds up to us; but much of women's lived experience is absent from those images. *Women and Work* attempted to attack stereotyped images by concentrating on those areas of women's lives which are usually invisible. They were alternative images but because of their form were unable to contradict the dominant notions of women's role in our society. *Women and Work* was a series of black and white photographs – it used naturalism, the "window on the world" technique, assuming transparency. But the visible world doesn't so easily yield up the reality of power relationships and institutions. In order to challenge images that serve to maintain women's subordination it is necessary to question the ideas and myths *behind* such images. For example, a working-class woman may recognise herself in a photograph of a woman working in a factory. While this self-recognition is important in terms of validating *individual* lived experience, it cannot negate the power of what advertising and other media images represent as *social* reality. These images are not simply a distortion of how we "really" are, but are part of a process of constructing us and prescribing our feminine role.

While this process starts even before we're out of our pink baby clothes, it's during adolescence that the ideological onslaught really hits us hard. Magazines aimed at the teenage market call upon girls to recognise themselves as "feminine". We can probably all remember the effect of those glamorous images alongside the barrage of advertisements that guaranteed to rid us of the imperfections that blighted our lives, but our miserable failure to ever recognize ourselves in what was constituted as attainable perfection, despite all the cosmetic paraphernalia we consumed, induced more than enough self-loathing to prepare us for a

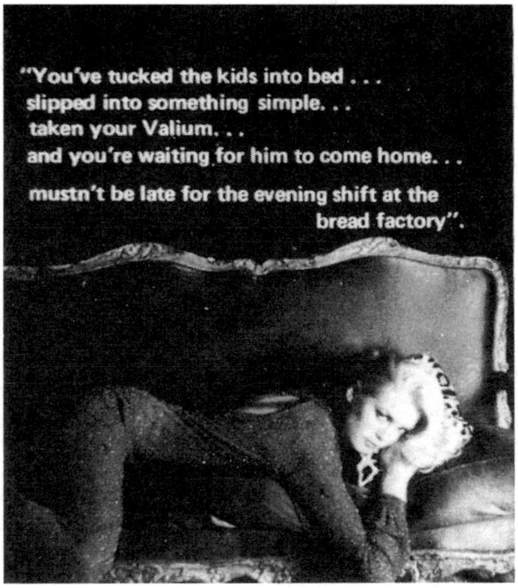

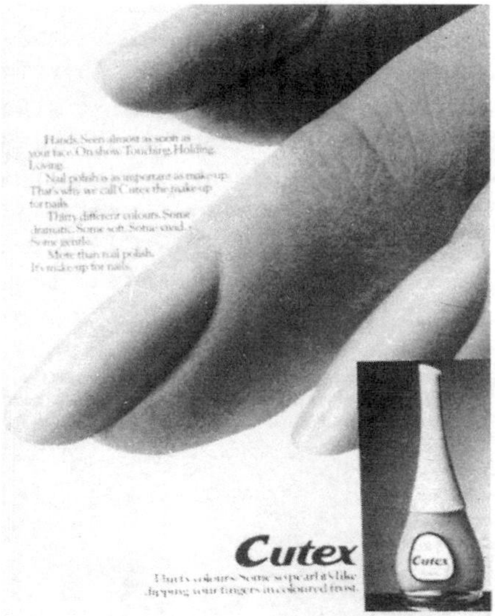

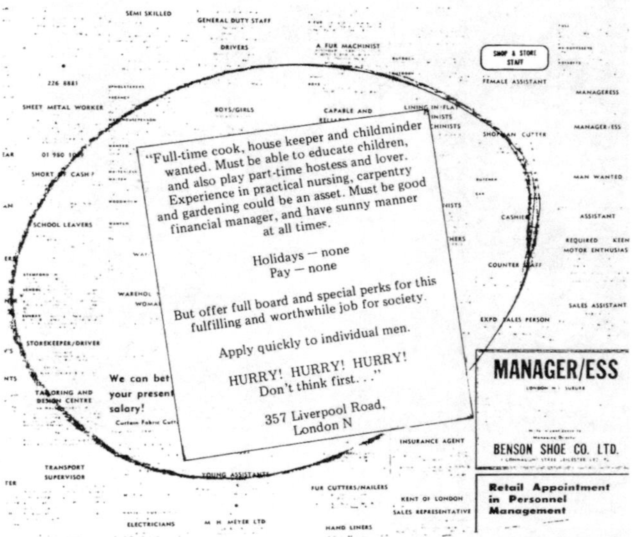

We began to subvert advertisements. Advertising doesn't present us with a false or distorted image of ourselves; it places us in relation to its images in such a way that it thereby defines us.

lifetime of subordination. The learning of femininity was also a lesson in inferiority.

Of course this symbolic oppression continues. Images of women as "workers" emphasise the feminine qualities indispensable to the job – the efficient well-groomed secretary, the nurse's hygienic glamour, the numerous other caring and servicing occupations where the way you look, smell and smile is vitally important. Job expectations are influenced by definitions of work as "masculine" and "feminine". For boys, some kinds of work acquire "masculine" status through the exclusion of women.

signify the same thing as the mother about to leave for the nightshift at the factory if there is nothing connecting them? By looking like an ad our "ad" refers to advertisements and their contradictions.

Naturalistic images of women in advertisements, acknowledging the pressures women have to cope with *are* to be found not, however, between the covers of *Woman* or *Cosmopolitan*, but between the covers of the medical journals. Here women are represented as helpless victims of bad housing and oppressed by the burden of two jobs – "the working mother".

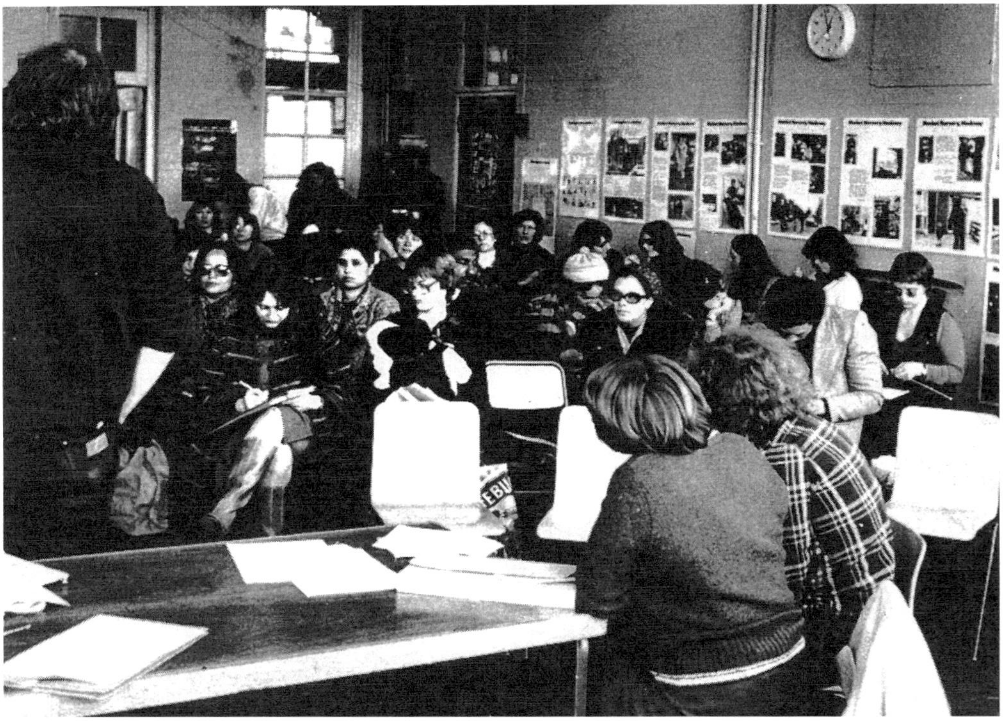

The current exhibition is used in a variety of situations, here at a one-day conference on childcare in Bethnal Green, East London.

For girls the reality of monotonous unskilled work is obscured by notions of glamour and femininity. Even the ads aimed at "working girls" use economic independence to reinforce ultimate dependence on a man – the pay packet can buy perfume, clothes, beauty, a man. There is also a recent trend in identifying women as potential house buyers, investors and bank account holders, which incorporates the acknowledgement of women's changed legal status in some areas. Recognition of changing roles and "Women's Liberation" is implicit in much of the "beauty" consumerism – the sexually independent woman. Here women are not simply sex-objects for men, but for themselves. Sensual images of voluptuous breasts, pouting lips and dewy skin surfaces can evoke a response that goes beyond just "wanting to be like that" as the object of a man's look, and is more like "wanting to feel like that". Images like that cannot simply be dismissed as "sexist exploitation" but demand some exploration of how advertisements use unconscious structures.

Images of women vary according to class – down-market and up-market products demand different images of femininity, but images of women consistently cut across class differences and disguise them. Shared roles of wife and mother create the illusion of shared experience, though they may differ vastly in their degrees of economic manoeuvrability. Our panel showing a nanny, an *au pair*, a child minder, and a mother, each with children, attempts to point out that money (or the lack of it) can make motherhood an easier or more difficult reality. Economic privilege is negated in newspaper and magazine stories about famous and wealthy women where, as a wife, a mother or a daughter, their experiences of the day-to-day joys and sorrows of family life are equated with Mrs Average and a day in her life – the message is that be it in the palace or the council flat the "female condition" is universal. Another panel takes an ad image of a smiling family outside their suburban middle-class home and puts it with a black-and-white photograph of a Hackney family in damp, overcrowded housing. We are not denying that middle-class women are also oppressed by their subordination to men and the gender-based discrimination they encounter, but we are attempting to expose the class differences that are usually hidden in representations of family life.

As well as fragmenting women's bodies, the media fragments women into different types and roles in order to define and locate the market for its products. The housewife is the prime consumer. Here, in the breakfast-to-bed-time role of cleaning the house and servicing the family, women's economic activity is absent. The proportion of married women in the labour force increases every year yet the need for more, not less, childcare provision goes officially unrecognised. The ideology of motherhood is one of the things we attempted to expose in *Who's Holding the Baby*; a collage of consumer goods answers the question *What are mothers made of?* Separate panels use graphics with photographs of wartime provision for children while their mothers worked in the factories, alongside contemporary photographs of children playing unsupervised because official policy has now relocated women in the home, although in reality they're still in the factories. We used speech bubbles with a photograph of a homeworker and her child to give information about her pitifully low piece-work earnings. Invisible not only in imagery but also in employment statistics, these women are a hidden category of workers, forced to do this kind of work because they need the money, but are also forced to stay at home to look after children.

Advertising is able to incorporate new images and contain contradictions – the reliable whiter-than-white mum can even hint at dissatisfaction and non fulfilment, but what could be a dangerous acknowledgement of certain needs and desires is apparently resolved by the offer of the product and the fantasy or the joke that comes with it. However, the same techniques can be employed to expose contradictions – without the ideological polyfilla. That's what we tried to do in our "advertisement". How can the vamp on the couch

The products that solve these problems are drugs – making it possible to cope with the "strain of modern living". In the exhibition we used a cartoon strip to tell the story of a woman in search of childcare – her only possible solutions are taking drugs to forget the problems, or taking action to attack them.

We started juxtaposing images with photographs when we worked on putting together two sets of slides. One member of the group had collected and classified a wide range of media images and had put them on slide. Photographs from *Women and Work* had also been put on slide and were being used as a basis for discussions at meetings and conferences. We discussed how the two sets of images could be used together and the idea of collage and montage came out of that. A workshop produced our first collective efforts – a photograph of a women working in a garment factory juxtaposed with an advertisement showing a glamorous evening dress with a three-figure price tag. It became clear that the context in which an image was used could dramatically alter its meaning. In *Who's Holding the Baby?* we've tried to subvert images and question their meaning.

We've also tried to question the unchangeability of "motherhood" by demonstrating that there are alternative possibilities for looking after children: collective childcare, childcare shared by men and women, and by giving information about the campaigns around nurseries, abortion and contraception, violence against women, and other related issues. The section made up of photographs and interviews with the families involved in the Market Nursery reveals a network of support in coping with problems like homelessness, illness, poor housing, unemployment and the difficulties experienced by the growing numbers of single-parent families.

We don't see the Market Nursery as a "solution", but there was a strong feeling among some members of the collective that it was vital to document an example of united action around childcare provision that had been successful. Even though it was only on the level of making demands on the Council for funding, it was also about taking control. Unfortunately, because it amounts to such a large proportion of the exhibition it makes the analysis ambiguous. We now see the possibility of the exhibition being used in different ways depending on its audience – with the removal of certain panels or sections. For example, to people directly involved in nursery campaigns the Market Nursery section could be of practical use, while in other contexts the exhibition could possibly be used with only three or four of the Market Nursery panels. Whatever its failings, though, the exhibition can nonetheless be a valuable educational and agitational tool.

The cost of materials and lamination for the exhibition was met by part of a grant which we received from the Gulbenkian Foundation. The remainder of the grant is set aside to pay an administrator one day a week. She has responsibility for exhibition bookings and deals with correspondence and enquiries we get for pictures and slides, as well as working to generate an income so that the group will be self-financing after the grant has run out. There is also money for materials to produce educational packs for use in schools. The grant came just in time, when we were uncertain about how we were going to pay for producing the exhibition and feeling that we ourselves would never be able to finance future projects.

In fact our future activity is currently under discussion. One decision has been unanimous – no more long-term projects. The variety of different emphases within the group made us feel that *Who's Holding the Baby?* was too much of an unhappy compromise for everybody. The arguments and the problems are beginning to fade from memory and we're already feeling more positive, but we have also decided to be more realistic about how we work together in future. We'll probably work on a number of smaller projects – producing educational materials, doing agit-prop posters and postcards, montage and collage and, for some of us, spending more time on study and discussion. Our experiences of working in the group have been useful and educative – contributing to the development of individual confidence and the acquisition of practical skills, part of a learning process in how we see images and how we see ourselves. Hopefully that process will continue for all of us.

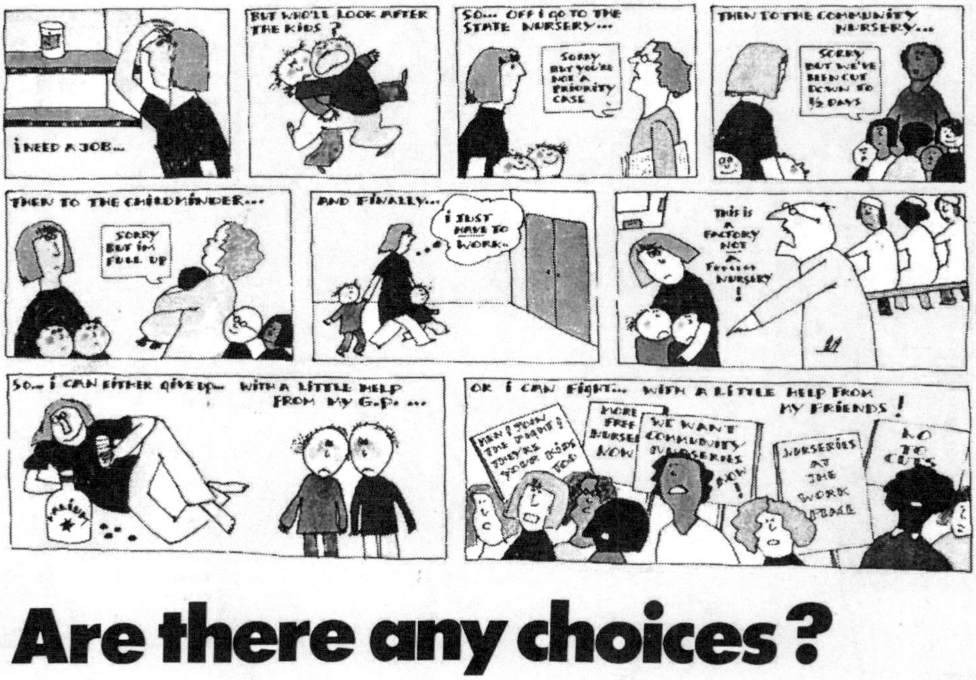

We used cartoons when we felt that the camera was inappropriate or inadequate.

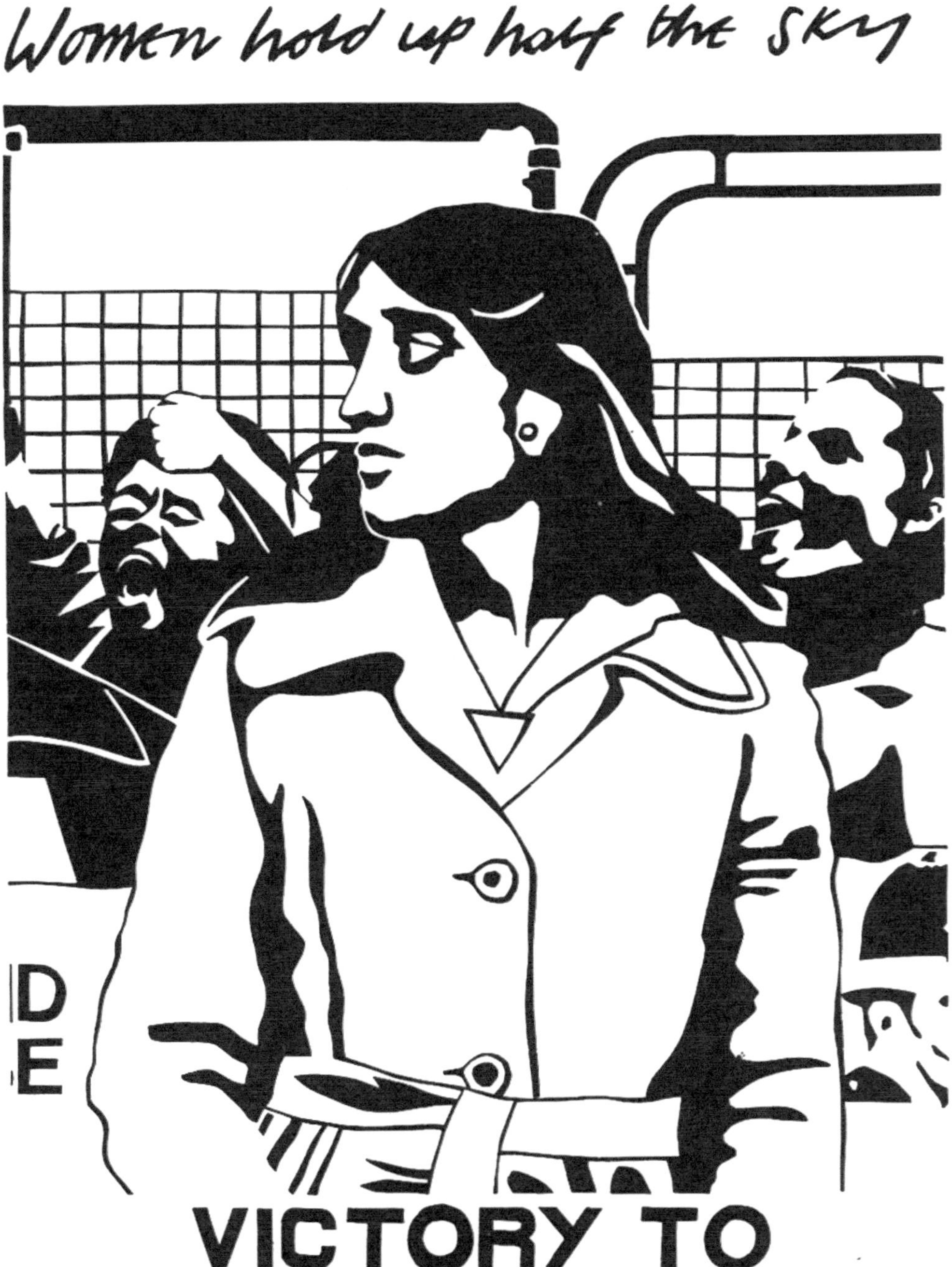
Women hold up half the sky
D
E
VICTORY TO
GRUNWICK STRIKERS

Film and Poster Collective

Interview

YOU WORK AS A COLLECTIVE; *how is the group organised?*
The group in its present form has developed principally over the last three years, although different individuals have been active over a much longer period. We work very much on a day-to-day basis, and this means that members have a total working commitment. There is no formal structure to the group other than a fully associated working basis, and most decisions and responsibilities are developed in a direct manner. Overall there is no division of labour, but it is the case that certain tasks have a tendency to be carried out on an uneven basis. In a sense responsibility is there to be taken, the more responsibility over different questions and matters that are taken up the more we can move forward. Often when we have problems with our work, we might tend towards systematizing it and dividing our responsibility formally, and to a schedule, but it would be difficult for us to move forward totally on a formal basis as that would not provide the necessary dynamic. At different stages, different individuals or even the whole group might get frustrated with this process, but it necessitates the eventual seizure

of initiative and the realization of the process we're involved with.

How do you maintain yourselves financially?
Overall we have managed to maintain economic self-sufficiency although on two occasions we have applied for separate project grants. When we first set up the present studio we discussed in detail the whole question of grant-aided structures, and overall we rejected the idea of becoming reliant on continuous grants (even assuming that it would be possible). First of all, this would have meant that we would have had to shape our structure to maximise the possibility of getting a grant, and then continue to maintain this initial framework in order to sustain the grant. For us, it was very important to create a structure based on free association, with total political and cultural commitment, and from there mobilise people to join on that basis (grants often serve only to create hierarchies and divisions of power).

How do you see the role of the artist?
In most respects we have rejected the traditional cultural role of the artist. Fundamentally, the artist's role within capitalist society is not really one of creating illusions about the class, but rather has become structurally an illusion of the class. The artist is a kind of emblem of freedom, someone who is negatively free to do anything in the name of art. The adoption of a preconceived, historically constructed, model (in the avant-garde tradition) moves against any radical rupture with the existing state of things. But at the same time, the manner in which an alternative practice is constructed and developed constitutes a problematic. There is no easy answer; the question can only be resolved over a protracted period and in conjunction with the unfolding of class struggle.

Do you see yourselves as "political interventionists", or rather as a "resource"?
We wouldn't pose the question in those terms. One seems to imply an active role, and the other passive. There are many difficulties in taking up a stance in relation to the question. As soon as you attempt to create a revolutionary structure it becomes a societal intervention. By definition you stand as a critique of something. But to proceed beyond that point there are many different elements to the question of political intervention. First of all, essentially the main form of our intervention is cultural, although the determination is primarily political. If we pose culture against politics, resource against intervention, we can get ourselves into many problems. The attempt is to unify a practice across these different elements in a concrete way to be both a resource whilst we attempt to intervene; both elements come into play at any given instance as complementary. Quite simply, if the attempt is to direct any apparatus in the direction of socialism you are addressing yourself not only to the development of emancipative forms socially but also towards the transformational element within your own given practice.

Who do you see as your "audience"?
As a group we hold together an apparatus of production which lends itself to be used to give a form of voice to those in struggle. At the same time the posters, slide shows, film shows, themselves create a basis for struggle. The question of audience is difficult in the sense that we have very little empirical information on, say, how the posters eventually get used.

With the advent of the first truly revolutionary means of reproduction, photography, simultaneously with the rise of socialism, art sensed the approaching crisis which has become evident later. At the time art reacted with the doctrine l'art pour l'art, that is with a theology of art. This gave rise to what might be called a negative theology in the idea of "pure" art, which not only denied any social function of art but also any categorizing by subject matter.

BENJAMIN

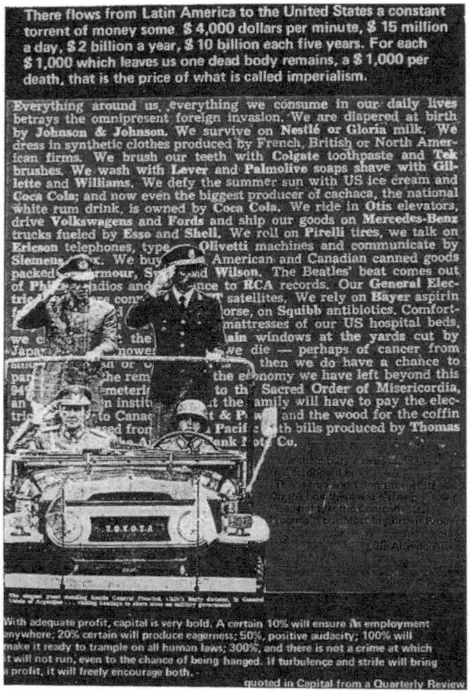
There flows from Latin America to the United States a constant torrent of money some $ 4,000 dollars per minute, $ 15 million a day, $ 2 billion a year, $ 10 billion each five years. For each $ 1,000 which leaves us one dead body remains, a $ 1,000 per death, that is the price of what is called imperialism.
Everything around us, everything we consume in our daily lives betrays the omnipresent foreign invasion. We are diapered at birth by Johnson & Johnson. We survive on Nestlé or Gloria milk. We dress in synthetic clothes produced by French, British or North American firms. We brush our teeth with Colgate toothpaste and Tek brushes. We wash with Lever and Palmolive soaps shave with Gillette and Williams. We defy the summer sun with US ice cream and Coca Cola; and now even the biggest producer of cachaca, the national white rum drink, is owned by Coca Cola. We ride in Otis elevators, drive Volkswagens and Fords and ship our goods on Mercedes-Benz trucks fueled by Esso and Shell. We roll on Pirelli tires, we talk on Ericson telephones,
With adequate profit, capital is very bold. A certain 10% will ensure its employment anywhere; 20% certain will produce eagerness; 50%, positive audacity; 100% will make it ready to trample on all human laws; 300%, and there is not a crime at which it will not run, even to the chance of being hanged. If turbulence and strife will bring a profit, it will freely encourage both.
quoted in Capital from a Quarterly Review

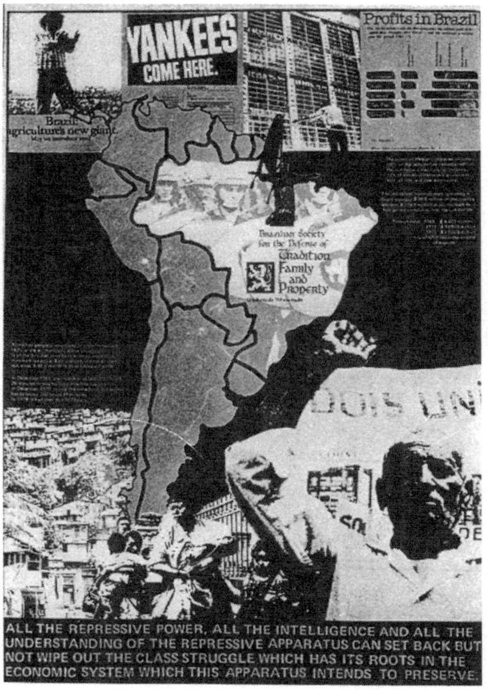
YANKEES
COME HERE.
Profits in Brazil
Brazil:
agriculture's new giant
Brazilian Society
for the Defense of
Tradition
Family
and
Property
ALL THE REPRESSIVE POWER, ALL THE INTELLIGENCE AND ALL THE UNDERSTANDING OF THE REPRESSIVE APPARATUS CAN SET BACK BUT NOT WIPE OUT THE CLASS STRUGGLE WHICH HAS ITS ROOTS IN THE ECONOMIC SYSTEM WHICH THIS APPARATUS INTENDS TO PRESERVE.

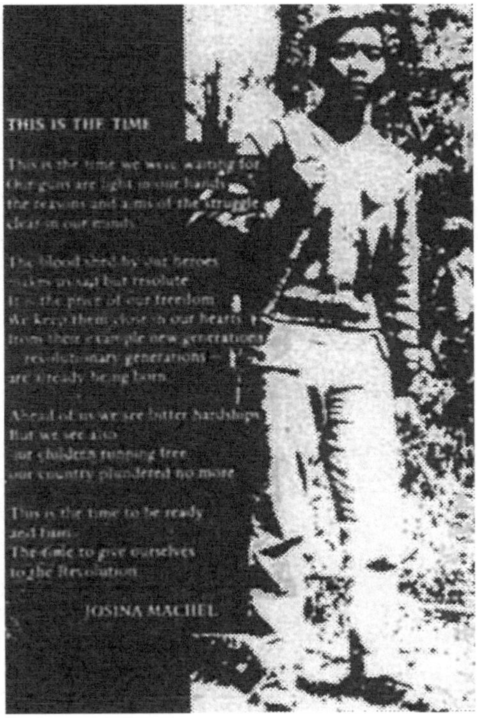
THIS IS THE TIME
JOSINA MACHEL

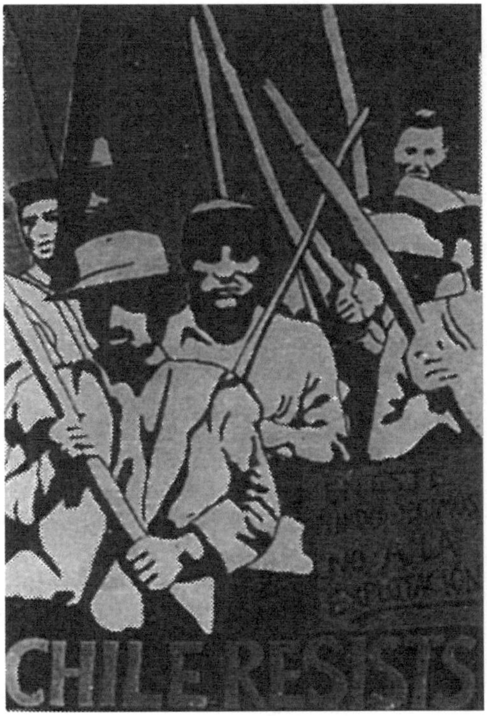
CHILE RESISTS

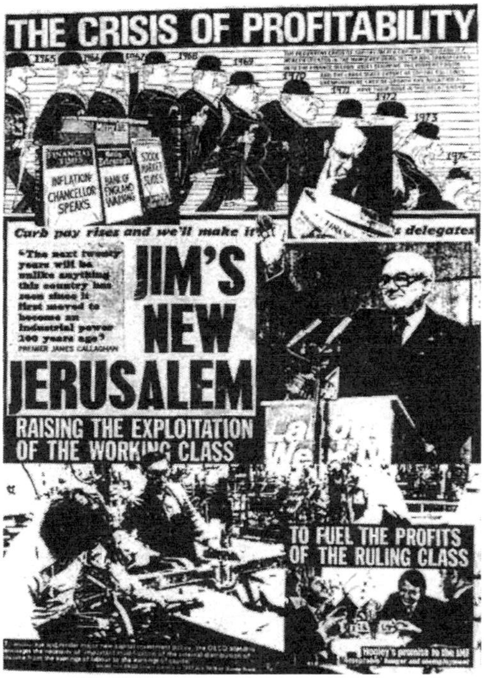

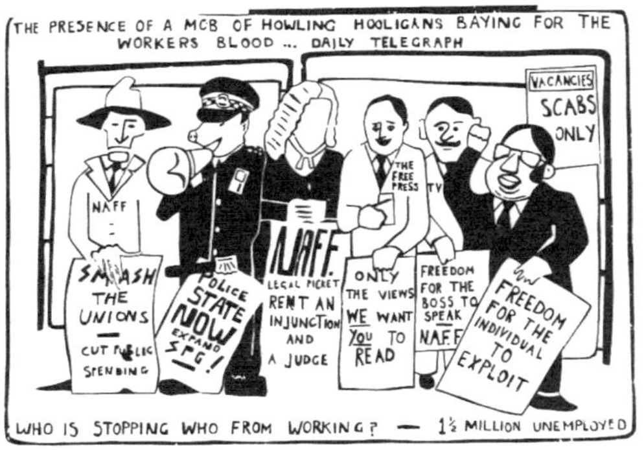

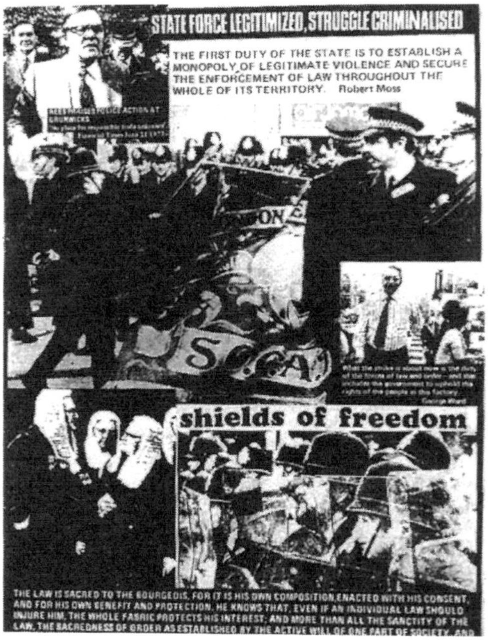

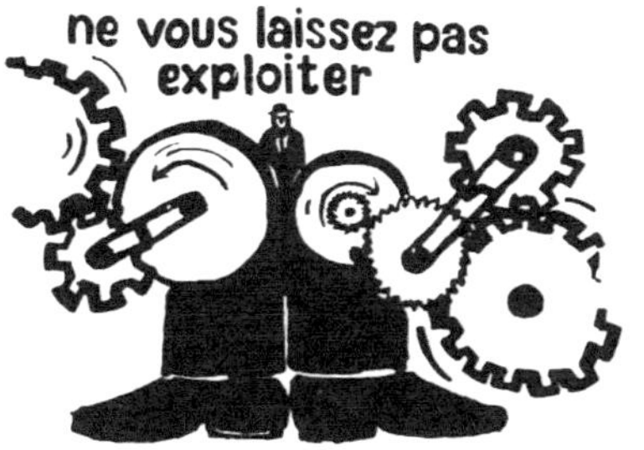

Brecht has coined the phrase "functional transformation" to describe the transformation of forms and instruments of production by a progressive intelligentsia – an intelligentsia interested in liberating the means of production and hence active in class struggle. He was the first to address to the intellectuals the far reaching demand that they should not supply the production apparatus without, at the same time, within the limits of the possible, changing the apparatus in the direction of Socialism.

BENJAMIN

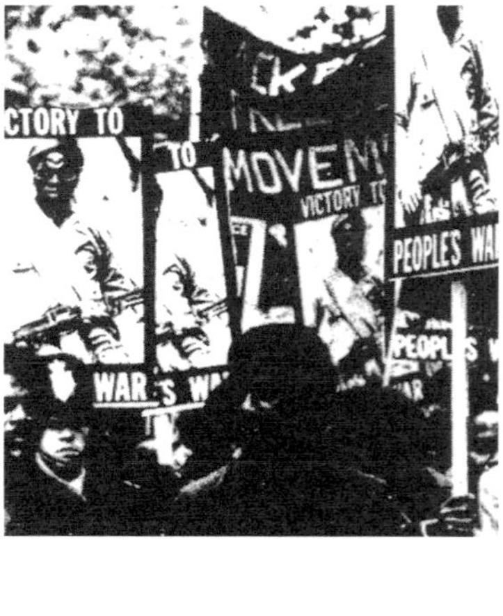

Our posters are distributed through many different sources – bookshops, meetings, demonstrations, groups. Also, there are many people who have large selections of posters for showing in exhibition form. Probably the majority of this form of display is abroad. Although the more politically structured showing and use of posters is important we also feel that the availability of posters for people to put up, either in their home or in the workplace, is also vital. Alongside the distribution of posters we have also attempted to use forms which more directly involve the immediate audience. Generally the use of film and slide shows have developed with either very particular political conjunctures or with particular political groups. Also, in the future we will attempt to develop the use of magazines where established distribution outlets exist – although we will obviously engage in attempting to extend methods of distribution for ourselves in this area as well.

How do you see the "message" of your posters? How do you decide what to tackle at any given time?
Most of the posters have a fairly unambiguous message, but we don't feel that this is the same as a closed or determined message. It is probably more the manner in which the posters have a relationship to fairly defined political events that determines this factor. Overall we have discussion and study around various questions and an attempt to formulate an approach to given questions, both in anticipation of how we see that things might be developing or as a response to a particular situation. Once we decide to do a particular poster we go through a process of drawing out a rough, then discussing it. From that point we will either resolve the problem or attempt a solution from another angle.

Your work seems to be evolving along several different lines: how has this come about?
This reflects the fact that, structurally, we work on different levels. First of all we work on given projects over a long period of time, alongside doing work with particular groups, as well as printing very basic information posters. At present we feel that we have been working in a very limited way and now that we have established the pre-conditions, both in terms of our working relationships and our resources, we will be able to explore the different areas of work in a much more developed way.

One large area of work that is being evolved is producing posters showing various historical developments that inform the present. This work has an importance in that the dominant culture severs links with the past, in a sense attempting to create a constant "now-ness" around people.

On a broader level the question of being able to develop new forms and approaches is extremely important in that we have to constantly evolve a language and technique capable of addressing themselves to new situations. Our working situation can often blunt awareness of the importance of this factor but we feel that we are beginning to address ourselves to it much more consciously now.

You seem to have moved away from the idea of a single, unproblematic, picture and slogan. Why is this?
Almost all the posters we have done combine text and image: many of the early posters were made up of just one image and a slogan, as they were often used as placards on demonstrations. Probably one of the main reasons why many of the posters have become much more dense in terms of text and image is that we want to produce posters that have a possibility of staying up on a wall in order to be viewed over a longer period of time. Instead of making an emphatic statement we wanted to explore something which could open out much more in terms of processes of reading, not just within the poster itself, but also in relationships with the specific conjuncture the poster is addressing itself to.

What do you think is the political and cultural role of the poster?

Historically, the role of posters and wall newspapers has varied enormously. Five sets of examples come immediately to mind: the Rosta posters from the Soviet Union, Heartfield's photo-montages, wall newspapers from the People's Republic of China, the Cuban posters, and the posters of May '68.

If we look first at the Rosta posters, we can see how the poster was used very consciously as a form of communication in a society with low literacy. These posters combined simple graphic technique, utilising popular folk form, with slogan and text. Heartfield's are still upheld today as being, in many respects, the highest form of political propaganda that has yet been attained. With the use of the most advanced forms of production, Heartfield developed forms far more advanced than those in use in the commercial sphere of that society. These posters attempted to expose the development of Nazism in a total manner and it is interesting that even today, when we think in general of how to characterise fascism, images of Heartfield's work come to mind. The use of the Chinese wall newspaper is an example of large scale participation in a public form of polemic, using a combination of large character text and cartoon form. The Cuban posters give us an example of how rich in visual terms the poster can be. Originally many of the artists involved in producing the posters had been trained in American graphic design schools and synthesised the various arts of billboard painting and commercial design into the politicised national culture of Cuba after the revolution. The May '68 posters, again, cannot be separated from the political event that they represent. They speak of total attack, rejection of bourgeois class rule in a language which is unique and particular to a very strong spontaneous movement. In each of the five cases, the posters served different purposes, and are formally very different, as each of the situations were.

What is interesting is that we carry a mental image in each instance of a general style, something within the approach and the form which has a powerful unity with a political event. Going briefly through some of the historical examples of particular cultural forms often helps to highlight different relationships and possibilities, but it is essential to develop new forms according to the particularities of our own culture and traditions.

Do you ever hold workshops, or pass on your skills to others?
We don't hold formal workshops as such, but when groups want to do a poster we attempt to work through as much of the process as possible with them. Also, various people have worked over a longer period of time, learning the processes without necessarily being fully part of the overall group. Probably, the most important part of the skill is thinking through the whole way in which people represent themselves. Once that process is learnt, then it has far greater transformational implications than the learning of the particular skills involved in printing, although they are obviously still very important.

Where do you get your basic imagery from?
We collect material from various sources, although the majority comes from either books or other publications. We use very few photographs that we have ourselves taken, although we are gradually learning better photographic skills. This is because we usually work very quickly on any given poster, and therefore attempt to reach a solution with the material we have most readily available at that particular time (we have a large image file which has been built up over a number of years) – though this is far from ideal and leads to many shortcomings in the posters. Unless you have a situation in which you can work over a long period of time resolving graphic problems, then a more pragmatic approach to the use of various images is going to be dominant. The other main factor determining the overall image is an economic one. Most of our posters tend to be two colours because we are working within certain cost and time limitations.

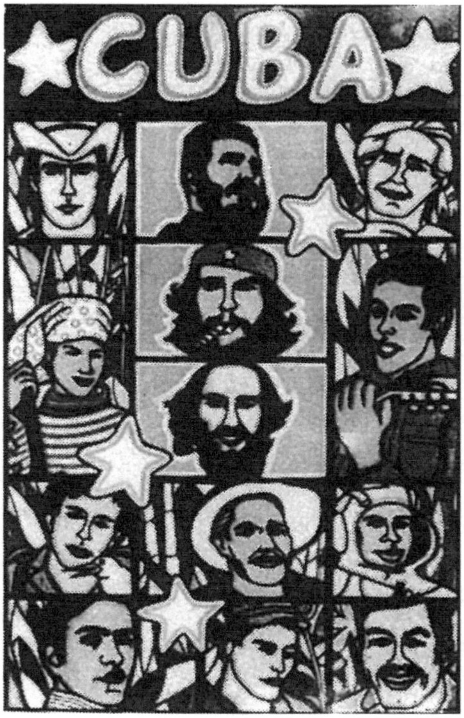

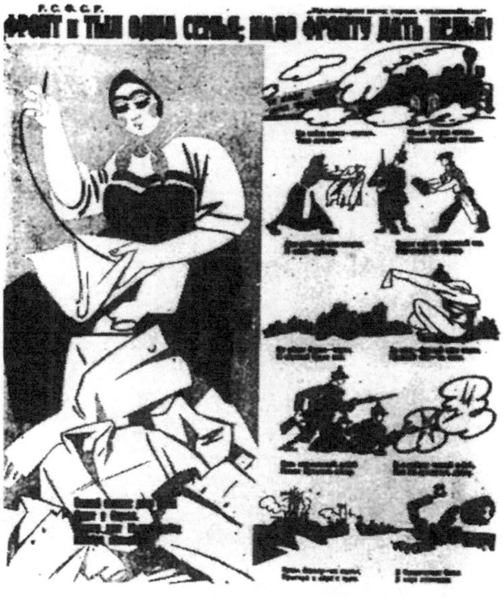

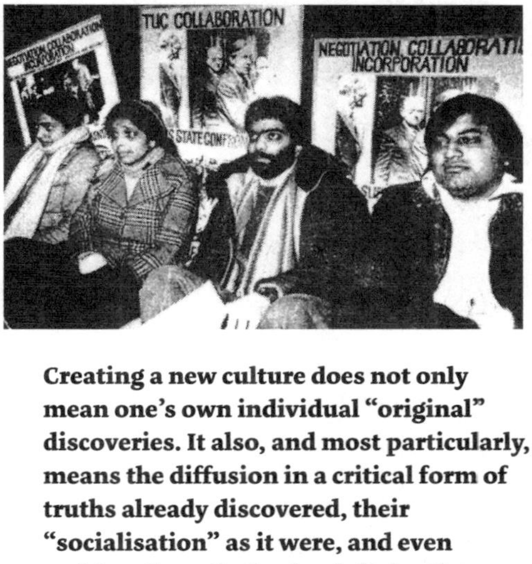

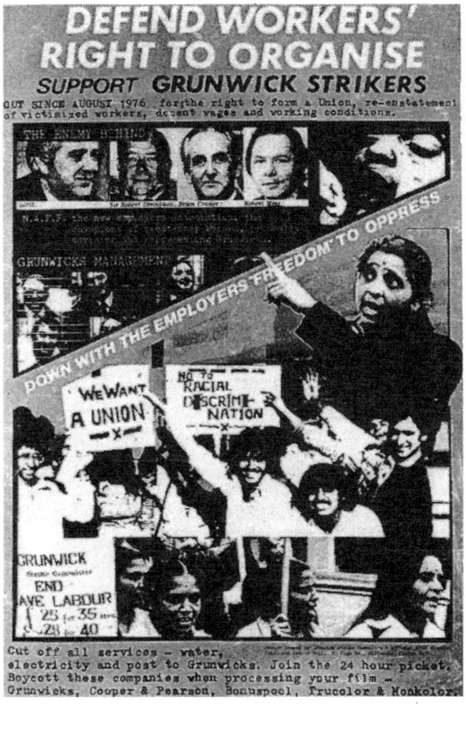

Creating a new culture does not only mean one's own individual "original" discoveries. It also, and most particularly, means the diffusion in a critical form of truths already discovered, their "socialisation" as it were, and even making them the basis of vital action, an element of co-ordination and intellectual and moral order. For a mass of people to be led to think coherently, and in the same coherent fashion about the real present world, is a "philosophical" event far more important and "original" than the discovery of some philosophical "genius" of truth which remains the property of small groups of intellectuals

GRAMSCI

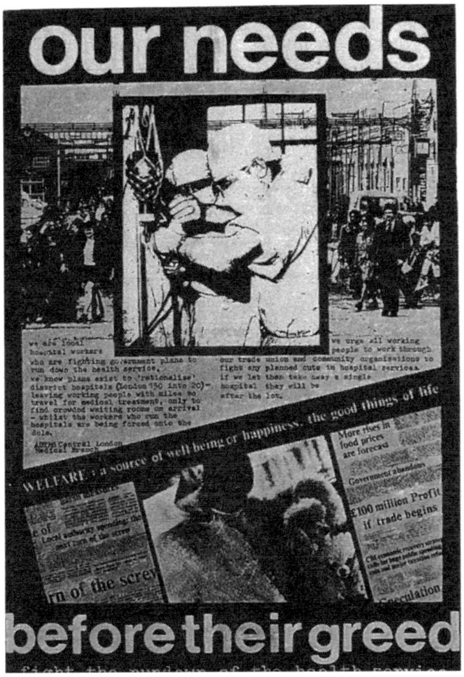

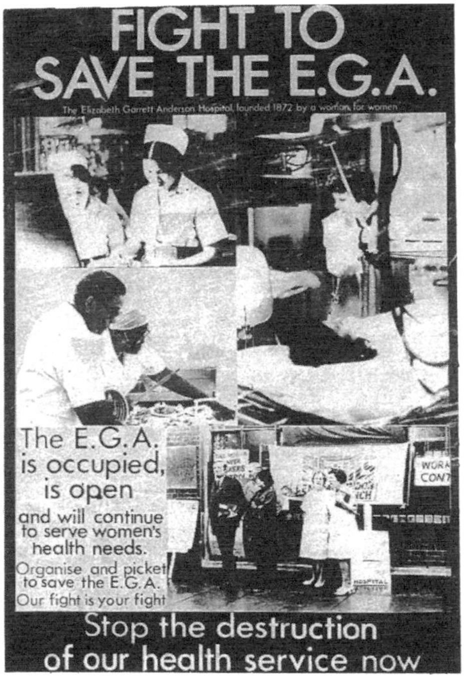

To wind up, can you tell us why you have added film to the group's work?

On the whole, our main concern is not *particular* media but rather it is in finding ways to work around different questions with the most appropriate means. Within that we do not have a totally free choice as we do not have free access to all the means of production at any given time. One of the reasons we started making posters was because it was the cheapest way in which we could make statements, and from there built up permanent means to continue doing so. From that point, we have attempted to expand outwards: first, with a slide projector and then by borrowing film equipment. We think that it is very important to build up independent means of production, and with it, the skills necessary to fully utilize the means. In general, film can be a far more powerful medium than that of the printed image, but very often posters and pamphlets can work far more effectively, especially within limited economic circumstances. We would like, over a period of time, to be able to work in various media in an overall manner on given questions, in such a way that we are using more of a complementary, totalising, approach. We were very aware of the way in which certain forms of media classification, such as film, theatre, poster groups, tend towards isolating the way in which various different groups work. In the long term, we want to work towards a situation where many different skills and media can be used in conjunction with one another, under a single umbrella.

For further information and price sheet, please send s.a.e. to Poster-Film Collective, Box No. 50, 182 Upper Street, London N1.

MINDA

PRIOR TO THE FORMATION of the Anti-Nazi League, the anti-fascist/anti-racist movement in Britain had no overall strategy in the fight against the National Front. There were no leaflets, posters or newspapers produced on a national basis available to all groups – and suitable for all political tendencies within the Labour movement. There were also few coordinated activities on a regional or national basis – all main activities were "local"... and often divisive and sectarian.

CARF – originally the paper of a South London Campaign Against Racism and Fascism – was launched as part of an attempt to co-ordinate the work of the various anti-fascist/ anti-racist groups in London. It aimed to provide a regular news coverage of racist and fascist activity – both in the London area and nationally – together with analysis and discussion of events. Its pages were open to all the London groups – and later those outside London – who were encouraged to provide local stories and reports.

From its concept, CARF was designed and "put together" by two people who went under the pseudonym of MINDA. From the beginning,

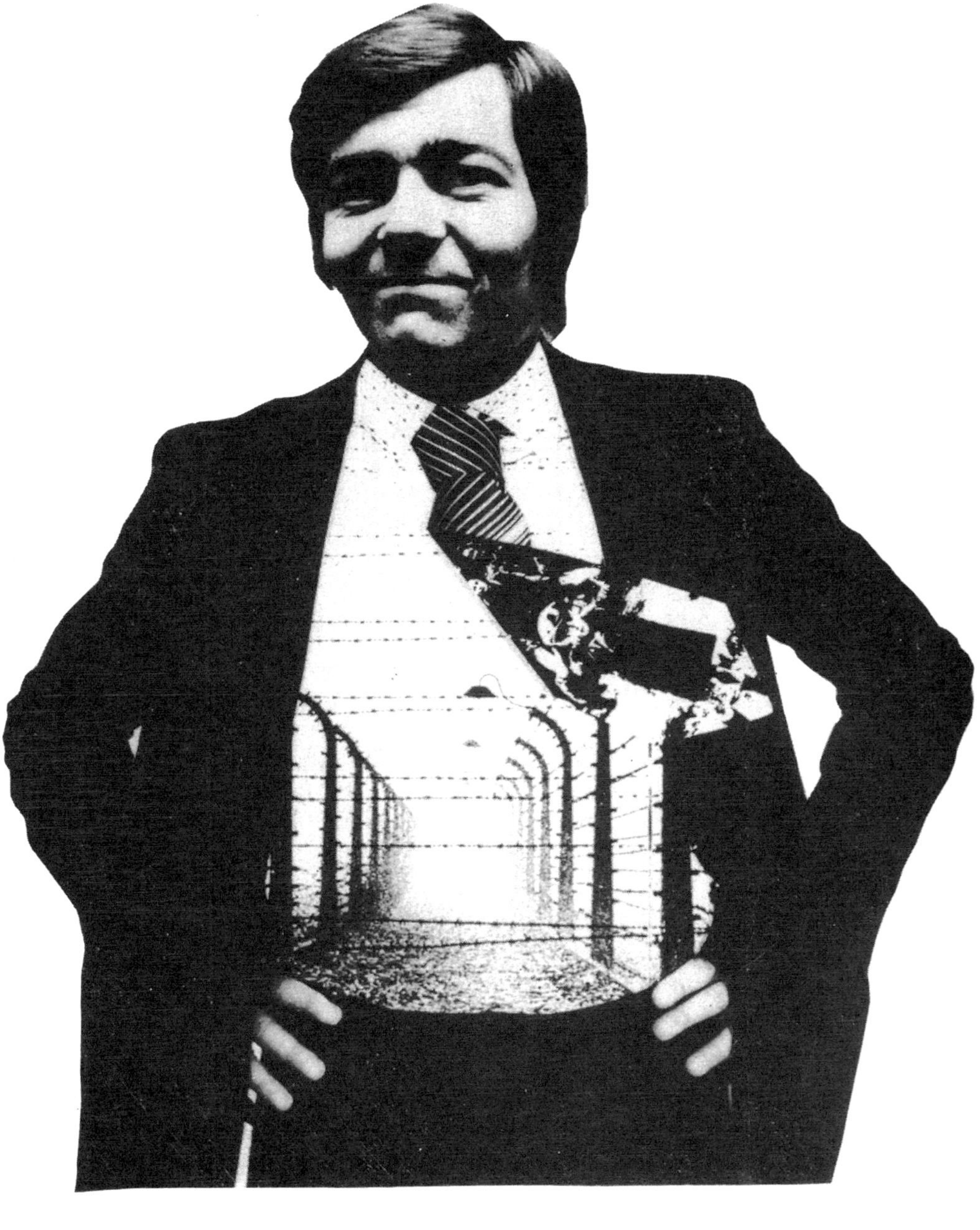

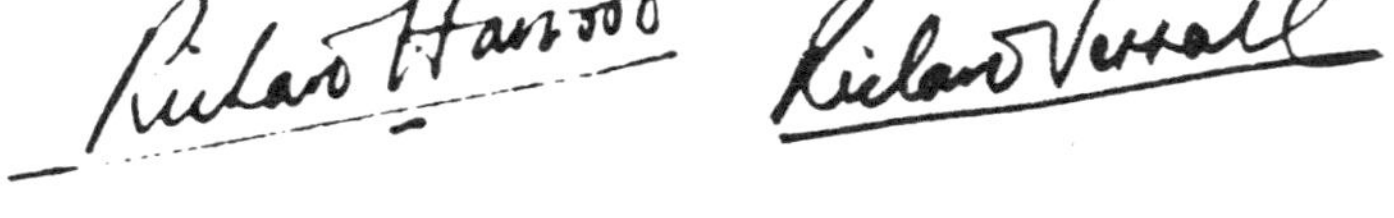

photographs and photomontages were always regarded as of equal importance to the text. Large areas of grey type with long and rambling theoretical articles were avoided. The aim was to produce a "fast-looking" paper with lots of photos, with clear large type and narrow columns and no "left jargon". Using photos as fillers and fullstops was out. The front pages were given over to strong photographic images – sometimes without text explanations or headlines. They were designed to "grab hold of people" immediately – thousands of copies of each issue were sold on street sales.

We look back at the earlier issues designed by MINDA.

The first montage we did. It was first used as a poster in South London and then adapted as a CARF cover. The idea came well before the National Front's recruitment drive for youth in 1978, when the YNF was launched. Richard Verrall, a leading NF spokesperson, was quoted then as saying, "When we are knocking at the gates of power in Britain, there will be a new generation, the 14 and 15 year-olds, who are joining us now. They will see us for the force we are, a new force, a virile force.

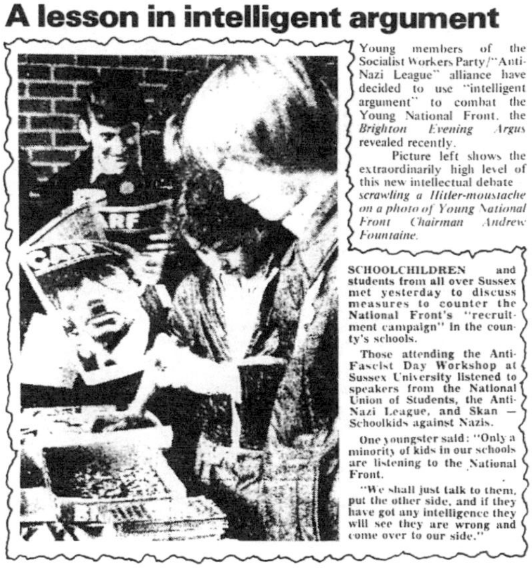

A lesson in intelligent argument

Young members of the Socialist Workers Party/"Anti-Nazi League" alliance have decided to use "intelligent argument" to combat the Young National Front, the *Brighton Evening Argus* revealed recently.

Picture left shows the extraordinarily high level of this new intellectual debate *scrawling a Hitler-moustache on a photo of Young National Front Chairman Andrew Fountaine.*

SCHOOLCHILDREN and students from all over Sussex met yesterday to discuss measures to counter the National Front's "recruitment campaign" in the county's schools.

Those attending the Anti-Fascist Day Workshop at Sussex University listened to speakers from the National Union of Students, the Anti-Nazi League, and Skan — Schoolkids against Nazis.

One youngster said: "Only a minority of kids in our schools are listening to the National Front.

"We shall just talk to them, put the other side, and if they have got any intelligence they will see they are wrong and come over to our side."

But battles against how the paper should look – with people in the All London Coordinating Committee Against Racism and Fascism, the publishers of CARF – began to grow both in number and intensity. Eventually a serious political rift developed, concerning not just the design of the paper, but also its political direction. MINDA were unable to carry on in the face of a vociferous opposition, who opposed CARF's "popular image" both in its use of graphics, photomontages and text photos, etc. A "cropped" version of the paper now appears with long theoretical articles and almost no visual content.

And when that happens, they won't give a damn who was a fascist and who was a Nazi."

A year earlier we personally had a first-hand view of their recruitment methods. It was in Stetchford, Birmingham, during a by-election. The Front were holding a large march and rally. As they gathered at a housing estate, three NF characters, one of them Derrick Day, a well-known East London NF "personality", were filming the event. A Scots pipe band was tuning up and a crowd of kids began to gather. Day took several kids aside and began to talk to them:

"Now what shall we do with the blacks... we don't want them here do we... shall we send

them all back home?"
"Umg ... well I don't... um... yes... yeah, send them back home."
"Right that's it, now repeat after me... if they're white, they're alright... if they're black, send them back!"
"That's it, nice and loud... right start the camera."

They filmed the kids chanting the Front's racist slogans and persuaded them to join the march. We went home and worked out the montage.

In terms of its effect on the National Front, this montage of YNF leader Andrew Fountaine really worked. It appeared in the April '78 edition of *Spearhead* under the title *A Lesson in Intelligent Argument* (see illustration below). If you look carefully you'll see that it's the Front who have "scrawled a Hitler moustache" on Fountaine – not us!

Some people street-selling this CARF were also worried about the montage. They said passers-by mistook them for Nazis. There were discussions about the problem of using "ambiguous" images on the covers. We were conscious of the problem when we were doing the montage, but thought the left were always far too cautious.

Fountaine is a Nazi. We wanted to illustrate just that. We did the obvious and put a Hitler moustache on him – but not a "scrawled-on moustache" – something more. Really it's a sort of follow-on from "Beware the National Front is a Nazi Front". This montage was done at the time of the forming of the YNF. More and more kids were appearing on NF demos. They were taking their politics into the schools. We were seeing the birth of a fascist youth movement – the parallels with the Hitler Youth Movements were no longer theoretical. The NF were forming their own. For good measure, they put in charge one of the Nazi old guard, ex-National Socialist, Fountaine.

If you go to a National Front demo you'll see the kids there – not in uniform yet, but in an assortment of army fatigues. We've taken it to the next stage. A full uniform. A Hitler salute. A line of kids. And we've stuck them on the face of their leader.

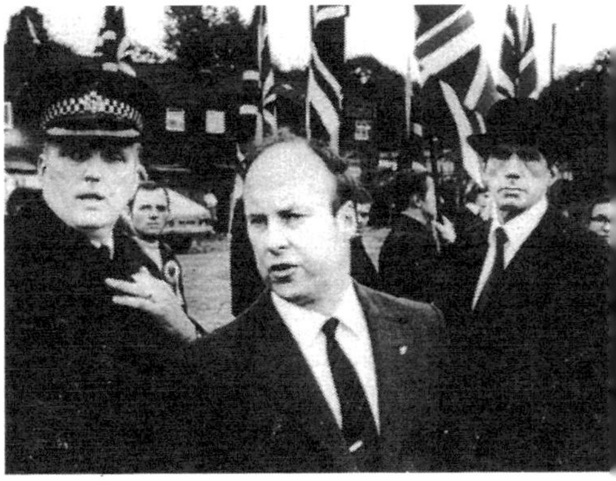

1

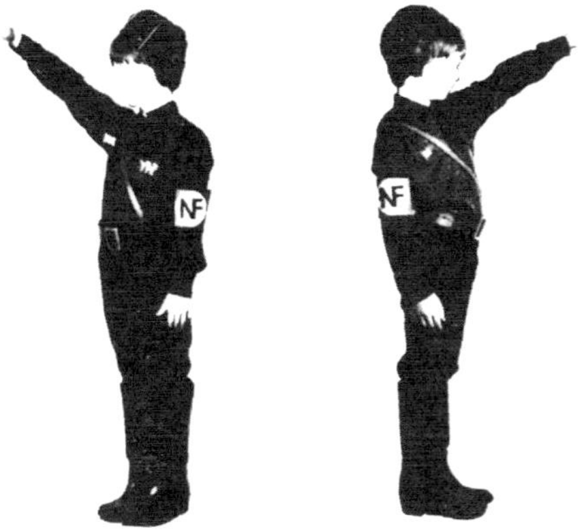

2

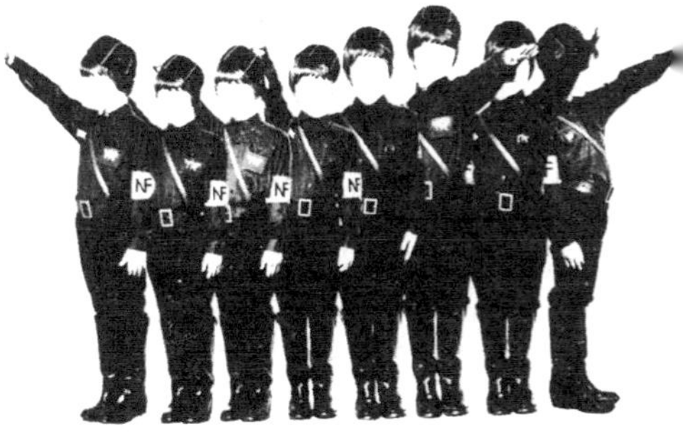

3

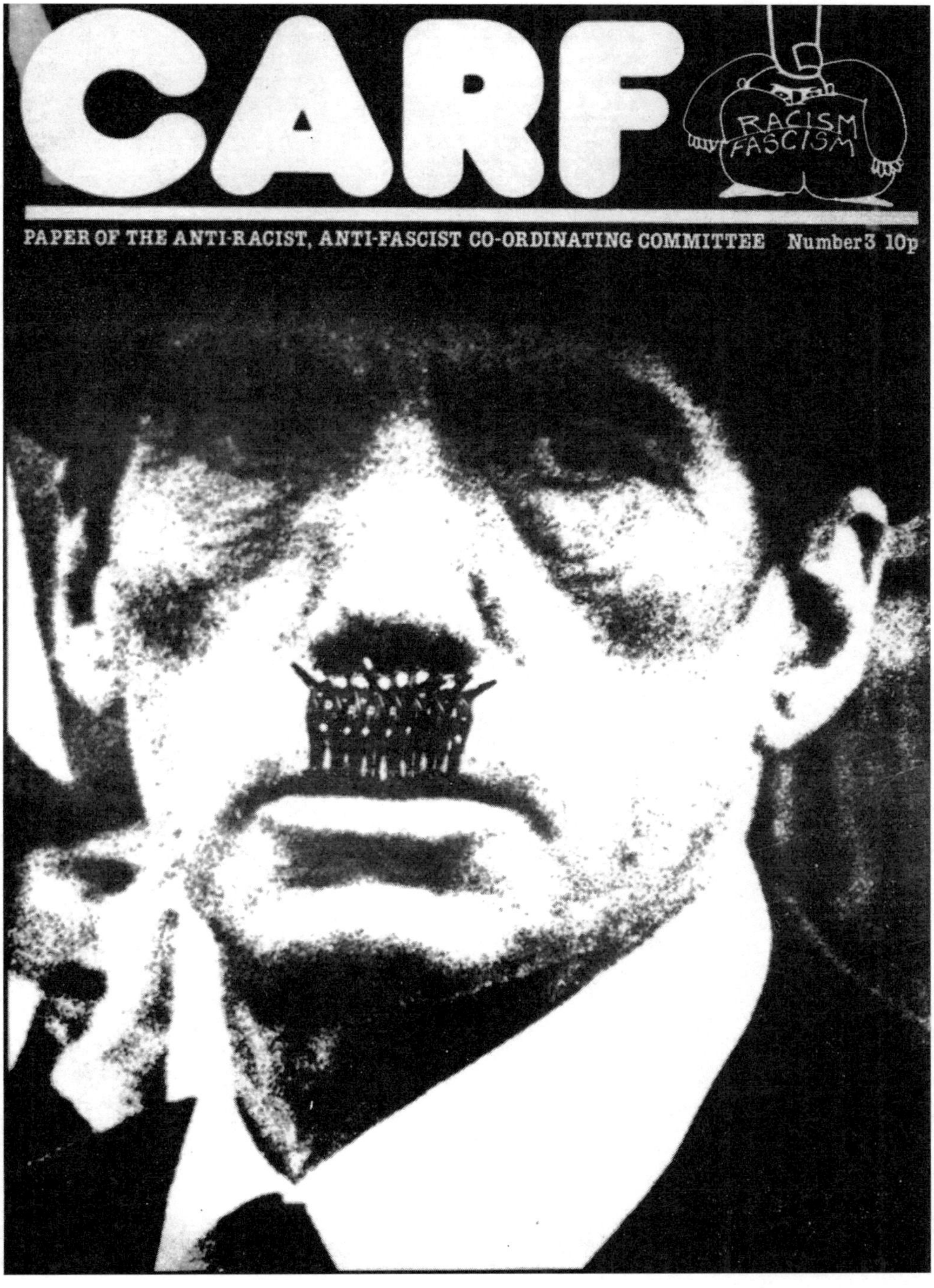
CARF
RACISM
FASCISM
PAPER OF THE ANTI-RACIST, ANTI-FASCIST CO-ORDINATING COMMITTEE Number 3 10p

4

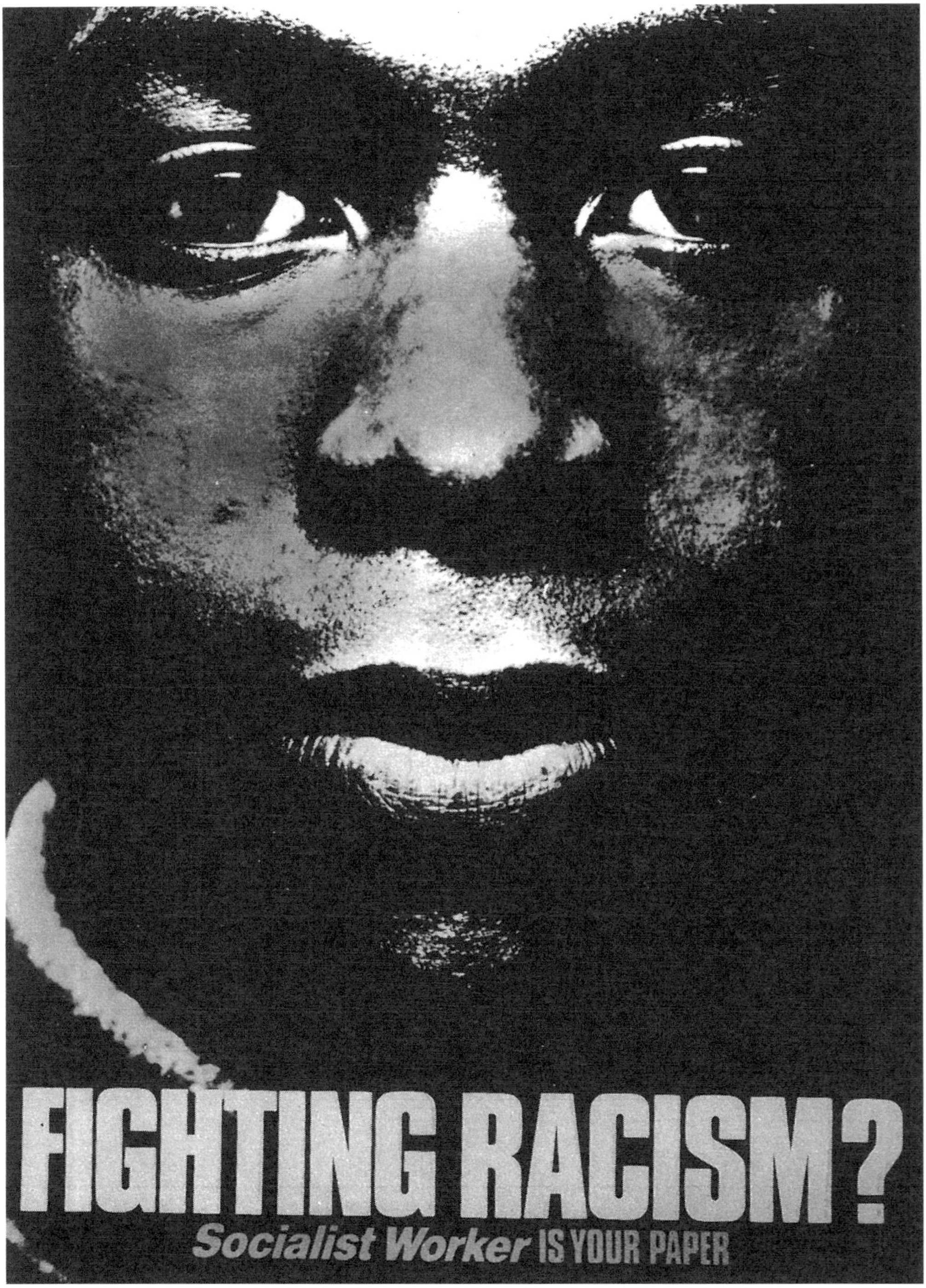

1. Fighting Racism?

Why Socialist Photography?

Robert Golden

IN 1963, IN THE BLACK ghetto of Detroit, I was photographing a child playing with a bit of industrial waste. A grey-haired ex-auto worker, a black ex-auto worker, a representative, though he did not know it, of all blacks, all workers and all the prejudice I had been raised with, sidled up to me and enquired, "Boy, what you doin' filmin' tha' child?" As I stuttered an answer, he arched his back away from me, brought his thumb and forefinger to his stubbly chin and said "You college boys got booksmarts, but tha' ain't the same as streetsmarts." He laughed and said I should come to his family's 4th of July barbecue party as I was a neighbour.

Aesthetic methods used to combat racism are at the moment more difficult to analyse than aesthetics applied to less immediate issues. As in anything which presently involves us we need time to see clearly the consequences of our actions. Nonetheless to have a look at what I have been doing for the past while, as you have requested of me, may prove of some value to others who are involved or wishing to be involved on the propaganda front against racism.

We know that racism is not an independent animal but an organic part of class divided society. As such, to formulate adequate aesthetic means to confront racism is also to form adequate means to challenge bourgeois assumptions about life. We must challenge not only the matrix of social institutions but, more to the point, the underlying ideological assumptions inculcated in people by these institutions.

The truth – that is, bourgeois or state capitalist truth, common knowledge (that is, assumptions which appear true because we work which effectively combats racism are outside ourselves and yet a part of us as they impinge upon our lives. The imperative for our work is not formulated out of our need to create, nor out of our inspiration, but out of the imperatives of a class, or a section of a class, or a party within that class to combat a particular aspect of contemporary social life. It is this imperative, this condition and the struggle against it which calls forth the objective elements of our work – i.e. subject matter, treatment vis-a-vis audience and techniques of presentation.

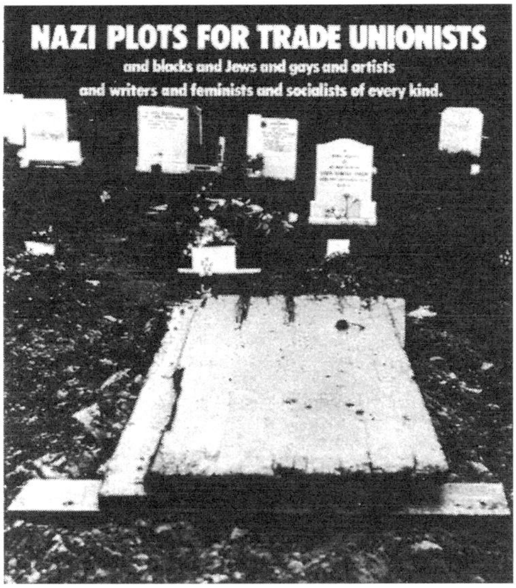

have been told so often that they are such) beliefs, morals, apparent self interests – must be revealed for what it is. And what it is, is an opaque film which blurs our view of reality. Our window on the world, formed as it is by the interests of the dominant class, intercedes between us and reality, rendering the latter a set of obscure shadows open to profoundly inaccurate interpretations. The aim of our applied aesthetic is to dissolve this opacity.

This window cleaning operation is both objective and subjective. It is the former in that the forces which call forth our need to create

The subjective component, that which bourgeois society places on the pedestal of ART, dissociated from immediate problems and acclaimed as a product of "their" civilization, is the particular cluster of skills, assumptions, attitudes, commitments and experiences the individual artist brings to the objective problems.

What we must do is drag aspects of reality which are at the moment unrecognised by the majority, or reality which is buried in the archives of the law courts, social workers' notebooks and back pages of popular newspa-

2. Nazi Plots For Trade Unionists.

pers, into the centre of the arena of common ideas. As with an audience in any arena, our audience will only view our work if we solicit their attention effectively. We must educate, but we must also entertain. We must surprise, delight, perhaps shock, but we must provide the view that their interests are the interests of others. That is, others which the class sees as allies. Our most effective resources are veracity and humour; our closest ally is the truth.

All this is well and good, but we in the field of visual propaganda, like other professionals, have a client – our comrades on the left – to satisfy. They provide us with a specific message to communicate, in a particular form and size and with an exact budget; and they confront us with their particular prejudices about visual communication. Here arises both an obvious and also a subtle problem. The former is that the left in general, and in Britain particularly, tend often to overlook the possibility of visual communication in favour of text. Fact and analysis, it is asserted, is best explained with words; words are clear, concise, exact, specific; words can best deal with describing facts. So design is reduced to the functional or decorative; and visual images are reduced to showing obviously superficial fact, clearly, concisely, exactly and specifically, as is expected of words. Invariably, a photograph of a strike will show a line of pickets holding placards standing in front of the works entrance which bears the name of the company. The photograph is used to affirm the fact of the strike, the fact of the picket and the facts of the place. How much more powerful, more loaded with our own understanding and commitment would be a photograph of one striker's face in close up, or a low angle shot of hand with placard, or hands locking a gate! In the rare moments when the visual means of communication are given some attention we encounter a reliance upon old visual techniques, especially socialist realist and photomontage methods of the twenties and thirties and advertising styles of the fifties. This implies a cultural conservatism which is out of step with progressive political views. It is perhaps a result of the relatively small amount of energy which has been devoted to the questions of aesthetics and propaganda by the left (compared, for instance, with the amount of enquiry into economic theory and practice); partly a result of the limited means and so the possibility for the employment of those talents which are to be found in the left as a whole, and partly a result of the fact that members of the left and the working class movement in general suffer, as do we all, from the pervasive culture of bourgeois society. Unfortunately, this means that the art organs of the dominant class, which are more self-assured, make progress while we cannot, and that we who are committed to the development and extension of culture as a voice of the mass of people must rely heavily upon such methods as photo montage, constructivist design and dadaist typography thrown up in the last widespread revolutionary periods.

The more subtle problem is that there is a tendency on the left to isolate underlying social analysis from personal life. We see an appeal to either the intellect or the emotions but usually not both at once. In the first case it is assumed that the art of convincing people lies in the proof of the fact and in its documentation – booksmarts. Being primarily concerned with the instruction of fact, professional revolutionaries, race leaders etc., forget that others need both facts and the emotional handles to grasp them: we must relate to their streetsmarts.

There are those on the left who believe that we must communicate on the level of daily life using popular (and therefore bourgeois) mass media language and trust in assumptions which are broadly known and accepted. Emotionalism (in appeals to our prejudices, outraged sensibilities, "natural" class responses) is used in lieu of analysis. The scope of the propaganda reaffirms that which is known, or at best tells us in emotional but not analytical terms what is happening.

Life is presented as a set of weekly events rather than as an organic whole. Here we have the stuff of daily life, but not the underlying fact of social life. Analysis is dismissed in favour of the view that people want only to be reaffirmed in their suspicions and prejudice. We must refer this assumption back to the very heart of the political analysis and ask whether elitism of some form is implied.

From my point of view I accept an historical materialist analysis of history and class war, and believe that the various parties and groups which today represent this view in the actual struggle of the working class are more or less correct in their analysis. Nonetheless, to accept and understand economic, social and political aspects of historical materialism does not mean, necessarily, to understand the fullness of our cultural lives or of the reality of most people's daily routines, assumptions or concerns. Operating in ignorance of this dense fabric of experience, a poster, newspaper front page etc., which isolates the analysis of the underlying social reality from the substance of our daily lives will fail utterly to communicate to all but those who assume the analysis. The fact of the underlying structure of society must be placed in the fuller context of the fact of daily life, and the aspirations inherent to it. It is, after all, the desire to understand and gain

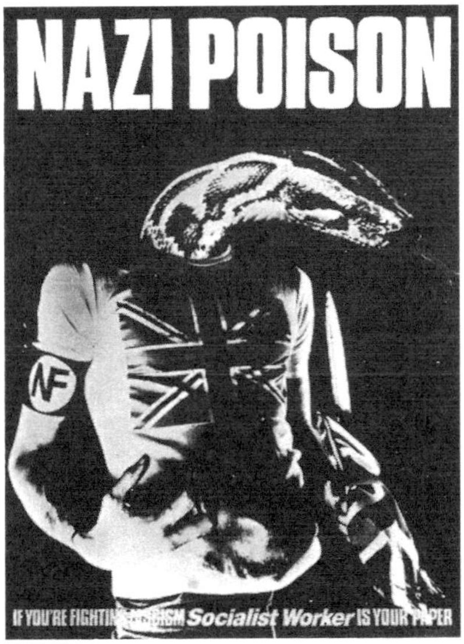

3. Nazi Poison

our aspirations which brings us to the difficult subjects of economics, politics etc.

This unity of need between analysis and the emotional content of life must be fused to describe ideas fully. And, as will be seen below, design and photographs are well suited to communicate this fusion.

In order to communicate an idea which is by and large not consciously understood by working class people yet an explanation of their lives, we must rely upon a visual vocabulary and style which is recognisable, knowable and entertaining. We are therefore immediately reliant to a degree on the methods of advertising if we are to attract people's eyes away from the seduction of the snappy competition we face. Our work must be as good or better than the competition which is selling cigarettes etc. This does not mean, though, that our work is identical. The iconography and construction of contextual and formal matter is profoundly different and must be if it is to announce our point of view. By necessity advertising is simplistic – the plush surroundings of the cigarette smoker are a result of the life which is led or can be gained by consuming Brand X;

whereas for us, we approach questions in their complexity – what we present is the result or aim of struggle for or against a situation, we surprise with juxtapositions which assault common belief, which confront the accepted.

Even though we rely to a degree on the formal methods of our adversaries, we are presented with a far greater question in matters of content. How do we create a telling visual equivalent to a problem like racism which is diffused, attitudinal, philosophical and rarely obvious for photographic documentation except in situations like demonstrations?

– which is where the montage of image with image or image with text occurs.

At the moment, I am using monumental realism, montage and the photo essay. Each of these serves a slightly different purpose and can express, in the order mentioned, more complex ideas.

In the A2 size *Fighting Racism* poster, (image 1) which was made as part of a series of five posters to promote the sales of *Socialist Worker*, the paper of the Socialist Workers Party, the intention was to stun the passer-by with the monumental size of the youth's face. He looked

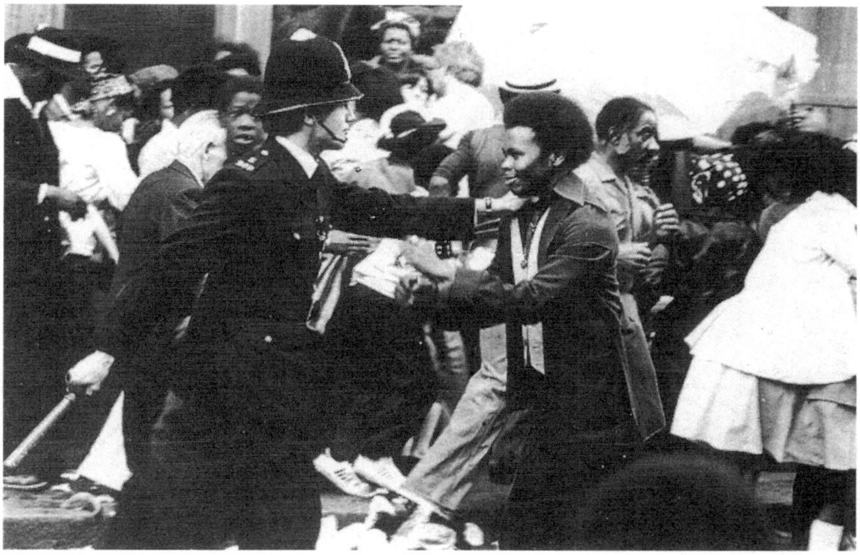

If we have the opportunity to place events in an extended context, juxtaposing photograph with photograph or with text, then the problem of exposition becomes somewhat simplified. But for the poster, book cover or pamphlet we must illustrate quickly, incisively, in one image and with few words. We have two possibilities. First, we may have the good fortune to be in the right place at the right time with the right lens on the camera and the right film in it and with the right light falling on the subject to capture that precise moment. Short of that, we must fabricate the visual equivalent of our ideology

directly at the camera lens in order to appeal directly to the viewer with the loaded question. The sharp rendering of detail and the dark ground intensifies the visual impact, dramatises the effect, and charges the face, the question, then the reaction with emotional undertones. Bold white lettering out of a dark ground also helped to ensure that racists would find it harder to write their messages on our posters and also find it harder to cover up our message as they would have to fill in our lettering with some material which was denser and darker than our background.

The poster *Nazi Plots for Trade Unionists* (image 2) offers the view that gays, blacks, feminists, trade unionists etc. have a common enemy in Nazism. It therefore implies unity of need. The photograph itself of the fresh grave reveals the power of juxtaposition. The grave, while loaded with personal connotations for each viewer, is in political terms neutral – but as it is placed against the text with its pun it becomes politically active. The double meaning of the text against the photograph uses irony to stir the imagination and affect the viewer's mind through humour. The thrust of the message – the need for unity – is disguised, left to be discovered and acted upon.

The *Nazi Poison* poster (image 3) was another in the series for *Socialist Worker* mentioned above and printed to the same size. While all of the posters sold out, this proved to be the most popular, probably because of the reliance by the left on the proven methods found in Heartfield's techniques and humour. I wished to emphasise "Nazi" while playing down NF, as I had observed that early on in the propaganda war against the NF all too many posters so boldly employed their initials that from a distance it simply

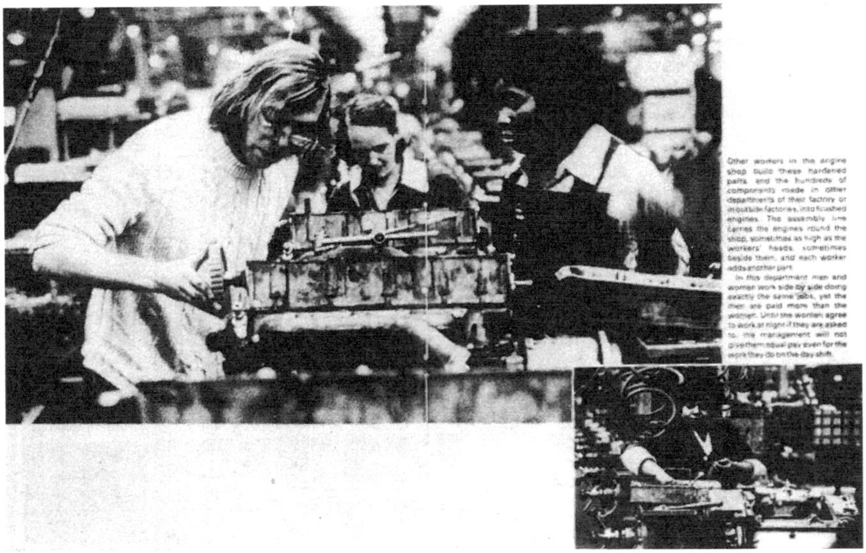
Other workers in the engine shop build these hardened parts and the hundreds of components made in other departments of their factory or in outside factories, into finished engines. The assembly line carries the engines round the shop, sometimes as high as the workers' heads, sometimes beside them, and each worker adds another part.

In this department men and women work side by side doing exactly the same jobs, yet the men are paid more than the women. Until the women agree to work at night if they are asked to, the management will not give them equal pay even for the work they do on the day shift.

5. Pages from *Carworker*

announced their presence, thus serving effectively as propaganda for them. The stark nature of the montage, describing a macho nationalist as a violent beast with a venomous bite, a purveyor of (social) poison surprises the passer by. The only problem with this poster is that it perpetrates an injustice on a beast far more noble than a racialist.

Some photographs, especially those which describe an event particularly clearly, find many uses. For instance the picture of the police attack upon the black youth, with its frozen action, peculiar expressions and clarity of detail, has been employed, often without my knowledge, by various groups and in various ways. It has been used in an SW article on the Notting Hill riots from where the image came, on a cover of a special *Flame* edition a year later and in several other places. The appeal of the image is based upon the way in which the clarity of the rendering allows the viewer vicariously to experience the action itself. Again, the use of this photograph reveals the neutrality of iconography and the importance of context. Certainly a racist, or the mass media could have used the image to show how blacks assault the police, or how well the police perform under difficult conditions. Though neither of these are in this case the facts of the event, the photograph in context could imply these notions. The questions of content must be seen in a twofold way. The first, as mentioned above, is the context of image with image or with text in a particular publication and medium. The second is the medium itself in the context of the wider society. In all propaganda, while we must lead with our ideas, we must resort with delicacy to the level of consciousness and the nature of receptivity of our audience.

The photograph of the youth and the cop (image 4) was made while working on *The People of Britain* – an in-depth study of the culture, work, religion, struggles and successes of various immigrant communities. This series of books has been undertaken for the purpose of describing to children of the subject culture their objective condition with a view to enhancing their self-pride and dignity while helping them to understand the life they lead, and at the same time showing to children of other cultural backgrounds the richness of the subject culture studied. These will be photo and text books. The images will describe a broad panorama of life – schools, churches, various jobs, home life, unemployment and the dole, cultural activity and the text will include the words of the people themselves. Through the breadth and veracity of our approach we hope to convince people with fact, but to enhance that fact through our own sensibility. We wish to create a dramatic document, not a factual guide through the byways of historical minutiae.

In ten other children's books called *The People Working Series* (*Dockworker, Mineworker, Carworker, Textileworker, Farmworker, Potteryworker, Newspaperworker, Railway worker, Buildingworker, Hospitalworker*), the writer Sarah Cox and I approached the question of racism and the relationship between black and white workers in an understated way. (image 5) This was because the content of these books centred around the life of the working class as a whole at the point of production, with an emphasis on the value of the individual worker as a producer of social wealth and their conflict with the ownership class. As the books are only 32 pages it meant that the questions of racism and sexism had to be largely ignored. We did approach these questions in places where not to mention them would have been to distort our main content.

People black, white, men and women were photographed because their position, function, or activity at the moment I encountered them described something necessary to our central narrative. We believed that this understatement. while being necessary for the clarity of our central content, would also serve as a subtle anti-racist statement. The very fact of showing the multi-racial and bi-sexual nature of the workforce without comment would imply the unexceptional, indeed natural, fact of it. And while very important distinctions were obscured these facts presented with the authority of the printed page might, we hope, implant a sense of class identity with people of different races and the opposite sex.

In all of this work the underlying effort is to stimulate through visual means a yearning for social and personal liberation, uncompromised by bourgeois assumptions which by nature attempt to invade and dominate.

The struggle against racism, even in the area of the production of visual work, is always a struggle against a class divided society. Even while this struggle is carried on in the domain of consciousness, we must remember that consciousness is not alone a matter of fact and programme, but of the totality of human life. The old man was right about the diversity between those who pass as booksmarts and those who pass as streetsmarts – it's up to the workers' movement to fuse them and to the propagandists to communicate this.

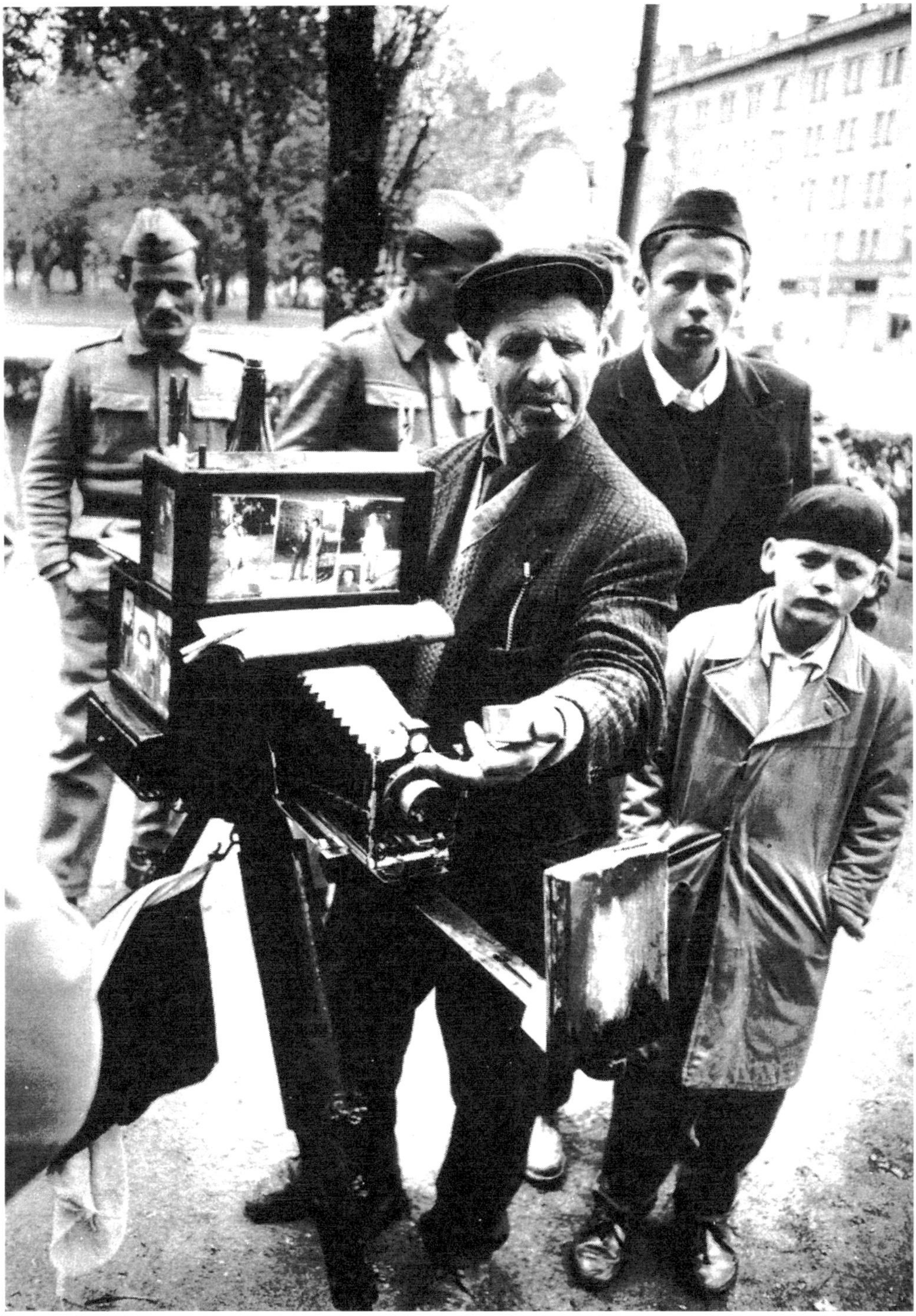

JEAN MOHR

JOHN BERGER

WHEN I THINK OF JEAN MOHR, I think of a traveller, not a tourist, not a commissioned journalist, but a traveller: a man who is driven by a kind of conscience to traverse the world in order to see for himself what is happening. Unlike most other travellers he neither leaves nor returns with romantic expectations. This is not to say, however, that he is objective. In face of an intolerable world, only those with a vested interest in it as it is can be objective. Objectivity pretends to justice whilst being compliant with injustice.

To recognise Jean Mohr's lack of objectivity is to begin to recognise his exceptional value as a photographer. He travels to see faces not places. Faces are for him events which reflect all other events. He is not a portraitist. The function of portraits has always been to celebrate. Whereas the faces Jean Mohr photographs aspire to, or appeal for, a different experience to that which they have undergone. In each face there is the shocked potential which suggests a different life and a different world. Even in the eldest of them there is still the furious memory of what the child had a right to expect. And all this is so evident because there is a complicity between the photographer and that shock of fury or disappointment. There is both the silent protest of experience in the face, and the mute protest of the photographer. The two can never be equal, but they can join and touch one another.

He offers photographs to the photographed not to us... and therein lies their delicate non-objectivity, their authenticity.

John Berger

1. *A Seventh Man*

In *A Seventh Man* there is a photograph, which is in a wooden barracks where Portuguese and Yugoslavs live. They work in a tunnel, they live in a wooden barracks, they have bunks two above the other. Around the bunks, on the roof of the bunk above, all the way round are pictures, sexy pictures, which they did not of course bring with them. They bought them in Germany or Switzerland or somewhere. The room is absolutely plastered with these. We wanted to use that picture because it was important, first of all because it was like that,

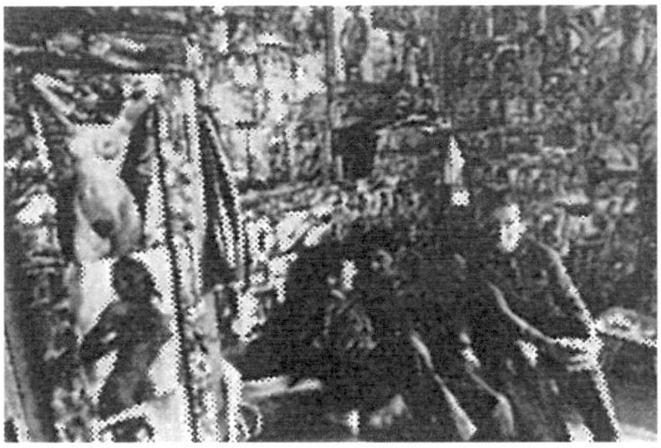

secondly because it is, in a sense, an indirect index of the sexual deprivation suffered by these men. How to do it? Because you put that picture on a page and what does it say? How is that image going to work?

It firstly, maybe, approves of the virulent sexism of the images stuck up. It's going to confirm the superstition that these men are all sex maniacs and it's probably also going to give a vicarious thrill to some. You see, it's not going to work and it was a problem which we actually worked on for about a week. How could we use this in order to escape this automatic and false meaning? We tried juxtaposing that picture with pictures of the men's faces; it didn't work because it doesn't really mean anything – it really only adds the personalities of these people. We tried putting in a photograph of something in the street, some sex shop in the street where the bourgeois of the city go. But again that says it is okay, the petty bourgeois go to the sex shop the same as the migrant workers. It doesn't help. I'm not saying that the solution we found is the ideal one, but finally we found a photograph of an old peasant woman in her village who could have been the page and in that context we put the picture of the barracks with the sexy pictures all round. Beginning to relate, to talk about a life story, beginning to talk about women in more than one dimension, beginning to talk about the experience of those men. And then finally we chose to put opposite that barracks picture an extraordinary photograph that Jean took of a young Polish peasant girl – at that time totally uninfluenced and untouched by sexist consumerist glamour, who at the same time has a very beautiful face, young and questioning, the exact opposite in fact of the women in

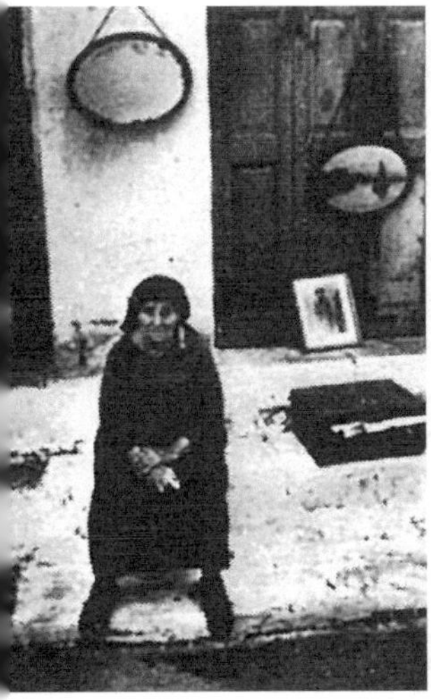

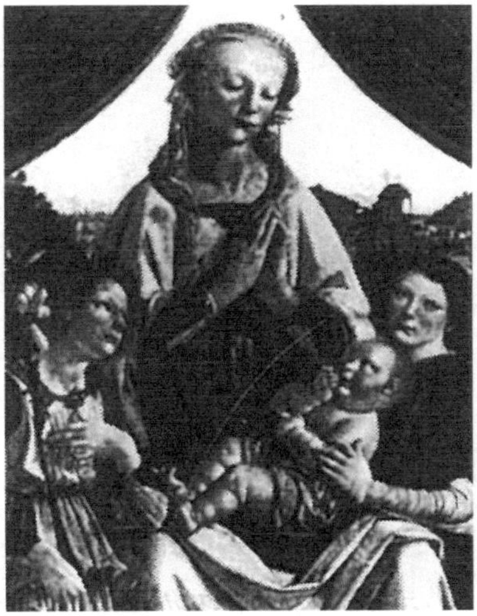

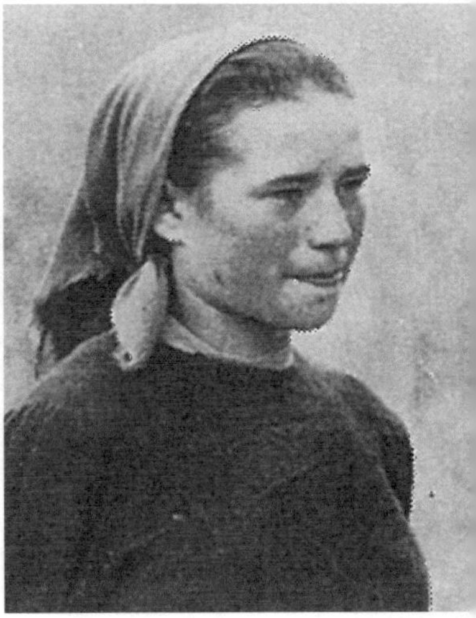

mother of any of those workers – in fact she wasn't – but she could have been. It was a picture of a mother, quite influenced in some respects by Catholic iconography with the Madonna and so on. The kind of picture that one of those workers might have carried around with him. It had a kind of icon value, it was sacred. We then put next to it, not a photograph but a reproduction of a Madonna, a painting by Perugino. There begins to be a juxtaposition between idealised maternity and real maternity – that's to say a woman of 45 looking like 65 and probably with eight children. Then we turn the the barracks picture but corresponding very likely to one of the girls in the village. Now with those four pictures we perhaps began to put back the first one – that is to say the barracks one – in a context.

John Berger
From a discussion at the BSA Conference, April 1978

2. Bricks

First of all John is a very militant person, although now he has withdrawn from precise parties and he is as much attacked by the left and the extreme left, or some factions of it, as he is from the right. I've never been like that. For a long time I must admit that I have been nearly non-political and I have never been part of a party. It was just that having worked after leaving university, for two years with Palestinian refugees, I became aware of a certain number of things, and let's say, it just happened that I always had the heart on the left side. But it wasn't definite, it wasn't precise. I found that I could work with some magazines and not with others. But still, when I met John, I was shooting in all directions. I still do in a way, but I shoot in experimental ways; or else I shoot pictures dealing with something else than just human beings. Indirectly it is still with human beings, but not directly. So I was shooting in all directions. When John looked at my pictures he has always made very clear choices. These pictures were of interest to him; the others, although he liked them because he has been a painter, he just put them aside, they had nothing to do with what he was doing...

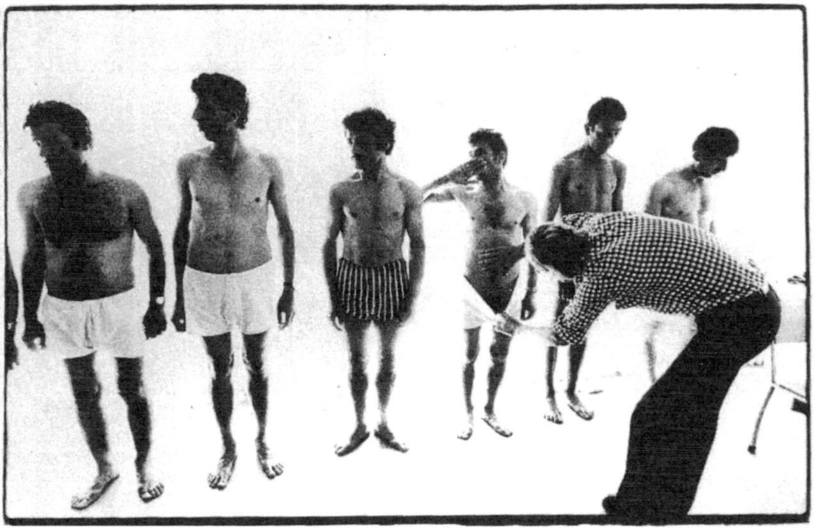

John recently compared the making of pictures with the making of bricks. He said that all photographers are making bricks and they have to be used to make a building, and sometimes photographers are involved in making the building, but very often they aren't. I'm thinking of photographers who are working for agencies (and I'm thinking of the great French agencies actually). They are not involved in making the building because most of the time they have to send their films from the country where they are working. If they are lucky they will see the contact sheets months later, and maybe they will see what has been done with their work. But very often if they see the magazine itself they won't recognize their own pictures. In that case they have very little to do with the building. I am happy enough to be sometimes building myself – if I make an exhibition, or in some cases when I publish something in magazines or journals – but at the same time working with a builder like John of course means a lot... We are fighting sometimes, but that kind of fight when it goes on with a real friend – and John is a real friend – then it's alright.

Jean Mohr in conversation, London, May 1973

3. Sunday Photography
A photographer, like I am, if he's working six days a week doing photography in which he believes, has sometimes to violate himself because he has to serve a certain – not ideal – but prospect.Then on Sunday, on the seventh day, he may just give himself away and do whatever he wants and feels; in my case having practised painting for a very short time, there is always a kind of nostalgia. First about colours and then about pictures which do not serve a precise aim. My *Sunday Photographs* are

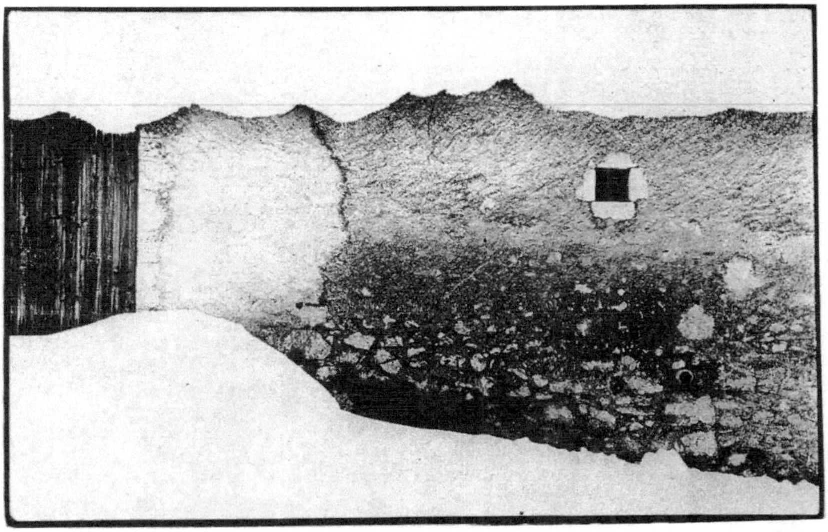

somehow raw material which is connected with the exhibitions, and which during the time I was working with John I thought could be used as a counterpoint to the black and white pictures. He convinced me that at that point it would just weaken our demonstration. My *Sunday Photographs* show nature, the environment in which the peasants are living and working and which could have been used, but then were mostly put aside...

Jean Mohr, Goldsmiths College Workshop, London, December 1978

4. Gaston and the forest
"Take pictures," he said to Jean, "to show what the work consists of..."

"This is the photo I've been dreaming of ever since I was a woodcutter," said Gaston. "The moment when the pine falls, and falls, if the woodcutter knows his job, exactly where he wanted. Within 20 centimetres."

Gaston, unlike most woodcutters, works by himself. He considers that this is much more dangerous. He has, however, a passion for the

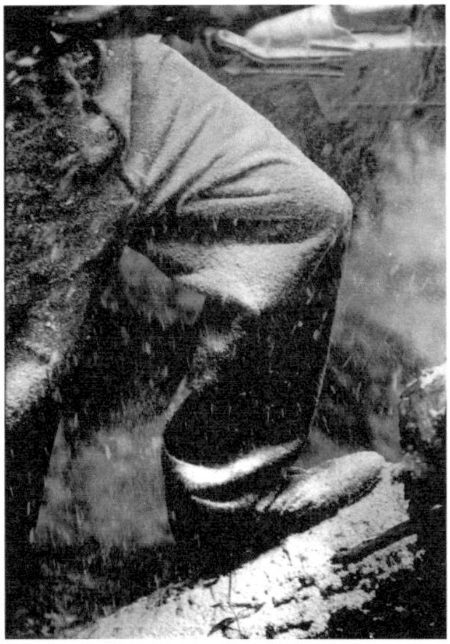

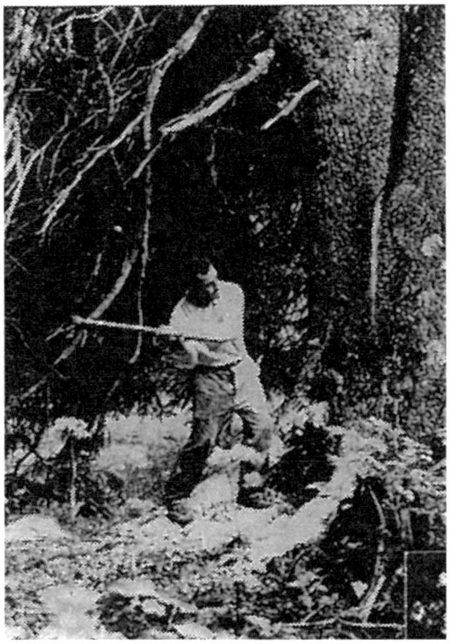

forest and likes to be alone in it. He also works too fast for most others to follow.

These pictures do not pretend to show his whole life, but show him when he is working in the forest and they are merely technical pictures of him.

Gaston is paid by the cubic metre of timber deposited on the side of the road for the lorries. To help bring the timber down the mountain-side, he himself pays a haulier, again by the cubic metre. To get the most out of the money invested in his expensive Canadian forest tractor, the haulier's one idea is to get the timber down to the road as fast as possible.

Peasants make up the majority of the world population. Peasant experience has mostly been left out of history books; it has also been left out of social theory. Even revolutionaries, even those who are concerned with the popular classes, have mostly misunderstood the experience of peasants. They've misunderstood it because they have seen that experience from an urban point of view. I'm not saying that peasants aren't also people – people first – they are not totally different from other people. But their experience and the way they meet that experience, and the way they give meaning to it for themselves, that is different. And that has been misunderstood. Although our exhibition only deals with a few aspects of peasant experience, this is the reason why we believed it was important to try to make an exhibition which showed to people (rather than explaining to them in words) something about peasant experience, and the ways peasants themselves see that experience.

The exhibition, apart from trying to say something about peasant experience, is also trying to suggest certain ideas, and perhaps to question certain pre-conceived ideas about photography. In the two portrait stories we try to show with pictures the attitude of the people themselves towards their own portraits. That's why we call one *Marcel – or the right to choose*. It's his right to choose the portrait that he wants of himself. It's his right to preserve in the world the image of himself. It's his right to preserve in the world the image of himself as he wants it to be preserved. And, of course, this is very much against current practice because most public photographs are in some way or another stolen. They are taken despite or even against the wishes of those who are photographed. Jean is one of the very few photographers who takes pictures on behalf of the people he is photographing. He is not taking them of them for other people, completely cut off from the experience of those who are photographed; he's taking them on behalf of the photographed.

John Berger
Fragments from an exhibition

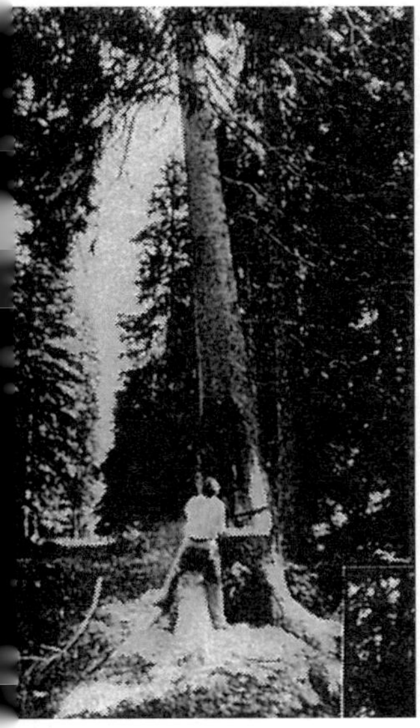

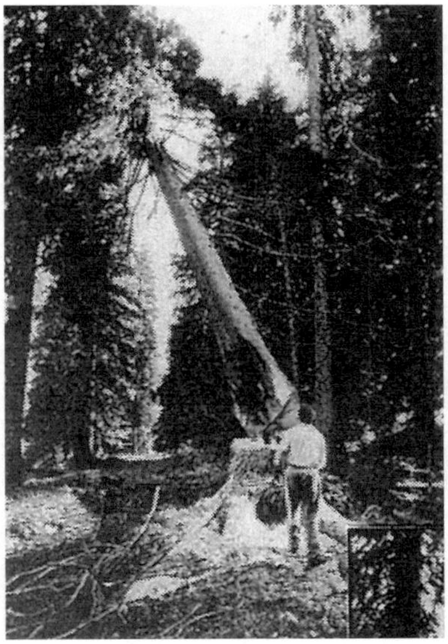

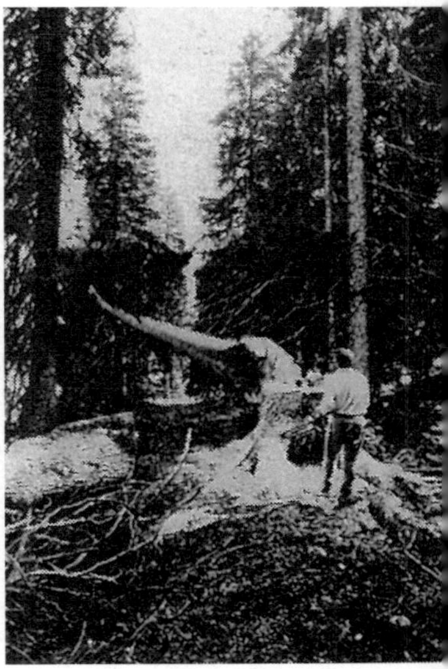

"To go into the forest is to go to war." A village saying

5. Marcel – or the right to choose

...When the following Saturday Jean brought him a pile of prints, Marcel studied them carefully on the kitchen table. "That's no subject for a picture," he said as he came to the close-up of the cow's eye, "but don't imagine I don't know which cow it is! It's Marquise..."

"It's the same for people", Marcel continued, "If you're taking a picture of somebody's head, you should be able to see the whole head and shoulders not just a piece...

"That's beautiful!" he said, "Everything's there." He picked out the photos he liked best of what means most to him: his herd, his grandson beside him, his dog.

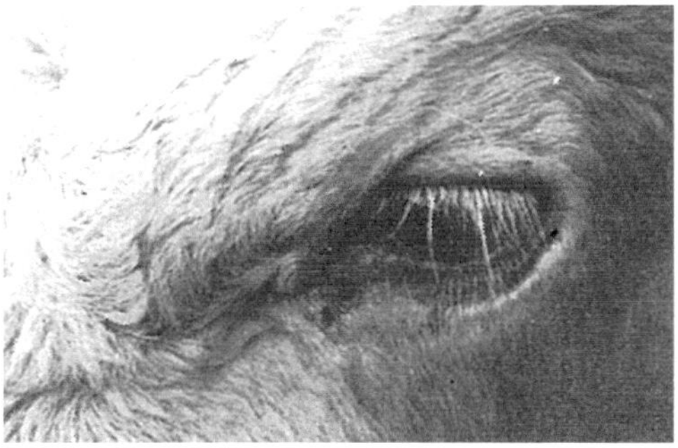

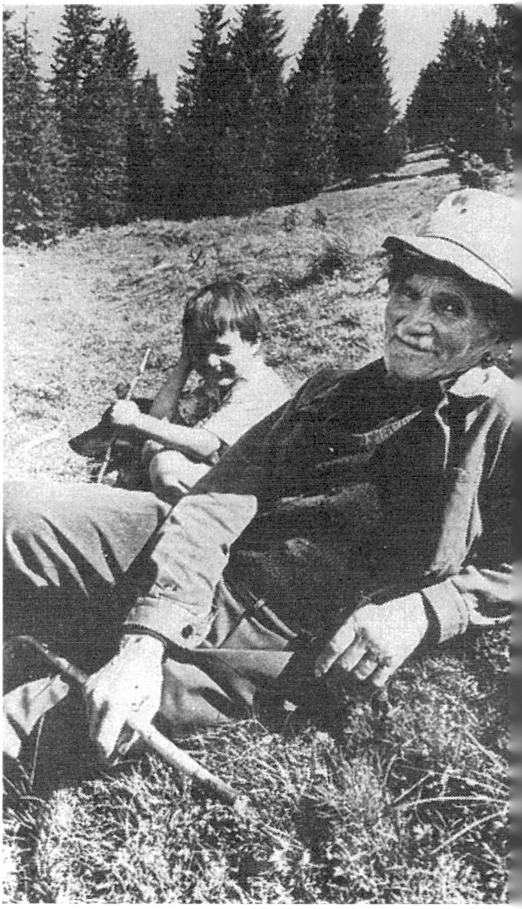

Early next morning, Sunday, Marcel knocked on the door. He was wearing an ironed dark shirt and was shaved and combed. "Now's the time," he said to Jean, "to take a picture of the head and shoulders, the bust, down to here." He held a hand across his waist. Below were the usual trousers and boots which he wore for the stable. Work on Sundays was the same as any other day. He stood in the middle of the kitchen, concentrating on the camera.

When Marcel saw the portrait he has chosen, he said with satisfaction: "Now my great grandchildren will know what I was like.

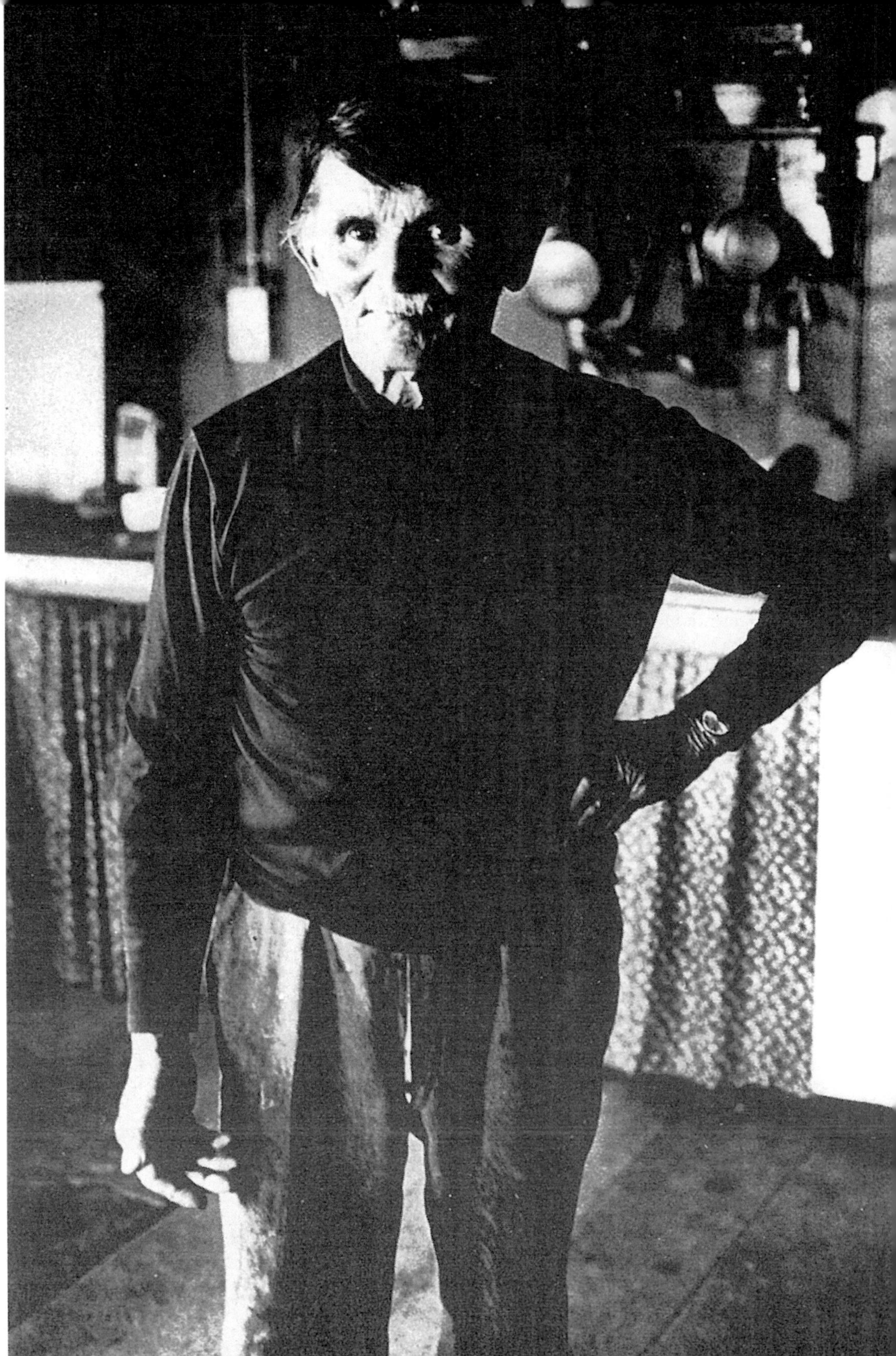

6. A context for a photograph

How in practice can we use photographs, so that, even though we are using them publicly, they are replaced in a context which is comparable to that of private photographs? This is what Jean Mohr, Sven Blomberg and myself have tried to do in our books. What we have achieved is only a tentative beginning, others later will make us look like primitives.

The problem is to construct a context for a photograph, to construct it with words, to construct it with other photographs, to construct it by its place in an ongoing text of photographs and images. How? Normally photographs are used in a very unilinear way – they are used to illustrate an argument, or to demonstrate a thought which goes like this:

Very frequently also they are used tautologically so that the photograph merely repeats what is being said in words. Memory is not unilinear at all. Memory works radially, that is to say with an enormous number of associations all leading to the same event. The diagram is like this:

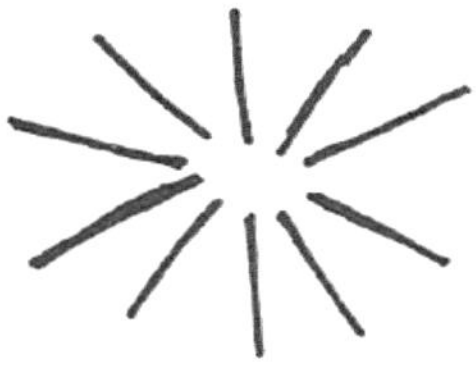

If we want to put a photograph back into the context of experience, social experience, social memory, we have to respect the laws of memory. We have to situate the printed photograph so that it acquires something of the surprising conclusiveness of that which *was* and *is*.

There are a few great photographs which practically achieve this by themselves. Any photograph may become such a "Now" if an adequate context is created for it. In general the better the photograph, the fuller the context which can be created.

Such a context replaces the photograph in time – not its own original time for that is impossible – but in narrated time. Narrated time becomes historic time when it is assumed by social memory and social action. The constructed narrated time needs to respect the process of memory which it hopes to stimulate.

There is never a single approach to something remembered. The remembered is not like a terminus at the end of a line. Numerous approaches or stimuli converge upon it and lead to it. Words, comparisons, signs need to create a context for a printed photograph in a comparable way; that is to say, they must mark and leave open diverse approaches. A radial system has to be constructed around the photograph so that it may be seen in terms which are simultaneously personal, political, economic, dramatic, everyday and historic.

John Berger
From a lecture at the BSA Conference, April 1978

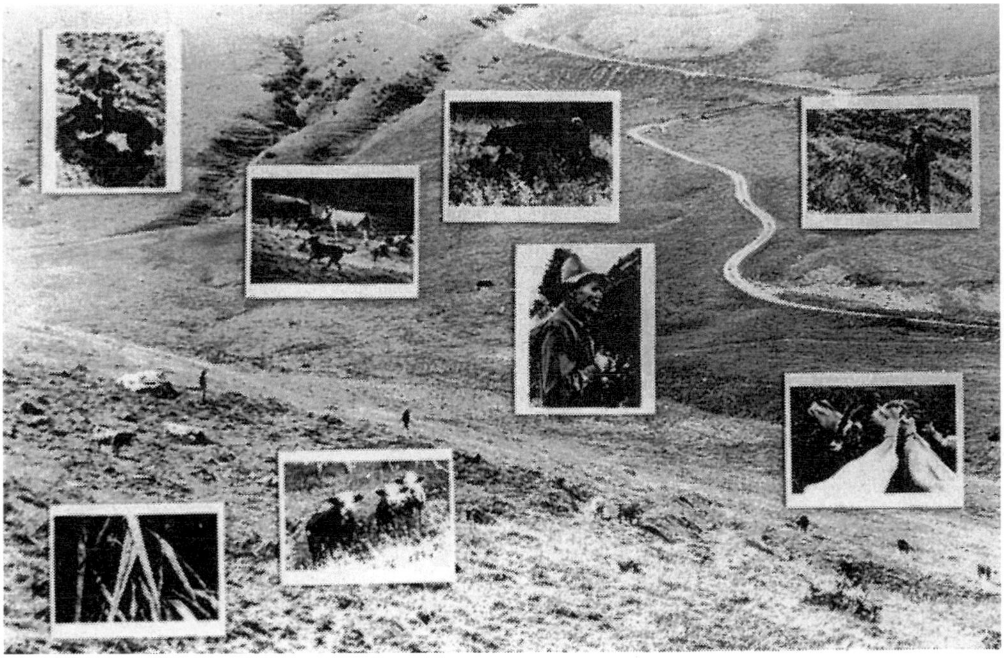

233

Fragments from an exhibition.

Charity Begins at Home: The Shelter Photographs

Nick Hedges

THE CONCEPT OF UNIVERSAL truths is out of fashion. It has Sheltered many of the generous and misguided claims made for photographed reality. On one level the universal truths of humankind represented in, for instance, *The Family of Man* (truths of birth, death, love and hate) are ever-present facts of life, and photography can deal successfully with such personal experience by representing them as symbolic truths. But most photographed reality which is made public is not concerned solely with private relationships, but rather with how the public world impinges on those relationships, and the context of those relationships within the public world. The same criteria for transmitting and receiving the private world as symbolic truth cannot be employed. Much of the misunderstanding has come from those photographed areas which in a sense represent the overlapping of the private arena and the public stage. Any photographer working with people will spend most of his or her life wandering in this area of overlap.

To be specific, I worked for the charity Shelter for four years from 1968-1972, as photographer and researcher. To understand a charity's photographs you need to understand the motives and intentions of a charity. Shelter staff were motivated by:

1. A genuine desire to change radically the housing priorities of a nation.

2. To raise as much money as possible, to enable housing associations to rehouse as many families as they could into secure tenancies.

3. To educate the public – both adult and child – to appreciate the needs of a substantial minority within the nation.

That is one way of representing their motives, but on another level you could say that their motives were concerned with preserving the status quo. As William Stott, in his book *Documentary Expression and Thirties America* writes; "the central motive of the New Deal was the preservation of the American socio-economic system by reforming it." Similarly with Shelter, although an independent charity rather than a government department, it afforded the middle classes the illusion that they were contributing to the reform of our society without ever questioning the reason for the need to reform.

In purely physical terms, the housing waiting lists are as long now as they were in 1966 when Shelter started; there are more families actually homeless now. On the positive side, thousands of homeless have been rehoused and many pioneering ventures (Housing Aid Centres, Neighbourhood Action Projects) have been adopted nationally. Charities are in that long and worthy British tradition of reform; most people who work there have a genuine concern, and seek out charities as the only practical expression for that concern. The magic ingredient that is missing is political will. Charities by definition cannot be political.

All photographs used in mass media are propaganda – conscious or unconscious. Even family albums are propaganda about the happy state of family life; children recognise this from the age of four onwards. Confront any child in any neighbourhood with a camera and the riposte is *Smile*. It seems that the very act of photography has become synonymous with happiness.

Taking photographs for a charity proves no exception to the propaganda concept. When I first worked for Shelter I had a naive motive and intent: I thought that by presenting to the general public the "real" world of bad housing that the truth of these observations would effect a change in their attitudes. Retrospectively I was confusing many things.

In order to raise money from the public, the propaganda that Shelter needed to present read as follows:

...there were three million people living in slums (indisputable fact);
...these people were depressed, their family life ruined by their living circumstances
(true and untrue, a convenient generalisation which serves to allow the middle class to donate).

As a generalisation it missed out 75% of the wholeness of the personality of any badly housed family, and suggests that the cure for under-privilege is a donation from the middle class pocket.

When I first started taking photographs for Shelter I was required to use models from a model agency to enact the stereotype that the advertising agency had designed. I was horrified at this perversion of the "truth", and won what I thought at the time was a major battle by getting the director to use only "real life" situations in future. But what happened to the truth now was that instead of being manufactured (using models), it was selected and edited in a very singular fashion.

A good example of what I mean (Illustration 1) is used in the exhibition *Children Photographed* organised by Ikon and Childrens' Rights Workshop. A contact sheet of the Tandy family in Sheffield shows a number of frames of mother and children, conveying a variety of emotional responses. Frame numbers 27a to 30, and 32a were of use to Shelter, whereas frame 31 a suggests a dissolute, and frames 33a to 36a had no bearing on the particular "truth" that Shelter wanted to convey. Love and affection would break the rules in the game that Shelter was playing, and you do not raise money by showing a "chain-smoking dissolute". Despair in Mrs Tandy's case was quite genuine, and poor housing had a large part to play in that despair. But the bits that you miss out, the tremendous feeling of love in that family (and Mrs Tandy going off to the local for a quick pint at lunch-time), all of this adds up to so much more than the stereotype that the charity leaves you with.

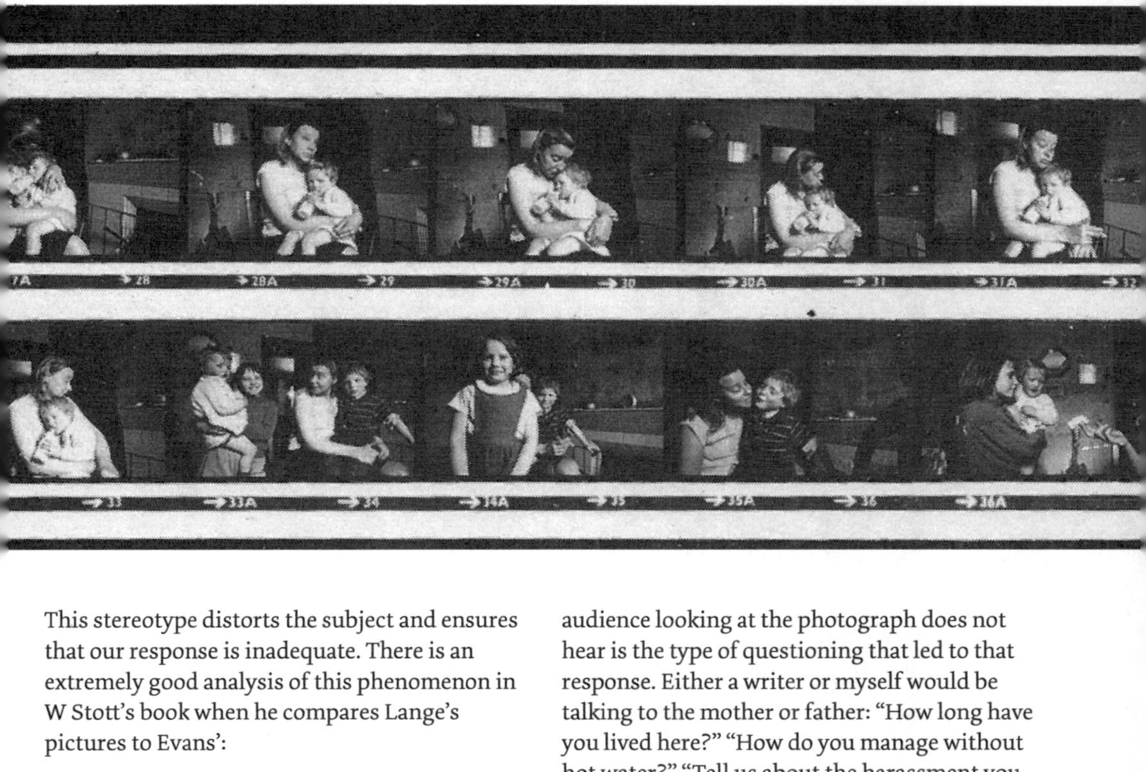

This stereotype distorts the subject and ensures that our response is inadequate. There is an extremely good analysis of this phenomenon in W Stott's book when he compares Lange's pictures to Evans':

> Lange's finest photographs are of people, and these show a tendency towards the sentimental. Everyone in her portraits had character; nearly all were handsome...
>
> Evans' version of the thirties, his cool yet disquieting vision of America, has prevailed. It has prevailed against the sentimental simplifying of the propagandists and the anecdotalists. Evans exercises taste and respect on behalf of his viewers as well as his subjects. The latter are not degraded by being made objects of pity or revulsion or fun, and the former are not degraded by being thus solicited.

On the practical level none of the family photography that I did for Shelter was posed or set up. The fact that people look depressed in the photographs is a genuine representation of their emotion at that time. However, what the audience looking at the photograph does not hear is the type of questioning that led to that response. Either a writer or myself would be talking to the mother or father: "How long have you lived here?" "How do you manage without hot water?" "Tell us about the harassment you have had from the landlord" "What is the health of your children like?" All these types of questions will evoke a particular response, which will convey – in terms of facial expression – depression. Another set of unrelated questions might have evoked a joyous response, but joy is not our business.

Illustration 1.

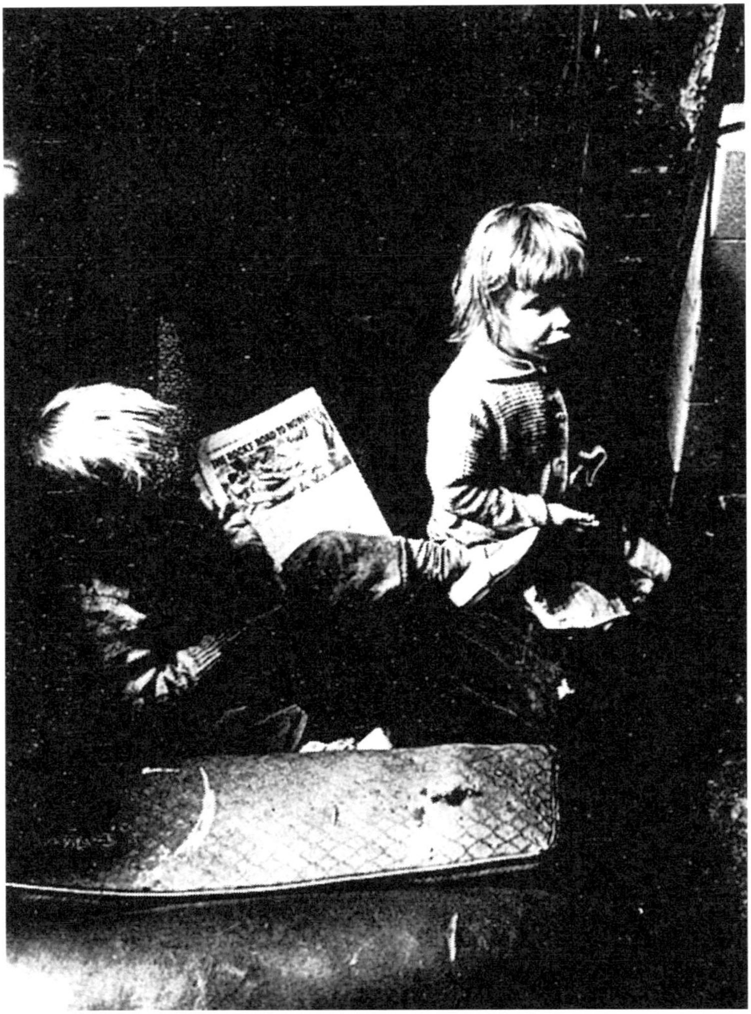

Forlorn child (innocent victim). 1968.

Going through one report, *Condemned*, published in 1971 by Shelter, I've come across the following stereotypes we used:

a. Forlorn child (innocent victim)
b. Mother and baby (madonna and child)
c. Anxious old age pensioner (helpless innocent)
d. Depressed family group (object of pity)
e. Resigned father (victim of society)

Another guideline which was employed was "try not to include too many immigrants as they will affect the fund-raising".

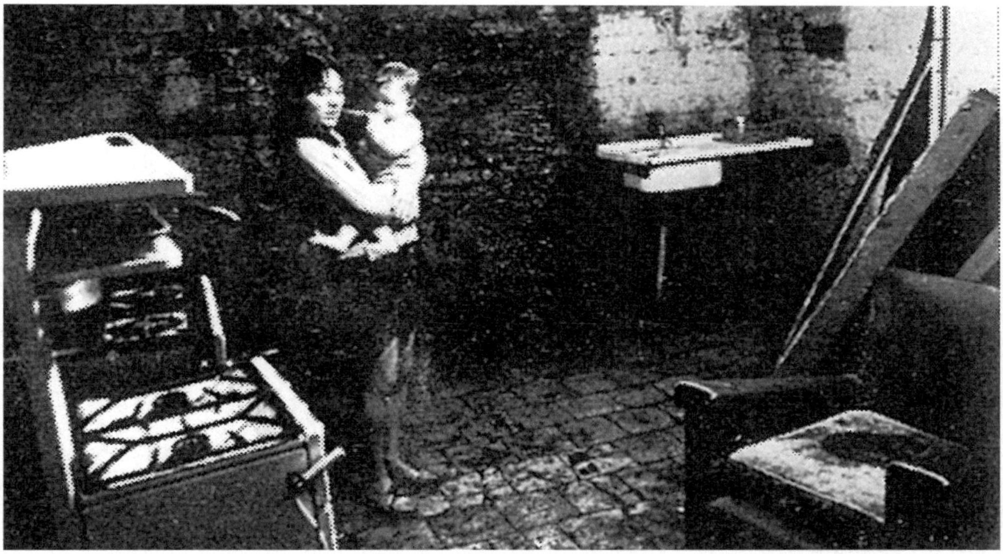

I'm not writing Shelter off, all I am saying is that it sought to present an edited version of reality which conformed to a vague, woolly, middle-of-the-road liberalism. Equally both the right-wing voice and the left-wing voice use "reality" to tell their version of the "truth". The propaganda of the National Front, and the very different propaganda of the Socialist Workers' Party, is as singular in its presentation of reality as Shelter. Reality is complex and multi-faceted, the mass media cannot be. The mass media disguise and distort most of the truth of the working class experience. I do believe that the

Mother and baby (madonna and child). 1971.

consumers of the mass media recognize the rules and conventions of the media game (that's not meant as a defence of the mass media). Passive reception, and distant grumblings at the disguises and distortions of the media will get no nearer to the truth of a working person's experience. The mass media, whoever control it, will reinforce conventional wisdom.

Shelter photographs reinforced conventional wisdom about poorly housed humans; any change in attitude can only come through actual experience, rather than simulated experience. The public who read Shelter reports knew that

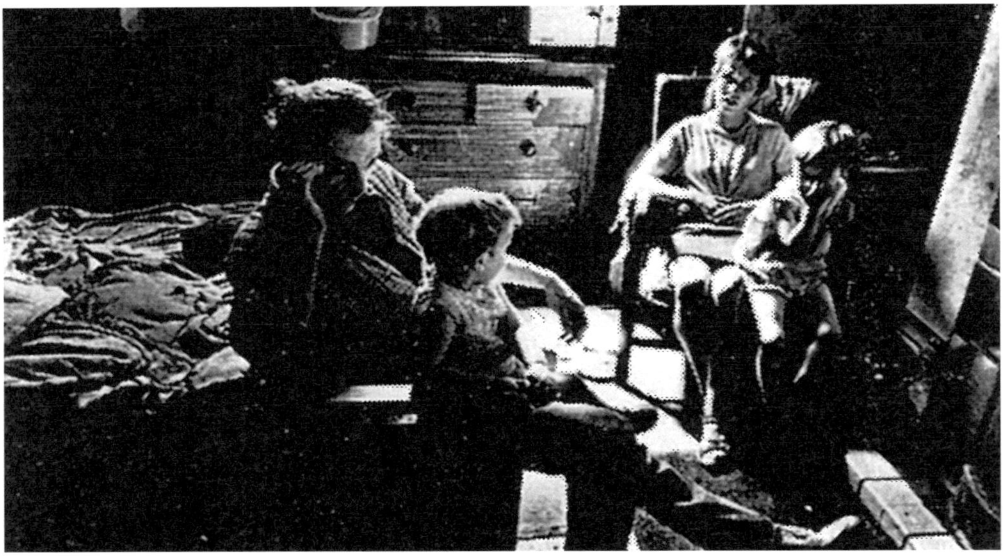

they were going to see one kind of truth. In that sense a charity wears its propaganda on its sleeve, it does not disguise its intention, or claim objectivity.

I was talking to a Jamaican steelworker recently who said that he prefers the politics of Enoch Powell because he can see where he stands. "I prefer Enoch to the silent politician. He is the snake you can see; the dangerous snake is the snake hidden in the grass." When you work for a charity you soon understand that you are concerning yourself with special pleading and stereotyping. Even if you take great care to

Depressed family group (object of pity). 1971.

establish authenticity, accept responsibility for the invasion of privacy, and materially improve the living conditions of certain families, in the end you realise that you have failed to preserve the dignity and humanity of the reality that you are illustrating. You also fail to bring out their true class position in relation to the rest of society. And anyway you weren't there to do that.

If there is one truth that propaganda reveals, it is that it tells you the truth about the people who manufacture it. And concerning the mass media and its audience, remember that everyone, on both sides, is an editor.

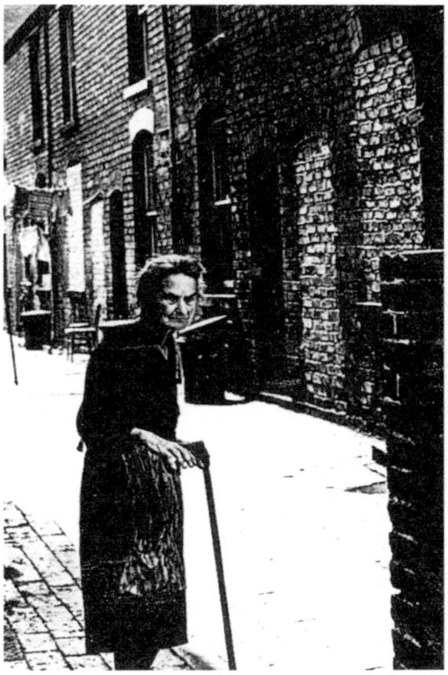

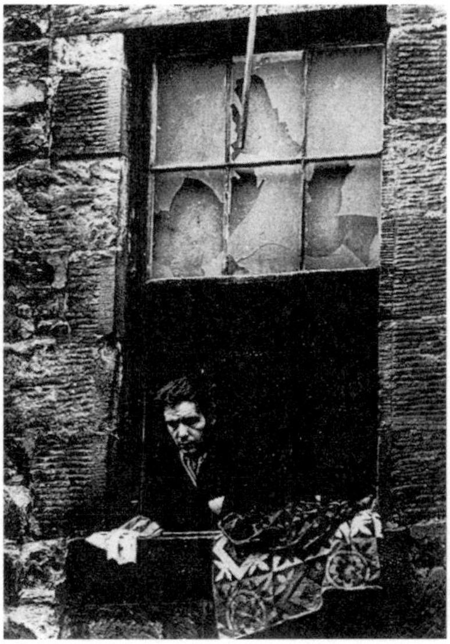

FURTHER READING

William Stott, *Documentary Expression and Thirties America*, Oxford University Press.
John Berger, "Moment of Cubism" in *The Look of Things*.
James Agee and Walker Evans, *Let Us Now Praise Famous Men*, Peter Owen and Panther.
Michael Frayn, *Towards the End of Morning*, Penguin.
Keith Dewhurst, "Images of War" in *The Guardian*.
Michael Duane, "Freedom – a biological imperative" in *Peace News*, 29.10.71.
John Szarkowski, in *Creative Camera*, February 1969.
Charles Harbutt, in *Album*, No. 9.

Anxious old age pensioner (helpless innocent). 1971; Resigned father (victim of society). 1971.

Working for the Council

Trisha Ziff

INITIALLY, THE PROSPECT of working as a photographer and a teacher for a social services department appeared to be a bizarre idea. It has however, given me the opportunity to carry out a specific photographic practice, which would not have been possible to develop in another situation.

I think it is important to try and explain the reasons why I have chosen to work in this area, and show how I am trying to map out a specific practice. I have reached no conclusions and l have no specific "line" as a socialist photographer. The method which I am trying to develop results from my own personal history as a photographer and is part of both a personal as well as political process.

My first job was working for a community arts group. As a photographer I was very aware of my "professional skills" and how these skills embodied specific values which automatically separated me from the people whom I met. In order to deal with this problem I took on the role of (neutral) technician hoping this act in itself would close the space which I felt existed and enable a photographic practice to develop amongst the people with whom I worked.

At that time I thought with my technical assistance it would be possible for a group of people to picture themselves. I chose this way of working because I felt personally alienated by the practice of the documentary photographer. The difference being that a documentary photographer goes into a situation with his/her own analysis of that specific situation and produces a sequence of images which hopefully elucidates a viewpoint. The people are "pictured" and "revealed". They remain passive to the camera and accept that rendering of themselves. No exchange takes place. The essential problem still remained: How to develop a socialist photographic practice. To become purely a technician only removes that problem without solving it.

Since I began working in Southwark I have tried to deal with this problem. As a feminist I am very aware of relationships which one imposes and are imposed on one as a woman. I find, though, by trying to tackle this problem both in my personal as well as public "at work" life, I am able to begin to solve problems to do with how I work as a photographer. I do try to work collectively wherever possible and to relinquish my position as "teacher" and "leader". It isn't easy to always do this but for my work I now find this to be the most satisfactory way of solving many of the problems which deal with my practice.

Obviously a lot of the work done in Southwark would not have taken place without my original input of work, but the type of work produced could not have happened without a collective practice. I now choose to work with other people – that is, we take pictures together and through this process, our consciousness develops faster as a collective group. I can only picture people if they choose to reveal themselves and they, in turn, now refuse to passively accept my interpretations of them.

Of course I am still employed by the council and it would be wrong to neglect the status which my job will not allow me to relinquish. On the other hand, I am no longer just a photographer but part of a group of people trying to use photography to look at their own lives. Whereas I play an essential role in the groups, without the groups as a whole this work could not be produced.

Working for the council

Working for a local council has many advantages. Firstly, it is a secure employer and for a photographer who is trying to make a living by his/her own work this is an important advantage. Though one's income is not comparable to that of a commercial photographer it is still a living wage. The structure of the Social Services Department is extremely varied and complex and provides many different outlets for a photographer to work in, from hospitals to luncheon clubs for the elderly, nurseries, teenage clubs and mentally – and physically-handicapped day centres.

Before working for the Social Services Department in Southwark, I was unaware of the diversity of the department, neither was I aware of the important role which it has within a community. For example, in Southwark where I work, the council as a whole is the largest employer within the borough; over 80% of housing is owned by the council; Southwark has a high percentage of unemployed people, especially in the dockland area, who are dependent on social security and the Social Services Department; Southwark also has one of the highest percentages of retired people in London, especially in Bermondsey, the majority of whom are dependent on the social services for their meals and welfare. I have mentioned all these facts to illustrate that the majority of people in Southwark come into contact with the council frequently and in turn are known to the Social Services Department.

On the one hand, this structure provides a way of gaining access into a community, for example on one estate I run a photographic group for the elderly and the young, and we are about to start a group for women who are at home either looking after young children or are isolated from other women as a direct result of their physical environment. As a result of this I would argue that the photographic workshops play a real part within the community, in recording community life, as a tool to improve the quality of life, and as a means of uniting a community.

On the other hand, a Social Services Department is an organisation which functions as a means of surveillance, by keeping people dependent on its institutions and handouts. Though a Social Services Department has the means to give a community its own autonomy, it rarely does. The urban aid scheme for the docklands in Southwark is a prime example of this, where the local community has little choice in deciding how this money should be spent. Apart from major issues like this, the department has filing cabinets full of files on individuals, which are handed from department to department. As a photography teacher I can gain access to files on individual clients in day centres if I felt it necessary, it is up to my own discretion whether I wish to or not, and my personal opting out of this aspect of the system changes nothing.

However, given that this institution exists and, as part of the state apparatus, obviously functions in both the interest of the state and the ruling class, there are still opportunities to work within it, with the possibility of producing important work. The nature and control of a Social Services Department will only change as a result of a massive redistribution of both wealth and power. However, as it exists at present there are still important opportunities to be used in the interest of working people.

In stating this I do not see myself as a naive utopianist, on the contrary, I am trying to map out an area of work which until recently has not been possible.

Having worked in the locality prior to working for the social services, it was possible to build up a rough knowledge and patchy relationship with the local community. Yet for the most part it was quite unsatisfactory. Perhaps this will appear to be contradictory; while working with the local community arts group, one met a lot of community workers, people not unlike myself, who were paid to do a job within a given locality (community); however, one met very few local people. Since working for the social services it has been possible to work with and meet all sorts of people, especially women and older people, by using the services which exist, who perhaps could be described as the most isolated members of a community. Without access to various institutions, I believe it would have been extremely difficult to make contact with these groups of people.

Teaching photography as part of the social services creates a great variety of work – it is possible for me to work with people from the ages 11 to 90-plus! As it is an expanding and new area of work, I have as yet faced no financial limitations nor have I had a specific request to buy equipment turned down.

On top of this I have access to transport and ambulances for photographic outings, museums and libraries for exhibition spaces and for research.

I work for two sections of the Social Services Department, the Activities Section (which provides staff to run activities in the various social services institutions from basketry to film making) and for Intermediate Treatment (an area of mainly social workers and youth workers who deal with children at risk, that is to say children with various social problems who do not fit into the existing structure i.e., non attendance at school, petty thieving children from "problem homes").

My brief is very broad. As far as the council is concerned I am there to provide activities for the members of the institutions which I visit. Their main concern is that I do this for the enjoyment of the clients concerned. As regards photography they are happy to develop a new area of work which gives some prestige to the borough.

However, for myself and for the people I work with directly, my brief is more specific. I work to develop photography as a tool for both communication, self- and group-development, as well as for personal and group expression. My timetable changes regularly, though perhaps a brief sketch of an average week might help to clarify what I do.

	MONDAY	TUESDAY	WEDNESDAY	THURSDAY	FRIDAY
NINE TILL FIVE	I teach in a centre for disabled people. I have a group of between 6-10 physically handicapped people aged between 18 and 25.	Day Centre for retired people near Kennington. I teach a group of people photography and film making, tape/slide and oral history.	Day Centre in Walworth, mainly women, at present produce a documentation piece + work + history of women's work.	Centre for the handicapped and retired in Surrey Docks.	Return to the day centre in Walworth to work on history of local women and document on the history of the local public baths.
EVENING (5-8 pm)	Intermediate Treatment girls' group 11-14 yrs old.		Mixed children's group 11+		

I earn an annual salary of approximately £3,500. I work a 42-46 hour week and have 4 weeks' paid holiday a year.

DIAGRAM OF BUDGET

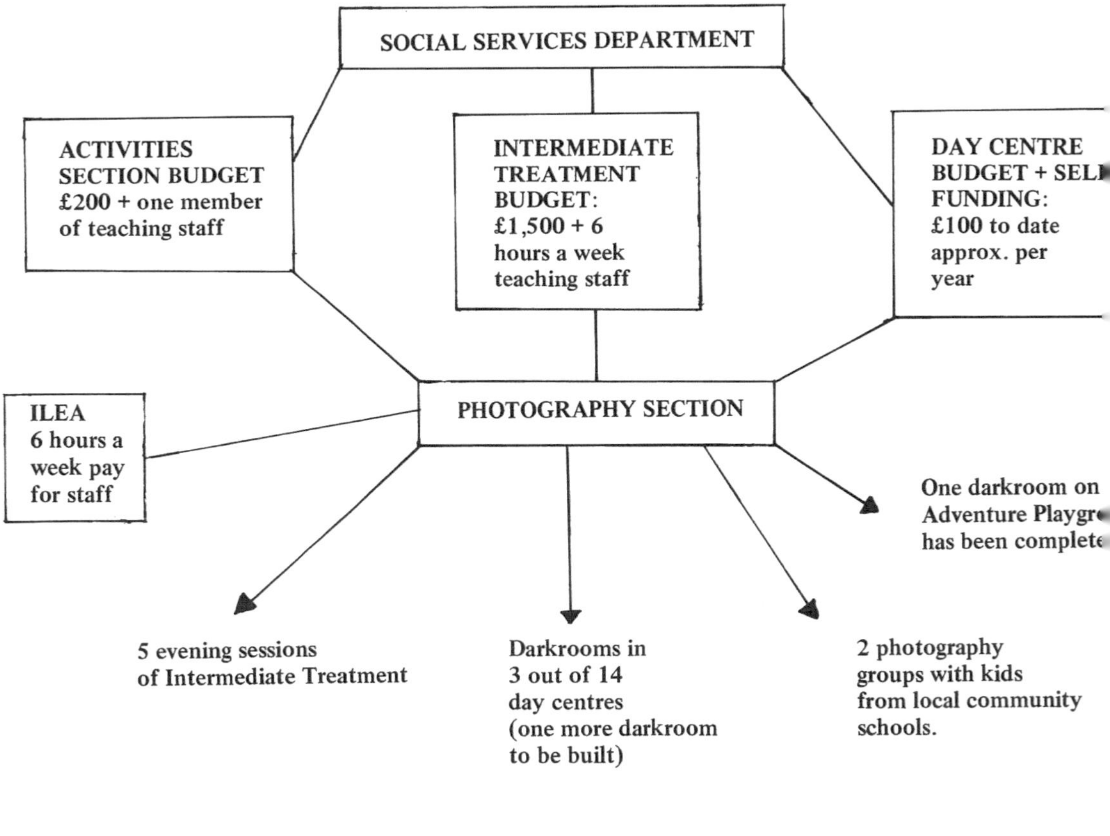

Because most of these operations have been in existence for only one financial year, the figures are not precise, but give as accurate a position as possible.

Background

I started working for Intermediate Treatment in May 1977 as an assistant for an evening group – at that time there was one evening IT group only. The darkroom which had been built within a day centre was seldom used for anything else.

Since then Intermediate Treatment photography, that is the kids' groups, have expanded so that the darkroom (now darkrooms) is used on three nights a week, and on two nights a week there are two groups. So approximately 50 children per week do some photographic work at this centre. There are three of us teaching (myself plus two ILEA sessional payments teachers).

This financial year we have been trying to expand our base, by inviting an outside group to join one of the sessions for a few months. We do this by inviting a group of kids plus a social worker, a teacher or play-leader from somewhere else in the borough. They need have no photographic skills at all. After about six months they return to their base, whether it be a school, an adventure playground, youth club, etc., with new skills plus a lump sum to build a darkroom on the condition that they run regular groups, which we will regularly visit and supply with both advice and materials.

It is a slow but practical way of growing, and this way we do not lose contact. So far one new group has been started and two are at the point of still working with us.

All the teaching which takes place makes use of photographic images. The work done by the children and the young handicapped group involves mainly practical work, that is they produce most of their own images. In the day-centres we work with a combination of found images and constructed images. I have found that using old photographs and working on projects about local history has been very popular in working with the elderly. Perhaps it would be useful to say why.

The camera for them pictures reality. The photograph is an unquestionable document of truth; and the photographs of themselves or of their friends which highlight their wrinkles and deformities only confirm what their bodies tell them, all of which is a reality that they prefer to put from their minds.

On the other hand, working with old photographs has been very popular. The first project which we carried out was to collect pictures of the street on which the day-centres stood, going back to the turn of the century. From these pictures we put together a tape-slide show of their memories of the changes which have occurred throughout their lives. Having done this, several of my group went on to make personal documents about their own lives with photographs, drawings and texts. Some of these documents are highly detailed, others are very simply lists of important events. What is interesting is that for both men and women alike the First World War was the most significant, whereas the Second World War is hardly mentioned, as if the 1939-45 war did not belong to their lives but to a different generation. Though a lot of these memoirs discuss personal events, common struggles such as the General Strike of 1926 and the Battle of Long Lane (when Mosley tried to march through Bermondsey) evoke vivid memories of struggle and hardship which they are able to put into a modern context. Many of the men remember Mosley and are able to argue against the racist National Front, because of their previous experiences. Similarly, a lot of the women remember how they were discriminated against in both the work place and at home, and as a result have a great deal of sympathy for the women's movement. In many cases they wish they could begin their lives again, because they feel life has improved so radically in the interests of women since they were young and they would like to be more actively involved in making things progress even more.

As I have said, all the old people I work with are working class, the centres to which they come are situated in working class areas of the borough where most of them have lived throughout their lives. Consequently, these people are deeply rooted in both local culture and history. This is not obvious but is part of the fabric which constructs their lives. Both the women and men have struggled constantly in and out of employment throughout their working lives. None of them have received salaries and the majority of them have not even been paid weekly. The men as well as the women were paid either for a day's work or were on piece-work. Very few of them have anything to show for this in terms of material gain, though their memories are of vital importance if we are to preserve and construct a history of working people.

At the moment we are in the process of putting together a document of photographs and text about the history of Surrey Docks, 1900-1972. The work is being produced by local people and is a combination of tape recordings, old photographs, written personal memoirs, new photographs and official Port of London documents. Dockworkers describe what their work physically entailed and what it was like to wait for work each morning outside the dock gates, hoping the ganger would spot you, having bought him a couple of pints the night before. Women describe how they worked canning and bottling on the dockside. Many remember how dangerous the factories were and how many lost fingers and received other industrial injuries. For married women there was little chance of employment whether your husband had a job or not.

These memories and photographs are not official histories. In many cases the stories become anecdotal and are of little more than entertainment value. Yet they do have an important use: not only does the recalling of personal struggles serve to re-politicise individuals themselves, but also in a group context they are able to produce a great deal of interest and energy which is relevant to local and national political struggles going on around them now.

It would be true to say that people's consciousness develops faster in action; for confirmation of this one would only have to turn to Jayabin Desai or indeed any of the Grunwick strikers. However, action does not always occur on a picket line and that process of self-development can occur as a direct result of personal crisis, or as a result of the realisation that the life that the media presents and one's reality have little in common. I especially notice this with several of the older women who watch their own family structures in which they have been the matriarch, disintegrate around them. Often as a result of unemployment, members of the family are forced to find work elsewhere, they watch the stress of modern city life cause divorce and illness within their own families. All of which forces them to rethink fundamental values and ideas such as "the family" which they have spent the whole of their own lives preserving and perpetuating.

These are important areas of struggle, and through the group work we do, a lot of new ideas are developed which help us to question capitalism and its complex ideological structure.

Recent developments

The Social Services Department provides a structure whereby one can meet various groups of people, which I have already mentioned. Yet the institutions do not reflect a cross section of a community. Every centre caters for its specific "type", "problem" or age group. As a direct result of this people are isolated and ghettoised; they are seen, and consequently see themselves, as a specific kind of problem.

Recently, having established a base I have been attempting to "cross-fertilise" the photographic groups, where possible. This is obviously limited given the structure in which I work. Yet it has produced positive effects. For example, the Intermediate Treatment kids have been on outings with groups of handicapped people. The kids' groups have helped the old people print their new pass photographs. We are also trying to keep records of all the work we do and some of the handicapped group are helping me make copy-negatives of the old people's work for the local history library (each group keeps its independent records of the work it produces – as well as sending copies of relevant work to the local history library).

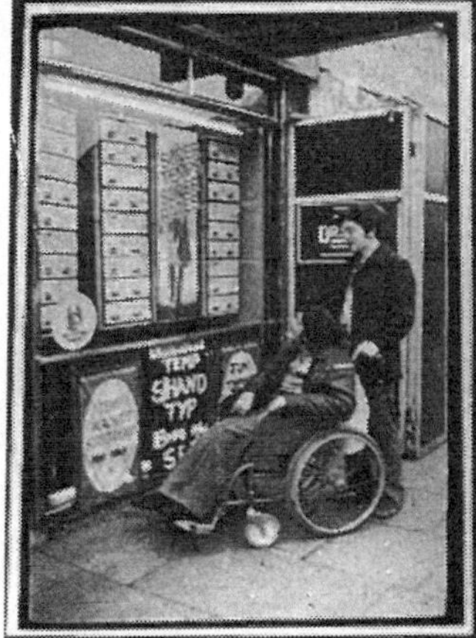

FRUSTRATED WE RETURN TO THE AYLESBURY.
ALL THOSE SHOPS - ALL THOSE THINGS TO SELL AND YET WITHOUT HELP FOR THOSE OF US IN WHEELCHAIRS OUT CHOICE IS VERY LIMITED.

WE FEEL VERY ANGRY ABOUT THIS.
AFTER ALL IF THIS COUNTRY IS REALLY FREE THEN GIVE US THE FREEDOM OF ACCESS TO GO WHERE WE WANT.
SURELY WITH RECORD PROFITS THIS YEAR MANY COMPANIES MUST HAVE MONEY AVAILABLE FOR RE-DESIGNING SHOPPING ACCESSABILITY FOR PEOPLE IN WHEELCHAIRS.
AND AS FOR SOCIAL SERVICES THE CUTS HAVE MADE OUR LIVES NO BETTER

FIGHT THE CUTS IN PUBLIC EXPENDITURE

WE DEMAND THE RIGHT TO ACCESS.

NO MONEY SO WE WENT TO LOOK FOR A JOB. THE JOB MARKET HAD NOTHING FOR US EITHER - DON'T PEOPLE IN WHEEL-CHAIRS HAVE A RIGHT TO WORK TOO? APPARENTLY NOT!

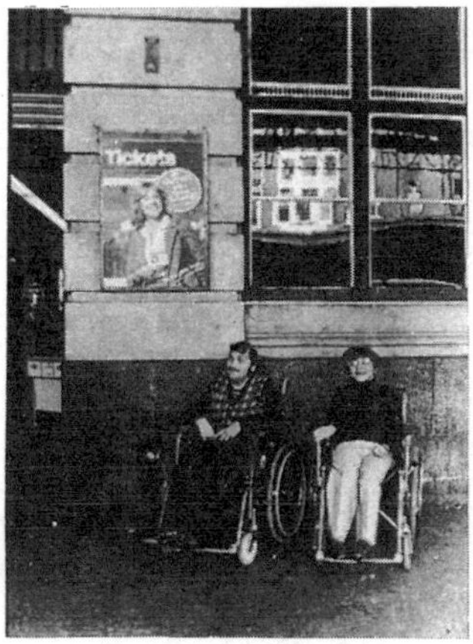

"AWAYDAY CHEAPWEEKEND"...have a good trip,
If you're handicapped Like us you'll have to travel with the luggage.
Ther's first class, second class and the luggage van, but with todays prices and not, so cheap weekends, travel does not just become just a question of access. If you can't afford to travel, then it doesn't make much difference if you are in a wheelchair or if you can walk.

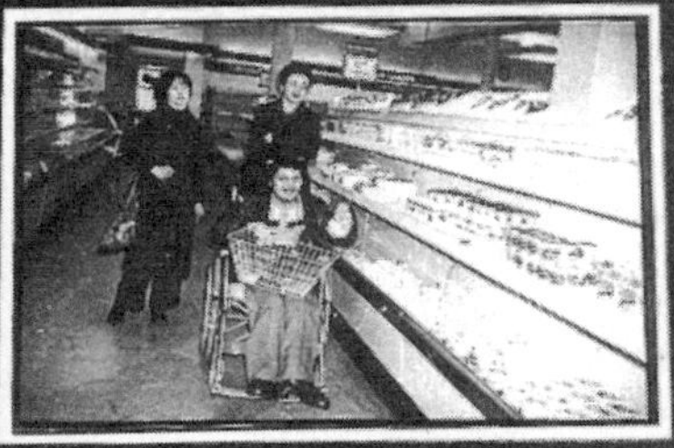

BALANCING THE BASKET ON HIS LAP WASN'T TOO EASY!

SOME OF THE SHELVES WERE FAR TOO HIGH FOR PETER TO REACH SPECIFIC FOODS THAT HE WANTED WITHOUT ASKING FOR HELP.

BUT THE BIGGEST PROBLEM WAS TRYING TO PAY - THE CASH DESKS WERE TOO CLOSE TOGETHER. PETER HAD TO WHEEL HIMSELF ALL THE WAY AROUND ALL THE TILLS IN ORDER TO COLLECT HIS SHOPPING.

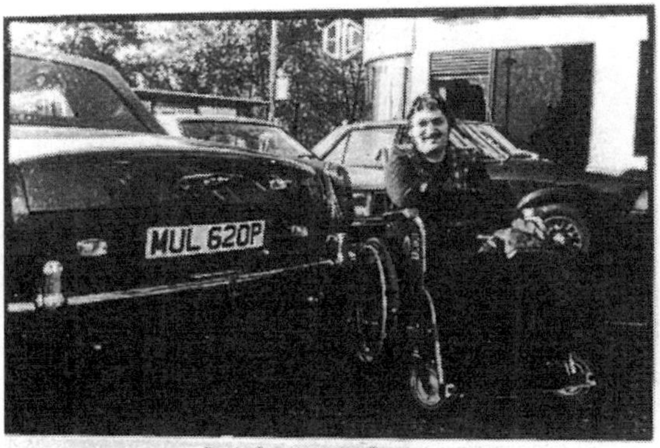

Part 2 extracts from,

ACCESS IS MORE THAN JUST BEING HANDICAPPED, IT'S OFTEN A QUESTION OF CLASS.

Project with handicapped group.

This Christmas we had a party for the old people organised by local anti-fascists. Around the walls we put large panels picturing the Battle of Long Lane as well as local current anti-fascist demonstrations. The children's groups began to plan how they were going to do this long beforehand.

In February we put on an exhibition about *Access* which the handicapped group completed, and which we hope will travel around the local libraries. It will be part of a wider exhibition which will contain paintings and other works done by day-centre members too.

Perhaps it will be through common struggles such as fighting racism, and developing access, (not only for handicapped people but in a broader dimension), that we will be able to begin to unite the "hidden" as well as "problem" members to the "community" itself. It is only through self- and collective-awareness that people can begin to develop concrete changes within the existing social structure.

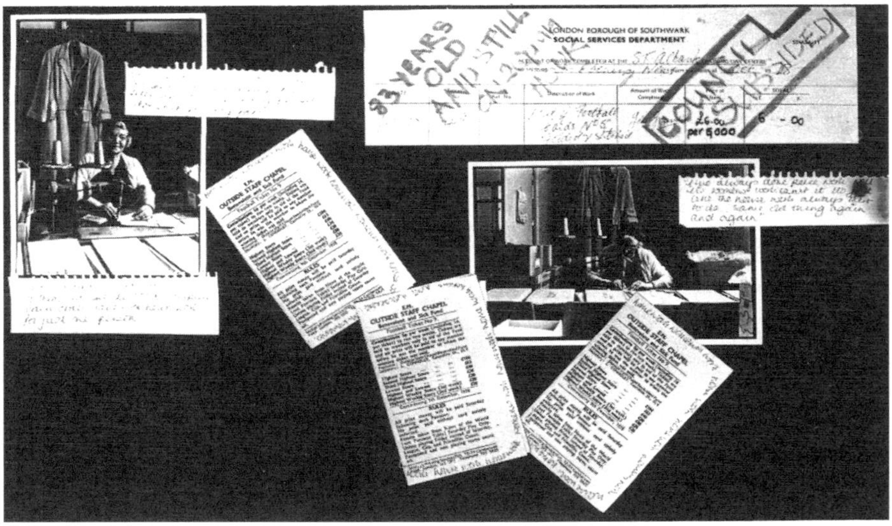

Project on work.

Dismantling Modernism, Reinventing Documentary (Notes on the Politics of Representation)

Allan Sekula

SUPPOSE WE REGARD ART as a mode of human communication, as a discourse anchored in concrete social relations, rather than as a mystified, vaporous, and ahistorical realm of purely affective expression and experience. Art, like speech, is both symbolic exchange and material practice, involving the production of both meaning and physical presence. Meaning, as an understanding of that presence, emerges from an interpretive act. Interpretation is ideologically constrained. Our readings of past culture are subject to the covert demands of the historical present. Mystified interpretation universalizes the act of reading, lifting it above history.

The meaning of an artwork ought to be regarded, then, as *contingent*, rather than as immanent, universally given, or fixed. The Kantian separation of cognitive and affective faculties, which provided the philosophical basis for Romanticism, must likewise be critically superseded. This argument, then, calls for a fundamental break with idealist aesthetics, a break with the notion of genius both in its original form and in its debased neo-romantic appearance at the centre of the mythology of mass culture, where "genius" assumes the trappings of a charismatic stardom.

I'm not suggesting that we ignore or suppress the creative, affective and expressive aspects of cultural activity; to do so would be to play into the hands of the ongoing techno-cratic obliteration of human creativity. What I am arguing is that we understand the extent to which art redeems a repressive social order by offering a wholly imaginary transcendence, a false harmony, to docile and isolated spectators. The cult of private experience, of the entirely affective relation to culture demanded by a consumerist economy, serves to obliterate momentarily, on weekends, knowledge of the fragmentation boredom, and routinization of labour, knowledge of the self as a commodity.

In capitalist society, artists are represented as possessing a privileged subjectivity, gifted with an uncommon unity of self and labour. Artists are the bearers of an autonomy that is systematically and covertly denied the economically objectified mass spectator, the wage-worker and the woman who works without wages in the home. Even the apparatus of mass culture itself can be bent to this elitist logic. "Artists" are the people who stare out, accusingly and seductively, from billboards and magazine advertisements. A glamorous young couple can be seen lounging in what looks like a Soho loft; they tell us of the secret of white rum, effortlessly gleaned from Liza Minnelli at an Andy Warhol party. Richard Avedon is offered to us as an almost impossible ideal: bohemian as well as his "own Guggenheim Foundation". Artist and patron coalesce in a petit-bourgeois dream fleshed out in the realm of a self-valorising mass culture. Further, the recent efforts to elevate photography to the status of high art by transforming the photographic print into a privileged commodity, and the photographer, regardless of working context, into an autonomous *auteur* with a capacity for genius, have the effect of restoring the "aura," to use Walter Benjamin's term, to a mass-communications technology. At the same time, the camera hobbyist, the consumer of leisure technology, is invited to participate in a delimited and therefore illusory and pathetic creativity, in an advertising induced fantasy of self-authorship fed by power over the image machine, and through it, over its prey.

The crisis of contemporary art involves more than a lack of "unifying" metacritical thought, nor can it be resolved by expensive "interdiciplinary" organ transplants. The problems of art are refractions of a larger cultural and ideological crisis, stemming from the declining legitimacy of the liberal capitalist world view. Putting it bluntly, these crises are rooted in the materially dictated inequalities of advanced capitalism and will only be resolved *practically*, by the struggle for an authentic socialism.

Artists and writers who move toward an openly political cultural practice need to educate themselves out of their own professional elitism and narrowness of concern. A theoretical grasp of modernism and its pitfalls might be useful in this regard. The problem of modernist closure, of an "immanent critique" which, failing logically to overcome the paradigm within which it begins, ultimately reduces every practice to a formalism, is larger than any one intellectual discipline and yet infects them all. Modernist practice is organized professionally and shielded by a bogus ideology of neutrality. In political-economic terms, modernism stems from the fundamental division of "mental" and "manual" labour under advanced capitalism. The former is further specialized and accorded certain privileges, as well as a managerial relation to the latter, which is fragmented and degraded.

An ideology of separation, of petit-bourgeois upward aspiration, induces the intellectual worker to view the "working class" with superiority, cynicism, contempt and glimmers of fear. Artists, despite their romanticism and their slumming, are no exception.

The ideological confusions of current art, euphemistically labelled a "healthy pluralism" by art promoters, stem from the collapsed authority of the modernist paradigm. "Pure" artistic modernism collapses because it is ultimately a self-annihilating project, narrowing the field of art's concerns with scientistic rigour, dead-ending in alternating appeals to taste, science and metaphysics. Over the past five years, a rather cynical and self-referential mannerism, partially based on Pop art, has rolled out of this cul-de-sac. Some people call this phenomenon "post modernism." (Already, a so-called "political art" has been used as an end-game modernist bludgeon, as a chic vanguardism, by artists who suffer from a very real isolation from larger social issues. This would be bad enough if it weren't for the fact that the art promotional system converts everything it handles into "fashion," while dishing out a good quantity of liberal obfuscation.) These developments demonstrate that the only necessary rigour in a commodified cultural environment is that of incessant artistic self-promotion. Here elite culture becomes a parasitical "mannerist" representation of mass culture, a private-party sideshow, with its own photo journalism, gossip column reviews, promoters, celebrity pantheon, and narcissistic stellar-bound performers. The charisma of the art star is subject to an overdeveloped bureaucratism. Careers are "managed". Innovation is regularized, adjusted to the demands of the market. Modernism, per se (as well as the lingering ghost of bohemianism), is transformed into farce, into a professionalism based on academic appointments, periodic exposure, lofty real estate speculation in the former factory districts of decaying cities, massive state funding, jet travel, and increasingly ostentatious corporate patronage of the arts. This last development represents an attempt by monopoly capital to "humanize" its image for the middle-managerial and professional subclasses (the vicarious consumers of high culture, the museum audience) in the face of an escalating legitimation crisis. High art is rapidly becoming a specialized colony of the monopoly capitalist media.

Political domination, especially in the advanced capitalist countries and the more developed neo-colonies, depends on an exaggerated symbolic apparatus, on pedagogy and spectacle, on the authoritarian monologues of school and mass media. These are the main agents of working class obedience and docility; these are the main promoters of phoney consumer options, of "lifestyle", and increasingly, of political reaction, nihilism, and sadomasochism. Any effective political art will have to be grounded in work against these institutions. We need a political economy, sociology, and a non-formalist semiotics of media. We need to comprehend advertising as the fundamental discourse of capitalism, exposing the link between the language of manufactured needs and commodity fetishism. From this basis, a critical representational art, an art that points openly to the social world and to possibilities of concrete social transformation, could develop. But we will also have to work toward a redefined *pragmatics*, toward modes of address based on a diological pedagogy, and toward a different and significantly wider notion of audience, one that engages with ongoing progressive struggles against the established order. Without a coherent oppositional politics, though, an oppositional culture remains tentative and isolated. Obviously, a great deal needs to be done.

2

A small group of contemporary artists is working on an art that deals with the social ordering of people's lives. Most of their work involves still photography and video; most relies heavily on written or spoken language. I'm talking about a representational art, an art that refers to something beyond itself. Form and mannerism are not ends in themselves. These works might be about any number of things, ranging from the material and ideological space of the "self" to the dominant social realities of corporate spectacle and corporate power. The initial questions are these: How do we invent our lives out of a limited range of possibilities, and how are our lives invented for us by those in power? As I've already suggested, if these questions are asked only within the institutional boundaries of elite culture, only within the "art world", then the answers will be academic. Given a certain poverty of means, this art aims toward a wider audience, and toward considerations of concrete social transformation.

We might be tempted to think of this work as a variety of documentary. That's all right as long as we expose the myth that accompanies the label, the folklore of photographic truth. This preliminary detour seems necessary. The rhetorical strength of documentary is imagined to reside in the unequivocal character of the camera's evidence, in an essential realism. The theory of photographic realism emerges historically as both product and handmaiden of positivism. Vision, itself unimplicated in the world it encounters; is subjected to a mechanical idealization. Paradoxically, the camera serves to ideologically *naturalize* the eye of the observer. Photography, according to this belief, reproduces the visible world: the camera is

an engine of fact, the generator of a duplicate world of fetishized appearances, independently of human practice. Photographs, always the product of socially-specific encounters between human-and-human or human-and-nature, become repositories of dead facts, reified objects torn from their social origins.

I shouldn't have to argue that photographic meaning is relatively indeterminate; the same picture can convey a variety of messages under differing presentational circumstances. Consider the evidence offered by bank holdup cameras. Taken automatically, these pictures could be said to be unpolluted by sensibility, an extreme form of documentary. If the surveillance engineers who developed these cameras have an aesthetic, it's one of raw, technological instrumentality. "Just the facts, ma'am." But a courtroom is a battleground of fictions. What is it that a photograph points to? A young white woman holds a sub-machine gun. The gun is handled confidently, aggressively. The gun is almost dropped out of fear. A fugitive heiress. A kidnap victim. An urban guerrilla. A willing participant. A case of brainwashing. A case of rebellion. A case of schizophrenia. The outcome, based on the "true" reading of the evidence, is a function less of "objectivity" than of political manoeuvring. Reproduced in the mass media, this picture might attest to the omniscience of the state within a glamorized and mystifying spectacle of revolution and counter-revolution. But any police photography that is publicly displayed is both a specific attempt at identification and a reminder of police power over "criminal elements". The only "objective" truth that photographs offer is the assertion that somebody or something – in this case, an automated camera – was somewhere and took a picture. Everything else, everything beyond the imprinting of a trace is up for grabs.

Walter Benjamin recalled the remark that Eugene Atget depicted the streets of Paris as though they were the scene of a crime. That remark serves to poeticize a rather deadpan, non-expressionist style, to conflate nostalgia and the affectless instrumentality of the detective. Crime here becomes a matter of the heart as well as a matter of fact. Looking backward, through Benjamin to Atget, we see the loss of the past through the continual disruptions of the urban present as a form of violence against memory, resisted by the nostalgic bohemian through acts of solipsistic, passive acquisition. Baudelaire's *Le Cygne* articulates much of that sense of loss, a sense of the impending disappearance of the familiar, that Benjamin attributes indirectly to Atget. I cite this example merely to raise the question of the *affective* character of documentary. Documentary photography has amassed mountains of evidence. And yet, in this pictorial presentation of scientific and legalistic "fact", the genre has simultaneously contributed much to spectacle, to retinal excitation, to voyeurism, to terror, envy and nostalgia, and only a little to the critical understanding of the social world.

A truly critical social documentary will frame the crime, the trial, and the system of justice and its official myths. Artists working toward this end may or may not produce images that are theatrical and overtly contrived, they may or may not present texts that read like fiction. Social truth is something other than a matter of convincing style. I need only cite John Heartfield's overtly *constructed* images, images in which the formal device is absolutely naked, as examples of an early attempt to go beyond the phenomenal and ideological surface of the social realm. In his best work, Heartfield brings the base to the surface through the simplest of devices, often through punning on a fascist slogan (*Millions stand behind me*). Here, construction passes into a critical *deconstruction*.

A political critique of the documentary genre is sorely needed. Socially conscious American artists have much to learn from both the successes *and* the mistakes, compromises, and collaborations of their Progressive Era and New Deal predecessors. How do we assess the close historical partnership of documentary artists and social democrats? How do we assess the relation between form *and* politics in the work of a more progressive Worker's Film and Photo League? How do we avoid a kind of aestheticized political nostalgia in viewing the work of the Thirties? And how about the co-optation of the documentary style by corporate capitalism (notably the oil companies and the television networks) in the late 1940s? How do we disentangle ourselves from the authoritarian and bureaucratic aspects of the genre, from its implicit positivism? (All of this is evidenced in any one second of an Edward R Murrow or a Walter Cronkite telecast. How do we produce an art that elicits dialogue rather than uncritical, pseudo-political affirmation?

Looking backward, at the art-world hubbub about "photography as a fine art," we find a near-pathological avoidance of any such questioning. A curious thing happens when documentary is officially recognized as art. Suddenly the hermeneutic pendulum careens from the objectivist end of its arc to the opposite, subjectivist end. Positivism yields to a subjective metaphysics, technologism gives way to auteurism. Suddenly the audience's attention is directed toward mannerism, toward sensibility, toward the physical and emotional risks taken by the artist. Documentary is thought to be art when it transcends its reference to the world, when the work can be regarded, first and-foremost, as an act of self-expression on the part of the artist. To use Roman Jakobson's categories, the referential function collapses into the expressive function. A cult of authorship, an auteurism, takes hold of the image, separating it from the social conditions of its making and elevating it above the multitude of lowly and mundane uses to which photography is commonly put. The culture journalists' myth of Diane Arbus is interesting in this regard. Most readings of her work careen along an axis between opposing poles of realism and expressionism. On the one hand, her portraits are seen as transparent, metonymic vehicles for the social or psychological truth of her subjects; Arbus elicits meaning from their persons. At the other extreme is a metaphoric projection. The work is thought to express her tragic vision (a vision confirmed by her suicide); each image is nothing so much as a contribution to the artist's self-portrait. These readings coexist, they enhance one another despite their mutual contradiction. I think that a good deal of the generalized aesthetic appeal of Arbus's work, along with that of most art photography, has to do with this indeterminacy of reading, this sense of being cast adrift between profound social insight and refined solipsism. At the heart of this fetishistic cultivation and promotion of the artist's humanity is a certain disdain for the "ordinary" humanity of those who have been photographed. They become the "other", exotic creatures, objects of contemplation. Perhaps this wouldn't be so suspect if it weren't for the tendency of professional documentary photographers to aim their cameras downward, toward those with little power or prestige. (The obverse is the cult of celebrity, the organized production of envy in a mass audience.) The most intimate, human-scale relationship to suffer mystification in all this is the specific social engagement that results in the image; the negotiation between photographer and subject in the making of a portrait, the seduction, coercion, collaboration, or rip-off. But if we widen the angle of our view, we find that the broader institutional politics of elite and "popular" culture are also being obscured in the romance of the photographer as artist.

The promotion of Diane Arbus (along with a host of other essentially mannerist artists) as a "documentary" photographer, as well as the generalized promotion of introspective, privatistic, and often narcissistic uses of photographic technology both in the arena of art photography and that of the mass consumer market, can be regarded as a symptom of two countervailing but related tendencies of advanced capitalist society. On the one hand, subjectivity is threatened by the increasingly sophisticated administration of the daily life. Culture, sexuality, and family life are refuges for the private, feeling self in a world of rationalized performance demands. At the same time, the public realm is "depoliticized" to use Jurgen Habermas's term; a passive audience of citizen-consumers is led to see political action as the prerogative of celebrities. Consider the fact that the major television networks, led by ABC, no longer even pretend to honour the hallowed separation demanded by liberal ideology between "public affairs" and "entertainment." News reporting is now *openly*, rather than covertly, stylized. The mass media portray a wholly *spectacular* political realm, and increasingly provide the ground for a charismatically directed, expressionist politics of the right. Television has never been a realist medium, nor has it been capable of narrative in the sense of a logical, coherent account of cause and effect. But now, television is an openly *symbolist* enterprise, revolving entirely around the metaphoric poetry of the commodity. With the triumph of exchange value over use value, all meanings, all lies, become possible. The commodity exists in a gigantic substitution set; cut loose from its original context, it is metaphorically equivalent to all other commodities.

The high culture of the late capitalist period is subject to the unifying semantic regime of formalism. Formalism neutralizes and renders equivalent, it is a universalizing system of reading. Only formalism can unite all the photographs in the world in one room, mount them behind glass, and *sell* them. As a privileged commodity fetish, as an object of connoisseurship, the photograph achieves its ultimate semantic poverty. But this poverty has haunted photographic practice from the very beginning.

3

I'd like, finally, to discuss some alternative ways of working with photographs. A small number of contemporary photographers have set out deliberately to work against the strategies that have succeeded in making photography a high art. I've already outlined the general political nature of their intentions. Their work begins with the recognition that photography is operative at every level of our culture. That is, they insist on treating photographs not as privileged objects but as common cultural artifacts. The solitary, sparely captioned photograph on the gallery wall is a sign, above all, of an aspiration toward the aesthetic and market conditions of modernist painting and sculpture. In this white void, meaning is thought to emerge entirely from within the artwork. The importance of the framing discourse is masked, context is hidden. These artists on the other hand, openly bracket their photographs with language, using texts to anchor, contradict, reinforce, subvert, complement, particularize, or go beyond the meanings offered by the images themselves. These pictures are often located within an extended narrative structure. I'm not talking about "photo essays," a cliché-ridden form that is the non-commercial counterpart to the photographic advertisement. Photo essays are an outcome of a mass-circulation picture-magazine aesthetic, the aesthetic of the merchandisable column-inch and rapid, excited reading made subservient to visual titillation. I'm also not talking about the "conceptual" and "post conceptual" art use of photography, since most such work unequivocally accepts the bounds of an existing art world.

Of the work I'm dealing with here, Martha Rosler's *The Bowery in two inadequate descriptive systems* (1975) comes the closest to having an unrelentingly metacritical relation to the documentary genre. The title not only raises the question of representation, but suggests its fundamentally flawed, distorted character. The object of the work, its referent, is not the Bowery per se, but the "Bowery" as a socially mediated, ideological construction. Rosler couples 24 photos to a near-equal number of texts. The photographs are frontal views of Bowery store fronts and walls, taken with a normal lens from the edge of the street. The sequence of street numbers suggests a walk downtown, from Houston toward Canal on the west side of the avenue, past anonymous grates, abandoned shop fronts, flop house entrances, restaurant supply houses, discreetly labelled doors to artists' lofts. No people are visible. Most of the photos have the careful geometric elegance – they seem to be deliberate quotations – of Walker Evans. The last two photographs are close-ups of a litter of cheap rosé and white port bottles, again not unlike Evans's 1968 picture of a discarded pine deodorant can in a trash barrel. The cool, deadpan mannerism works against the often expressionist liberalism of the find-a-bum school of concerned photography. This anti-"humanist" distance is reinforced by the text, which consists of a series of lists of words and phrases, an immense slang lexicon of alcoholism. This simple listing of names for drunks and drunkenness suggests both the signifying richness of metaphor as well as its referential poverty, the failure of metaphor to "encompass," to explain adequately, the material reality to which it refers.

We have nautical and astronomical themes: "deck's awash" and "moon-eyed." The variety and "wealth" of the language suggests the fundamental aim of drunkenness, the attempted escape from a painful reality. The photographs consistently pull us back to the street, to the terrain from which this pathetic flight is attempted. Rosler's found poetry begins with the most transcendental of metaphors, "aglow, illuminated" and progresses ultimately, through numerous categories of symbolic escape mingled with blunt recognition, to the slang terms for empty bottles: "dead soldiers" and "dead marines." The pool of language that Rosier has tapped is largely the socio-linguistic "property" of the working class and the poor. This language attempts to handle an irreconcilable tension between bliss and self-destruction in a society of closed options.

The attention to language cuts against the pornography of the "direct" representation of misery. A text, analogous formally to our own ideological index of names-for-the-world, interposes itself between us and "visual experience."

Most of Rosler's other work deals with the internalization of oppressive namings, usually with the structuring of women's consciousness by the material demands of sex and class. Her videotape, *Vital Statistics of a Citizen, Simply Obtained* (1976) portrays documentation as the clinical, brutal instrumentality of a ruling elite bent on the total administration of all aspects of social life: reproduction, child-rearing, education, labour and consumption. A woman is slowly stripped by white-coated technicians, who measure and evaluate every component of her body. A voice-over meditates on violence as a mode of social control, on positivism, on the triumph of quantity, on the master's voice from within. Rosier refers to the body as the fundamental battleground of bourgeois culture.

Since I've mentioned video, I ought to point out that the most developed critiques of the illusory facticity of photographic media have been cinematic, stemming from outside the tradition of still photography. With film and video, sound and image, or sound, image and text, can be worked *over* and *against* each other, leading to the possibility of negation and meta-commentary. An image can be offered as evidence, and then subverted. Photography remains a primitive medium by comparison.

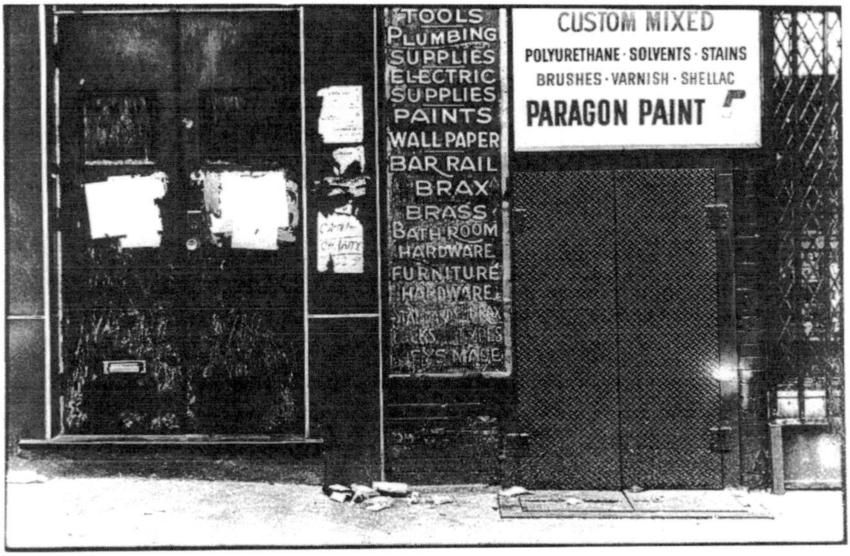

lush wino rubbydub
inebriate
alcoholic
barrelhouse bum

From Martha Rosler, *The Bowery in two inadequate descriptive systems*, 1975. Photographs and text.

Still photographers have tended to believe naively in the power and efficacy of the single image. Of course, the museological handling of photographs encourages this belief, as does the allure of the high-art commodity market. But even photojournalists like to imagine that a good photograph can punch through, overcome its caption and story, on the power of vision alone. The power of the overall communicative system with its characteristic structure and mode of address, over the fragmentary utterance, is ignored. Brecht's remarks in *The Modern Theatre is the Epic Theatre* are worth recalling on this issue, despite his deliberately crude and mechanistic way of phrasing the problem:

> The muddled thinking which overtakes musicians, writers and critics as soon as they consider their own situation has tremendous consequences to which too little attention is paid. For by imagining that they have got hold of an apparatus which in fact has got hold of them they are supporting an apparatus which is out of their control...

The critical anti-naturalism of Brecht, continued in the politically and formally reflexive cinematic modernism of Chris Marker, Godard, and the team of Jean-Marie Straub and Danielle Huillet, stands as a guide to ideologically self-conscious handling of image and text. Americans, schooled in positivism from infancy, tend to miss the point. It was Americans who mistranslated the reflexive documentary methods of Dziga Vertov's *Kino-Pravda* and Jean Rouch's *cinema vérité* into "direct cinema," the cult of the invisible camera, of life caught unawares. The advent of the formalist reflexivity of "structural film" hasn't helped matters either, but merely serves as a crude antithesis to the former tendency.

Jon Jost's film *Speaking Directly* (1975) and Brian Connell's videotapes *La Lucha Final* (1976) and *Petro Theater* (1975) stands as rare examples of American works that write a developed left-wing politics with an understanding of the relation between form and ideology within the documentary genre. *La Lucha Final* dissects the already fragmented corpus of television news by constructing (perhaps deconstructing is the more appropriate word) a detective story narrative of American imperialism in crisis. The story emerges on the basis of scavenged material: State Department publicity photos, Tet offensive news footage, bits of late night television movies. American agents are always asking the wrong questions too late. Another of Connell's tapes, *Petro Theater*, decodes mysterious photo-postcard islands floating off the coast of Long Beach, California. These man-made oil drilling operations are disguised as tropical paradises, complete with palm trees and waterfalls. The derricks themselves are camouflaged as skyscrapers, made to pose as corporate headquarters. Connell's tape reads the island as an image of colonial territory, as nature dominated by an aggressive and expansionist corporate order. The islands are named for dead astronauts, allowing the derricks to assume the glamour of moon rockets. Connell plays the offshore mirage against the political economy of the "energy crisis." Photography like that of Lewis Baltz, to give a counter example, suggests that the oxymoronic label "industrial park" is somehow natural, an unquestionable aspect of a landscape that is both a source of Pop disdain and mortuarial elegance of design. Baltz's photographs of enigmatic factories fail to tell us anything about them, to recall Brecht's remark about a hypothetical photograph of the Krupp works. Connell, on the other hand, argues that advanced capitalism depends on the ideological obliteration of the base. In California, we are led to believe, no one works, people merely punch in for eight hours of Muzak-soothed leisure in air-conditioned condominium-like structures that are somehow sites for the immaculate conception of commodities.

Jost's *Speaking Directly* is a rigorously phenomenological attempt at political autobiography, setting Jost's own subjectivity as film-maker, as he-who speaks, as: particular and emblematic male, as American, as war resister, as rural dropout, as intellectual, as lover, friend, and enemy to numerous Others. Against its determinations and constraints, Jost is continually exposing the problematic character of his own authorship, suggesting his own dishonesty in attempting to construct a coherent image of "his" world. The film skirts solipsism; in fact, Jost resists solipsism through an almost compulsively repetitive rendering of a politicized "outer world". American defoliant bombers waste a section of Vietnam again and again, until the viewer knows the sequence's every move in advance. Magazine advertisements pile up endlessly in another sequence. The "politics" of Jost's work lies in an understanding it shares with, and owes to, both the Women's Liberation Movement and sections of the New Left; the understanding that sexuality, the formation of the self, and the survival of the autonomous subject are fundamental issues for revolutionary practice.

These concerns are shared to a large extent by Philip Steinmetz in a six-volume sociological "portrait" of himself and his relatives. The entire work, called *Somebody's Making a Mistake* (1976), is made up of more than 600 photographs taken over several years. The pictures are well-lit, full of ironic incident and material detail, reminiscent of Russell Lee. Steinmetz pays a great deal of attention to the aesthetics of personal style, to clothing and gesture, to interior decoration. His captions vary between sociological polemic and personal anecdote. The books are a curious hybrid of the family album and a variety of elegantly hand-crafted coffee-table book. The narrative span of the family album is compressed temporally, resulting in a maddening intensity of coverage and exposure.

While covering intimate affairs, Steinmetz offers a synecdochic representation of suburban middle-class family life. At the same time the work is a complex autobiography in which Steinmetz invents himself and is in turn invented, appearing an eldest son, ex-husband, father, alienated and documentation obsessed prime mover, and escapee with one foot in a suburban petit-bourgeois past. The work pivots on self-implication, on Steinmetz's willingness to expose his interactions with and attitudes toward the rest of the family. The picture books are products of a series of discontinuous theatrical encounters; the artist "visits the folks". Some occasions are full of auspicious moments for traditional family-album photography: a birthday, a family dinner. Here Steinmetz is an insider, functioning within the logic of the family, expected, even asked to take pictures. At other moments the camera is pulled out with less fanfare and approval, almost on the sly, I imagine. Other encounters are deliberately staged by the photographer: on a weekend visit he photographs his daughter in front of an endless toy-store display of packaged games. She smiles rather quizzically. Judging from the titles, the games are all moral exercises in corporate virtual male aggression, and female submission. I'm reminded of a frame from Godard, but this picture has a different affect, the affect of real, rather than emblematic, relationships. Eventually the artwork became a familial event in itself. Steinmetz visited his parents with a handful of his books, asking them to talk captions into a tape recorder. Other artists and photographers have done this sort of thing with family archives; Roger Welch is an example. The difference here is that Steinmetz is not particularly interested in memory and nostalgia in themselves. His pictures are geared to elicit ideological responses; they are subtle provocations. The work aims at revealing the power structure within the extended family, the petit-bourgeois ambitions of the men. Their sense of ownership, and the supportive and subordinate role of the women. Steinmetz's father, a moderately successful building contractor, poses by the signpost for a subdivision street he named: Security Way. The photographer's mother sits in the kitchen reading a religious tract entitled *Nervous Christians*. He comes closest to identifying with his daughter, with the possibility of her rebellion.

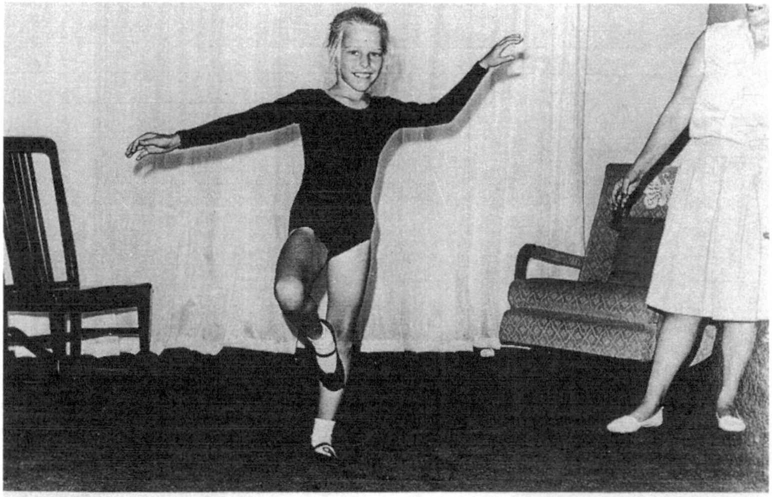

Mom: "Traci has learned how to set a beautiful table. She has your artistic abilities."

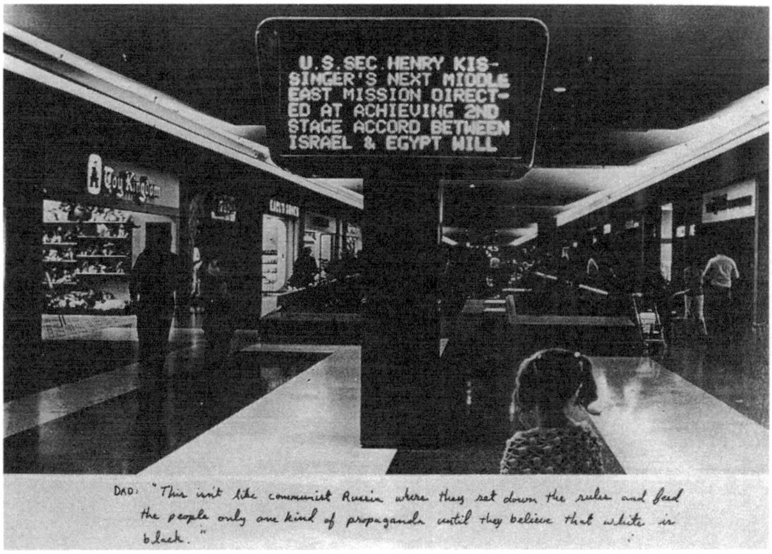

DAD: "This isn't like communist Russia where they set down the rules and feed the people only one kind of propaganda until they believe that white is black."

From Philip A Steinmetz, *Somebody's Making a Mistake*, 1976. Photographic books with text.

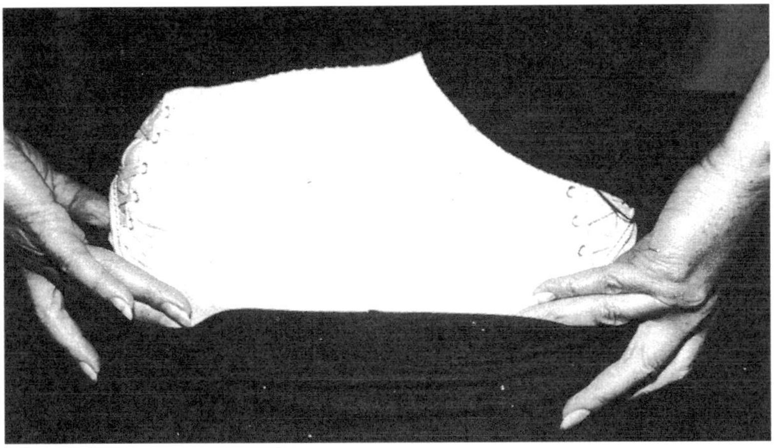

262

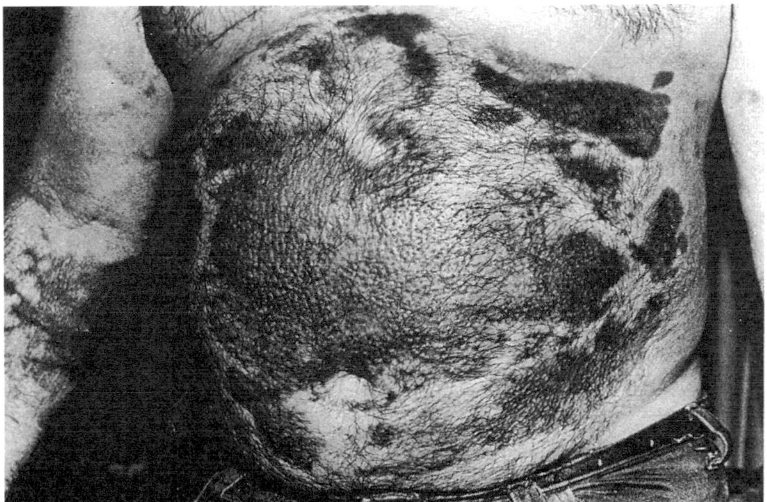

The last of the six books deals with his ex-wife's second wedding. Steinmetz appears at a dress rehearsal – as what? Guest, interloper, official photographer, voyeur, ghost from the past? His wife's new in-laws look troubled. The pictures have a curious sense of the absurd, of packaged roles poorly worn, of consumer ritual. The camera catches a certain awkwardness of tuxedo-and-gown-encased gesture and movement. The groom is late, and someone asks Steinmetz to stand in for him. The affair takes on a television situation comedy aspect as familial protocol lapses into absurdity.

Fred Lonidier deals more with public politics than with the family. *The Health and Safety Game* (1976) is about the "handling" of industrial injury and disease by corporate capitalism, pointing to the systemic character of everyday violence in the workplace. Some statistics: one in four American workers is exposed on a daily basis to death, injury, and disease-causing work conditions. According to a Nader report, "job casualties are statistically at least three times more serious than street crime." (So much for TV cop shows.)

An observation: anyone who has ever lived or worked in an industrial working-class community can probably attest to the commonness of disfigurement among people on the job and in the street. Disease is less visible and has only recently become a public issue. I can recall going to the Chicago Museum of Science and Industry and visiting the "coal mine" there. Hoarse-voiced men, retired miners, led the tourists through a programmed demonstration of mining technology. When the time came to deal with safety, one of the guides set off a controlled little methane explosion. No one mentioned black-lung disease in this corporate artwork, although the evidence rasped from the throats of the guides.

Lonidier's "evidence" consists of twenty or so case studies of individual workers, each displayed on large panels laid out in a rather photo-journalistic fashion. The reference to photojournalism is deliberate, I think, because the work refuses to deliver any of the empathic goodies that we are accustomed to in photo essays. Conventional "human interest" is absent. Lonidier is aware of the ease with which liberal documentary artists have converted violence and suffering into aesthetic objects. For all his good intentions, for example, Eugene Smith in *Minamata* provided more a representation of his compassion for mercury-poisoned Japanese fisherfolk than one of their struggle for retribution against the corporate polluter. I'll say it again: the subjective aspect of liberal aesthetics is compassion rather than collective struggle. Pity, mediated by an appreciation of "great art," supplants political understanding. Susan Sontag and David Antin have both remarked that Eugene Smith's portrait of a *Minamata* mother bathing her retarded and deformed daughter is a seemingly deliberate reference to the *Pieta*.

Unlike Smith, Lonidier takes the same photographs that a doctor might. When the evidence is hidden within the body, Lonidier borrows and copies x-ray films. These pictures have a brute, clinical effect. Each worker's story is reduced to a rather schematic account of injury, disease, hospitalization, and endless bureaucratic run-around by companies trying to shirk responsibility and liability. All too frequently we find that at the end of the story the worker is left unemployed and under-compensated. At the same time, though, these

Opposite:

Waitress's Back. "He said he had known other comp. attorneys in the past that would work for the workers and really get in there and get for them what they deserved.Then the first thing you know they'd be becoming more pro-company, pro-company because it's easier."

Oil Worker's Burns. "When it really comes down to the nitty-gritty it's the employees themselves who won't really make a stand on safety. When it comes down to the bread-and-butter issue, if you make a strike issue over a safety matter, it's going to take a lot more education, in my opinion."

From Fred Lodinier, *The Health and Safety Game: Fictions Based on Fact*, 1976. Photographs, text and videotape.

people are fighting. A machinist with lung cancer tells of stealing samples of dust from the job, placing them on the kitchen griddle in a home-made experiment to detect asbestos, a material that his bosses had denied using. The anonymity of Lonidier's subjects is a precaution against retaliation against them; many are still fighting court cases; many are subject to company intimidation and harassment if they do make their stories public.

Lonidier's presentation is an analogue of sorts for the way in which corporate bureaucrats handle the problem of industrial safety, yet he subverts the model by telling the story from below, from the place occupied by the worker in the hierarchy. The case-study form is a model of authoritarian handling of human lives. The layout of the panels reflects the distribution of power. Quotes from the workers are set in type so small that they are nearly unreadable. The titles are set in large type: *Machinist's Lung*, *Egg Packer's Arm*. The body and the life are presented as they have been fragmented by management. Injury is a loss of labour power, a negative commodity, overhead. Injury is not a diminishing of a human life but a statistical impingement on the corporate profit margin.

The danger exists, here as in other works of socially conscious art, of being overcome by the very oppressive forms and conditions one is critiquing, of being devoured by the enormous machinery of material and symbolic objectification. Political irony walks a thin line between resistance and surrender.

Above the case studies, Lonidier presents an analysis of strategies employed by corporations and unions in the struggle over occupational health issues. The final corporate resorts are closed factories and runaway shops. But implicit in Lonidier's argument is the conclusion that work *cannot*, in the long run, be made safe under capitalism, because of the absolute demand for increasing capital accumulation under escalating crisis conditions. Most businessmen know this, and are resisting reforms for that very reason. The health issue exposes an indifference to human life that goes beyond ethics, an indifference that is structurally determined and can only be structurally negated.

Lonidier's aim is to present his work in a union hall context; so far showings have included a number of art school galleries, a workers' art exhibition at the Los Angeles Museum of Science and Industry, the Whitney Museum, AFSCME District Council 37 AFL-CIO in New York City (AFSCME, the American Federation of State, County, and Municipal Employees, is the largest union of workers in the state sector in the United States), and at the Center for Labor Studies at Rutgers University. Since the late 1940s, anti-communism has been a dominant ideology within American organized labour. Thus, for obvious reasons, *The Health and Safety Game* only makes explicit a critique of the current monopoly stage of capitalist development, without pointing directly to the necessity of socialist alternatives. This is only one of the problems of working through labour bureaucracy and toward a rank-and-file audience. At the same time, it should be noted that a number of progressive unions, mostly in New York, are beginning to develop cultural programmes. Potentially, this could amount to an attempt to counteract the hegemony of corporate culture and restore some of the working-class cultural traditions that were obliterated with the onslaught of the 1950s. Recent documentary films like Barbara Kopple's *Harlan County USA* and *Union Maids* by Julia Reichert and Jim Klein keep alive a tradition of working-class militancy, emphasizing the active role of women in struggle. Both films reveal the importance of oral history and song for maintaining working-class traditions; both emerge from the film-makers' partisan commitment to long-term work from within particular struggles. Neither of these films qualifies as the standard "neutral" airplane ticket-in-the-back-pocket sort of documentary.

Nearly all the work I'm discussing here demands a critical re-evaluation of the relationship between artists, media workers, and their "audiences». I'm not suggesting that the mass media can effectively be infiltrated. Mass

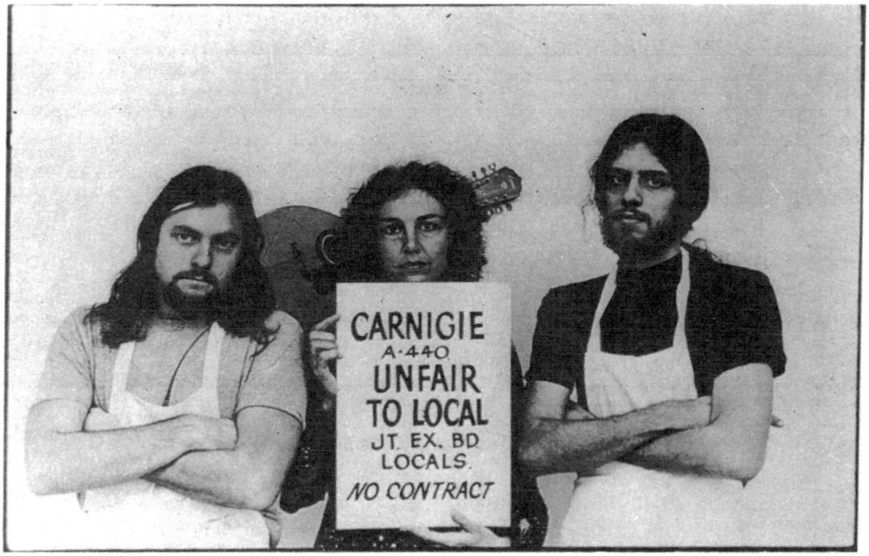

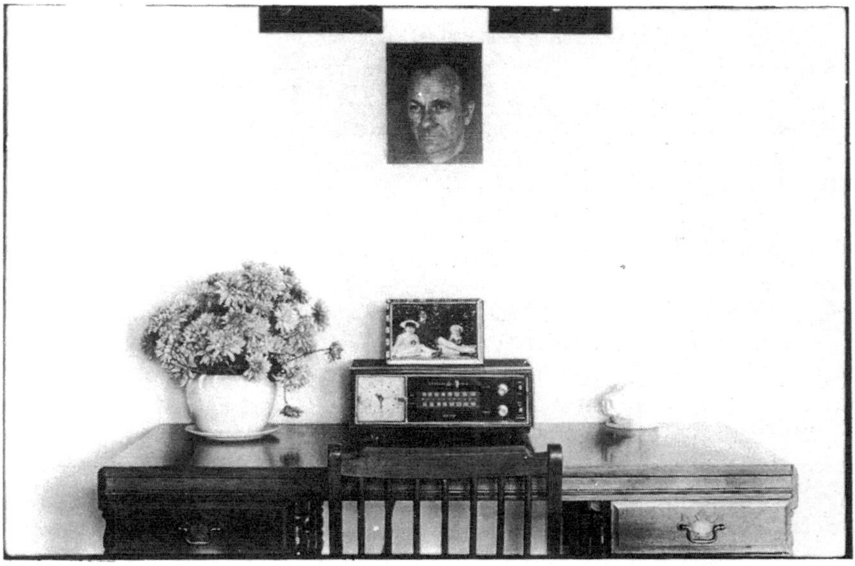

" ...a political novel in which the workers were denied the privilege of psychological treatment... a psychological novel in which the boss invented the workers...a political novel in which the workers were allowed the privilege of psychological treatment..."
From Allan Sekula, This Ain't China: a photonovel, 1974. Photographs and text.

"...i photographed the inside of the apartment... i photographed his resume..."
From Allan Sekula, *Aerospace Folktales*, 1973. Photographs, text and audiotape.

"communication" is almost entirely subject to the pragmatics of the one-way, authoritarian manipulation of consumer "choices". I think "marginal" spaces have to be discovered and utilized, spaces where issues can be discussed collectively: union halls, churches, high schools, community colleges, community centres, and perhaps only reluctantly, public museums. Still photographers ought to consider "vulgar" and "impure" formats, such as the slide shows; but formal questions can only follow a more fundamental and re-definition of political priorities. A number of cultural workers in the Oakland area are using slide shows didactically and as catalysts for political participation. Bruce Kaiper has produced work on the capitalist image of labour using a critical reading of *Fortune* magazine advertisements and historical material on scientific management. Ellen Kaiper has done a piece on the forced layoffs and "domestication" of women industrial workers after the Second World War. These shows are designed primarily for audiences of working people by people who are themselves workers. Fern Tiger is working on an extended documentation of class structure and conflict in Oakland. Her working method involves a lot of prolonged interaction with the people she photographs. She makes return visits with prints as part of an attempt to overcome the traditional aloofness of the merely contemplative sociological observer or journalistic photographer. Mel Rosenthal is involved in a similar project in the South Bronx.

My own work with photographs revolves around relationships between wage-labour and ideology, between material demands and our imaginary coming-to-terms with those demands. I use "autobiographical" material, but assume a certain fictional and sociological distance in order to achieve a degree of typicality. My personal life is not the issue; it's simply a question of familiarity that forms the necessary basis for an adequate representational art. I've tended to construct narratives around crisis situations: around unemployment and workplace struggles, situations in which ideology fails to provide a "rational" and consoling interpretation of the world, unless one has already learned to expect the worst. What I've been interested in, then, is a failure of petit-bourgeois optimism, a failure that leads to either progressive or reactionary class identifications in periods of economic crisis. *Aerospace Folktales* (1973) is a family biography which focuses on the effects of unemployment on white-collar technical workers, on people who have internalized a view of themselves as "professionals" and subsequently suffer the shock of being dumped into the reserve army of labour. I was interested in the demands unemployment places on family life, in the family as refuge, training ground and women's prison. As Max Horkheimer has noted, unemployment blurs the boundaries between the private and the social. Private life becomes mere waiting for work, just, I might add, as work is increasingly a mode of waiting for life, for a delayed gratification. For men who have internalized the demands of production, forced idleness can breed both small and large insanities, from the compulsive straightening of lamps to despair and suicide.

This Ain't China (1974) is a photo-novel which grew out of an attempt to unionize a restaurant. The work is a comedy about theatricalized food, about food as a central fetishized image in an organized drama of "service." Among other things, I wanted to portray the conditions under which people stop obeying orders, and in the way repetitive alienated work colonizes the unconscious, particularly work in crowded, greasy "backstage" kitchens.

Formally, I use long edited sequences of still photographs, usually broken up into "shots" of varying length, as well as lengthy novelistic texts and taped interviews. The photographs deliberately quote a variety of stylistic sources: from motion studies to a deadpan, clinical version of colour food photography. The narrative moves self-consciously between "fictional" and "documentary" modes. A lot of scenes are staged. Both *Aerospace* and *China* have been shown on the wall, as books and, most effectively in a political sense, as live slide shows

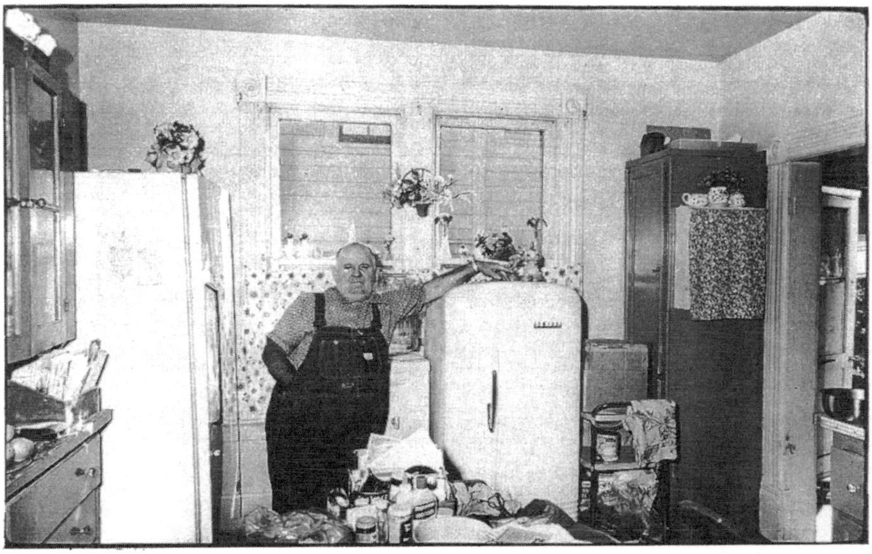

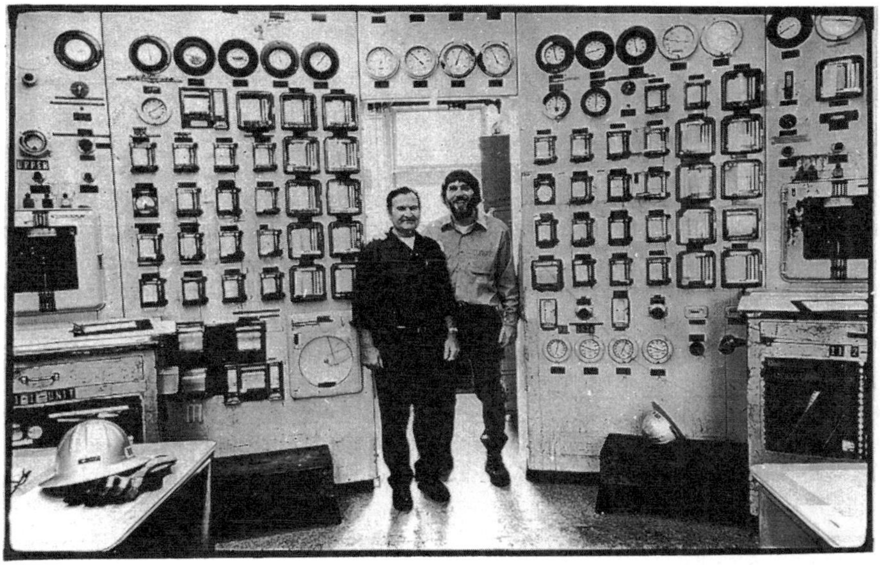

Point Richmond, California, 1976. "I was a refinery stage rigger and was hurt permanently. I get no compensation from the oil company. I still pay for my own medicines. They use you and when they are done, well... it's tough for you!" (signed) Orville England, Standard Oil Co.

Control Room of a Crude Oil Distillation Unit, Standard Oil Refinery, Richmond, California, 1977.

From Chauncey Hare, *A Study of Standard Oil Company Employees 1976-77*. Photographs and audio-taped interviews for people who have something other than a merely aesthetic relation to the issues involved.

Chauncey Hare is a photographer who happens to have spent twenty years of his life as a chemical engineer. This biographical note is central to the meaning of his work. Of all the people I've discussed, he has the least relation to a hybridized pictorially disrespectful narrative approach to the photographic medium. His photography grows out of a by now established documentary tradition, characterized by a belief in the efficacy of the single image, and a desire to combine formal elegance with a clarity of detail. The radicalism of Hare's work lies in his choice of a terrain and his identification with its inhabitants.

Hare is beginning to be known for work done over the past ten years while traveling across the United States, taking careful, tripod-mounted portraits of people, mostly working people, in their home environments. These images depict home life as a source of dignity and grace (his portrait-subjects are always on balance, sharing none of the grotesquery of Arbus or Bill Owens) and as something flawed, something invaded by the horrific sameness of a consumer culture. It is in the grasping of this dialectical character of family and private life, that Hare partakes of the same general critique I've been noting in the work of other politically aware photographers. This earlier work of Hare's exhibited in 1977 at the Museum of Modern Art and published by Aperture as *Interior America*, continues in these contexts to reinforce the dominant American myth of the documentary photographer as a rootless wanderer, of art as the project of a contemplative, but voracious eye.

Of course, Hare with his careful, sympathetic interactions, doesn't share the transcontinental anomic *flaneurerie* of the Robert Frank tradition. For the moment, then, I'm more interested in a more recent project of Hare's, entitled *A Study of Standard Oil Company Employees* (1976-77). It is unlikely that this work will even be exhibited at the Rockefeller-backed Museum of Modern Art which is, after all, a cultural edifice built on Standard Oil profits, not withstanding the "relative autonomy" of John Szarkowski's curatorial decisions. Using credentials as a Guggenheim photography fellow, Hare asked his employers for a year's leave of absence from his engineering job, only that he might return to work every day and take photographs that would begin to expose what he saw as the relation between "technology and alienation." Somehow, corporate public relations agents saw the project in a positive light and approved it. After only three months of independent work, Hare's investigations were terminated by a suddenly threatened management. During his wanderings in this familiar territory, Hare photographed and interviewed at every level of the corporate hierarchy, ranging from refinery operators, maintenance workers and headquarters keypunch operators, to supervisors and executive engineers. His photographs form a kind of metonymic map of an abstract bureaucratic structure. Each portrait suggests a life and a position. One sees evidence of the elaborately coded privileges and humiliations of autocratically managed large enterprises. An executive inhabits a large office on an upper floor with a plate glass view of San Francisco's financial district. In a corner, a far corner, behind an expensive potted plant, he keeps a small photographic shrine to his wife and kids. Refinery operators, unable to leave their job sites for lunch, eat sandwiches as they stare at walls of gauges. A woman's head is barely visible in a labyrinthine word-processing cubicle. A line of refinery operators sits glumly on a bench while their supervisor lectures them about a failed valve, exhibited prominently in the foreground of the picture.

Hare's photographs demand extended captions. His interviews serve to reveal the subjective aspects of the work experience, something photographs can only suggest indirectly. Interviews allow for a kind of self-authorship that portraiture offers only in an extremely limited and problematic way. The photographer always has the edge; and a moment is, after all, only a moment, and only a visible moment at that. Speech allows for critical reflection, for complaints, for the unfolding of personal histories, for the voicing of fears and hopes. Hare was trained as a technocrat and a pragmatist, trained to submit all problems to the logic of an efficiency defined solely in terms of profit. This is hardly a personal attack, but merely a remark on the historical role of the engineering profession under capitalism. Hare brings an engineer's knowledge, coupled with an ethical integration of "fact" and "value", to his critique of the petrochemical industry. And yet he sees in the refinery workers an image of his own, previously unacknowledged, prolet- arianization. He overcomes the contempt commonly felt by professional and technical staff for the people who actually run the everyday operations of a large refinery complex. Refineries are increasingly dangerous, both to workers and to the surrounding communities. Under-staffed and poorly maintained, many plants are potential bombs. Pipes wear thin and explode; operators have to contend with doubled and tripled workloads. This crisis situation is evident in Hare's pictures and interview transcripts. A lone worker is photographed in the midst of a large tank truck loading complex for which he alone is responsible, rather than the normal crew of three. A number of the workers photographed by Hare have since died of cancer. The Richmond, California area, where Hare both works and lives, is a petrochemical centre with the highest *per capita* rate of cancer in the country. As a known member of the community and friend, Hare photographs many of the workers in their homes, in private life and retirement. It is among these older retired workers that he discovers the most variations on the theme of uncompensated injuries and epidemic carcinoma. The younger workers know what awaits them, and talk about their options.

Like Lonidier, Hare has had to protect many of his subjects from the potential consequences of their remarks, from company reprisals. However, he has chosen an altogether different approach to the problems of visual representation, preferring portraiture to a deadpan, clinical style of photography. Lonidier accepts the reified form of visual depiction, and works toward its subversion through storytelling and political analysis. Hare begins with a "humanized" image, but embeds the portrait within a larger frame, within the very midst of a bureaucratic labyrinth and a modern "automated" version of the dark, satanic mill with its routine, its boredom, its sterility and its invisible poisons.

4

I'm arguing, then, for an art that documents monopoly capitalism's inability to deliver the conditions of a fully human life, for an art that recalls Benjamin's remark in the *Theses on the Philosophy of History* that "there is no document of civilization that is not at the same time a document of barbarism." Against violence directed at the human body, at the environment, at working people's ability to control their own lives, we need to counterpose an active resistance, simultaneously political and symbolic, to monopoly capitalism's increasing power and arrogance, a resistance aimed ultimately at socialist transformation. A naive faith in both the privileged subjectivity of the artist, at the one extreme, and the fundamental "objectivity" of photographic realism, at the other, can only be overcome in a recognition of cultural work as a praxis. As Marx put it in *The Economic and Philosophic Manuscripts of 1844*:

> It is only in a social context that subjectivism and objectivism, spiritualism and materialism, activity and passivity cease to be such antinomies. The resolution of the theoretical contradictions is possible only through practical means, only through the practical energy of man.

A didactic and critical representation is a necessary but insufficient condition for the transformation of society. A larger, encompassing praxis is necessary.

POSTSCRIPT

Contacts/Worksheets. Notes on Photography, History and Representation

John Tagg

READING FOR PLEASURE

Working in the library, I find a reproduction of a little-known photograph by Lewis Hine, taken around 1936 for the National Research Project of the Works Progress Administration. It shows a young couple in what we may take to be their sitting room. He, on one side, in a wooden-armed upright; she, to his left, in a padded armchair with bulging, curving lines and elaborate wooden feet; they sit opposite each other. The man does a crossword. The woman reads. Something that may be a paper knife is held in her right hand. Both are smiling, half flattered, half afraid. He wears a short sleeved shirt and holds his pen with confidence but, nervously perhaps, his other hand fingers his collar and the base of his neck.

To his right is a small side table and on its top lies what could be an ashtray with a special device for holding matches. On the stand beneath is another object but it is not possible to make it out. Next to the table, moving left, is a metal standard lamp, strangely wrought, on a square-legged base and supporting a large fringed shade whose decoration shows a stylised hunting scene: the hound is on the right, the stag in the centre and, to its left, in the direction it is running, is a clump of grass. Each motif occupies one face of the hexagonal shade. On its other sides, if the pattern continues, it is not visible to us, though it would be to the man in the chair were he to look up.

Diagonally in front of him, but parallel to the picture plane, is a square pouffe on cabriole legs, and between him and the woman, though to the rear of the room and set across a corner so as to obstruct a dark painted door with a round white handle, someone has set a wardrobe or cupboard on which stands a small two visible walls would be in line on the picture plane with the vertical axis of the cupboard or wardrobe: the junction of its two closed doors.

The floor covering may be rush matting but it is difficult to tell from the suggested texture of the image and the regular squares whose closely abutting edges recede parallel to the walls of the room. Rush matting or not, they seem comfortably off: he wears a watch and a signet ring; her hand relaxes without difficulty on the arm of her chair and her eyes are not reading the magazine in her lap. Yet the room cannot be serving the use for which it was planned. Perhaps it is a

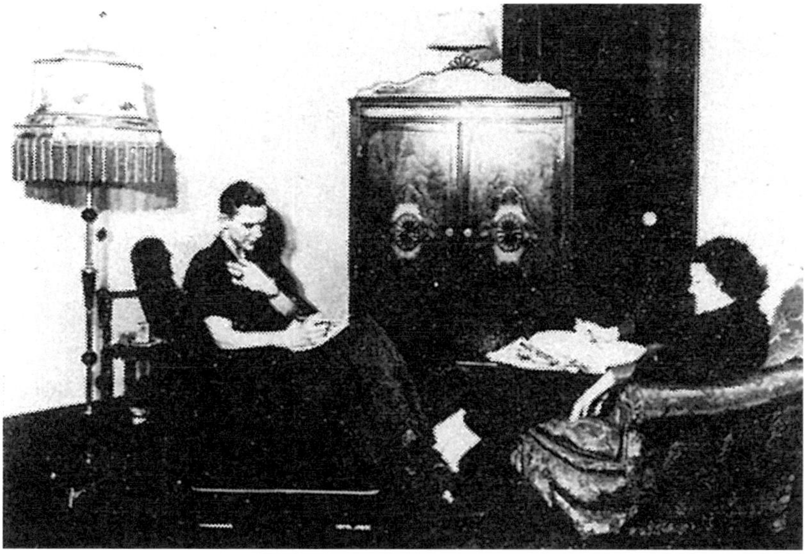

table lamp fitted, like the standard lamp, with an hexagonal shade. The wardrobe or cupboard avoids being parallel to the camera plane so that, although it marks a caesura, not quite the furthest plane in depth, it mediates between the plane of the pouffe and the diagonally receding wall in which the dark painted door would open and which meets the other visible wall at ninety degrees in a corner the wardrobe obscures. The image must be over-exposed at this point or else it has lost too much in definition in the process of being reproduced, but we may guess that the plane of intersection of the room in a house divided into flats. Perhaps the photographer moved them here, arranging the furniture in a plain, deflected symmetry.

We are invited to speculate: is this their first home? (He finds himself dreaming into the picture – sliding into the picture beneath this assemblage of objects and meanings – a look, his self, a reconstituted world). They are young, nice folks; clean, hair neatly brushed; making a start. The connotations hang without seeming to find an object: have these things been brought here or is this a home? These things – the personal jewellery, the furnishings,

1. Lewis Hine, Young couple, 1936.

the room or "home", their ankles which seem to be touching (she needing reassurance, he the sense of command), his bare arms unmarked by labour, her stockingless legs, their unglancing awareness of each other, scarcely absorbed in their carefully divided but inconsequential domestic pursuits (he doesn't read for learning, she doesn't sew or knit) – are so many moments, retrievable only with difficulty, instated here as Hine's young couple: the generation of the New Deal, healthy, leisured, free from the factory, ignorant of child labour, assembling the signifiers of family and home, stabilizing society in its fundamental unit, content, hopeful, shut in by the cupboard up against the door. Perhaps, however, it is a wardrobe. Though that would be unlikely in a sitting room. Something is not right. Some flaw in the ensemble. 1936: seven years after the Wall Street Crash and a year before the "Roosevelt Depression". The style of the furniture undatable; perhaps second-hand. The image unplaceable; perhaps Hine's late period. Unexpected. Unreliable.

How many tracks converge on this point and seem at once to have petered out at their nodal point? Does Hine's personal disappointment cut across his reformist script and its public, political enactment: a sudden movement of light over these few objects and this closed stage? The flash that lit this image and set the shadow of the standard lamp on the pale, receptive surface of the wall beyond, revealed too much and the pleasure of the ideology is spoilt.

Notes for a panel discussion at Nottingham

In his essay *Understanding a Photograph*, written in 1968, John Berger has argued that "photographs are records of things seen", an "automatic record". "Photography", he has added, "has no language of its own". "There is no transforming in photography". The only decision is the choice of moment to record and isolate.

Clearly the pursuit of such views has put Berger on a collision course with a growing number of other writers on photography. It has been said, for example by Umberto Eco, that if photography is to be likened to perception, this is not because the former is a "natural" process but because the latter is also coded.

The photographer turns his or her camera on a world of objects already constructed as a world of uses, values and meanings, though in the perceptual process these may not appear as such but only as qualities discerned in a "natural" recognition of "what is there". By more or less conscious adjustment of an infinite field of significant determinations ranging from the arrangement and lighting of this "world of objects" to the mechanics and field of view of the camera and the sensitivity of the film, paper and chemicals, the photographer abstracts from the distribution of reflected light from the objects to procure a pattern of light and dark on paper which can in no way be regarded as a replication of the "given" subject. This pattern on paper is, in turn, the object of a perception – or reading – in which it is constituted as a meaningful image according to learned schemas.

The meaning of the photographic image is built up by an interaction of such schemas or codes which vary greatly in their degree of schematization. The image is therefore to be seen as a composite of signs, more to be compared with a complex sentence than a single word. Its meanings are multiple, concrete and, most important, *constructed*.

In common, too, with other language-like systems, photographs may be exhaustively analysed as projections of a limited number of rhetorical forms in which a society's values and beliefs are naturalised and which may not be dispelled simply by analysis since, following Freud's discussion of desire and censure, we may see rhetorical forms as mock transgressions of notional, simple, underlying propositions which may be rejected but which still provide, through their very rejection, a source of unpunished satisfaction.

It is the underestimation of the degree to which the photographic image itself already needs to be read as a rhetorical construction which gives rise to the idea that the meaning of the photograph is too imprecise in itself and needs to be anchored by a caption, if it is not to drift in ambiguity. The same underestimation gives rise to the rigid separation of verbal and visual which semiotics, by revealing the complex interpenetration of visual and verbal codes, has shown to be spurious: the purely visual image is nothing but an Edenic fiction.

If there cannot be found any ontological or semiological basis for the privileging of photography as a means of representation which renders a direct transcription of the real, how are we to account for the real force which photography exerts in modern social life? In the first place, the production and attribution of photographic meanings is not an arbitrary or voluntaristic process. Encoding and decoding in photographs is the product of work by concrete historical individuals who are themselves reciprocally constituted as the subjects of ideology in the unfolding historical process. Moreover, this work takes place within specific social and institutional contexts. Photographs are not ideas. They are material items produced by a certain elaborate mode of production and distributed, circulated and consumed within a given set of social relations; images made meaningful and understood within the very relations of their production and sited within a wider ideological complex which must, in turn, be related to the practical and social problems which sustain and shape it.

What I am trying to stress here is the absolute continuity of the photograph's ideological existence – its coalescence and codification of value-filled meanings – with its existence as a material object whose "currency" and "value" arise in certain distinct and historically specific social practices and are ultimately a function of the state. When we deal with photography as ideology, we are not dealing with something "outside" reality – a looking-glass world related to the real world by laws of reflection and reversal. As Louis Althusser has argued: "an ideology always exists in an apparatus, and its practice or practices. This existence is material." Therefore, as Pierre Macherey has shown, to study the ideology of a society is not to analyse the system of ideas, thought and representations (the "history of ideas" approach) or to produce a new metaphysics of the image. It is to study the material operation of ideological apparatuses, to which correspond a certain number of specific practices.

We are now in a position to displace the question about photography's privileged status as a guaranteed witness of the actuality of the objects or events it represents from the level of internal relations – the alleged intrinsic nature of the photographic process – to the level of the operation of certain privileged apparatuses within the given social formation, such as, in our case, scientific establishments, government departments, the police and the law courts. This power to bestow authority and privilege on photographic representations is not given to other apparatuses within the same social formation – such as amateur photography or "art photography" – and it is only partially held by photojournalism. Ask yourself, under what conditions would a photograph of the Loch Ness Monster or a UFO become acceptable as proof of their existence. Not if they were "frontal and clear", to use Barthes' term, that is if they deployed the allegedly "natural" rhetoric of documentary images.

Here, we pass into the area of the constant articulation of power on knowledge and knowledge on power which the French philosopher and historian Michel Foucault has explored. Foucault argues that each society establishes what he calls its "regime of truth": "its 'general politics' of truth: that is, the types of discourse it harbours and causes to function as true; the mechanisms and instances which enable one to distinguish true from false statements... ; the techniques and procedures which are valorized for obtaining truth; the status of those who are charged with saying what counts as true".

It is within this "regime of truth" that we must situate the photograph if we are to understand not how photographic truth may be emancipated from every system of power, but how we may construct a *new politics of truth* by detaching its power from the specific forms of hegemony in the economic, social and cultural domains within which it operates at the present time. This, I think, is very different from the development of a "world historical consciousness" which John Berger has called for.

Part of a proposal for study

The work will involve a reconsideration of how representations are articulated, circulated and consumed within certain specified social apparatuses, how they have an effect, and what it means to say that, in this circulation, the ideological level is constituted. This, in turn, entails a critique of the conception of ideology as "false consciousness" but also of the notion of ideology as a mode of vision (thought, value) whose boundaries do not constitute part of (appear within) the field of sight. What these theories share is a conception of ideology as an internally consistent, if not coherent, system which may be "unmasked" by the revelation of the ideology's non-correspondence with a pre-given reality, or by confronting it with some other ideology, reflecting an opposed class outlook.

This work, by contrast, will attempt to construct a theory of ideology which will accommodate the non-conflictual coexistence and interpenetration of divergent ideological elements and representations, and which will give an account of ideology as something "seen through" yet whose enforcement stabilizes contradictions between the existing social order and the conflicting projection of desires by a double effect in which it, simultaneously, installs the idea of a prior, "normal" level which constitutes "truth", while allowing a release of phantasy in a pretended transgression of this "truth" which, because it is only pretence, yields unpunished – because unrealized – gratification. From this point of view, ideology will be seen as a mode of accommodation between the regime of truth and the domain of prohibited desires, whose effectivity lies in the manner in which it can bring both into play: on the one hand, naturalizing the regime of truth and, on the other, ameliorating the disruptive effects of desire, the sources of whose prohibition is, in the process, completely erased. It is this form of collusion of power and the unconscious which remains entirely unmoved by "rational" analysis

(Addendum on Hine's photograph and Russell Lee's picture of FSA clients in Hidalgo County Texas)

Where would one begin one's analysis of the constitution of "family" and "home" in these photographs? Before the photographic phase? ...with the marking out of the landscape by the designation, through the complex codes and relations of power of urban planning, of a regular hierarchy of "residential" areas? ...with the division of these areas by the further elaboration of related codes and the constitution of an orderly sequence of plots or "private sites" along the avenues of a continuous and unobserved surveillance? ...with the subdivision of these sites and the articulation, in architecture, of a set of domestic functions, together with their relations: the "sitting" room, "lounge" or "living" room marked out in separation from the functions of cooking, eating, washing, sleeping, excreting, as clearly as the house itself marks out the domain of "family life" from that of work? This is the "living room", the centrepiece of the "family home", the arena of its life, a space of leisure, recreation and interpersonal relationships. uncluttered by social functions and work, on the one hand, or bodily functions, on the other. (The woman, wife-and-mother, for whom the "home" is arena of being and place of work is, of course, the exception in this. How often in such photographs she sits sewing or knitting or engaged in some other "homely" labour) ... with the elaboration, extension and refinement of these architecturally defined functions in the subcodes of decor and furnishing: two chairs which face each other, the radiogram between them, the lamp arranged for reading or sewing, the identically framed photographs restating the symmetry and duality of the entire arrangement; this appalling topography of the "family"; this production and marriage of an hierarchy of needs and gratifications within a single setting?

Only now, on this *mise-en-scène*, does the photographer begin to act, deploying a whole set of skills and techniques, the entire power of an artistic method and the apparatus or apparatuses within which it is inscribed, to inflect, reveal, conceal, draw out or curtail the densely overlaid discourses of the "Family home" which become "what was there", a second "nature", the "truth" of the photograph.

assault on the ruling codes and a replenishing of those dissident or disengaged codes which survive or coexist within the dominant and dominated formation.

The goal of Clark's argument is a Realism that is constructed as a specific artistic or representational reality, not that spurious after-the-event realism which is embedded in the ruling discursive formation and which in no way merits the name "socialist". The moment he scrutinises is that of the historical failure of this enterprise in painting and of the emergence of a modernism, critical on the level of the sign

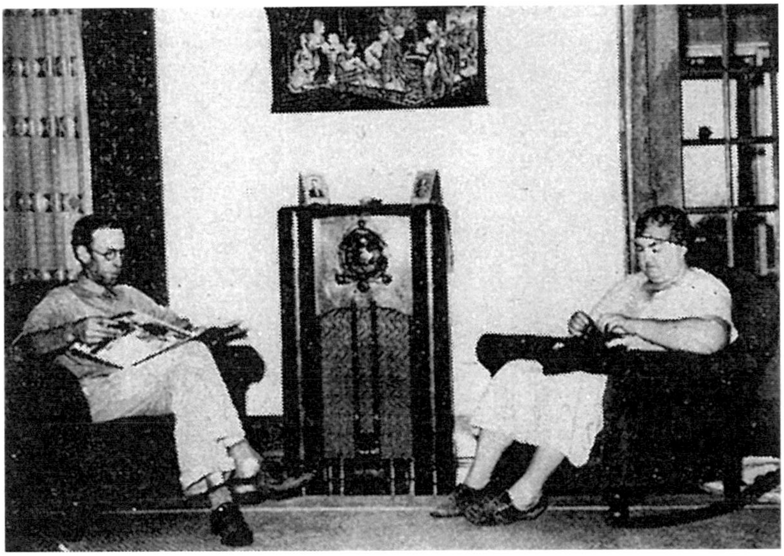

13.vii

What Tim Clark argues is that the question of a Realist representation concerns not only the confluence of crucial and necessary conditions and codes in the Realist work, but also outlawing, the refusal of signification of certain "realities" in the dominant and dominated discourses of the same historical moment. Therefore, the possibility of a conjuncturally Realist discourse is dependent not only on the assemblage of the disparate elements of a new code at the point of historical conflict, but also a double entry into the regime of discourse: an alone, within the very work that seems to reinstate the Realist challenge: Manet's *Olympia*.

(But Foucault might challenge that the realism of a representation is not just a matter of codes or of their insertion in and traversal of a ruling formation of discourses. No more has it solely to do with the function of the definite apparatuses or institutions within which it is inscribed but it is incited by a whole technology through which power is accrued, transmitted and exercised in the social body. What is poignant about the assertion of "Realism" in nineteenth century painting is that it occurs at

2. Russell Lee, FSA clients at home, Hidalgo County, Texas, 1939.

the very moment when painting was losing its role within the technology of power which determined the regime of truth in western European countries and in the USA. It was "technologically" superseded by the camera in more than the literal sense. Though it played some part in the early elaboration of this new technology of power, it was already stretched and already assuming a different function, leaving the field for photography to dominate, for a time, the image production of the "panoptic" societies, that is to assume its fullest role as the first medium of surveillance.)

Hine does not show a "lost" rural America with its simple, homely ways – the America of Stryker's childhood which he sought to recall – even though he had in common with Stryker a utopian, social democratic idea of a perfectable capitalism: reformed, free from injustice and social inequalities. For Stryker, this reform was to be achieved by the release or restoration of capabilities vested in all people. For Hine, before the Roosevelt era of state intervention, it seemed that these capabilities would only be found among the skilled workers. The others – children, women,

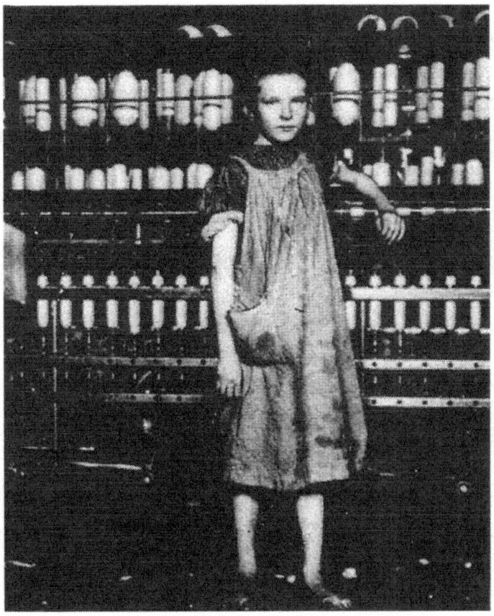

Lewis Hine at the Side Gallery, Newcastle
1. Consider Hine as a photographer who, in his earlier work, completely avoids "humanism" in his representations of people. He is neither humanist nor anti-humanist; neither empathetic nor alienated. Is this why Stryker ultimately rejected him as a photographer for the FSA, because there is no "positive" element; because he doesn't show people with a potential to recover?

(How could they, from causes beyond their effective reach as unorganised immigrants, homeworkers, children?)

immigrants from peasant economies – seemed entirely dependent upon enlightened reformers who might "rescue" them. In themselves, these groups were represented as entirely helpless.

(How different is Marx's view of poverty and exploitation, being neither sentimental and humanist, like Stryker's, nor paternalistic and reformist, like Hine's. From the point of view of Marx's analysis, Hine and Stryker want to retain the categories which express bourgeois relations, without the antagonism which constitutes them and is inseparable

3. Lewis Hine, Cotton mill worker, 1912.

from them. They have failed to comprehend that: "An oppressed class is the vital condition for every society founded on the antagonism of classes. The emancipation of the oppressed class thus implies necessarily the creation of a new society". Like Proudhon, they are beset by the "illusion of seeing in poverty nothing but poverty, instead of seeing in it the revolutionary, subversive side which will overthrow the old society.") (How should one see Hine's photographs of the construction of the Empire State Building in this light? Are they an exception?)

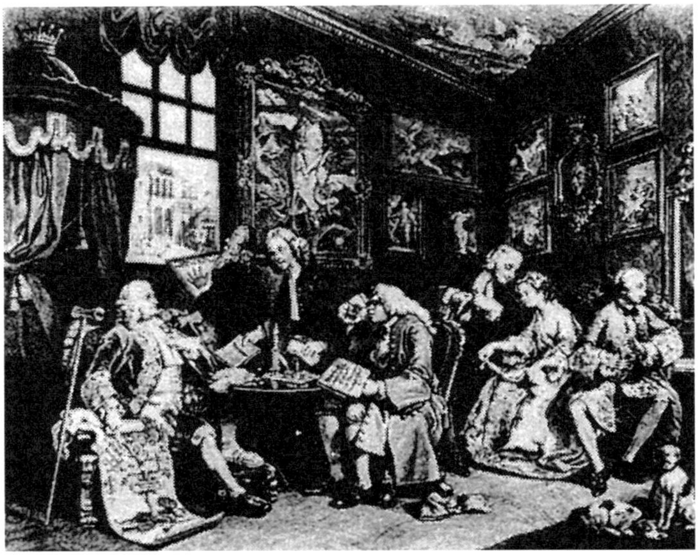

5. William Hogarth, *Marriage A-la-Mode: The Contract*, c.1742-4.

2. In the catalogue essay, Valerie Lloyd argues that Hine transformed accepted notions of what constituted a "picture", drawing on the mode of the "traditional commercial photographer", to produce images of an unprecedented systematic power and a new kind of aesthetic consciousness. What Lloyd misses is the *class content* of the frontal, symmetrically posed picture.

It would be entirely wrong to regard it as an unsophisticated genre or device without rhetoric. It draws, in fact, on a tradition going back, at least, to the painter Le Brun's treatise on expressions. One of its constituent elements is a social history of posture and the "language of gestures". Hogarth employed it in the contract scene of *Marriage A-la-Mode* in which the gout-infected, bankrupt Earl desports himself in elegant, mannered, asymmetrical pose, in contrast to the mean-minded, aspiring middle-class merchant with whom he has to barter, who sits square on, his feet and limbs parallel, in a squat and cramped posture.

Daumier was well-versed in the same depictive codes and used them in his telling contrast of "natural" and "civilised" man; though, in his two caricatures, the confident possessor of "culture" who arranges himself decorously against a table and stool, clearly belongs to the higher bourgeoisie, while the glowering, Neanderthal figure in the frontal pose emanates from the lowest stratum of the petty-bourgeoisie from the edge of the town, where it meets the country. These modes of behaviour, these clichés of portrayal of types, and the demand for unaffected depiction – "warts and all" – are vehicles of meaning which cluster together at the disputed boundary between two class territories. But Daumier had more than this in mind. The target of his satire is also the booming photographic trade. It is not only the two class stereotypes who are present. We are also shown the picture maker: the photographer. What we see is not only a comedy of class manners, but also the way representatives of different classes are imagined to present themselves to the camera. The significant differences which Daumier observed and drew still inform the photo-snapshot.

We must, of course, go on to ask why this frontal, symmetrical presentation of the subject to the camera is coupled with the desire for an unmediated and unadorned record. Here, we are concerned not only with the class co-ordinates of the search for realism but also with a certain view of the ontology of the photograph.

This is the point at which we may return to Hine who said that if he could have told the story in words, he would not have needed to lug a camera around. He saw the camera as a means to "vivify" empirical, scientific facts; to flesh them out, to prove them. The camera, for Hine, was fundamentally a source of truth. The photograph was an unmediated reflection of the world "outside", a true record of the subject stood before it. Technique was therefore an "intervention" which only falsified. However modified by secondary effects of light, balance, composition and contrast, the photographic image asserted itself as a primary fact: proof of the existence of a subject; an unshakeable witness bound to its subject by physical laws of chemistry and optics. The invention of the half-tone block further enabled the transference of these qualities directly onto the pages of magazines and newspapers, without the intervention of the interpreting engraver.

Daumier had clearly seen beyond this "naive" view yet, within its limits, Hine elevated and refined a photographic language which was to be deployed across a spectrum of self-conscious photography ranging from the "fine art" of Evans and Strand, through the work of what was later called a documentary genre, to the imagery of corporate advertising. We might still ask, however, whether Hine's achievement is any greater than that of Charles Van Schaick and countless other unremembered high street photographers. Doubtless, there are important departures in Hine's approach. Like Sander, in those of his images which portray the working class, he exchanged the fictive painted

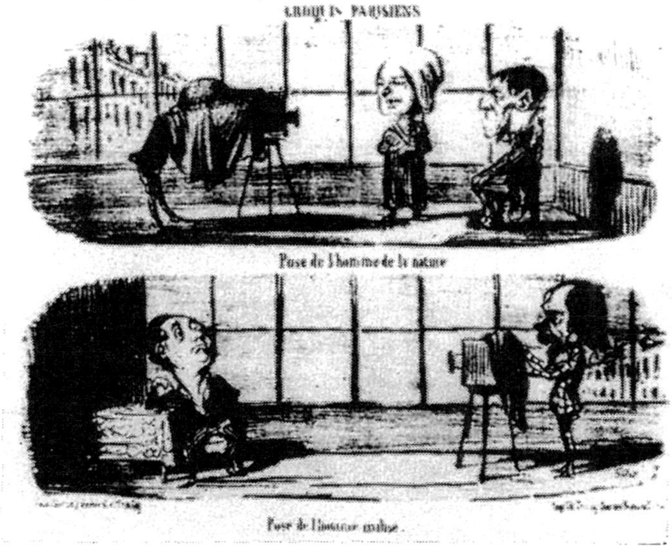

6. Honoré Daumier, *Natural and Civilised Man.*

backdrop for the background of the actual setting – though a problem with Hine's work is that it remains, precisely, a background, against which the figure is set. What may be looked on as a primarily aesthetic departure was, for Hine, simply a consequence of the fact that, following the tracks of Jacob Riis, he had to get out to find his subject, to record it on location often under the suspicion of the owners of the site. Any other strategy would have detracted from the evidential value of his photographs which was his primary concern and governed the way in which he used his images.

But this is not enough to explain why Hine should have sought to rehabilitate dissident or underprivileged signifying conventions. Hine's was an assumed naivety. He had to shed the pictorialism he learnt with his early photography in order to command a new rhetoric in keeping with the obdurate, intransigent nature of the problems he wished to picture. Contrary to the current misconception, Hine was a photographer first and had to learn his sociology later – the reverse of what was the case with the social reformer Jacob Riis whose photographs of the conditions of work and life in New York's tenements were published in his book *How The Other Half Lives* in 1890. Hine was undoubtedly a campaigner but we must be sceptical about the idea that his over-riding concern with his theme simply presented him with a ready-made form.

Perhaps this also begins to explain the development of Hine's post-war photography in which he wished to present those positive features of the "toiling classes": strength, skill, physique and courage; "positive features" characteristically marked as male. To realize his conception, Hine brought into play an elaborate pictorial code of heroism, familiar from nineteenth century academic classicism and genre painting. Not that his images are crude and ineffective. The writer of the catalogue notes dismisses them too easily. Hine's skill at manipulating art historical models should not be underestimated. His pre-war photograph of a Chicago man, bed-ridden through tuberculosis, is as solid in its sharply illuminated forms, yet as ambiguous as any de Latour. Where the loss of effectivity of his later work lies is not in his resort to an old, though still current rhetoric – this is the basis, too, of all his "documentary" work – but in his return to a humanistic and

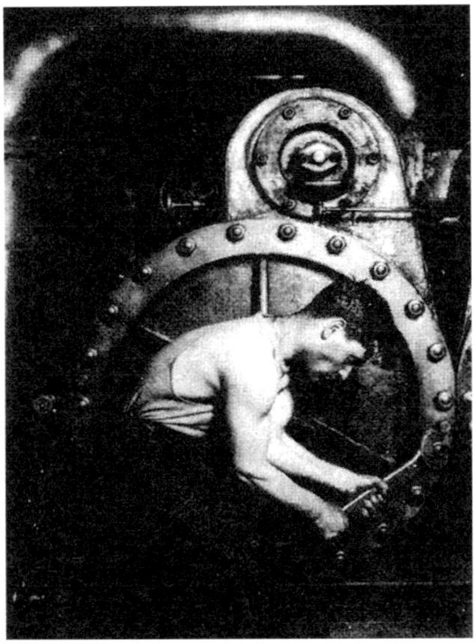

4. Lewis Hine, Power house mechanic, 1920.

sentimental view of working people which, for reasons not always progressive, had had no place in the representational conventions through which he constructed his picture of child workers, immigrants and homeworkers.

A fragment

I consider my historical researches always to be fragmentary and incomplete; not just like a series of sketches of a landscape, but like a series of sitings, authenticated reports, rumours, glimpses, prolonged observations, and second-hand accounts which are evaluated and re-evaluated, categorized and re-categorized, brought to some kind of order in which the contradictions are suppressed, then broken up and reformed into unexpected configurations. All through this process, the concepts and theories with which the records and accounts are to be articulated are themselves refined, adjusted or replaced.

But for all the provisional nature of the work, certain categories and concepts remain as those which reveal more in the material on which they are brought to bear, which allow more questions to be asked, which expose more passages of half-light and suggest more far-reaching spaces beyond; in short, which exert a greater power to produce representations dense with meanings disclosed and undisclosed. The concepts and theories which emerge and re-emerge are those of the tradition of Marxist thought and the representations of history which are tentatively and partially formed in this manner are, I believe, fragments of an historical materialist view.

17 vii

If we say that the mechanisms of control in a society, in which the respective capacities for action of social classes are established and measured, arise from specific struggles in specific arenas which have their own particular given conditions for action, how are we to account for and analyse the presence of certain regularities in a number of social institutions which, if they do not constitute an organic system, at least constitute a cluster of apparatuses somehow related, somehow functioning towards the same or a convergent end, somehow structurally isomorphic?

The terms in which this question is raised do not entail the positing of an Hegelian essence working itself out in the forms of an organic social structure. But they do problematise the relations of coexisting apparatuses or institutions: How does action in one affect the others? Does action in one infect the others? In what way may they be said to constitute collectively a *technology of power*? And if the apparatuses interlock, interact or interfunction in some way, does this not raise difficulties for a political practice which confines itself to establishing and intervening in the specific conditions of struggle in specific arenas?

If the institutions or apparatuses which constitute the technology of power in a particular society form a cluster, not an organic system, then an intervention in one apparatus, or around the conditions of possibility of struggle within it, does not threaten to collapse the whole structure nor necessarily entail any effects in the other apparatuses or mechanisms which make up that structure. This is not to say, however, that such an intervention *may* not affect the others, which may be non-continuously directed towards some common or convergent, emerging or incoherently defined end, without sharing a common ruling and prior-existent "purpose" in the Hegelian sense, even where a consciously arrived at "plan" may exist.

The hegemony of socialism will have to emerge in general conditions comparable to those which governed the emergence of the capitalist class's capacity to exert control, in a diverse and fluctuating topography of arenas of conflict and struggle. The capitalist class had to construct its "interests" in an incoherent and episodic fashion in which its success was not guaranteed from one domain to another, where the conditions of action applying might be very different. The "homology" of the apparatuses elaborated by the emergent class and in which that class emerged was not one of "essence" and "form"; nor was the historical fact, moment or order of their elaboration strictly determined. What is opened up is the *possibility* of the emergence, construction, restructuring or reorientation of the various apparatuses. What is given are the conditions or pre-conditions. But what cannot be given is the guarantee of realization: the accomplishment of the emergence, construction, restructuring or reorientation of each apparatus.

Each apparatus or its terrain becomes the object of a specific struggle whose possibilities and limitations are set by the conditions particular to the apparatus or terrain in question or by the particular form certain general conditions take in relation to this apparatus or terrain. Nor are such struggles merely the unfolding or realization of "interests" preformed and present before the struggles themselves, as a "formless content" waiting to be poured into the particular apparatus as into a vessel. Rather, these interests are themselves constituted only in the process of struggle.

(What this solution seems to leave hanging is the original question. Yet, to say that the conditions of possibility of struggle in a given arena are particular to it does not exclude the possibility of their having much in common with those governing other arenas. It says nothing about the existence or non-existence of common or dissimilar features. Such a topography cannot be given in theory. Theory can only describe the spectrum of possibilities. To establish what is the case, one must "look and see", that is, trace the topography of concrete institutions in the geography of the specific conjuncture...)

(But this again leaves in suspension the question of whether there are any necessary common features. Are there any highly general preconditions governing the possibilities of struggle in all arenas? Or is history discontinuous on the plane of synchrony?)

10 vii

All the time, it seems that I am trying to stem the flow of phantasy. Not because I wish to suppress it but the reverse: because I do not want to dissipate it by resorting to it too directly. I do not want to lose that proximity of phantasy which puts pressure on conscious thought, causing it to be suddenly diverted, making it run desperate risks for avoidance. It is almost as if the telling of the dream would sap its strength and dispel the strange force it exerts over the day. It is there to be savoured but not explained. (Yet the dream conceals a wish).

I look at an image and it is flooded with a half-forgotten dream, bulking out its figures with the forms of desire, opening up its vistas to a physically sensed space and presence. Now it can emerge, exciting my interest, inciting my curiosity for this very different object.

29 vi

"A dreary exhibition of students' photographs". We leave and hail a cab. In the one we choose, the driver has two photographs fixed to his dashboard, in front of the windscreen and vertically below his rear-view mirror. One shows a young girl; the other a naked baby, perhaps another girl, in its bath. They are not for show but are positioned so that *he can see them at all times*.

Why does he need them whilst he drives? What reflections of the past do they provide? What fragments of his life fall in their frames? What does he see in them? Or *through* them? ...the screen, the mirror, the photograph.

6 vii

He studied the images of the naked woman very carefully. He thought he knew the girl. Crouching over the light box, it was hard to tell. What was her body like? What kind of nipples did she have? What sort of breasts and thighs? How strangely light and bold the tuft of pubic hair. He has a predatory curiosity which directs his look but what he is offered remain pictures of a girl he thinks he knows. They do not gain entry to that subterranean genre of the erotic, least of all its most urgent sub-form, the pornographic. As in Bellocq's portraits of New Orleans prostitutes, which remain pictures of working women posed out of context like Hine's workers set alongside their machines or the tools of their trade, so, in these pictures, the ensemble is not completely articulated, not unfolded. The realization falls short of *suture*: desire does not fuse the discrepant elements of the image, even for a moment, in the orgasmic pleasure of illusory wholeness. There is no response on the level of the body, so easily deceived yet so constantly awake to stimulation. The masculine gaze is denied satisfaction.

Perhaps, even in the most fully realized erotic image, suture cannot be sustained since the contradiction of the flat actuality of the paper and the fullness of the body of desire is too great. There must be a mechanism to reimmerse the distanced subject. Either the image must cleave to the sadistic first-person captions characteristic of hard pornography or else it must give itself over to the excitation of delay; it must, as in the Japanese print, intertwine the disavowal of the printed image in the courtesanship of style, the formal etiquette of sexual foreplay: the invitation in art that is never consummated.

And yet, the final solution to this problem in art – accepting entirely the look which is sexed as male – has been to turn away from the insistence of bodies, to embrace and penetrate space, to give oneself up to the illusion of recession, the flawless conduit of suture, to find oneself again in the unfolding of the image, opening on an endless vista of wholeness and harmony, passing like an insatiable longing beyond the capabilities of the eye to infinity. And, as our passage is uninterrupted, flowing into the picture; so is the illusion we enter without disharmony or contradiction. For the moment, we accept everything and do not wish to see beyond it; we cannot see beyond it; it is the limits of our vision and the co-ordinates of our space.

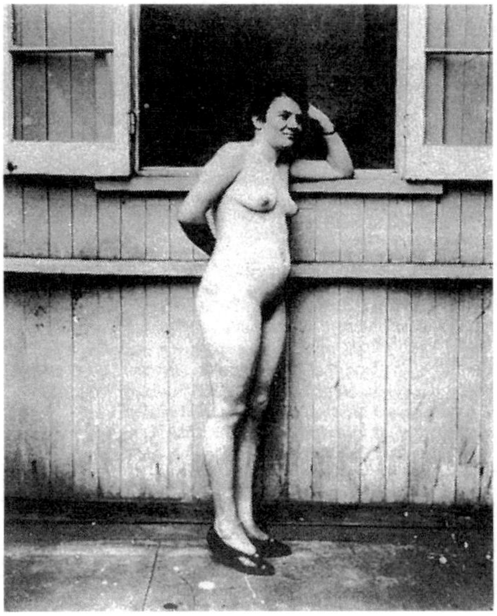

(What happens in the *Rape of Europa*, which Titian painted for Philip II of Spain, is that the amplitude of the woman's body is set against an infinite, atmospheric space – mediated at their junction by the varying degrees of realization of the bull's obliquely thrusting body – a space that is also entirely abstract, resolved into a colour circle whose centre is the white of Europa's body; a mythological space possessed only of extension, emanating from specific locations, revolving around specific actions of

7. E J Belloc, Nude.

bodies. In this way, Titian binds the unfolding of the mythological events to the unfolding of space and of bodies, moving from an unbounded background through increasing degrees of emergence, to the fullest bodying forth of the woman: the object of myth and rape; the culmination of our phantasies; the physical climax for the male owner/viewer.)

But this is a moment far removed from those – in Italy in the Quattrocento, in Holland in the seventeenth century, in France in the mid-nineteenth century – in which, most typically in landscape painting, release was sought from all bodily bounds through the infinite recession of central vanishing point perspective: the path or road which leads from the lower edge of the frame to a point on the depicted horizon. This is also the mode of representation deployed so often in "road pictures" in American photography from the thirties on, though here too, as in Dutch landscape painting or the paintings of the Barbizon and Impressionist schools, the schema is capable of variation:

... As we look at Evans' post office, here at Sprott, Alabama, we find ourselves at a crossroads. Beyond the symmetrical front of the wooden frame building, with its tin plaques and single petrol pump, the dusty road stretches, curving slightly and cut by the unflinching shadows of solitary trees. Some way down the track, it bends again. We cannot see as yet which way it will turn but, before we go on, we may pause to look again at the spare-lined post office. We may pause and feel the temptation to move round – round the simple gabled frontage and the pitched roofed block behind. The invitation is there, to pass round its plain solidity laid bare for our inspection in the flat, bright light.

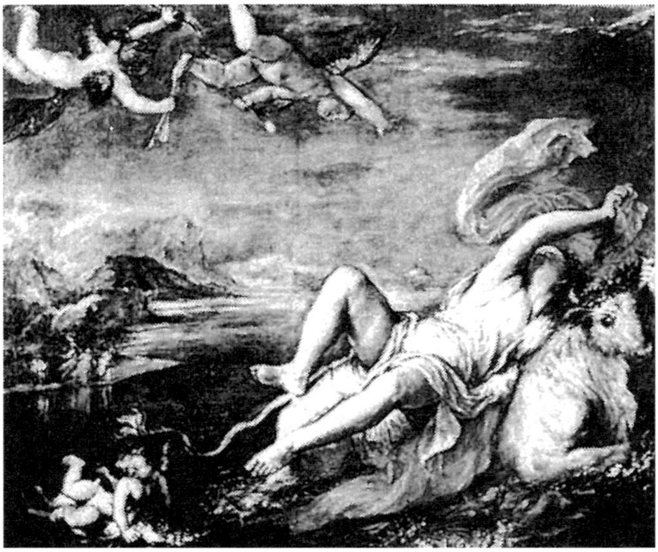

It is this pause, this moment of choosing, that we are offered: on the one hand, the post office with its satisfying symmetry and unadorned forms; on the other, the road beyond, running away from us and turning out of sight. For a moment, we pause – here at the crossroads – an unmeasurable moment of longing. As we do so our longing is displaced: to the place, to the time, to the vision of the man whose gaze is, we believe, constructed in the camera viewfinder. Still we cannot choose, and the longer we wait the more the picture seems to see us, drawing us into its space, holding us there, filling us with a

8. Titian, *The Rape of Europa*, 1559-60.

doubtful contentment, offering us over to the dangerous "inexhaustibility" of art.

In our dream, which passes for the timelessness of art, the site, the picture, the artist seem beyond doubt. They appear so "real" and in their "reality" we find the consolation of a confirmation of ourselves. If there is pleasure in ideology, then there is also the nostalgia of self enjoyment.

Bodies and space
Imagine a history of photography as an insistent practice, inserted into the very heart of the modern social order and characterised by a double momentum: an ever more intimate and exacting attention to bodies, dividing them, apportioning them, observing them, supervising them and, in the same movement, exerting a control over them; and a diverse constitution of space as itself a realm of phantasy and control, submission and consent, a space of the Imaginary and the Ideological. On one side, time and motion studies, criminal records, sociological dossiers, humanist documentaries, medical photography, ethnographic records, reportage, sports pictures, pornography, identikit faces, all kinds of portraiture, and photographs in official documents, papers and files. On the other, the landscape tradition, aerial surveys, astronomical photography, micro-photography, topographical records, certain kinds of advertising images and so on. Two kinds of longing. Two kinds of subjection. (The gaze has both passion and perspective).

(no date)
For Barthes, the writer uses words the way a tourist handles money: not entirely blind to its value but with a pleasurable unfamiliarity, for its strangeness, its foreign-ness; for the pleasure of its passing through the hands; with a *delay* in value. But not at all like the miser, that is without any trace of fetishism.

In everyday life, this pleasure is squeezed out by the drive of desire, the ceaseless to and fro of exchange. But as a tourist, one has no regularised place in the social structure, though one's presence is now entirely necessary to the economy: a place at the "base" but none at all in the co-extensive structures?

Folies Bergère
What Berger and Sontag have in common,

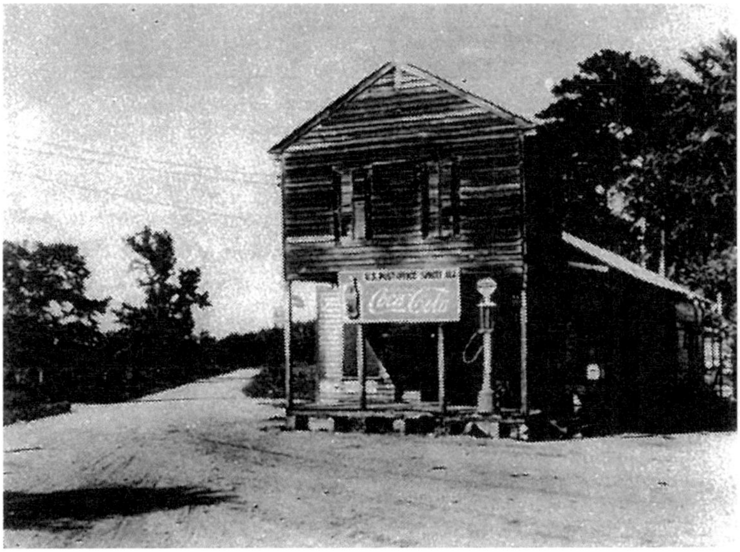

9. Walker Evans, The Post Office at Sprott, Alabama, 1936.

stylistically, is that their prose moves by a series of sudden, dramatic and epigrammatic assertions. These pithy statements, which are neither supported historically nor developed theoretically, spurt the argument forwards, carrying the reader with them by the force of their flat conviction. This gives their style an illusion of "simplicity with grandeur", a "profundity" modestly born within a readily intelligible prose.

The first step in breaking with the pretentious role of critical overseer and commentator must be to undertake real historical research. The conceptual and descriptive demands this makes of themselves render the assertive style redundant. More than this, they erode the entire ground on which a certain critical stance has set itself and, with that, goes a view of history and a view of the process of social change.

What Berger appeals to is a "future" which serves both as a hope, a profession of faith, and a standard by which present actions may be judged. What historical research produces is no such grand plan but a constantly changing ground of tactical actions whose strategy may be stated only in terms so generalised as to be of little analytical use, though they may have a function in political rhetoric. What such historical analysis offers practitioners is not the heroic chance to measure themselves against the future, but a multiplicity of points of intervention, limited objectives, courses of action open now, ends that can be achieved through struggle: an unremitting "war of position" in which the smallest gain may hold significance for a chain of related struggles. The sexist macro-image of the "Big Push" is abandoned for a spectrum of specific interventions in a micro-physics of power.

Such a prospectus for action may lack the emotional appeal and attraction of the Utopian projection. It may not offer the guarantees of historicism. But it does have the incomparable advantage that it begins in the present, in the topography of existing apparatuses and institutions, in a concrete analysis of the uneven terrain in which the struggles must be waged. Its "revolution" is not to be put off till the millennium. Its forces are not to be gathered for the "moment of becoming". Its "revolution" is a potential now and everywhere.

18.ix.78

I began my work on the emergence of the USA from World War Two into global, neo-imperial power, as a result of a series of compulsory steps back. The project came out of a need to understand the origins of the American painting and sculpture which still dominated the remodelled art education I began to receive in British art schools in the late sixties. It was pursued through a study of the emergence of a coherent East-coast American school of modernist painting which provided the platform for the unerring push into the heartland of European art, for which Britain itself was a staging base. This, in turn, opened out onto the whole question of the massive insertion of US mass culture into European life and the effective re-culturation of Western Europe which was bound up with the effects of Marshall Plan "aid" and the spread both of US military bases and US-controlled multinational corporations. The re-examination of the economic growth, political fluctuations and cultural transformation this entailed was itself a retracing of uncertain recollections and distorted images from the years of my own childhood and primary education through the fifties. What kept the project alive was this direct connection with my own formative life, together with the need constantly to gauge and regauge the relationship of representations of this period to an always changing, elusive and incoherent historical present.

But the problem which began to be formulated in my mind as *the* problem to be solved was how to describe, to follow, to plot and explain the emergence of American cultural hegemony, the process of transformation of American power and American life, this period of passage in American history which saw the disappearance of the goals and beliefs of the thirties and their mutation into the hysterically militarised and hysterically privatised society of the fifties. Here began a track which led back to the New York of the Eight Street Club and the Cedar Tavern, to the Greyhound bus queues of recently demobilised young men, to Kerouac and Cassady's disorganised pads, to smoke-filled jazz clubs, Harlem brothels, Greenwich Village and the slow drift uptown. Further and further beyond the bounds of my memory and childhood on Tyneside; deeper and deeper into what I did not know, but all the time staying here, in the years of my own life; moving away from an account of myself to an encounter with the life of another: finding with a shock that Kerouac was born in the same year as my father.

26.x
There is something morbid about looking at pictures, something frigid, and something furtive.

We shuffle from one image to the next like the buyers of old books. Once I imagined a collective looking, argued out aloud. But the exhibiting institutions allow no space for such a practice. Now, like the other Johns, I move from one picture to another, alone. Sometimes I make a transaction, out in the open, here in this public space. But to the moment of intimacy, the image is entirely indifferent and I am alone once more.

(My friends tell me it is because intellectuals have lost contact with the Movement. "The Movement" – as if to conjure up the strict but forgiving Mother was a solution.)

There is a scene, familiar from a certain type of sentimental movie and from television advertisements for cigarettes, proprietary pills or diamond rings: it is on the road and she (never he) is coming towards me (always a he). Suddenly, she begins to run. Now, she is coming towards me, running, her arms outstretched. (We must repress the memory of that child, running on a road in Vietnam, arms outstretched, napalm burning her skin). I feel myself move. This is the final denouement. I feel myself towards her and we are both running. The hoped for moment when I shall truly enter the picture, or whatever the picture promises, and be immersed within it – when I shall find myself in its space, embraced by it – closes upon me as if some memory of an ideal Mother stirred. But it never comes. The running never stops. The moment never arrives. Always the promise, never that moment of joining: real wholeness; distance gone.

In the overblown image is something of what it is to look at pictures; something of why they leave one listless, inadequate and incomplete yet, strangely, with an appetite for them uncloyed. This is why they find one so ready to be deceived. This is the source of their ideological effectivity which the world of real actions and effects could never enjoy. It is precisely what is lacking in them that prolongs their influence; precisely their disavowal of the desires which they incite and which remain unchecked and unreproached, ready to be excited again.

(There is something unhealthy about looking at pictures and the kind of dependence they produce. Yet our way of looking is neither universal nor eternal. Rather, it is installed in the particular modes and apparatuses of exhibition in our culture. It has not always been the same.)

Two pictures of women in "men's" clothing
A photograph by Dorothea Lange from around 1937 shows a migrant labourer pausing from work in a field and leaning on a hoe. The format is vertical and the figure fills the frame with a softened roundness and solidity reminiscent of Millet. Behind this standing figure, the furrows of a ploughed field recede to a low horizon and the light sheet of the sky which throws forward the darkened upper forms of the labourer's body.

The dress is familiar from other photographs: battered, stitched and patched-up dungarees, an outsize denim jacket, boots and a cap. But, looking closely, we see that the figure is a woman, or possibly a woman. It is not that the body is de-sexed. The more we look, the more clues we gather: breasts perhaps rounding the cotton plaid shirt; the stance; the face – worn and creased like a man's, or like a woman's.

What we have in this image is a theme to which Lange was to return. Here, it is social conditions of poverty and unemployment which have degraded bodies to a uniform appearance; though, in the work of other contemporary photographers, the different sexual significations of dress remain evident. There is, however, another image by Lange from another moment, showing two wartime workers having just left a supermarket, stopping for the camera, still wearing their workplace dungarees and helmets,

Yet, she was not immediately concerned to make a general point. She was interested, as always, in the warmth of these people: women, in relative affluence or depression, somehow freed from stereotyping, wearing "men's" clothing from necessity but also from a seeming desire to lay hold on a production of meanings, doing "men's" work and temporarily, rupturing that restrictive social categorization.

In the case of the wartime worker, she is pictured alongside a man. He is taller than she and further to the fore of the picture space but he leans back on his heels with an elegant swagger,

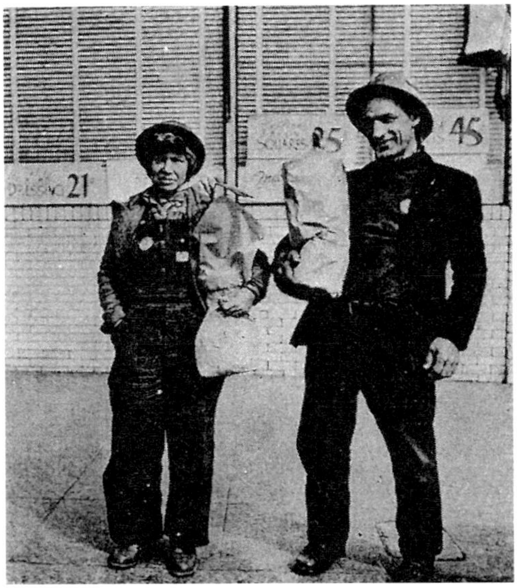

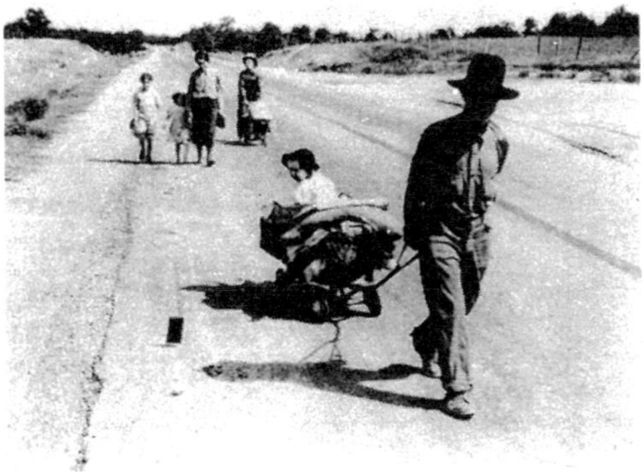

their union buttons pinned to their clothing, each clutching a well-packed paper grocery bag. One is a woman. The other is a man. The usual cues are removed – removed by a situation as dramatic in its effects as the Depression. In this case, what we see is the result of a wartime shortage of labour which necessitated the absorption of women into better-paid, skilled industrial jobs which had never before been open to them. In poverty and wartime, Depression and Boom, the sexual division of labour and its significations in dress, in places, broke down and Lange saw it.

as if to reduce his size and to allow her to advance. Despite the ample evidence of the hostility of the unions and male workers to the employment of women in heavy industry, there is something in their expressions which suggests a pleasure in their sameness, a mutual enrichment and enjoyment of this moment of ambiguity; a rediscovery of sexuality not a loss of it.

Lange: Oklahoma. June 1938

The picture renews itself in dreams. This is its dream life, that it erects so many barriers to the

10. Dorothea Lange, Workers Richmond, California, 1942.

shock of waking. We turn but we are pushed back into its imagery. A wash of memories and expectations always hanging on the present: this couple will always be walking on the road, the children always running. The tension with which I fill them, drawn from the waking world in which I dream, gives their actions a real and vivid poignancy for behind them is the knowledge I must refuse: that this picture of people walking is only a still.

10.x

So much "marxist" art history has been caught in the circular trap of trying to explain the image production of a society by reference to a "mental outlook" or "world view" which is itself only present in the *representational activity* of that society. These "world views" are then allotted to social "classes", defined in the most general terms, the only progression over the view that history is the enactment of racial or national mentalities being that national cultures are seen as divided and heterogeneous: the sites of contention between rival "world views" in which one is dominant.

Just as the development of cultures cannot be explained as the conflict of "mainline" traditions or tendencies (aristocratic v. bourgeois; agrarian v. mercantile; peasant v. urban) but must be seen as the product of conflict and interaction within an hierarchy of heterodox and overlaid (sub) cultures, each with its characteristic institutions, each catering for a more or less defined and distinct "public"; so, the complex topography of these "publics" cannot be *reduced* to a simple "class" map. Nor can the kinds of image production sustained and consumed by these "publics" be explained away by reference to "outlooks", "mentalities" or "world views" somehow present at another level.

We must not forget these imaginary entities, these thought-bubbles floating above the heads of the supposed "real actors" of history. We must not allow ourselves the expedient of imagining something existing "before" representation by which we may conveniently explain the representation away. Where we must start is with concrete material activity and what it produces. We must begin to analyse the real representational practices that go on in a society and the concrete institutions and apparatuses within which they take place. We must plot the network of material, political and ideological constraints which bear on these institutions and constitute their conditions of existence and operation. We must describe the function of "specific" individuals within them and their production of "operatives" to staff them. We must establish the material, social and symbolic contexts in which they are sited, in which they operate and in which they intervene.

Only in this way will we come to understand how ideologies are produced in real representational practices, in material apparatuses; how these representations are disseminated, consumed, elaborated, modified and sustained; how they are meaningful; how they affect and are affected by other productive activities within the same social complex. And all this is to be done by studying actual material entities and processes, entirely without the need for pre- given mental or spiritual phenomena. This, then, would be the beginnings of a materialist account.

The women editors take exception to certain parts of this article.

The research on which these notes are based was carried out with the aid of a grant from the Arts Council of Great Britain, as Fellow in Photographic Arts at the Polytechnic of Central London.

Further work by John Tagg:
"American Power and American Painting: The Rise of Vanguard. Painting in the US since 1945", *Praxis* 1:2, Winter 1976, pp.59-79.
"The World of Photography of Photography of the World?" *Camerawork* 6, April 1977, pp.8-9.
"Marxism and Art History", *Marxism Today* 21:6, June 1977, pp.183-92.
"The Currency of the Photograph", *Screen Education* 28, Autumn 1978, pp.45-67.
"A Socialist Perspective on Photographic Practice" in *Three Perspectives on Photography*, London: Arts Council, 1979.

11. Dorothea Lange, Family bound for Krebs, Oklahoma from Idabel, Oklahoma, 1939.

APPENDIX 1
ADVERTS

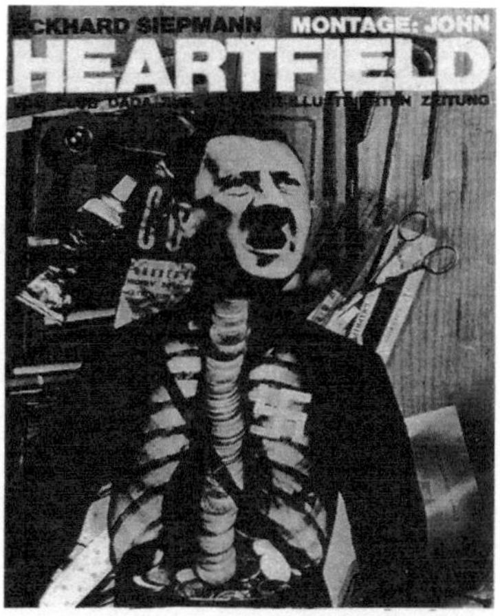

Eckhard Siepmann, Montage: John Heartfield: Vom Club Dada zur Arbeiter-Illustrierten Zeitung. Published by Elefanten Press, Berlin (West) 1977. With texts by Grosz, Hausmann, Tretyakov, Dimitrov, Münzenberg, Gertrud Heartfield, Aragon and many others. The most comprehensive book ever to have appeared on Heartfield. 245x310mm, 300pp., more than 1000 illustrations presented by J. Holtfreter. Available from "Zweitausendeins", Postfach 710249, D 6000 Frankfurt/M. 71, West Germany.

bfi
British Film Institute Publications and Membership Services
81 Dean Street, London W1V 6AA

Capital and Culture: German Cinema 1933-45
by Julian Petley
Price £2·45, £2·70 including p. & p. ($6·40)

Chilean Cinema
edited by Michael Chanan
Price £1·50, £1·65 including p. & p. ($4·30)

Gays and Film
edited by Richard Dyer
Price £1·50, £1·65 including p. & p. ($4·30)

Ideology and Realism in Film
by Terry Lovell August 1979.
Price £1·50, £1·65 including p. & p. ($4·30)

May '68 and Film Culture
by Sylvia Harvey
Price £1·50, £1·75 including p. & p. ($4·50)

Pasolini
edited by Oswald Stack and Paul Willemen
Price £1·75, £1·95 including p. & p. ($4·90)

Stars: a study text
by Richard Dyer
Price £2·25, £2·45 including p. & p. ($5·90)

Traditions of Independent Cinema: Britain in the Thirties
edited by Don Macpherson August 1979.
Price £2·45, £2·70 including p. & p. ($6·40)

Women in Film Noir
edited by E. Ann Kaplan
Price £1·75, £1·95 including p. & p. ($4·90)

Television Monograph No. 8
Television and History
by Colin McArthur
Price £1·20, £1·35 including p. & p. ($3·70)

Television Monograph No. 10
Everyday Television: Nationwide
by Charlotte Brunsdon and David Morley
Price £1·20, £1·35 including p. & p. ($3·70)

PHOTOGRAPHY WORKSHOP
152, UPPER STREET, LONDON, N.1.

WORKING LIVES 2

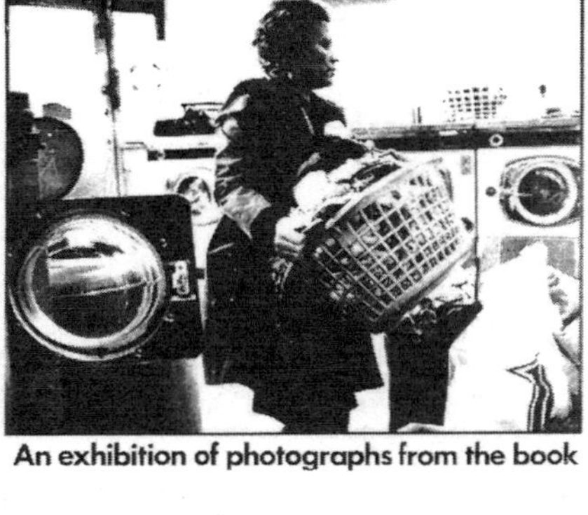

An exhibition of photographs from the book

Besides its publishing project Photography Workshop is also involved in a number of other activities:

Labour History Research
Alternative Technology
Educational projects
Critical analysis of the photographic image
British socialist photography
(a number of exhibitions have been initiated on these and other themes)

The following touring shows are currently available for hire/loan:

Who's Holding the Baby? by Hackney Flashers Collective
Working Lives II by Centerprise photography project
Beyond the Family Album by Jo Spence
The (British) Workers' Film and Photo League 1934-39 by Terry Dennett
Alternative and Low Cost Technology in Photography by Terry Dennett
Struggles in the Thirties/The 1926 General Strike by Terry Dennett

(the panels of several of these exhibitions have been designed to be inter-changeable with each other, thus exhibitions can be modified to fit a specific event). Further details from Photography Workshop.

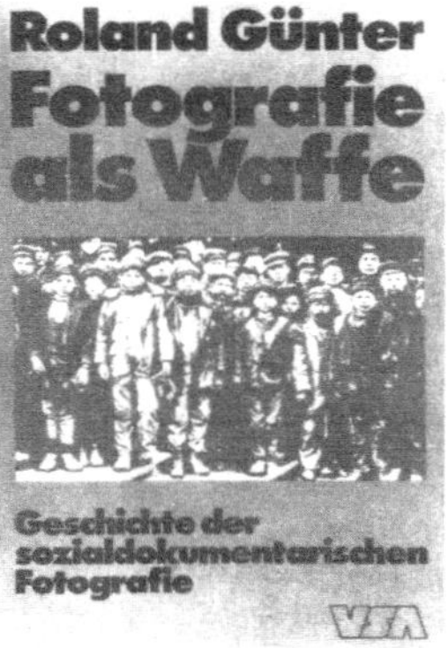

Roland Günter, Fotografie als Waffe. Geschichte der sozialdokumentarischen Fotografie. Published by VSA-Verlag, Hamburg 1977. A history of social documentary photography.

Roland Günter (ed.), Alltag 1. Published by VSA-Verlag, Hamburg 1978. This is a yearbook of social photography with the title "Every day life". It contains approx. 30 articles about the life and problems of the "man in the street" with an emphasis on West Germany's main industrial area, the Ruhrgebiet. Many illustrations.

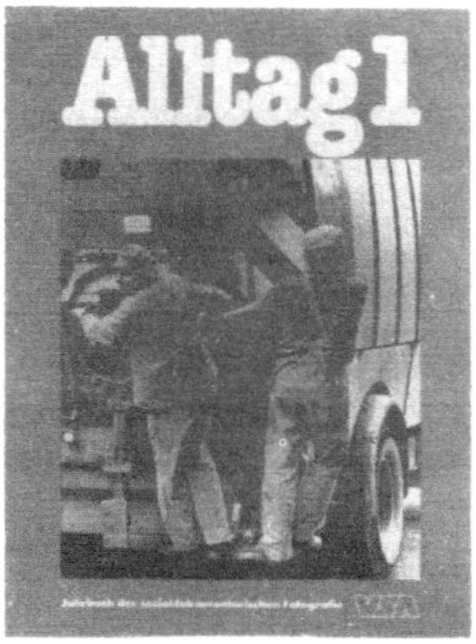

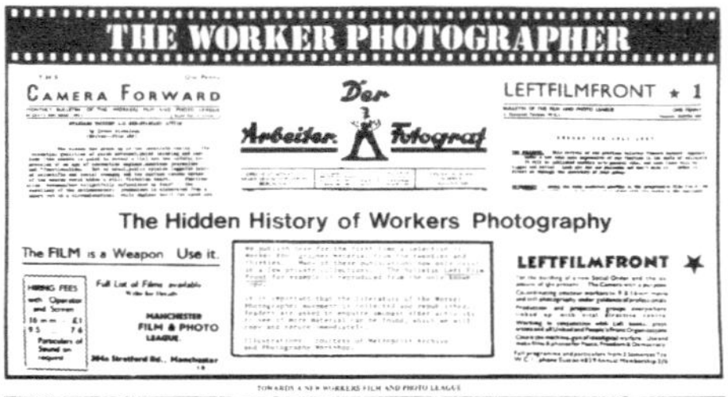

The Worker Photographer is published to provide a platform for photography made by working people in struggle. It also publishes information and documentation on the earlier traditions of socialist photography and journalism from various countries.

A subscription costs £1.00 for 4 issues. All enquiries to THE WORKER PHOTOGRAPHER, c/o 152 Upper Street, London, N.1.

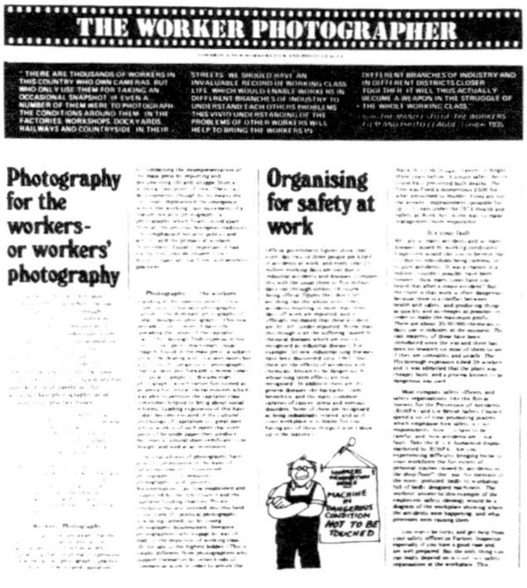

HISTORY WORKSHOP

A Journal of Socialist Historians

Issue 7 (June 1979) includes:

Sickles & Sythes: Women's & Men's Work at Harvest-time	Michael Roberts
The **Batteurs** & and the Informer's Eye: a Labour Dispute under the French Second Empire	William M. Reddy
Morris Motors in the 1930's, Part II	Arthur Exell
A Clown in Regal Purple: Social History & the Historians	Tony Judt
The English Folk Revival	Frankie Armstrong & Brian Pearson
Crime, Poverty & the Streets of New York City: the Diary of William H. Bell 1850-51	Sean Wilentz
Women in Australia: a Guide to Records	Kay Daniels
Male Fantasies: Comments on a New Study in History & Psychoanalysis	Lutz Niethammer

plus Debates on Socialist History and Comprehensive Schooling 1945 - 51
Enthusiasms ; Noticeboard ; Readers' Letters ; Index

Subscriptions £5 a year (2 issues), £6 overseas, from History Workshop, P.O. Box 69, Oxford OX2 7XA.

Back numbers also available.

RUSKIN COLLEGE

offers places and scholarships for working class adult students (men and women) without formal educational qualifications.

Courses in Labour Studies, Social Studies, Modern History, Literature, Development Studies, etc. (normally two years, full time, residential).

Admission by essay, record (trade union and community activity, adult education etc.), and interview.

Details from Gen. Sec. Ruskin College, Oxford. Applications for entry in October normally required by 1 March.

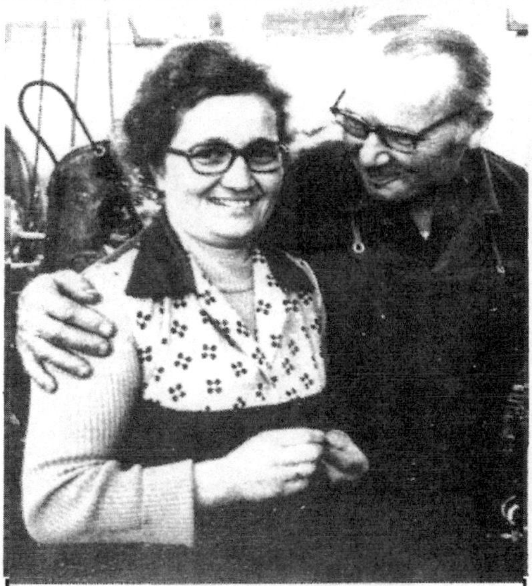

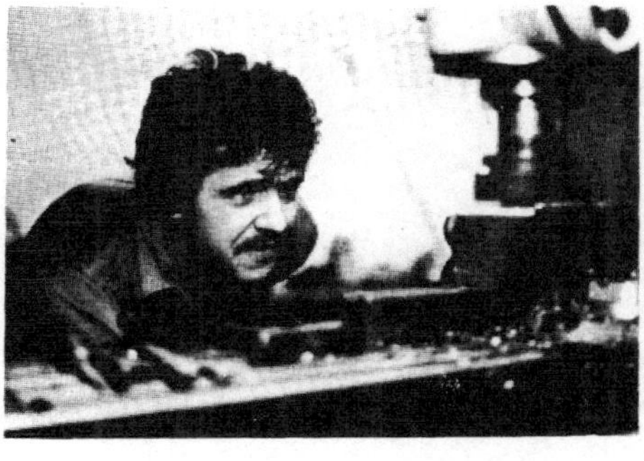

PHOTOGRAPHY/POLITICS: ONE

How does photography contribute to the defence of the old order?
How may it be used to help hasten the arrival of the new?

Against the Dominant Ideology: Sylvia Harvey, Gen Doy, Stuart Hall, Jo Spence, Eckhard Siepmann, Judith Williamson.

Left Photography Between the Wars – the International Worker Photographer Movement: W. Korner & J. Stuber, Bert Hogenkamp, Russell Campbell, Douglas Allen, Terry Dennett, Victoria Wegg-Prosser.

Left Photography Today: Hackney Flashers Collective, Film and Poster Collective, Minda, Robert Golden, Jean Mohr/John Berger, Nick Hedges, Trisha Ziff, Allan Sekula.

Postscript: John Tagg

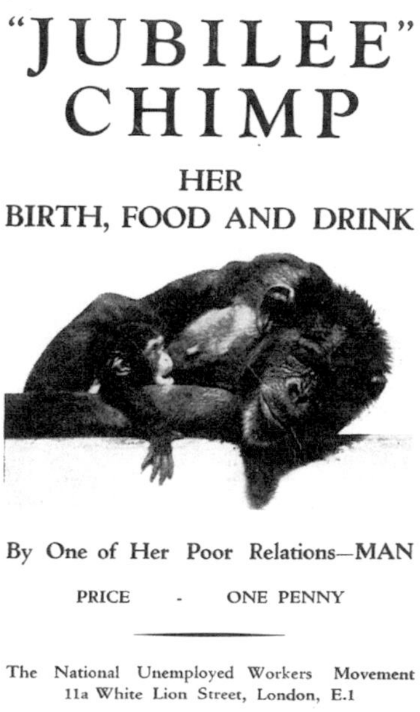
"JUBILEE" CHIMP

HER
BIRTH, FOOD AND DRINK

By One of Her Poor Relations—MAN

PRICE - ONE PENNY

The National Unemployed Workers Movement
11a White Lion Street, London, E.1

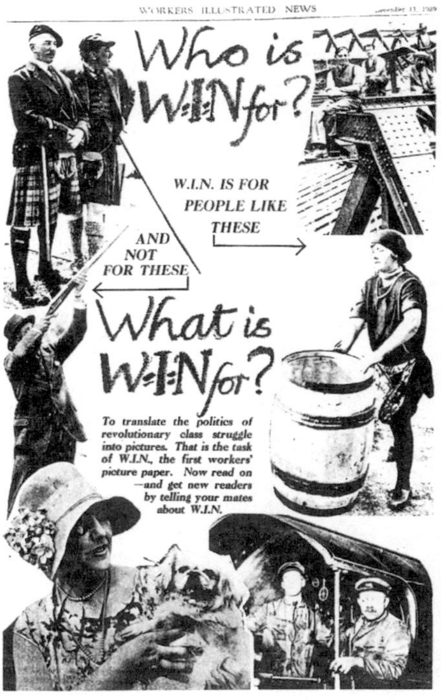

Cover Illustrations:
Garment worker, whose wages don't allow her to buy what she makes. From *Women–Work in Hackney by Hackney Flashers Collective, 1976.*

(left) Agitational pamphlet with photos by Workers Film and Photo League member John Maltby, 1935.

(right) A page from *Workers' Illustrated News (WIN)*, **1929.**

The back cover of the original edition of Photography/Politics: One

APPENDIX 2
AUTHORS' NOTES

Gen Doy

I GOT INVOLVED in writing for *Photography/Politics: One* though meeting Jo Spence at a conference, and getting to know her photographic activist work and the work she was doing with Terry Dennett. Jo was always really encouraging to me and I met her for discussions in the small flat above shops in Upper Street, Islington, which was absolutely full of photography stuff, books and all their belongings. The article on *Photography and the Paris Commune* was the first thing I wrote, and thanks to Jo's encouragement and light-touch editorial comments, I gained the confidence to go on to write many more things about images and politics. Through researching the Paris Commune and feeling great admiration for what the Communards did, and their sacrifices, I became, and remain, a Trotskyist, though with less energy than I possessed many years ago.

I went on to write books and articles about images and issues of class, race and gender whilst being active in various political campaigns, notably participating in Women against Pit Closures, our support group being based in Keresley Village near Coventry, where there was a pit.

WWW.GENDOY.COM
SOUNDCLOUD.COM/GUINEVEREDOY

Robert Golden

I'VE NO RECOLLECTION of how I became involved with the first edition of this book. My vague memory reflects that it was probably via Jo Spence at the Half Moon Gallery.

And there is no way of me knowing how my subsequent working life was affected by the publication. I had no reactions afterwards. I suspect that I've been made *persona non grata* by the photographic establishment.

My work since has taken numerous twists. Late in the 1970s it became clear that I could not work for newspapers and magazines as a photojournalist. I decided I'd find another way to make a living. With innocence I chose to do work that was far from the lives of people. Instead of a Leica I would use an 8 x 10 tripod-based camera; instead of light that happened to be available I'd teach myself studio lighting; instead of the life of society I'd put things in front of my lens. Bringing together my documentarist experiences with my knowledge of western art history I created a new style of food photography and went from photographing cookery book covers to shooting corporate food campaigns. Soon I was asked to shoot commercials. I began discovering how bad the products were for the conditions of labour around the world, for people's health and for the earth itself. My innocence faded. I decided to turn my back on that career and return to documentary, but with a video camera. Since 1999 I've made over 40 documentaries (winning some awards) about food and culture, about Bosnia's afterlife of the Srebrenica genocide, and with various theatre companies. Although I regret my lost years in commercial work, I learned a high level of filmic skills that have served in making documentaries.

Re-reading my text today, the outstanding change is that then there was a viable unionised working class on which much of what I assumed was based. Now, after financialisation of the economy, off-shoring of the industrial base and the use of austerity to further weaken both the unions and the working/middle classes while destroying the welfare state, the presumption of that audience no longer exists. With this lack of class identity and the imposition of political correctness, recognising the sectors of society capable of forcing change through peaceful action is very difficult. For me there are three indistinct groups: the largest being the middle ground of people who are too busy, too borne down or too self-preoccupied to care about abstractions like justice, equality or fairness; there are the humanists who do care about those things; and there are the small and powerful groups of wealthy people who have purchased our political parties and politicians with little care about the social world they live in and the earth upon which it sits – these are the psychopaths who dominate all social, economic and cultural life. For me this leads to asking, not what is the potential of this or that class, but rather what is our potential as a very faulty species?

ROBERTGOLDENPICTURES.COM

Nick Hedges

MY INVOLVEMENT with *Photography/Politics: One* (PP1) followed on from working with Jo Spence on the *Camerawork* publication that she was involved with in the late 1970s. At that time *Camerawork* was the most significant radical journal that debated and published issues that dealt with photography and feminism, photography and the representation of the working class, and photography and its role in depicting the Third World.

Jo approached me with the idea of my writing an article about my experience working for Shelter in the late 1960s and early 1970s. I was sufficiently distanced from the charity to raise issues about the depiction of poverty and about whose voice was being heard.

When PP1 was published it became a crucial textbook for the growing number of degree courses in photography and multimedia. I was able to use it myself in degree courses that I taught in the 1980s and 1990s.

What it did for me and other colleagues was give us the confidence to suggest that there were issues to do with the depiction of reality in documentary photography that should not and could not be avoided. It scrutinised what had previously been an accepted virtue of documentary.

My working life since then has been a mixture of lecturing in higher education and publishing books that owe their themes and legitimacy to the arguments first proposed in PP1.

It was one of the most significant publications that changed the way in which the working class, women, and the underdeveloped world were given a voice. Who is speaking, who is making images, has become central to our vision of the world and its inequalities. PP1 is to be forever thanked for its original initiative.

WWW.NICKHEDGESPHOTOGRAPHY.CO.UK

Liz Heron

IN THE SUMMER of 1979, *Three Perspectives on Photography*, a major exhibition at the Hayward Gallery, featured the work of the Hackney Flashers. There was some unease about our decision to take part, since we saw ourselves as producing agitprop, not art. The collective dissolved in the early 1980s as members pursued different commitments. Since then, the exhibition *Who's Holding the Baby?* has led a double life, its panels circulating for some years as intended, but also, without our knowledge, because of our individual anonymity, and through the vagaries of life, death and administration, finding its way into a number of international exhibitions and public collections. In 2012, those of us remaining were alerted to this by young academic researchers.

We had never named ourselves as individuals, preferring to present our work as a collective endeavour. This was a significant principle in our activism. Nowadays, anyone interested in the details of our history and the names of all those involved can find links on our website, listing an abundance of relevant publication and archive material, including interviews.

Our work appeared again at the Hayward Gallery in 2015, as part of *History Is Now*, and in 2023 Tate Britain's *Women in Revolt: Art and Activism in the UK 1970-1990* showed a substantial part of *Who's Holding the Baby?* It remains, in our view, an example of feminist agitprop, though this is a designation still often resisted by the art world. It's clear that more curators in recent years have been opening gallery doors to cultural forms that occupy the terrain between art and activism.

As of now, January 2024, five of us from the collective that produced *Who's Holding the Baby?* remain alive and in touch. We are Sally Greenhill, Michael Ann Mullen, Maggie Murray, Christine Roche and myself. Jo Spence, a fellow Hackney Flasher, asked me to write my contribution to *Photography/Politics: One*.

A Glaswegian by birth, I had lived in various European countries before settling in London in 1976, the year I joined the Hackney Flashers Collective, and around the time I was starting out as a freelance writer for several publications, among them *Spare Rib* and *Camerawork*. Collectives were flourishing across the political and cultural spectrum, and like many others I was involved in more than one. It was a time of great excitement and hope.

Later I contributed literary and arts journalism to a wide range of newspapers and magazines. My first book was *Truth, Dare or Promise: Girls Growing Up in the 50s* (1985). Others include a novel, *The Hourglass* (2018), and a short-story collection, *A Red River* (1996), as well as non-fiction and anthologies (one of these, *Illuminations*, was a co-edited volume of women's writing on photography over 150 years).

WWW.HACKNEYFLASHERS.CO.UK
WWW.LIZHERON.CO.UK
WWW.LIZHERON.WORDPRESS.COM

Maggie Murray

AS A MEMBER of the Hackney Flashers, *Photography/Politics: One* provided me with ongoing food for thought, political understanding and action.

I continued as a documentary photographer whilst interrogating that way of working and became a founder member of Format Photographers (1983-2003), which started as a collective representing women photographers. The archives of Format and of the Hackney Flashers are both now held in The Bishopsgate Institute Archives.

A partial copy of The Hackney Flashers' exhibition *Who's Holding the Baby?* is at the Reina Sophia Museum in Madrid, while the Arts Council England Collection has a version of all the panels.

John Tagg

I FIRST MET JO SPENCE when I was Arts Council of Great Britain Fellow in Photographic History at what was then the Polytechnic of Central London. Jo was an incomparable figure in the emerging, diverse and highly polemical photography culture of the time and we became fast friends. It was Jo, then, who asked me to contribute an essay to the collection on politics and photography she was editing, along with Terry Dennett, David Evans and Sylvia Gohl. I always felt they were expecting something more muscularly militant, more Althusserian and Foucauldian, rather than the Barthesian fragments they received, reworked as they were from the notebooks I kept at the time. Certainly, what they carefully segregated as a *Postscript* was a far cry from the paradigm of worker photography and ideology critique that prevailed over the rest of the book. Yet, these fragmentary notes were also the only space where issues of vision and writing, desire and sexuality were raised, pointing in a direction that was to become much more prominent in the photo-theory of the 1980s.

I left Britain in 1985, and am now SUNY Distinguished Professor of Art History at Binghamton University, State University of New York. I've written a number of books, as well as numerous catalogue essays, articles and book chapters; have taught and lectured widely; and am currently working on a new collection provisionally titled, *Everything and Nothing: Essays on Photographies and Photographers*.

Trisha Ziff

I BECAME INVOLVED in PP1 in my early twenties through the influence of two people, John Tagg and Jo Spence, both important contributors to this publication. Having studied at Goldsmiths and moved into community arts, I saw what I had learnt in those years as being relevant to my activism at the time. I worked a little with the *Spare Rib* collective, was an arts worker in Southwark on a large housing estate, collaborated with the Hackney Flashers and the Poster Film Collective, and with Sylvia Stevens who is still family. From Southwark I joined the Camerawork Collective and that focused my energy on photography. Those years defined my visual arts activism and, now in my late 60s, that has been in different guises the work of my life.

During the seventies, there was a paranoia for real reasons around bombs going off on the streets of London – and I had little understanding of why. The organizations I was close too did little to inform my curiosity. Then in 1980, the women in Armagh prison in Ireland who had been on the No Wash Protest went on hunger strike – I joined the Armagh Women's Group and began a correspondence with one of the women, Breige Brownlee, and also Mary Nelis, a Derry woman activist, a mother of sons on the blanket in the H Blocks of Long Kesh prison. My life changed. The following summer during the tumultuous hunger strike of 1981, I moved to Derry and established Derry Camerawork – a place with a darkroom and cameras so that young people could tell their own stories and not depend on the international photographers, who would come and go. My plan had been to stay a year, I stayed five years. I returned to London in 1986 and ran the collective of Network photographers. I worked with two of them, Mike Abrahams and Laurie Sparham on a book, *Still War: Photographs from the North of Ireland*. They were wonderful photographers; it was a moment when photojournalism thrived. Of course, that would change too.

I moved to Mexico and Los Angeles and began working with Mexican photographers and then into film. I felt film allowed me to reach a wider audience than did exhibitions and have been an independent film maker ever since, making documentaries with a focus on photography. Currently, I am finishing a film that has taken 40 years to make. It's a documentary about the conflict in Ireland and the road to peace seen through the eyes of Gerry Adams – a film about him, but also a film about photography, from personal albums to the work of both local and international photographers. I would say its premise goes right back to *Photography/Politics One*. Those ideas – ways of seeing, activism and the image – have always supported me to understand what is in front of me, a kind of guidebook, a blueprint to where I live in struggle.

ISBN 978-1-912528-43-1

www.5x7editions.com

5 x 7 Editions is an imprint of
MuseumsEtc Ltd
Hudson House, 8 Albany Street
Edinburgh EH1 3QB, Scotland

The paper used in printing this book
comes from responsibly managed
forests and meets the requirements
of the Forest Stewardship Council™

Design: SecMoCo, London
Type: Dolly Pro and PMN Caecilia
Print and thread-binding:
Halstan, Amersham
Cover: Callisto Pearl 250 gsm
Text: Munken Print White 90gsm